W9-CZS-793

Fodor's 2008

BERMUDA

Where to Stay and Eat
for All Budgets

Must-See Sights
and Local Secrets

Ratings You Can Trust

Fodor's Travel Publications   New York, Toronto, London, Sydney, Auckland
www.fodors.com

FODOR'S BERMUDA 2008
Editor: Molly Moker

Editorial Production: Evangelos Vasilakis
Editorial Contributors: Suzy Buckley, Linda Coffman, Michael de Zayas, Sirkka Huish, Dale Leatherman, Susan MacCallum-Whitcomb, Andrew Raine, Keisha Webb-Gibbs
Maps & Illustrations: David Lindroth, *cartographer*; Bob Blake and Rebecca Baer, *map editors*
Design: Fabrizio LaRocca, *creative director*; Guido Caroti, Siobhan O'Hare, *art directors*; Tina Malaney, Chie Ushio, Ann McBride, *designers*; Melanie Marin, *senior picture editor*; Moon Sun Kim, *cover designer*
Cover Photo (Bermuda): Caroline Commins/Alamy
Production/Manufacturing: Angela L. McLean

COPYRIGHT
Copyright © 2008 by Fodor's Travel, a division of Random House, Inc.

Fodor's is a registered trademark of Random House, Inc.

All rights reserved. Published in the United States by Fodor's Travel, a division of Random House, Inc., and simultaneously in Canada by Random House of Canada, Limited, Toronto. Distributed by Random House, Inc., New York.

No maps, illustrations, or other portions of this book may be reproduced in any form without written permission from the publisher.

ISBN 978–1–4000–1896–3

ISSN 0192–3765

SPECIAL SALES
This book is available at special discounts for bulk purchases for sales promotions or premiums. Special editions, including personalized covers, excerpts of existing books, and corporate imprints, can be created in large quantities for special needs. For more information, write to Special Markets/Premium Sales, 1745 Broadway, MD 6-2, New York, New York 10019, or e-mail specialmarkets@randomhouse.com.

AN IMPORTANT TIP & AN INVITATION
Although all prices, opening times, and other details in this book are based on information supplied to us at press time, changes occur all the time in the travel world, and Fodor's cannot accept responsibility for facts that become outdated or for inadvertent errors or omissions. So **always confirm information when it matters,** especially if you're making a detour to visit a specific place. Your experiences—positive and negative—matter to us. If we have missed or misstated something, **please write to us.** We follow up on all suggestions. Contact the Bermuda editor at editors@fodors.com or c/o Fodor's at 1745 Broadway, New York, NY 10019.

PRINTED IN THE UNITED STATES OF AMERICA
10 9 8 7 6 5 4 3 2 1

Be a Fodor's Correspondent

Your opinion matters. It matters to us. It matters to your fellow Fodor's travelers, too. And we'd like to hear it. In fact, we need to hear it.

When you share your experiences and opinions, you become an active member of the Fodor's community. That means we'll not only use your feedback to make our books better, but we'll publish your names and comments whenever possible. Throughout our guides, look for "Word of Mouth," excerpts of your unvarnished feedback.

Here's how you can help improve Fodor's for all of us.

Tell us when we're right. We rely on local writers to give you an insider's perspective. But our writers and staff editors—who are the best in the business—depend on you. Your positive feedback is a vote to renew our recommendations for the next edition.

Tell us when we're wrong. We're proud that we update most of our guides every year. But we're not perfect. Things change. Hotels cut services. Museums change hours. Charming cafés lose charm. If our writer didn't quite capture the essence of a place, tell us how you'd do it differently. If any of our descriptions are inaccurate or inadequate, we'll incorporate your changes in the next edition and will correct factual errors at fodors.com immediately.

Tell us what to include. You probably have had fantastic travel experiences that aren't yet in Fodor's. Why not share them with a community of like-minded travelers? Maybe you chanced upon a beach or bistro or B&B that you don't want to keep to yourself. Tell us why we should include it. And share your discoveries and experiences with everyone directly at fodors.com. Your input may lead us to add a new listing or highlight a place we cover with a "Highly Recommended" star or with our highest rating, "Fodor's Choice."

Give us your opinion instantly at our feedback center at www.fodors.com/feedback. You may also e-mail editors@fodors.com with the subject line "Bermuda Editor." Or send your nominations, comments, and complaints by mail to Bermuda Editor, Fodor's, 1745 Broadway, New York, NY 10019.

You and travelers like you are the heart of the Fodor's community. Make our community richer by sharing your experiences. Be a Fodor's correspondent.

Happy Traveling!

Tim Jarrell, Publisher

CONTENTS

ABOUT THIS BOOK

Our Ratings

Sometimes you find terrific travel experiences and sometimes they just find you. But usually the burden is on you to select the right combination of experiences. That's where our ratings come in.

As travelers we've all discovered a place so wonderful that its worthiness is obvious. And sometimes that place is so experiential that superlatives don't do it justice: you just have to be there to know. These sights, properties, and experiences get our highest rating, **Fodor's Choice**, indicated by orange stars throughout this book.

Black stars highlight sights and properties we deem **Highly Recommended**, places that our writers, editors, and readers praise again and again for consistency and excellence.

By default, there's another category: Any place we include in this book is by definition worth your time, unless we say otherwise. And we will.

Disagree with any of our choices? Care to nominate a place or suggest that we rate one more highly? Visit our feedback center at www.fodors.com/feedback.

Budget Well

Hotel and restaurant price categories from ¢ to $$$$ are defined in the opening pages of each chapter. For attractions, we always give standard adult admission fees; reductions are usually available for children, students, and senior citizens. Want to pay with plastic? **AE, D, DC, MC, V** following restaurant and hotel listings indicate if American Express, Discover, Diners Club, MasterCard, and Visa are accepted.

Restaurants

Unless we state otherwise, restaurants are open for lunch and dinner daily. We mention dress only when there's a specific requirement and reservations only when they're essential or not accepted—it's always best to book ahead.

Hotels

Hotels have private bath, phone, TV, and air-conditioning and operate on the European Plan (aka EP, meaning without meals), unless we specify that they use the Continental Plan (CP, with a Continental breakfast), Breakfast Plan (BP, with a full breakfast), or Modified American Plan (MAP, with breakfast and dinner) or are all-inclusive (including all meals and most activities). We always

list facilities but not whether you'll be charged an extra fee to use them, so when pricing accommodations, find out what's included.

Many Listings
- ★ Fodor's Choice
- ★ Highly recommended
- ⊠ Physical address
- ⊹ Directions
- ⌂ Mailing address
- ☎ Telephone
- 🖷 Fax
- ⊕ On the Web
- ✎ E-mail
- 💳 Admission fee
- ☻ Open/closed times
- Ⓜ Metro stations
- ▭ Credit cards

Hotels & Restaurants
- ▥ Hotel
- ⇌ Number of rooms
- ⚴ Facilities
- ¶⊙¶ Meal plans
- ✕ Restaurant
- ⚑ Reservations
- ↘ Smoking
- ₲₽ BYOB
- ✕▥ Hotel with restaurant that warrants a visit

Outdoors
- 🏌 Golf
- ⚠ Camping

Other
- ♿ Family-friendly
- ⇨ See also
- ⊠ Branch address
- ☞ Take note

WHAT'S WHERE

BERMUDA PARISHES	When Bermuda was developed back in the early 1600s, surveyors carved out the area around St. George's (then the capital) and divided the rest of the archipelago into eight districts. These parcels of land were deeded to—and named after—the Bermuda Company's original investors: Hamilton, Smith's, Devonshire, Pembroke, Paget, Warwick, Southampton, and Sandys. Although parish boundaries no longer delineate property ownership, they continue to function as the island version of state or province lines, and Bermudians remain parochially proud of them. Whether from the *West End* (anything west of the city of Hamilton), the *East End* (anything east of the city of Hamilton), or the *Town* (the city of Hamilton and its surrounding parishes), allegiances are quite publicly paraded when Cup Match—the annual cricket festival where east faces west—rolls around in July/August.
ST. GEORGE'S	Air travelers and many cruise ship passengers first make land in this East End parish, just as the crew of the *Sea Venture* did. Their 1609 shipwreck kick-started Bermuda's settlement, and the town they erected (St. George's) is today a UNESCO World Heritage Site. History lovers admire its centuries-old churches, offbeat museums, and colorful cottages; those more interested in the here and now enjoy the boutiques and lively British-style pubs. When cruise ships arrive, crowding can obscure St. George's charm, but luckily the parish also boasts accessible beaches and forts. It has challenging golf courses, too: the public St. George's Club lies just north of town, and two private ones—Tucker's Point and the famed Mid Ocean—are in Bermuda's most exclusive residential enclave, Tucker's Town (home to billionaire Ross Perot).
HAMILTON	Don't confuse Hamilton Parish with the city of Hamilton (in Pembroke Parish) or you'll be in for a shock. Unlike the capital, this district is quite low-key and appeals primarily to families. Several of Bermuda's most kid-friendly attractions are here, namely the Bermuda Aquarium Museum & Zoo (which has cool hands-on displays aimed squarely at children) and the stunning Crystal Caves. Shelley Bay Park, with its shallow waters and adjacent playground, appeals to youngsters as well. But otherwise, beaches here aren't the best. Moreover, there are limited entertainment options apart from the Fodor's Choice Swizzle Inn (motto: "Swizzle Inn, Swagger Out"), which hosts popular music nights throughout the summer.

WHAT'S WHERE

SMITH'S 	Mainly a sleepy residential area, Smith's Parish hugs Harrington Sound and has a few attractions that can be covered in a matter of hours. Nature lovers should visit Spittal Pond, a 64-acre nature reserve that hosts scores of migratory and indigenous birds. History buffs will appreciate Verdmont: an 18th-century house-cum-museum administered by the Bermuda National Trust. Smith's Parish has a handful of affordable lodgings and a gorgeous, family-friendly public beach at John Smith's Bay Park. But if it's nightlife or dining you're after, head east to St. George's.
DEVONSHIRE 	Hilly Devonshire Parish may be the geographical center of the island, but it is far off the beaten track compared to the attractions—and distractions—of Hamilton or St. George's. Hence most travelers merely pass through it. Serious sports enthusiasts are an exception to the rule; the National Equestrian Centre, National Sports Centre, and Bermuda Squash Racquets Association Club (site of the world-class Bermuda Masters tournament) are all here. Others who linger will be rewarded by pastoral "away from it all" walks in small preserves like the Montpelier Arboretum and Edmund Gibbons Nature Reserve.
PEMBROKE 	Bermuda's most populous parish is anchored by the city of Hamilton: a bustling little capital referred to as "the town" by locals. Along with major historical attractions, Hamilton has by far the broadest array of restaurants, shops, clubs, and cultural venues. Plus, there are top-rated resorts (among them, the Fairmont Hamilton Princess and Waterloo House) as well as a host of smaller properties that put you within walking distance of it all. Because of its small size, the city can feel crowded once cruise ships dock. However, nearby sites like Fort Hamilton and the Bermuda Underwater Exploration Institute offer a peaceful respite not far from the standard tourist route. Many sightseeing boats and water-bound excursions also depart from Hamilton Harbour.
PAGET 	Paget Parish is best known for its enviable selection of south shore beaches, yet even if you're not a beach bum you'll find plenty to do. Take a walk on the wild side in Paget Marsh or let your nose lead your toes around the perfume-filled Botanical Gardens. Alternately, you can rent a bike (the flatter terrain here is a boon to cyclists) and check out Paget's neighborhoods. Convenient bus and ferry connections also enable visitors to tour the rest of the island with compara-

tive ease. These factors, and its location a stone's throw from Hamilton, make Paget an ideal home base: especially when you consider that available accommodations run the gamut from upscale resorts (like Elbow Beach or Horizons & Cottage) to affordable housekeeping units.

WARWICK

The claim to fame here is Warwick Long Bay Beach, a ½-mi of prime pink sand with a camera-ready coral outcropping just offshore. Bermuda's longest beach is rarely crowded, so it's likely you'll find a private patch to lounge on even in peak season. If you're feeling energetic, explore the scenic seaside parklands. A little inland, Warwick Pond welcomes birdwatchers. Golfers flock to the Belmont and Riddell's Bay Golf Clubs. Although Warwick remains a little isolated from restaurants and nightlife, things are looking up with the recently opened—and consistently packed—Swizzle South Shore (a sister to the original Swizzle Inn in Hamilton Parish).

SOUTHAMPTON

Southampton is a good place to park yourself for a "fun in the sun" vacation. Horseshoe Bay, the most popular—and arguably the best provisioned—pink sand beach is a big draw. Area resorts have further amenities for active types. The Pompano Beach Club has a water-sports concession that rents gear (including SunKat cruisers and glass-bottom kayaks), while the Fairmont Southampton has both a dive center and an executive golf course. Duffers will be pleased to know that the parish is also home to one of the world's finest public courses (Port Royal). So you can hit the links in the morning and bask on the beach in the afternoon.

SANDYS

This West End parish (pronounced *Sands*) has something of a split personality. Much of it is bucolic: an unspoiled mix of small farms, pristine nature reserves, and craggy coastlines that loop into beautiful bays. Yet its furthest tip also happens to be the site of Bermuda's single largest tourist attraction: the Royal Naval Dockyard. A former British bastion, the complex has been converted to house a maritime museum, dolphin swim program, and snorkel park, plus various shops and restaurants. Sandys remains geographically isolated, so if your plan is to bop or shop 'til you drop, base yourself in Hamilton and visit Sandys on a Tuesday (when you can take in the evening street festival) or on a Sunday (when most stores elsewhere in Bermuda are closed).

Bermuda

WEST END

Royal Naval Dockyard

Ireland Island N.

Cruise Ship Dock

Ireland Island S.

Admiralty House Park

Boaz Island

Lagoon Park

Cobbler Island

Clarence Cove

Watford Is.

Malabar Rd.

Spanish Point

Spanish Pt. Rd.

Somerset Long Bay

Watford Br.

PEMBROKE

Daniel's Head

Somerset Village

Hamilton

Somerset Island

Somerset Rd.

SANDYS

Great Sound

Front

Fort Scaur

Hawkins Island

Cruise Dock

Somerset Br.

Middle Rd.

Hamilton Harbour

Hamilton Harbour Rd.

Middle

Spring Benny's Bay

Riddle's Bay Golf & Country Club

Little Sound

Belmont Hills Golf Club

PAG

Port Royal Golf Course

WARWICK

West Whale Bay

Middle Rd.

SOUTHAMPTON

Fairmont Southampton Golf Club

South Rd.

Warwick Long Bay

South Shore Park

Gibbs Hill Lighthouse

Horseshoe Bay

Church Bay Park

Church Bay

KEY

⚓ Cruise Ship Dock

🚢 Ferry

┼┼┼ Railway Trail

0 ——————— 2 miles

0 ——————— 3 km

QUINTESSENTIAL BERMUDA

Pretty in Pink

According to local lore, Bermuda's sand has a faint rosy hue because it's so romantic here that even the beaches blush. Scientists, conversely, contend the coloring is derived from calcium carbonate and crushed bits of coral combined with the pulverized skeletons of microscopic scarlet protozoa (*Foraminifera* to be exact) that thrive on the surrounding reefs. Whatever the reason, this fine sand remains a Bermuda trademark. The pink-o-meter hits highest along the south shore, where "blushing beaches" include Horseshoe Bay Beach (a classic curving strand) and Warwick Long Bay Beach (Bermuda's longest expanse of sand). Yet other pocket-size beaches and secluded coves are easy enough to find. Bermuda may only cover 21 square mi, but the islands comprising it have a combined 75 mi of coast, so wherever you stay the beach is never more than a mile away.

The Long & Short of It

When it comes to the island's most recognizable symbol, Bermuda shorts might trump the infamous Bermuda Triangle. Originally part of a military uniform, the garment is a source of amusement to visitors—and a matter of national pride to natives. Elsewhere the term "Bermuda shorts" is loosely applied to any casual knee-length shorts. But real ones are characterized by their fabric and tailoring (linen or wool blends, hitting 2 inches above the knee). Worn by businessmen with knee socks and a blazer, they're considered the smartest of attire. If you want to join the local fashion and flash a little leg, just be sure to play by the rules. Rather than going for the seersucker-and-sandals look, get outfitted at a traditional retailer—like the English Sports Shop on Front Street in Hamilton, where genuine Bermuda shorts start at $40.

Although it's only 650 mi east of the United States, Bermuda seems like a world apart. Feeling at home on this oh-so friendly archipelago, however, isn't hard. Just sample a few local pleasures and you'll be kicking back like a native "Onion" in no time.

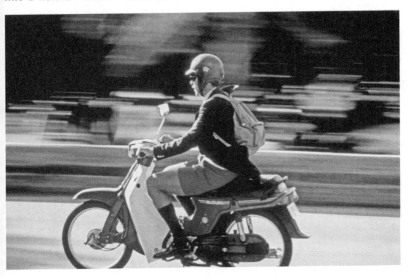

A Perfect Match

On the Thursday and Friday before the first Monday in August, Bermuda takes a two-day holiday ostensibly to let residents watch the Cup Match: an annual cricket game pitting the West End against the East End. Locals clearly take the event seriously. Cup Match fever, for instance, takes hold weeks in advance when team colors start flying from houses and vehicles island-wide. But Cup Match is also an excuse for some serious partying. While the players concentrate on whacking a leather ball through a wicket, the spectators generally focus on fun. Pulsating music, outrageous fashions, and delectable foods (anyone for mussel pie?) add to the carnival-like atmosphere. The Bermuda Government even relaxes its antigambling laws so that locals can indulge in Crown & Anchor, a betting game first brought here by British sailors in the 19th century.

The Beat of a Different Drum

Bermuda has its own musical mélange that embraces both British and African traditions. Sample the former when the Bermuda Regiment's brass-and-drum corps "Beat Retreat." The pomp-filled sunset ceremony—a military staple since the 1700s—runs at least once a month in rotating venues around the island. Red coats and pith helmets are replaced by peacock-color capes and mile-high headdresses when local Gombey troupes take center stage. The hypnotic dancers and drummers, whose distinctive style dates back to the days of slavery, pop up unexpectedly. November through March, however, you'll see them at a revue held Tuesday afternoons in Hamilton's No. 1 Passenger Terminal. Other months, you can catch them in action on Wednesday during the city's Harbour Nights festivities.

IF YOU LIKE

Life in the Past Lane

You don't have to be here long to realize there's much more to Bermuda than sea, sand, and rum swizzles. As one of Britain's oldest colonies, the island has more than 400 years of history and, thanks to thoughtful preservation policies, the architecture to prove it.

The jewel in the crown, in terms of period charm, is the UNESCO-designated town of **St. George's**. As Bermuda's original capital, it has a distinctly colonial feel, and wandering its crooked, cottage-lined lanes is akin to time travel. See the statue of Sir George Somers (who was shipwrecked here in 1609), and tour a replica of his vessel before ambling over to King's Square to catch a "ducking stool" reenactment.

The British, understanding Bermuda's strategic significance, kept it well protected from 1612 to 1956—which is why this tiny country has the world's highest concentration of **historic forts**. Start working through the list at the Maritime Museum: a converted fortress that's now the centerpiece of the Royal Naval Dockyard. Fort St. Catherine, a 17th-century edifice, complete with moat and sprawling ramparts, is another must-see.

The **African Diaspora Heritage Trail**, part of the international Slave Route Project, shows Brits weren't the only ones who helped shape Bermuda. This self-guided tour crisscrosses the island, identifying 11 sites related to Black Bermudians. Highlights include the poignant slave graveyard at St. Peter's Church and Cobb's Hill Methodist Church, which was built by and for blacks before Emancipation.

Tee Time

Bermuda is a renowned golfing destination and close enough to the United States and Canada to be pitched as "putting distance" from the eastern seaboard. The courses are as scenic as the island itself. But don't let their pretty appearance fool you. Many have holes by the sea or atop ocean-side bluffs, so wind and that big water hazard (the Atlantic!) can play havoc with your game.

Laid out by Charles Blair Macdonald in 1921, the classic course at **Mid Ocean Golf Club** in Tucker's Town is one of the most spectacular on the island—and one of the most highly regarded in the world. If you can wrangle an introduction from a member (or have your concierge do it on your behalf) you might find yourself on the links with celebs like Michael Douglas and Catherine Zeta-Jones, who live in Bermuda.

The accessible, affordable **Port Royal Golf Course** in Southampton Parish is popular with locals and visitors alike. The government-owned property has an impressive pedigree: it's a Robert Trent Jones design and a favorite of Jack Nicklaus. Plus it boasts Bermuda's most recognizable hole (the sublimely beautiful 16th), which has been photographed for countless glossy golfing magazines.

You can see why they say "good things come in small packages" at the **Fairmont Southampton Princess Golf Course.** The property's 18-hole par-3 executive course, designed by Ted Robinson, is on a hillside, and its challenging terrain offers a good warm-up for Bermuda's full-length courses. Better yet, playing here for an afternoon won't break your piggy bank.

Just Add Water

Warm, clear water with visibility up to 150 feet, rich marine life, unique topography, and perhaps most importantly, reliable outfitters, combine to make Bermuda an ideal place for underwater exploration. Bermudians like to drop anchor, crack open a case of beer, and float the day away—an activity that should not be knocked until it is tried. But if waterskiing, kayaking, parasailing, snorkeling, kite-skiing, or scuba diving are more to your liking, the crystal clear waters of Bermuda offer endless opportunities.

Not all of Bermuda's history lessons can be learned on dry land. Due to the island's treacherous coral reefs, hundreds of shipwrecks from various eras lie beneath its waters—and companies like **Triangle Diving** and **Blue Water Divers** will take you out to see them. Both operate wreck tours for experienced scuba enthusiasts as well as lesson-and-dive packages for first-timers.

Not ready to dive in? Consider taking an underwater walk. **Bermuda Bell Diving** and **Hartley's Under Sea Adventures** let you don a specially designed helmet, then descend about 10 feet for some fish face time. The equipment may look strange, but the science is sound (helmets operate on the same principal as a tumbler overturned in water) and the experience is unforgettable.

From April to November, grab your fins and a mask to enjoy the Dockyard's **Snorkel Park.** This sheltered inlet features exotic sea creatures, submerged artifacts (such as centuries-old cannons), marked reef trails, and even floating rest stations. You can rent snorkel gear—along with an assortment of other equipment, including underwater scooters—at the site.

Suite Dreams

Many holiday hot spots invite visitors to bed down in ho-hum "all inclusives." Not Bermuda. Instead, the island is dotted with unique accommodations. Big names in luxury lodging (think Fairmont, Mandarin Oriental, Relais & Châteaux) are interspersed with posh family-run resorts, cottage colonies, and quaint, sometimes quirky, bed-and-breakfasts.

With its "British Manor meets the Beach" vibe, **Waterloo House** in the city of Hamilton routinely ranks among the world's best resorts. Aside from plush old-school rooms, this boutique hotel has a top restaurant, private boat launch, and terraced harbor-view gardens. As if that weren't enough, you also get introductions to the island's most exclusive golf courses, plus the otherwise private Coral Beach & Tennis Club.

You'd expect over-water lodgings in Bora Bora, not Bermuda. But **9 Beaches** in Sandys Parish has them: 16 funky canvas-covered cabanas (aka *tentalows*) set on stilts above the ocean. Each has a Plexiglas floor panel for viewing sea-life and a "refined rustic" decor. There are temptations outdoors, too. In addition to the titular nine beaches, the resort houses a Surf Shack equipped with all the requisite water toys.

The **Old Rectory** in St. George's is a divine B&B where breakfast comes with a side order of history. Built around 1699, the limestone cottage has classic Bermudian features (like cedar beams, multiple chimneys, and "welcoming arms" stairs) as well as an old-fashioned price. You can get a good night's sleep for $100–$150 . . . provided you're not bothered by the resident ghost!

GREAT ITINERARIES

BUMMING AROUND BERMUDA: SEA, SAND & SIGHTS

Day 1: Horseshoe Bay Beach

Chances are you came for that legendary pink sand, so don't waste any time finding it. If you think variety is the spice of life, spend the day bouncing from beach to beautiful beach along the south shore. (The No. 7 bus gets you there and back from the city of Hamilton.) Otherwise just choose one and settle in. Our pick is the flagship beach at Horseshoe Bay: a gently curving crescent lapped by turquoise water and backed by South Shore Park. It does get crowded here—but for good reason. Unlike most Bermudian beaches, Horseshoe Bay has lifeguards plus a snack bar, changing rooms, and beach gear–rental facilities. (Families should note there's also a protected inlet, dubbed Horseshoe Baby Beach, which is perfect for young children.) Looking for something more private? Picturesque trails through the park will lead you to secluded coves. Whichever you opt for bring a hat, plenty of water, and a light cover-up if you plan to stay until evening. Don't forget sunscreen either: a bad burn and road rash (from skimming the road on a scooter) are the two most common ailments among Bermuda's visitors. When the sun goes down—and you have sand in every crevice—stroll over to the lively Henry VIII pub and restaurant for an evening bite.

Day 2: The Town of St. George's

Founded in 1612, St. George's qualifies as one of the oldest towns in the Western Hemisphere and deserves a place on any traveler's itinerary. This UNESCO World Heritage Site has a smattering of worthwhile museums, the Bermuda National Trust Museum and Tucker House being chief among them. Historic buildings such as St. Peter's Church also shouldn't be missed. Yet the real delight here is simply wandering the walled lanes and quaint alleys lined with traditional shops, pubs, and cottages. All those roads eventually lead to King's Square, where you can try out the replica stocks. Nearby is another device formerly used to punish unruly folk—the seesawlike ducking stool—which serves as the focal point for reenactments starring the Town Crier and a wet wench. (These are staged at noon April through October on Monday, Wednesday, Thursday, and Saturday; other months on Wednesday and Saturday only.) If you have time and shoe leather to spare, continue your history lesson outside St. George's at Fort St. Catherine, a hilltop defense built in the 17th century. Stop for a little swimming or snorkeling just below it in snug Achilles Bay, then cap the day back in town by enjoying a casual meal at the White Horse Tavern on the water's edge.

Day 3: The City of Hamilton

With a permanent resident population of only 1,500 households, Bermuda's capital city is minuscule by mainland standards. Yet it dominates island life and has all the ingredients for a great day out. Because there's a little bit of everything here, you can plot a course according to your individual tastes. Shoppers should make a beeline for the Front Street area to spend a few hours—and a wallet-full of money—in the stores and galleries. Prefer sightseeing? Simply pick up a brochure for a self-guided tour at the Visitor Information Centre (VIC) and start walking. (Free guided strolls from the VIC are also available at 10 AM Monday in low

Outside the city, visit Fort Hamilton, a must-see for history buffs and a great spot for photo ops. Alternately, you can investigate sunken treasure and seashells without ever getting wet at the Bermuda Underwater Exploration Institute (it's about a 15-minute walk from the city center), or get out on the water itself. Excursion options from Hamilton range from archipelago tours and glass-bottom boat trips to affordable ferry rides. Afterward, gear up to see Hamilton by night. Pubs and clubs start filling around 10 PM, leaving plenty of time for dinner at one of the city's surprisingly diverse restaurants.

Day 4: The Dockyard

Once a military stronghold, now a magnet for tourists, the Royal Naval Dockyard offers a full day of history mixed with a heaping helping of adventure. Its centerpiece is the Maritime Museum, where you can find exhibits on whaling, sailing, shipbuilding, and shipwrecks set within an imposing stone fortress. Once you've checked out the displays—and taken in the stunning views from the ramparts—head to the Old Cooperage. This for-

mer barrel-making factory houses both the Bermuda Craft Market (perhaps the island's best-stocked, best-priced craft outlet) and the Bermuda Arts Centre (a high-end co-op with gallery and studio space). It's the perfect place to stock up on one-of-a-kind souvenirs. After lunch in an area eatery, join one of the educational Dolphin Quest programs, or baby your budget with a swim next door at the inexpensive Snorkel Park. Spring through fall, adrenaline junkies should try parasailing at the Dockyard (through Skyrider Bermuda) or Jet Skiing (courtesy of Windjammer Watersports). Toast your achievements nearby at the Frog & Onion Pub. If you're interested in a more placid on-the-water experience, take the slow, scenic ferry to Somerset Island and disembark at Watford Bridge. From there explore Somerset Village or sit down for dinner at the Somerset Country Squire, a traditional tavern overlooking Mangrove Bay.

Day 5: Go Green

For many travelers, Bermuda is synonymous with golf greens, so dedicated duffers will want to spend at least one day putting around. Even neophytes can get into the swing of things at the Bermuda Golf Academy. However, for a different kind of "green experience," you can feel genteel at the Botanical Gardens or go wild at Paget Mash, both near the city of Hamilton. The former is a Victorian venue with formal flower beds and subtropical fruit orchards; the latter a 25-acre tract that covers five distinct ecosystems (including primeval woodlands that contain the last surviving stands of native palmetto and cedar). Spittal Pond, on Bermuda's south shore, is another ecodestination. November to May, it's a major draw for bird-watchers, thanks to the 30-odd species of waterfowl that stop here; in April it attracts whale-watchers hoping to spy migrating humpbacks from the preserve's oceanfront cliffs. You can access more "undiscovered" spots by traversing the Bermuda Railway Trail. (One of our favorite sections starts near the Southampton Post Office.) With its lush greenery and dramatic lookouts, this 18-mi recreational route is best seen on foot. But if your boots aren't made for walking, bicycling is permitted, too. When renting equipment, just remember to request a pedal bike, otherwise you might end up with a motorized scooter.

Tips:

Before going swimming, check Horseshoe Bay Beach's notice board for jellyfish updates. The Portuguese man-of-war variety looks like an innocuous blue plastic bag, but its sting is extremely painful and poisonous.

Bermuda has loads of beaches—but few lifeguards. The only places you can find them are at Horseshoe Bay, John Smith's Bay, Clearwater Beach, and Turtle Bay (from May to October).

The northern end of Court Street in the City of Hamilton is off the typical tourist trail so you can find some great local eateries and a taste of day-to-day Bermuda life. Be warned, this area is not advisable after dark.

In high season, Hamilton hosts Harbour Nights, a street festival complete with craft vendors and live entertainment every Wednesday evening. Similar events run Tuesday nights in the Dockyard and St. George's, Monday nights in Flatt's Village.

Certain outdoor activities are only offered seasonally, so confirm operating times to avoid disappointment. Also try to make any sporting reservations before you arrive in Bermuda—tee times and boat charters are especially in high demand.

Always be cautious if you're tooling around on a scooter. The island's notoriously narrow, twisting roads have a particularly high accident rate and drinking-and-driving is a problem. Don't be scared, just be aware.

WHEN TO GO

The important thing to remember when planning your trip is that subtropical Bermuda is in the Atlantic—*not* the Caribbean. High season here is April through October, when the sun shines brightest and the warm waters beckon. During the summer months particularly, the island teems with activity. Sightseeing options are plentiful and the "official" events calendar is full. (Hotels add to it by offering their own daytime programs and evening entertainment.) Off-season—November through March—the weather is often perfect for golf or tennis, and on sunny days you can take advantage of uncrowded beaches. Nevertheless, the pace is considerably slower. A few restaurants and shops close, some excursion boats are dry-docked, and typically only taxis operate tours of the island. Most hotels remain open, but with rates slashed by as much as 40%. As an added incentive for off-peak travelers, the Department of Tourism sponsors the Bermuda Heart & Soul program: a series of daily activities (the majority of which are free) that include guided walks, high teas, and golf tournaments.

Climate

Bermuda has a remarkably mild climate that seldom sees extremes of either heat or cold. In winter (December through March), temperatures range from around 55°F at night to 70°F in early afternoon. High, blustery winds can make the air feel cooler, however, as can Bermuda's high humidity. The hottest times are between May and mid-October, when temperatures generally range from 75°F to 85°F. It's not uncommon for the mercury to reach 90°F in July and August, but it often feels hotter due to humidity levels. Although summer is somewhat drier, rainfall is spread fairly evenly throughout the year. Bermuda depends solely on rain for its supply of fresh water, so residents usually greet a summer shower as "good tank water" in reference to the cisterns where rainwater is stored beneath many houses. In August and September, hurricanes moving north from the Caribbean occasionally hit the island, causing storm damage and flight delays.

Forecasts **Bermuda Weather Service** (☎ *441/297-7977 for a recorded update* ⊕ *www.weather.bm*). **Weather Channel** (⊕ *www.weather.com*).

ON THE CALENDAR

Bermuda is a year-round destination with an active events calendar, so we've highlighted the top annual offerings. For more options, consult Bermuda Tourism (☎*800/237–6832 ⊕www.bermudatourism.com*). Local publications are another reliable resource. The free widely distributed tourist magazine, *Preview,* provides a monthly overview; while the island's newspaper, the *Bermuda Sun* (⊕*www.bermudasun. org*) publishes a weekly calendar each Friday. Events are also listed on the paper's Web site. Further info can be found online at Thisweekinbermuda.bm and Bermudayp.com. For detailed entertainment listings try Bermynet.com or BlackandCoke.com.

WINTER

December

Foursomes made up of professional and amateur golfers swing into action during the **Bermuda Goodwill Tournament** (☎*441/295–4640 ⊕www.bermudagoodwill.org*). Debuting in 1922, it's the world's oldest pro-am competition and spectators are invited to watch the event for free.

During the annual **Christmas Boat Parade** (⊕*www.bermuda boatparade.bm*), decorated vessels of every size and description float through Hamilton Harbour. The event, which can draw 20,000 spectators, usually takes place on the second Saturday of the month and is topped off by festive fireworks.

The **Annual Christmas Walkabout in St. George's** (☎*441/236–6483 ⊕www.bnt.bm*) is an early-evening event hosted by the Bermuda National Trust. Properties specially decked out for the holiday season open their doors to the public. Choir concerts, Christmas-theme readings, and eggnog-sipping are also on the agenda.

Following Commonwealth tradition, Bermuda makes December 26 a public holiday: **Boxing Day.** Pugilists need not apply, but many other sporting activities—like harness racing and cycling competitions—are scheduled, and Gombey troupes mark the day by dancing in the streets.

Who needs Times Square? **St. George's New Year's Eve Celebration** (☎*441/297–1532*), held in King's Square and on Ordnance Island, has food stalls, kiddie rides, and continuous live entertainment by local musicians. A midnight count-

	down culminates in the much-anticipated dropping of the "onion." Fireworks follow.
January	For more than 30 years the **Bermuda Festival of the Performing Arts** (☎441/295–1291 ⊕*www.bermudafestival.org*), the largest of its kind on the island, has featured international *artistes*. Plays, ballets, chamber orchestras, and jazz jams are staged over two months at the City Hall Theatre and other venues.

On your mark! **Bermuda International Race Weekend** (☎441/236–6086 ⊕*www.bermudaraceweekend.com*) kicks off the third weekend of the month. The event begins Friday night with the Front Street Mile. It also includes a marathon, half-marathon, and a 10k (6.2-mi) charity walk. Top runners participate, but most races are open to all.

The 50-year-old **Bermuda Regional Bridge Tournament** (☎441/236-6466 ⊕*www.bermudaregional.com*) attracts more than 250 players from both home and abroad. Sanctioned by the American Contract Bridge League, it's generally held at the Fairmont Southampton the last week of January. |
| February | Grand masters assemble for the **Bermuda International Open Chess Tournament** (☎441/234–2322 ⊕*www.bermuda.bm/chess*). Part of the Association of Chess Professionals tour, this round-robin competition is open to both residents and visitors and awards $5,000 in prize money. Check, please. |
| **SPRING**

March | Horse lovers can watch a range of equestrian events, including dressage and jumping classes, when the two-day **Bermuda Horse & Pony Association Spring Show** (☎441/234–0485 ⊕*www.bef.bm*) comes to the National Equestrian Centre in Devonshire Parish in the middle of the month.

In mid-March, the prestigious **Bermuda International Film Festival** (☎441/293–3456 ⊕*www.bermudafilmfest.com*) screens dozens of independent feature, documentary, and short films from around the world, awarding prizes in four categories. In addition to nine days of screenings, you can expect panel discussions, parties, and popcorn.

Zoom Around the Sound (☎441/293–2727 ⊕*www.bamz.org*), an annual 7.2-mi trip around Harrington Sound sponsored by the Bermuda Zoological Society, invites walkers, joggers, |

	runners, bikers, and rollerbladers to go the distance. It's a fund-raiser for the Bermuda Aquarium, Museum & Zoo.
March – April	The **Virtual Spectator Bermuda Masters** (☎*441/292–6881* ⊕*www.bermudamasters.com*), held late March or early April, attracts the world's 31 top-ranked squash players with one "wild-card" local added to the roster. It's estimated that more than 600 spectators—and 625 million TV viewers—watch the action. The **Palm Sunday Walk** (☎*441/236–6483* ⊕*www.bnt.bm*) is an annual 5- to 8-mi stroll sponsored by the Bermuda National Trust. Following a different route each year, the event allows thousands of walkers to access private properties that would otherwise be off-limits. Good Friday is a public holiday and traditionally *the* day for kite-flying. Residents like to make their own from tissue paper, glue, and wooden sticks; then show them off during the annual **Bermuda Kite Festival** (☎*441/295–0729*). Held at Horseshoe Bay in Southampton, it includes a kite contest plus classic fun and games.
April	Much like a state fair, Bermuda's **Annual Exhibition** (☎*441/ 239–2351* ⊕*www.agshowbda.com*) showcases agriculture via livestock competitions, horticultural displays, and down-home entertainment. This three-day event at the Botanical Gardens typically runs the third weekend in April. The gardens (free other days) charge admission for the Exhibition. Members of St. George's Masonic Lodge pay their rent on the Old State House with great pomp and circumstance during the **Peppercorn Ceremony** (☎*441/297–1532*). A single peppercorn is solemnly passed over to the mayor in a stylish (if somewhat surreal) display that includes a march by the Bermuda Regiment. Tennis, anyone? The **XL Capital Bermuda Open** (☎*441/296– 2554* ⊕*www.xlcapitalbermudaopen.bm*) is an ATP Tour, USTA-sanctioned tournament hosted mid-month by the Coral Beach & Tennis Club. In past years top male tennis players like Andy Roddick and Patrick Rafte have competed for prize money.

April – May	Regatta season gets off to a roaring start with **International Invitational Race Week** (☎*441/295–2214* ⊕*www.rbyc.bm*), hosted by the venerable Royal Bermuda Yacht Club in late April and early May. Since 1927, it has pitted Bermuda's top sailors against the best of the rest in keel boat and dinghy-class races on the Great Sound.
May	May is **Bermuda Heritage Month** (☎*441/292–9447*), when a host of commemorative, cultural, and sporting activities are scheduled. The climax is Bermuda Day (May 24), a public holiday that includes a parade to the National Stadium, a cycling race, and dinghy races in St. George's Harbour. Traditionally, this is also the first day that locals swim, swearing the water is too cold earlier in the year—though most visitors don't seem to mind.

Prepare to go green with envy. Wednesday afternoons in May, the Garden Club of Bermuda leads to-die-for tours through private properties during their yearly **Open Houses & Gardens Event** (☎*441/293–0128* ⊕*www.gardenclubbermuda.org*). At least three different spots can be viewed each week.

The **Bermuda Senior Amateur Championships for Men and Ladies** (☎*441/295–9972* ⊕*www.bermudagolf.org*) are hosted by the island's oldest golf club—Riddell's Bay, in Warwick Parish. Women entrants must be at least 50 years old, men at least 55. |
| **SUMMER**

June | The Bermuda Philharmonic Society's June offerings are music to parsimonious ears. On the first weekend of the month, it presents free **Open Air Pops Concerts** (☎*441/238–1108*) at King's Square in St. George's and outside the Clocktower Mall at the Royal Naval Dockyard.

Queen Elizabeth II's Birthday is on April 21. But Bermudian's send belated best wishes by celebrating on the second Monday in June. The highlight of this public holiday is a military parade—complete with marching bands and cannon fire— along Hamilton's Front Street.

Seasoned yachtsmen chart a challenging 635-mi course from Rhode Island to St. David's Lighthouse during the biennial **Newport–Bermuda Race** (☎*441/295–2214* ⊕*www.bermuda race.com*). One of the sailing world's preeminent blue water |

events, it's held late June in even-numbered years and is hosted by the Royal Bermuda Yacht Club.

The smaller-scale **Bermuda Ocean Race** (☎410/849–8523 ⊕*www.bermudaoceanrace.com*) out of Annapolis also sets sail in even-numbered years. In odd ones, the **Marion-Bermuda Cruising Yacht Race** (☎441/236–2250 ⊕*www.marionbermuda.com*) runs instead from Plymouth County, Massachusetts.

Tuna tends to be the catch of the day at the **Bermuda Angler's Club International Light Tackle Tournament** (☎441/293–0875 ⊕*www.bermudaanglersclub.com*), held the first or second week of the month. Even if you don't like "Chicken of the Sea" it's fun to watch the weigh-ins at Spanish Point Boat Club.

July	The island keeps reeling in anglers with the back-to-back billfish tournaments that make up the **Bermuda Triple Crown** (☎407/571–4680 ⊕*www.bermudatriplecrown.com*). First up is the Bermuda Billfish Blast, followed by the Bermuda Big Game Classic and the Sea Horse Anglers Club Billfish Tournament.
	Up-and-coming young golfers from Europe and the United States take part in the **Ross "Blackie" Talbot Junior International Classic** (☎441/298–6950 ⊕*www.juniorgolf.bm*). It's a 72-hole competition played at Tucker's Point Golf Club in St. George's Parish.
July – August	The **Cup Match Cricket Festival** (☎441/234–0327 or 441/297–0374) is a spirited two-day celebration centered on the match between rival Somerset and St. George's cricket clubs. (Locals sport red-and-navy if they're Somerset fans, and dark blue–and–light blue if they're St. George's fans.) The highlight of Bermuda's events calendar, it's scheduled either the last Thursday and Friday in July or the first Thursday and Friday in August in conjunction with two public holidays: Emancipation Day and Somers Day.
August	The quirky **Non-Mariners Race** (☎441/236–3683) is decidedly nonsensical. On the first Sunday in August, landlubbers hastily cobble together "non-boats" on the beach; then attempt to race them in Mangrove Bay. No paddles, oars,

engines, or sails are permitted and contraptions that manage to float far are disqualified.

The **Byron Lee Soca Show** (☎*441/295–4839* ⊕*www.byron leemusic.com*) usually takes place in August. Featuring soca legend Byron Lee and his band the Dragonaires, the show at Tiger Bay (St. George's) can draw a diverse, mixed-age audience up of to 2,000 people

FALL September	Bermuda's fine pink sand is put to good use during Horseshoe Bay Beach's one-day **International Sand Sculpture Competition** (☎*441/295–4597*), held in early September. Teams of up to six people are encouraged to get creative and build the craziest castles possible on a 15x15-foot patch of beach. Prizes are awarded in seven categories. Cyclists gear up for the **CD&P Bermuda Grand Prix** (☎*441/799–8614* ⊕*www.bermudagrandprix.com*). More than 100 male and female professionals (plus some intrepid amateurs) take part in four days of timed trials, criteriums, and hair-raising road races. The finale of the Women's Prestige Cycling Series is also part of the lineup. Triathletes cap their calendar with the **Bank of Bermuda Foundation Triathlon Race Series** (⊕*www.bta.bm*). Entrants in the team event swim, bike, and run around the city of Hamilton on the last Sunday in September. The individual event is slated for the following Sunday, and duathlons for juniors are offered in both categories.
October	The **Bermuda Music Festival** (⊕*www.bermudamusicfestival. com*) brings together island and international entertainers for a weekend of jazz, soul, pop, and gospel. Past editions have starred Gladys Knight, Al Green, India.Arie, and Seal. The main venue—an over-the-water stage at the Dockyards—is pretty stellar, too. The weeklong **King Edward VII Gold Cup** (☎*441/295–2214* ⊕*www.kingedwardviigoldcup.com*) sees match-race skippers (America's Cup competitors among them) vie for the titular trophy and a $100,000 purse. Races are in Hamilton Harbour, and the Royal Bermuda Yacht Club opens its doors for the event, making this one especially appealing to spectators.

Go fore it! Mid-month the Mid Ocean Club proudly hosts the **PGA Grand Slam of Golf** (☎*561/624–8400* ⊕*www.pga.com*) for the second year running. Only an ultra-elite foursome—winners of the year's Masters Tournament, U.S. Open, British Open, and PGA Championship—qualify to play.

Professional and accomplished amateur golfers again tee off at the **Bermuda Open Championship** (☎*441/295–9972* ⊕*www.bermudagolf.org*). Held at the Port Royal Golf Club, it's considered to be the island's premier annual golfing event.

Pet lovers, rejoice! Felines rule during the **Bermuda Cat Fanciers' Association Cat Show** (☎*441/238–0112*), held in Hamilton's No. 1 Passenger Terminal at the tail of the month. The seven-day **Bermuda International Dog Show** (☎*441/291–4230*) runs about a week later in the Botanical Gardens.

| November | On the first Friday in November, the **Reconvening of Parliament** (☎*441/292–7408*) kicks off when the governor, in full regalia, arrives at Hamilton's Cabinet Building in a horse-drawn landau. His Speech from the Throne (detailing new policies and initiatives) usually begins around 11 AM, so arrive by 10:15 to secure a good spot. |

During the **World Rugby Classic** (☎*441/295–6574* ⊕*www. worldrugby.bm*) former pro players from around the globe come out of retirement to represent their respective countries in matches at the National Sports Centre in Devonshire Parish. Spectators can position themselves in the stands or a "tavern tent" behind the touchline.

Remembrance Day is a public holiday held in memory of fallen soldiers from Bermuda and its allied nations. A parade with Bermudian, British, and U.S. military units, the Bermuda Police, and war-veterans' organizations takes place on Front Street in Hamilton and commemorative wreaths are laid at the Cenotaph near the Cabinet Building.

The **Coral Beach & Tennis Club** (☎*441/236–2233* ⊕*www. coralbeachclub.com*) in Paget Parish is a busy spot this month. The Bermuda Lawn Tennis Club Invitational hits the clay courts early in the month, followed immediately by the Coral Beach Club Invitational.

Exploring Bermuda

WORD OF MOUTH

"I was not expecting such beauty. Bermuda is unlike any other island we have visited. I think it's the combination of great views, friendly people, really good restaurants, variety of things to do, and efficient transportation that makes Bermuda so special, in my opinion."

—mnag

"We loved the people we got to meet—initially more formal and reserved than we're used to, and always kind and interesting. I enjoyed the formality—it seems more believable and real than the forced buddy-buddy one sometimes gets in large resorts."

—cynstalker

By Susan
MacCallum-
Whitcomb

BERMUDA IS JUSTIFIABLY FAMOUS FOR pink-sand beaches, impossibly blue water, and kelly-green golf courses. But that's only the beginning. Thanks to its colorful past, this small sliver of land also has a surprising number of historic sites. In addition to countless quaint old cottages, it's said to have the oldest continually inhabited town of English origin in the Western Hemisphere and—because of its strategic Atlantic location—more forts per square mile than any other place on earth.

Bermuda has a distinctive culture, too: one that combines a reverence for British traditions dating back to colonial days with a more relaxed attitude befitting a subtropical island. In court, for instance, local lawyers may still wear formal flowing robes—yet there's a good chance that they're sporting Bermuda shorts beneath them. So while you're here, take time to look beyond the obvious and savor *all* that Bermuda has to offer.

There is certainly no shortage of things to see. The town of St. George's, at the island's East End, is the original 1600s settlement and a UNESCO World Heritage Site. The city of Hamilton (not to be confused with the parish of the same name farther northeast) is home to Bermuda's principal harbor and most of its shops. It's also the main departure point for sightseeing boats, ferries, and the pink-and-blue buses that ramble all over the island. The Royal Naval Dockyard, at the West End, is a former British shipyard that has been transformed into a stunning tourist attraction.

All three of these destinations can be explored easily on foot. The rest of the island, however, is best discovered by taxi, motor scooter, or bicycle—but only if you're fit, because Bermuda is hilly! The main roads connecting the parishes are North Shore Road, Middle Road, South Road (also known as South Shore Road), and Harbour Road. Their names make it easy for you to get your bearings and almost all the traffic traversing the island's 21-mi length is concentrated on them, although some 1,200 smaller roads also crisscross it.

To make the most of your money, as well as your time, consider buying a $25 Heritage Passport if you plan on visiting several of the following sites: the Bermuda National Gallery; Bermuda Underwater Exploration Institute; Bermuda Maritime Museum; Fort St. Catherine; Bermuda National Trust Museum in the Globe Hotel; Verdmont; Tucker House; and the Bermuda Aquarium, Museum & Zoo. The passport allows unlimited admission to all eight sites for seven consecutive days. You can purchase it online at ⊕ *www.bermudatourism.com* or in person at individual attractions. Passports are also available at the island's visitor information centres. Return travelers should note that these replaced the former visitor service bureaus in the spring of 2007. Along with a new name (and new hours) they also have new locations. If you want pamphlets and brochures—not quizzical looks—be sure to check our maps first to see where the new locations are.

ST. GEORGE'S

1

The settlement of Bermuda began in what is now the town of St. George's when the *Sea Venture*— flagship of an English fleet carrying supplies to Jamestown, Virginia— was wrecked on Bermuda's treacherous reefs in 1609. Today, nearly 400 years later, no visit to the island would be complete without a stop in this picturesque and remarkably preserved example of an early New World outpost.

Although St. George's is a living community—not a living-history museum—it retains the patina of authenticity. In fact, in 2000 it was named a UNESCO World Heritage Site. That designation puts it on a par with spots like the Great Wall of China and the Taj Mahal in India. But don't expect awe-inspiring edifices here. On the contrary, St. George's chief charm lies in tiny walled cottages, simple colonial churches, and labyrinthine alleys that beg to be explored.

TOP 5 BERMUDA

■ Lose yourself (and the crowds) on the winding side streets and mazelike back alleys of 400-year-old St. George's.

■ Head to the Dockyard's Maritime Museum for a crash course in island history and up-close animal encounters.

■ Kick back with the kids at the engaging—often interactive—Bermuda Aquarium, Museum & Zoo.

■ Glimpse a surreal subterranean world filled with stalactites and stalagmites at the Crystal Caves.

■ Hike through Paget Marsh: an unspoiled 25-acre nature preserve minutes from bustling Hamilton.

Numbers in the text correspond to numbers in the margin and on the Town of St. George's and Hamilton maps.

A GOOD WALK

Start your tour in **King's Square ❶**, then stroll out onto **Ordnance Island ❷** to see a replica of *Deliverance II*: the ship built as a replacement for the *Sea Venture*. Behind you, just up the street is the **Bermuda National Trust Museum at the Globe Hotel ❸**, and across the square is the **Town Hall ❹**. Venturing up King Street, notice the fine Bermudian architecture of **Bridge House ❺**. At the top of King Street is the **Old State House ❻**, the earliest stone building in Bermuda.

Walk up Princess Street to Duke of York Street and turn right, following the sidewalk to the **Bermudian Heritage Museum ❼**. Across Duke of York Street, you can find **Somers Garden ❽**, where Sir George Somers's heart is reportedly buried. After walking through the garden, climb the steps to Blockade Alley for a view of the **Unfinished Church ❾** on a hill ahead. To your left are Duke of Kent Street, Featherbed Alley, and the **St. George's Historical Society Museum, Printery & Garden ❿**. Next, cross Clarence Street to Church Lane and turn right on Broad Alley to reach the **Old Rectory ⓫**. Straight ahead (or as straight as you can go among these twisted streets) is Printer's Alley, which in turn links to **Nea's Alley ⓬** where a whiff of 19th-century scandal still lingers.

Return to Church Lane and enter the yard of **St. Peter's Church ⓭**, a centuries-old sanctuary that, until the building of the Old State House, did double duty as the colony's only public meeting place. (The main entrance is on Duke of York Street.) From the church, continue down Duke of York Street until you reach Queen Street on your right. A short walk up it brings you to the **Bermuda Perfumery & Gardens ⓮** at Stewart Hall, which will be on the left. Turn around and walk back to Duke of York Street and go right until you get to Barber's Alley, turning left to reach **Tucker House ⓯**, which has been transformed from a prominent merchant's home into a museum. From there continue along Water Street, veering left again on Penno's Drive to visit the new **World Heritage Centre ⓰** at Penno's Wharf.

TIMING   Given its small size, St. George's has a disproportionately large number of historical buildings, plus pleasant gardens and enticing shops. They say you can't get lost here—but you can certainly lose track of time. So give yourself a day to explore its nooks and crannies.

WHAT TO SEE

★ ➌ **Bermuda National Trust Museum at the Globe Hotel.** Erected as a governor's mansion around 1700, this building became a hotbed of activity during the American Civil War. From here, Confederate Major Norman

Walker coordinated the surreptitious flow of guns, ammunition, and war supplies from England, through Union blockades, into American ports. It saw service as the Globe Hotel during the mid-19th century and became a National Trust property in 1951. A short video, *Bermuda, Centre of the Atlantic,* recounts the history of Bermuda, and a memorabilia-filled exhibit entitled "Rogues & Runners: Bermuda and the American Civil War" describes St. George's when it was a port for Confederate blockade runners. ⊠*32 Duke of York St.* 🕾*441/297–1423* ⊕*www.bnt.bm* ⊠*$5; $10 combination ticket includes admission to Tucker House and Verdmont* ⊗*Nov.–Mar., Wed.–Sat. 10–4; Apr.–Oct., Mon.–Sat. 10–4.*

★ ⑭ **Bermuda Perfumery & Gardens.** In 2005 the perfumery moved from Bailey's Bay in Smith's Parish, where it had been based since 1928, to historic Stewart Hall. Although the location is new, the techniques it uses are not: the perfumery still extracts natural fragrances from island flowers, and manufactures and bottles all products on-site. Frangipani, jasmine, orchids, oleander, and passion flowers are only a few of the ingredients used in making the sweet-smelling Bermudian scents. Guides are available to explain the entire process, and there's a small museum that outlines the company's history. You can also wander around the gardens and stock up on your favorite fragrances in the showroom. ⊠*5 Queen St.* 🕾*441/293–0627* ⊕*www.bermuda-perfumery.com* ⊠*Free* ⊗*Mon.–Sat. 9–5.*

❼ **Bermudian Heritage Museum.** The history, trials, and accomplishments of black Bermudians are highlighted in this converted 1840s warehouse. Photographs of early black residents including slaves, freedom fighters, and professionals line the walls, and the works of black artisans are proudly exhibited. Look, in particular, for the display about the *Enterprise,* a slave ship that was blown off course to Bermuda while sailing from Virginia to South Carolina in 1835. Since slavery had already been abolished on the island, the 78 slaves on board were technically free—and the Local Friendly Societies (grassroots organizations devoted to liberating and supporting slaves) worked to keep it that way. Society members obtained an injunction to bring the slaves' case into court and escorted the "human cargo" to their hearing in Hamilton, where many spoke in their own defense. All except one woman and her four children accepted the offer of freedom. Today, countless Bermudians trace their ancestry back to those who arrived on the *Enterprise.* Appropriately enough, the museum building was once home to one of the Friendly Societies. It's now a Bermuda National Trust property. ⊠*Water and Duke of York sts.* 🕾*441/297–4126* ⊠*$4* ⊗*Tues.–Sat. 10–3.*

❺ **Bridge House,** a 17th-century building owned by the National Trust, currently contains apartments, an art studio, and a shop. But previously it was home to several of Bermuda's governors—and at least one ghost. Mistress Christian Stevenson, who was condemned as a witch in 1653, proclaimed her innocence at this spot and now seems reluctant to leave it. Other National Trust properties also qualify as "favorite haunts." For instance, the Old Rectory on Broad Alley is said to have a spirit

CLOSE UP

Law & Order: Colonial Style

Back in Bermuda's early days, colonists convicted of offenses such as drunkenness, blasphemy, and slander would be locked in the stocks or forced to stand in the pillory for a set length of time. Either way the punishment was uncomfortable and humiliating (especially when rapidly thrown rotten fruit was added to the equation!). Today, replicas of both stocks and pillory can be found on King's Square in St. George's, and curious souls are welcome to try them out.

It is, however, recommended that you stay well away from the other apparatus townsfolk used to chasten the unruly—the ducking stool—unless you fancy getting wet. Originally reserved for women who nagged or gossiped, the device is essentially an oversize wooden seesaw. The accused would be strapped to a seat on one end, then wheeled out over the harbor, and repeatedly dropped in.

It's a procedure that Alison Outerbridge knows well because, for more than a dozen years, she has played the part of St. George's resident nag in regularly scheduled reenactments. Outerbridge explains, "the punishment is carried out by the Town Crier who, with the assistance of the Town Constable, ducks me until I repent for my crime. I repent pretty quickly in the winter months, not so quickly in the sweltering heat of August. And I take as much time as possible if it is rain-

ing, so everybody in the crowd gets wet, too!"

These days, she adds, "the most tedious part of the job is all the laundry." But it's doubtful Outerbridge would be so philosophical if she was instead asked to demonstrate the "trial by water," otherwise known as "swimming the witch." In the 1600s suspected witches—typically women charged with such heinous crimes as bewitching hogs or having warts—would have their thumbs tied to their toes and be thrown into the harbor.

Those who sank, for whatever good it did them, were declared innocent. Those who floated were condemned. The unfortunates who fell into the latter category were hauled out to be hung. And when it comes to the executioners' preferred locations, place names like Gallows Island and Gibbet Island are a dead giveaway.

To learn more about colonial life in St. George's, sign on for one of the hour-long tours Outerbridge leads. As a descendent of Bermuda's first settlers, a trustee of the St. George's Foundation, and a former town councilor, she's sure to have the inside scoop. Tours are priced at $15 per person and run thrice weekly April to November. To reserve a spot, contact her at ☏441/297–2086 or by e-mail at alicatbda@yahoo.com.

–Susan MacCallum-Whitcomb

who plays the spinet in the wee hours of the morning. Verdmont, in Smith's Parish, also has its share of resident ghosts: among them, an adolescent girl who died of typhoid there in 1844. ⊠ *1 Bridge St.*

❶ **King's Square.** In a town where age is relative, King's Square is comparatively new. The square was created in the 19th century after a marshy part of the harbor was filled in. Today it still looks rather inauspicious, more a patch of pavement than a leafy common, yet the square is St. George's undisputed center. Locals frequently congregate here for civic celebrations. Visitors, meanwhile, come to see the replica stocks and pillory. Formerly used to punish petty crimes, these grisly gizmos—together with a replica "ducking stool"—are now popular props for photos ops. Reenactments of historical incidents, overseen by a town crier in full colonial costume, are staged in the square November through March on Wednesday and Saturday at noon, and April through October on Monday, Wednesday, Thursday, and Saturday at noon. In high season, King's Square also hosts St. George's Market Nights, a weekly street festival with craft vendors, Gombey dancers, and more reenactments from 6:30 to 9:30 on Tuesday nights, May through September.

⓬ While roaming the back streets, look for **Nea's Alley.** Nineteenth-century Irish poet Thomas Moore, who lived in St. George's during his tenure as registrar of the admiralty court, waxed poetic about both this "lime-covered alley" and a lovely woman he first encountered here: his boss's teenaged bride, "Nea" Tucker. Though arguably the most amorous, Moore wasn't the only writer to be inspired by Bermuda. Mark Twain wrote about it in *The Innocents Abroad,* and his exclamation "you go to heaven if you want to; I'd druther stay in Bermuda" remains something of a motto in these parts. Two 20th-century playwrights, Eugene O'Neill and Noel Coward, also wintered—and worked—on the island. More recently, Bermuda resident Peter Benchley took the idea for his novel *The Deep* from the ships lost off shore. ⊠ *between printer's alley and Old Maid's La.*

⓫ **The Old Rectory.** Built around 1699 by part-time privateer George Dew, this charming limestone cottage takes its name from a later resident, Alexander Richardson (the rector of St. Peter's Church), who lived here between 1763 and 1805. In addition to handsome gardens, the house with its cedar beams, multiple chimneys, and "welcoming arms" entrance is a lovely example of traditional Bermudian architecture. Want more than a quick look inside? The Old Rectory currently operates as a bed-and-breakfast. Rates for the two guest rooms run between $100 and $150 per night, based on double occupancy, with a minimum three-night booking. ⊠ *1 Broad Alley, behind St. Peter's Church* ☎ *441/297–4261* ⊕ *www.bnt.bm for tours, www.bermudagetaway. com for overnight stays* ⊡ *Donations accepted* ⊙ *Sightseeing visits Nov.–Mar., Wed. only 1–5.*

❻ **Old State House.** A curious ritual takes place every April in King's Square as one peppercorn, regally placed upon a velvet pillow, is presented to the mayor of St. George's amid much pomp and circumstance. The paltry peppercorn is the rent paid annually for the Old State House by the Masonic Lodge St. George No. 200 of the Grand Lodge of Scotland. This fraternal organization has occupied the building since Bermuda's Parliament—the third oldest in the world after Iceland's and England's—vacated it in 1815 when the capital moved to Hamilton. The Old State House was erected in 1620 in what Governor Nathaniel Butler believed was the Italian style, so it's one of the few structures in Bermuda to feature a flat roof. Builders used a mixture of turtle oil and lime as mortar, setting the style for future Bermudian buildings.

✉*4 Princess St.* ☎*441/296–8766* ⊕*members.northrock.bm/~lcenter/ Lodge/StateHouse.html* ☞*Free* ⊙*May–Nov., Wed. 10–2.*

★ ☾ ❷ **Ordnance Island.** Ordnance Island, directly across from King's Square, is dominated by a splendid bronze statue of Sir George Somers, commander of the *Sea Venture.* Somers looks surprised that he made it safely to shore—and you may be surprised that he ever chose to set sail again when you spy the nearby *Deliverance II.* It's a full-scale replica of one of two ships—the other was the *Patience*—built under Somers's supervision to carry survivors from the 1609 wreck onward to Jamestown. But considering her size (just 57 feet from bow to stern) *Deliverance II* hardly seems ocean-worthy by modern standards. You can scramble on board for a small fee; however, it's easy enough to imagine the cramped conditions by simply comparing the small vessel to the contemporary cruise ships that moor behind her. ✉*Across from King's Sq.* ☎*441/297–1459* ☞*$3* ⊙*Apr.–Oct., weekdays 9:30–5.*

❽ **Somers Garden.** After sailing to Jamestown and back in 1610, Sir George Somers—the British admiral charged with developing the Bermudian colony—fell ill and died. According to local lore, Somers instructed his nephew Matthew Somers to bury his heart in Bermuda, where it belonged. Matthew sailed for England soon afterward, sneaking Somers' body aboard in a cedar chest so as not to attract attention from superstitious sailors, and eventually burying it near his birthplace in Dorset. Although it can't be proven that Matthew actually carried out his uncle's wishes, it's generally believed that Admiral Somers' heart was indeed left behind in a modest tomb at the southwest corner of the park. When the tomb was opened many years later, only a few bones, a pebble, and some bottle fragments were found. Nonetheless, ceremonies were held at the empty grave in 1920, when the Prince of Wales christened this pleasant, tree-shrouded park Somers Garden. ✉*Bordered by Shinbone and Blockade alleys, Duke of Kent and Duke of York sts.* ☞*Free* ⊙*Daily 8–4.*

❿ **St. George's Historical Society Museum, Printery & Garden.** Furnished to resemble its former incarnation as a private home, this typical Bermudian building reveals what life was like in the early 1700s. Along with period furnishings, it has assorted documents and artifacts (like ax heads and whale-blubber cutters) pertaining to the colonial days. But it's the re-created kitchen—complete with palmetto baskets and calabash "dipping" gourds—that really takes the cake. Downstairs the printery (accessible from Featherbed Alley) features a working replica of a Gutenberg-style press, as well as early editions of island newspapers. The beautiful cottage gardens behind the museum are also worth a visit. ✉*Duke of Kent St. and Featherbed Alley* ☎*441/297–0423* ☞*$5* ⊙*Apr.–Nov., weekdays 10–4; Jan.–Mar., Wed. 11–4.*

⓭ **St. Peter's Church.** Because parts of this whitewashed stone church date
FodorśChoice   back to 1620, it holds the distinction of being the oldest continuously
★   operating Anglican church in the Western Hemisphere. It was not, however, the first house of worship to stand on this site. It replaced a 1612 structure made of wooden posts and palmetto leaves that was

CLOSE UP

Island Weddings

1

It's no wonder so many couples want to exchange their vows in Bermuda. For starters, this subtropical paradise has loads of pink beaches—and little red tape. Factor in easy access from the United States; a well-established infrastructure that includes English-speaking wedding personnel; and a remarkably high romance quotient (the island even has an honest-to-goodness Lover's Lane!) and you can understand why Bermuda is an ideal spot to tie the knot.

There are more than 100 places of worship on the island and you can be married in most of them. Two of the prettiest churches, especially for a small wedding, are Christ Church (Church of Scotland/Presbyterian) in Warwick Parish and St. Paul's (Church of England/Anglican) in Paget Parish. If you prefer to wed in a natural setting, you can choose from a nearly endless number of lovely locations, including beaches, gardens, parks, and the gorgeous grounds of historic properties. If you wish to bring your own minister to perform the ceremony, you need permission from the Department of Immigration. Civil weddings take place in the Marriage Room at the Registrar's office—a surprisingly attractive venue.

Want to add some local flavor to the festivities? Follow Bermudian tradition by serving two wedding cakes. In this part of the world the groom's cake is plain, often a pound cake, wrapped in

gold leaf to symbolize prosperity. The multitier bride's cake is a dark fruit-cake wrapped in silver leaf to symbolize purity. A cedar seedling, placed atop one of them, is later planted by the couple to represent their growing love. Another tradition is for the bride and groom to walk hand-in-hand beneath a Bermuda moongate—an archway made of limestone and coral usually found at the entrance to gardens. It's said that all who do so are assured everlasting luck. Afterward, it's customary for the couple to travel on to their honeymoon destination in a classic horse-drawn carriage.

If you're dreaming of a full-service wedding, it's a good idea to contact a local coordinator to handle the legalities and logistics. Knowledgeable wedding consultants at **Bridal Suite** (☎ 441/292–2025 ⊕ www.bridalsuite bermudaweddings.com), the **Wedding Salon** (☎ 441/292–5677 ⊕ www. bermudaweddingsalon.com), and **Bermuda Bride** (☎ 441/232–2344 ⊕ www.bermudabride.com) can help you plan the perfect day. Several of the larger hotels also have their own in-house coordinators. You'll need to request a "Notice of Intended Marriage" form from the Registrar General's Office and file it at least four weeks prior to the wedding. Obtain one by calling ☎ 441/297–7709 or download a copy at ⊕ www. bermudatourism.com.

—Susan MacCallum-Whitcomb

destroyed in a storm. The present church was extended in 1713 (the oldest part is the area around the triple-tier pulpit), with the tower and wings being added in the 19th century. Befitting its age, St. Peter's has many treasures. The red cedar altar, carved in 1615 under the supervision of Richard Moore (a shipwright and the colony's first governor) is the oldest piece of woodwork in Bermuda. The baptismal font, brought to the island by early settlers, is about 500 years old; and the late 18th-century bishop's throne is believed to have been salvaged from a shipwreck. There's also a fine collection of communion silver from the 1600s in the vestry. Nevertheless, it's the building itself that leaves the most lasting impression. With rough-hewn pillars, exposed cedar beams and candlelit chandeliers, the church is stunning in its simplicity. After viewing the interior, walk into the churchyard to see where prominent Bermudians, including Governor Sir Richard Sharples who was assassinated in 1973, are buried. A separate graveyard for slaves (to the west of the church, behind the wall) is a poignant reminder of Bermuda's segregated past. ⊠33 Duke of York St. ☎441/297-2459 ⊕www.anglican.bm ▱Donations accepted ⊗Mon.–Sat. 10–4, Sun. service at 11:15.

> ### ALL FIRED UP
>
> In 1775 the Continental Congress imposed a ban on exports to colonies not supporting their trade embargo against England. Bermuda depended on the American colonies for grain, so a delegation of Bermudians traveled to Philadelphia offering salt in exchange for the resumption of grain shipments. Congress rejected the salt, but agreed to lift the ban if Bermuda sent gunpowder instead. A group of Bermudians, including two Tuckers, then broke into the island's arsenal, stole the gunpowder, and shipped it to Boston. The ban was soon lifted.

❹ **Town Hall.** St. George's administrative offices are housed in a putty-color two-story structure that dates back to 1808. Inside the cedar-paneled hall—where the civic government still meets—you can see portraits of past mayors. Better yet, you can get some "face time" with the current one. At 11:45 on Wednesday and Saturday, November through March, the mayor greets visitors and gives a brief talk. ⊠5 King's Sq. ☎441/297-1532 ▱Free ⊗Mon.–Sat. 9–4.

★ ⓫ **Tucker House.** Tucker House is maintained, owned, and lovingly preserved as a museum by the Bermuda National Trust. It was built in the 1750s for a merchant who stored his wares in the cellar (a space that now holds an archaeological exhibit). But it's been associated with the illustrious Tucker family ever since Henry Tucker, president of the Governor's Council and a key participant in the Bermuda Gunpowder Plot, purchased it in 1775. His descendents lived here until 1809 and much of the fine silver and heirloom furniture—which dates primarily from the mid-18th and early-19th centuries—was donated by them. As a result, the house is essentially a tribute to this well-connected clan whose members included a Bermudian governor, a U.S. treasurer, a Confederate navy captain, and an Episcopal bishop.

The kitchen, however, is dedicated to another notable—Joseph Haine Rainey—who is thought to have operated a barber's shop in it during the Civil War. (Barber's Alley, around the corner, is also named in his honor.) As a freed slave from South Carolina, Rainey fled to Bermuda at the outbreak of the war. Afterward he returned to the United States and, in 1870, became the first black man to be elected to the House of Representatives. A short flight of stairs leads down to the kitchen, originally a separate building, and to an enclosed kitchen garden. ⊠5

Water St. ☎441/297–0545 ⊕*www.bnt.bm* 📧*$5; $10 combination ticket includes admission to National Trust Museum in Globe Hotel and Verdmont* ⊙*Nov.–Mar., Wed.–Sat.; Apr.–Oct., Mon.–Sat. 10–4.*

❾ Unfinished Church. Work began on this intended replacement for St. Peter's Church in 1874. But, just as it neared completion, construction was halted by storm damage and disagreements within the church community. Hence the massive Gothic-revival pile sat—unfinished and crumbling—until the Bermuda National Trust stepped in to stabilize the structure in 1992. With soaring stone walls, a grassy floor and only the sky for a roof, it's the sort of atmospheric ruin that poets and painters so admire. ⊠*Duke of Kent St.* ☎441/236–6483 ⊕*www.bnt.bm* 📧*Free* ⊙*Daily dawn–dusk.*

NEED A BREAK?

Return to the 21st century to check your e-mail—cup of gourmet coffee in hand—at **Caffè Latte** (⊠*8 Duke of York St.* ☎*441/297–8196* ⊕*www.caffelatte.bm* ⊙*Mon.–Sat. 7:30–5, Sun. 7:30–4*), located just west of Tucker House by St. George's main bus stop. While you're there you can stock up on brochures and bus tokens, too, because this cyber café shares its facilities with the town's new **Visitor Information Centre** (☎*441/297–8000*). If you're hungry for more than information, order a snack (bagels, pastries, hearty homemade soups, and deli sandwiches are all on the menu); then settle down on the sunny patio or in the comfortable air-conditioned shop.

⑯ World Heritage Centre. Housed in an 1860 customs warehouse next to the Penno's Wharf Cruise Ship Terminal, the center is still a work-in-progress. However, Phase One of this multiyear, multimillion-dollar project opened in the summer of 2006. You can now visit the ground-floor Orientation Exhibits Gallery showcasing several hundred years of civic history, and view a brief film (*A Stroll through St. George's*). Developed under the auspices of the St. George's Foundation, the World Heritage Centre is set to include further exhibition space, a library, theater, and retail outlets when completed. ⊠*19 Penno's Wharf* ☎441/297–5791 ⊕*www.stgeorgesfoundation.com* 📧*Free* ⊙*Tues.–Sat. 10–4.*

HAMILTON

St. George's and Hamilton are about 10 mi and 200 years apart. The latter wasn't even incorporated as a town until 1792; and by the time Hamilton became capital in 1815, St. George's had already celebrated its bicentennial. The age difference is apparent. The charmingly gnarled lanes of the island's first town straighten out here into proper streets, and topsy-turvy colonial cottages give way to more formal Victorian facades. As Bermuda's economic and social hub, Hamilton has a different vibe, too.

With a permanent resident population of 1,500 households, this city in Pembroke Parish still doesn't qualify as a major metropolis. Yet it has enough stores, restaurants, and offices to amp up the energy level. Moreover, it has a thriving international business community (centered on financial and investment services, insurance, telecommunications, global management of intellectual property, shipping, and aircraft and ship registration), which lends it a degree of sophistication seldom found in so small a center.

Numbers in the text correspond to numbers on the map.

A GOOD WALK

Any tour of Hamilton should begin on **Front Street ❶**, a tidy thoroughfare lined with ice-cream–color buildings, many with cheery awnings and ornate balconies. The **Visitor Information Centre** in the No. 1 Passenger Terminal (the most westerly of Hamilton's two cruise ship facilities) is a good starting point. Stroll toward the intersection of Front and Queen streets where you can see the Birdcage, a much-photographed traffic box named for its designer, Michael "Dickey" Bird; then continue west and swing down Point Pleasant Road to **Albuoy's Point ❷** for a splendid view of Hamilton Harbour. Afterward, retrace your steps, passing the Ferry Terminal Building where passengers board boats for sightseeing excursions. (You can also depart from here on more affordable round-trip rides to the Dockyard via the Sea Express ferry.)

Back at the Birdcage, turn up Queen Street to see the 19th-century **Perot Post Office ❸**. Just beyond it is the **Museum of the Bermuda Historical Society/Bermuda Public Library ❹**. Follow Queen Street away from the harbor to Church Street to reach the **City Hall & Arts Centre ❺**, which houses the Bermuda National Gallery, the Bermuda Society of Arts Gallery, and a performing arts center. Saturday mornings from November to June, you can continue on to the **City Market ❻**, which sets up about five minutes north on Canal Road.

Returning to the City Hall steps, turn east on Church Street and pass the Hamilton Bus Terminal. One block farther, the imposing **Cathedral of the Most Holy Trinity ❼** looms up before you. Next, past the cathedral near the corner of Church and Parliament streets, you'll come to **Sessions House ❽**. Keep going down Parliament to Front Street for a look at the **Cabinet Building ❾** and, in front of it, the Cenotaph for fallen Bermudian soldiers. From here, you might head back to Front Street for a leisurely stroll past (or into!) the shops, then linger over lunch in one of the many cafés overlooking the harbor.

If you're up for a longer walk (about 15 minutes east from the Cenotaph) or are traveling by scooter or taxi, head to the **Bermuda Underwater Exploration Institute (BUEI) ❿**. **Fort Hamilton ⓫** is another worthwhile destination, though the road to it—north on King Street, then a sharp right on Happy Valley Road—is a bit too steep for casual walkers. The moated fort has gorgeous grounds, underground passageways, and great views of Hamilton and its harbor.

TIMING   Although it's possible to buzz through Hamilton in a few hours, you should plan to give it a day if you're going to take in some of the museums, Fort Hamilton, and the Bermuda Underwater Exploration Institute. Serious shoppers should set aside another half day to browse around the shops.

WHAT TO SEE

❷ Albuoy's Point. It's always a pleasure to watch sailboats and passenger ferries zigzag around the many islands that dot Hamilton Harbour. For a ringside seat to the show, grab a bench beneath the trees at Albuoy's Point, a small waterside park. Nearby is the **Royal Bermuda Yacht Club,** founded in 1844 and granted the use of the word "Royal" by Prince Albert in 1845. Today luminaries from the international sailing scene hobnob with local yachtsmen and business executives at the club's 1930s headquarters. If you're around between April and November, you might catch one of the many club-sponsored racing events, such as the Newport–Bermuda Race in June or the King Edward VII Gold Cup Match Race Tournament in October. ✉ *Off Front St.*

★ ☾ ❿ Bermuda Underwater Exploration Institute (BUEI). The 40,000-square-foot Ocean Discovery Centre showcases local contributions to oceanographic research and undersea discovery. Guests can ogle the world-class shell collection amassed by resident Jack Lightbourne (three of the 1,000 species were identified by and named for Lightbourne himself); or visit a gallery honoring native-born archaeologist Teddy Tucker to see booty retrieved from Bermudian shipwrecks. The types of gizmos that made such discoveries possible are also displayed: including a replica of the bathysphere William Beebe and Otis Barton used in their record-smashing 1934 dive. (Forget the Bermuda Triangle: the real mystery is how they descended ½ a mile in a metal ball less than 5 feet in diameter!) A more modern "submersible," Nautilus-X2, lets wannabe explorers take a simulated seven-minute trip to the ocean floor. Special events, like lectures and whale-watching trips, are available, too, for an added fee. If all that activity makes you hungry, Harbourfront Restaurant (which replaced La Coquille as the on-site eatery in May 2007) is a lovely choice for lunch. Pedestrians may access the BUEI by following the sidewalk on the water side of Front Street. Motorists must drive out of town on Front Street, round the traffic circle, and exit at the lane signposted for the BUEI because it's only accessible to in-bound vehicles. ✉ *40 Crow Lane, off E. Broadway* ☎ *441/292–7219* ⊕ *www.buei.org* ✉ *$12.50* ☾ *Weekdays 9–5, weekends 10–5, last admission at 4.*

❾ Cabinet Building. Bermuda's Senate (the upper house of Parliament) sits in the dignified Cabinet Building built in 1841 and remodeled almost a century later. The most rewarding time to be here is during the formal opening of Parliament, traditionally held on the first Friday of November. His Excellency the Governor, dressed in a plumed hat and full regalia, arrives on the grounds in a landau drawn by magnificent black horses and accompanied by a police escort. A senior officer, carrying the Black Rod made by the Crown jewelers, next asks the speaker of the House, elected representatives, and members of the Senate chamber to convene. The governor then presents the Throne Speech from a tiny cedar throne dating from 1642. A more somber ceremony is held in front of the building every Remembrance Day (November 11), when the governor and other dignitaries lay wreaths at the Cenotaph: a limestone memorial to Bermuda's war casualties erected in 1920. At other times of the year, assuming Parliament is in session, you may visit the Senate chambers on Wednesday to watch debates that are alternately lively and long-winded. Note that the gallery to the left of the main entrance is intended for public use. ✉ *105 Front St.* ☎ *441/292–5501* ⊕ *www.gov.bm* ✉ *Free* ☉ *Weekdays 9–5.*

★ ❼ **Cathedral of the Most Holy Trinity.** After the original Anglican sanctuary on this site was torched by an arsonist in 1884, Scottish architect William Hay was enlisted to design a replacement. True to his training, he set out to erect a Gothic-style structure in the grand European tradition. Mission accomplished. Inside, the clerestory in the nave

---

HEEEEERE'S JOHNNY!

"Good morning. I love you!" Johnny Barnes calls, waving and smiling. And he means it. The eccentric retired bus driver has greeted motorists for more than two decades, standing on the Crow Lane roundabout at the entrance to the City of Hamilton every weekday morning from about 6 to 10 rain or shine. Late risers who don't get to see him in person can look for the bronze Desmond Fountain–designed statue of Johnny near the Bermuda Underwater Exploration Institute.

---

is supported by piers of polished Scottish granite; soaring archways are trimmed in stone imported from France; and the choir stalls and bishop's throne are carved out of English oak. The pulpit, meanwhile, is modeled on the one in Hay's hometown cathedral (St. Giles in Edinburgh), and the whole thing is crowned by a copper roof that stands out among Bermuda's typical white-topped buildings. Yet for all the European flourishes, Bermuda Cathedral still has a subtropical flair. After all, the limestone building blocks came from the Par-la-Ville quarry and one of its loveliest stained-glass windows—the Angel Window on the east wall of the north transept—was created by local artist Vivienne Gilmore Gardner. After sauntering around the interior, you can climb the 155 steps of the church tower for a heavenly view of Hamilton and its harbor. ✉ *Church St.* ☎ *441/292–4033* ⊕ *www. anglican.bm* ✉ *Cathedral free; tower $3* ☉ *Church daily 7:30–5 and for Sun. services, tower weekdays 10–4.*

★ ☺ ❺ **City Hall & Arts Centre.** Set back from the street behind a fountain and lily pond, City Hall contains Hamilton's administrative offices as well as two art galleries and a performance hall. Instead of a clock, its tower is topped with a bronze wind vane—a prudent choice in a land where the weather is as important as the time. The statues of children playing in the fountain are by local sculptor Desmond Fountain, whose lifelike characters you may encounter elsewhere on the island. The building itself was designed in 1960 by Bermudian architect Wilfred Onions, a champion of balanced simplicity. Massive cedar doors open onto an impressive lobby notable for its beautiful chandeliers and portraits of mayors past and present. To the left is City Hall Theatre, a major venue for concerts, plays, and dance performances. To the right are the civic offices where you can find the Benbow Stamp Collection and an exhibit of Bermudian antiques. A handsome cedar staircase leads upstairs to two second-floor art galleries. (An elevator gets you there, too.)

On the first landing, in the East Exhibition Room, is the **Bermuda National Gallery** (☎*441/295–9428* ⊕*www.bng.bm* ✉*Free*), home to Bermuda's national art collection. The permanent exhibits include paintings by island artists as well as European masters like Gainsborough and Reynolds; African masks and sculpture; and photographs by internationally known artists, such as Bermudian Richard Saunders (1922–87). The fine and decorative art pieces in the Bermuda Collection reflect the country's multicultural heritage. Temporary exhibits are also a major part of the museum's program, and on any given day you can see a selection of local work along with a traveling exhibit from another museum. For a comprehensive look at the collections, join one of the free docent-led tours offered Thursday at 10:30 or sign on for the $8 Cultural Art Tour that begins each Tuesday at 11 (reservations required). Lectures and other special events are listed in the gallery's online calendar. Farther up the stairs, in the West Wing, the **Bermuda Society of Arts Gallery** (☎*441/292–3824* ⊕*www.bsoa.bm* ✉*Donations accepted*) displays work by its members. Its frequently changing juried shows attract talented local painters, sculptors, and photographers. Art collectors will be pleased to learn that many pieces may also be purchased. ✉*17 Church St.* ☎*441/292–1234* ☉*City Hall weekdays 9–5; National Gallery and Society of the Arts Mon.–Sat. 10–4.*

❻ One of the best places to mingle with Onions and, yes, buy a few edible ones is the **City Market** held every Saturday, 8 to 1, from November to June. It features up to 50 vendors who sell only Bermuda-grown, -caught or -made products. Along with organic produce, fresh fish, and assorted homebaked items, goodies like handcrafted soaps and honey derived from the pollen of island wild flowers are up for sale. The market, at the Bull's Head Car Park on Canal Road, is about a five-minute walk north of City Hall. ☎*441/517–4101.*

★ ☾ ⓫ **Fort Hamilton.** This imposing moat-ringed fortress has underground passageways that were cut through solid rock by Royal Engineers in the 1860s. Built to defend the West End's Royal Naval Dockyard from land attacks, it was outdated even before its completion but remains a fine example of a polygonal Victorian fort. Even if you're not a big fan of military history, the hilltop site's stellar views and stunning gardens make the trip worthwhile. On Monday at noon, from November to March, bagpipes echo through the grounds as the kilt-clad members of the Bermuda Islands Pipe Band perform a traditional skirling ceremony. Due to one-way streets, getting to the fort by scooter can be a bit challenging. From downtown Hamilton head north on Queen Street, turn right on Church Street, then turn left to go up the hill on King Street. Make a sharp right turn (270-degree) onto Happy Valley Road and follow the signs. Pedestrians may walk along Front Street to King Street. ✉*Happy Valley Rd.* ☎*441/292–1234* ✉*Free* ☉*Daily 9:30–5.*

❶ **Front Street.** Running along the harbor, Hamilton's main thoroughfare bustles with small cars, motor scooters, bicycles, buses, pedestrians,

1

and the occasional horse-drawn carriage. When cruise ships are in port, it also bustles with tourists who tend to cram into the street's high-class low-rise shops. Return visitors will notice that Triminghams Department Store (a Bermuda institution since 1842) has closed; however, there are still plenty of places on Front Street offering retail therapy. Don't overlook small offshoots and alleyways, like Chancery Lane, Bermuda House Lane, and the Walkway, where you'll stumble upon hidden-away boutiques. The **Visitor Information**

WHAT'S IN A NAME?

Bermudians cultivated onions long before Americans did. In fact, throughout the 19th century they were one of the island's major exports, and its people were so closely identified with the tear-inducing plant that anyone born and bred here came to be known as an "Onion." Though competition eventually put an end to the lucrative trade, this nickname for locals stuck.

Centre (☎441/734–3233) is a good place to strike out from when you're ready to explore the rest of Hamilton. Open weekdays 9–4 and Saturday 10–4, it's the place to go for pamphlets, maps, or transit passes. It's also the departure point for a free city walking tour that leaves Monday mornings, November to March, at 10. In case you can't make it, the bureau has brochures for a self-guided walk as well.

★ ❹ **Museum of the Bermuda Historical Society/Bermuda Public Library.** Mark Twain admired the giant rubber tree that stands on Queen Street in the front yard of this Georgian house, formerly owned by William Bennet Perot and his family. Though charmed by the tree, which had been imported from what is now Guyana in the mid-19th century, Twain lamented that it didn't bear rubbery fruit in the form of overshoes and hot-water bottles. The library, about which he made no comment, was established in 1839 and its reference section has virtually every book ever written about Bermuda, as well as a microfilm collection of Bermudian newspapers dating back to 1784.

The museum is to the left of the library entrance. Established in 1955, it chronicles Bermuda's past through interesting—and in some cases downright quirky—artifacts. One display, for instance, is full of tools and trinkets made by Boer War prisoners who were exiled to Bermuda in 1901 and 1902. Another features an unusual 18th-century sedan chair. Check out the portraits of Sir George Somers and his wife, painted around 1605, and of Postmaster Perot and his wife that hang in the entrance hall. Time permitting, also ask to see a copy of the letter George Washington wrote in 1775: addressed TO THE INHABITANTS OF BERMUDA, it requests gunpowder for use in the American Revolution. ✉13 Queen St. ☎441/295–2905 library, 441/295–2487 museum ⊕www.bermudanationallibrary.bm ✑Donations accepted ☉Library Mon.–Thurs. 8:30–7, Fri. 10–5, Sat. 9–5, Sun. 1–5; closed Sun. in July and Aug.; museum Mon.–Sat. 9:30–3:30 ☞Tours by appointment.

❸ **Perot Post Office.** To some, this rather austere 1840s structure is simply a place to mail a letter. To stamp collectors, on the other hand, the lovingly restored, fully operational post office named for Hamilton's first

CLOSE UP

The Bermuda Triangle Demystified

Long before the myth of the Bermuda Triangle became legend, Bermuda had already earned a reputation as an enchanted island. It was nicknamed "The Devil's Islands" by early sea travelers, frightened by the calls of cahow birds and the squeals of wild pigs that could be heard on shore. But perhaps the most damning tales were told by sailors terrified of shipwreck on Bermuda's dangerous reefs. The island's mystical reputation is believed to have inspired Shakespeare's *The Tempest,* a tale of shipwreck and sorcery in "the still-vexed Bermoothes."

The early origin of the Triangle myth stretches as far back as Columbus, who noted in his logbook a haywire compass, strange lights, and a burst of flame falling into the sea. Columbus, as well as other seamen after him, also encountered a harrowing stretch of ocean now known as the Sargasso Sea. Ancient tales tell of sailboats stranded forever in a windless expanse of water, surrounded by seaweed and the remnants of other unfortunate vessels. It's true that relics have been found in the Sargasso Sea—an area of ocean between Bermuda and the Caribbean—but the deadly calm waters are more likely the result of circular ocean currents sweeping through the North Atlantic rather than paranormal activity.

In the past 500 years at least 50 ships and 20 aircraft have vanished in the Triangle, most without a trace—no wreckage, no bodies, nothing. Many disappeared in reportedly calm waters, without having sent a distress signal. Among the legends is that of Flight 19. At 2:10 on the afternoon of December 5, 1945, five TBM Avenger Torpedo Bombers took off from Fort Lauderdale, Florida, on a routine two-hour training mission. Their last radio contact was at 4 PM. The planes and 27 men were never seen or heard from again. The official navy report said the planes disappeared "as if they had flown to Mars."

The bizarre disappearances attributed to the Triangle have been linked to everything from alien abduction to sorcery. Although the mystery has not been completely solved, there are scientific explanations for many of the maritime disasters that have occurred in the Triangle. The most obvious answers are linked to extreme weather conditions with which any Bermudian fisherman would be well acquainted. "White squalls"—intense, unexpected storms that arrive without warning on otherwise clear days—are probable culprits, along with waterspouts, the equivalent of sea tornadoes. The most recent scientific theory on the infamous Triangle suggests that the freakish disappearance of ships and aircraft could be the result of large deposits of methane gas spewing up from the ocean floor. Huge eruptions of methane bubbles may push water away from a ship, causing it to sink. If the highly flammable methane then rises into the air, it could ignite in an airplane's engine—causing it to explode and disappear.

Fact or fiction, the Triangle is a part of local lore that won't disappear anytime soon. But don't let it scare you away—this myth isn't the only thing that makes Bermuda seem so magical.

–Kim Dismont Robinson

postmaster is a veritable shrine. William Bennet Perot was certainly a genial fellow: he would meet arriving steamers, collect the incoming mail, stash it in his beaver hat, and then stroll around Hamilton to deliver it, greeting each recipient with a tip of his chapeau. But it was his resourcefulness that made him most famous among philatelists. Tired of individually hand-stamping outgoing letters, Perot began printing stamps in 1848. Of the thousands he produced, only 11 still exist—and several of those are owned by Queen Elizabeth. If you'd like to get your hands on one, be prepared to dig deep. In June 2005 a Perot-era one-penny stamp sold at auction for a record-breaking $244,000. ⊠ *11 Queen St.* ☎ *441/292–9052* 🎫 *Free* ⊙ *Weekdays 9–5.*

NEED A BREAK?

Next to the Perot Post Office is the Queen Street entrance to Par-la-Ville Park (there's another entrance on Par-la-Ville Road). Once Perot's private garden, it has winding paths, luxuriant blooms, and park benches that are ideal for people-watching. At the park's west entrance is a fine example of a Bermuda moongate.

8 **Sessions House & Jubilee Clock Tower.** This eye-catching Italianate edifice, erected in 1819, is where the House of Assembly (the lower house of Parliament) and the Supreme Court convene. The Florentine towers and colonnade, decorated with red terra-cotta, were added to the building in 1887 to commemorate Queen Victoria's Golden Jubilee. The Victoria Jubilee Clock Tower made its striking debut—albeit a few years late—at midnight on December 31, 1893. Bermuda's Westminster-style Parliament meets on the second floor, where the speaker rules the roost in a powdered wig and robe. (The island has approximately 14 times as many politicians per capita as Europe or North America, so maintaining order is no small feat!) Sartorial splendor is equally evident downstairs in the Supreme Court where wigs and robes (red for judges, black for barristers) are again the order of the day. You're welcome to watch the colorful proceedings: bear in mind, though, that visitors, too, are required to wear appropriate attire. Call first to find out when parliamentary sessions and court cases are scheduled. ⊠ *21 Parliament St.* ☎ *441/292–7408 Parliament, 441/292–1350 Supreme Court* ⊕ *www.gov.bm* 🎫 *Free* ⊙ *Weekdays 9–12:30 and 2–5.*

THE WEST END & DOCKYARD

Bermuda is denser than you might imagine. But in contrast to Hamilton and St. George's, the island's West End seems positively pastoral. Many of the top sites here are natural ones: namely the wildlife reserves, wooded areas, and beautiful waterways of Sandys Parish. The notable exception is Bermuda's single largest tourist attraction—the Royal Naval Dockyard.

Its story begins in the aftermath of the American Revolution, when Britain suddenly found itself with neither an anchorage nor a major ship-repair yard in the western Atlantic. Around 1809, just as Napoleon was surfacing as a serious threat and the empire's ships were becoming increasingly vulnerable to pirate attack, Britain decided to construct a stronghold in Bermuda. Dubbed the "Gibraltar of the West," the Dockyard operated as a shipyard for nearly 150 years. The facility was closed in 1951, although the Royal Navy maintained a small presence here until 1976 and held title to the land until 1995.

The Bermudian government and development groups began to plan for civilian use of the Dockyard in 1980. Since then, $21 million in public funds and $42 million in private money has been spent to make the area blossom. Now trees and shrubs grow where there used to be vast stretches of concrete. Private yachts calmly float where naval vessels once anchored, and cruise ships dock at the terminal. Historic structures—like the Clocktower and Cooperage buildings—house restaurants, galleries, shops, even a movie theater. A strip of beach now serves as a snorkel park. And, at the center of it all, are the Maritime Museum & Dolphin Quest: two popular facilities that share a fortified 6-acre site. You can reach the Dockyard from Hamilton in 45 minutes by bus or a half hour by fast ferry.

> ## NO EXPERIENCE NECESSARY
>
> The Dockyard was largely built by convicts transported from Britain and the other colonies. Burglars and privateers from Nova Scotia were, for instance, sent here well into the 19th century. Murderers who had their death sentence commuted were also shipped over. But given the harsh conditions, some must have wished they had never been shown such "mercy." Almost one quarter of these forced laborers (some 2,000 in total) died and were buried, mostly in unmarked graves, in a cemetery at the approach to the Dockyard, just off Malabar Road.

A GOOD TOUR

To make the most of your visit to the West End, plan to combine sea and land transportation. If you've bought a bus pass (rather than tickets), it will work on both ferries and buses, allowing you to hop on and off wherever you please. If you have a bicycle or scooter, you can bring it on the ferry; however, you'll be charged an extra adult fare to take the scooter, and space is sometimes limited. Once you arrive, you can see the Dockyard itself can be covered easily on foot. But other sights are rather far apart. So plan to take a taxi, bus, or ferry if you're continuing on to Somerset or elsewhere.

The logical place to begin a tour is the Royal Naval Dockyard. Start your day by visiting the **Bermuda Maritime Museum & Dolphin Quest**, which are housed together in a stone fortress. Next to the entrance is the **Snorkel Park**, a small protected reef with underwater "trails" where you can get up close to marine life. Across from the museum entrance, the tempting art gallery and permanent art-and-crafts market in the **Old Cooperage** also warrant a visit. To the west are a pottery shop, glassblowing center and other businesses that occupy attractive old military warehouses; just south is the **Clocktower Mall & Clocktower Parade,** where you can find still more shops plus the new **Visitor Information Centre.** Finish your tour here, or continue via ferry to Somerset Island.

CLOSE UP

The Bermuda Railway

1

The history of the Bermuda Railway—which operated on the island from 1931 to 1948—is as brief as the track is short. Bermuda's Public Works Department considered proposals for a railroad as early as 1899, and Parliament finally granted permission, in 1922, for a line to run from Somerset to St. George's. But laying tracks was a formidable undertaking, requiring the costly and time-consuming construction of long tunnels and swing bridges. By the time it was finished, the railway had cost investors $1 million, making it, per mile, the most expensive railway ever built.

"Old Rattle and Shake," as it was nicknamed, began to decline during World War II. Soldiers put the train to hard use, and it proved impossible to obtain the necessary maintenance equipment. At the end of the war the government acquired the distressed railway for $115,000. Automobiles arrived in Bermuda in 1946, and train service ended in 1948 when the railway was sold in its entirety to British Guiana (now Guyana). Then, in the 1980s, the government gave new life to the ground it had covered by converting the tracks into trails.

Today the secluded 18-mi recreational Bermuda Railway Trail runs the length of the island, offering fabulous coastal views along the way. Restricted to pedestrians, horseback riders, bicyclists, and scooter drivers, the trail is a delightful way to see the island away from the traffic and noise of main roads. You might want to rent a bike or scooter if you plan to cover the entire trail, as many enthusiastic travelers do. Do note, though, that many portions of the trail are isolated—so you should avoid setting out alone after dark. Regardless of when you go, it's wise to first pick up a free copy of the Bermuda Railway Trail Guide available at visitor information centers.

–revised by Susan MacCallum-Whitcomb

For an interesting change of pace, opt for the slow boat (not the one heading directly to Hamilton) out of the Dockyard. You'll pass by Boaz and Watford islands on your way to Somerset Island, fringed on both sides with beautiful secluded coves, inlets, and bays. Getting off the ferry at Watford Bridge, you can make a quick jaunt into **Somerset Village**, which consistently ranks among Bermuda's prettiest communities.

The next sights, reached via Somerset Road, are best visited by bus or scooter. About 2 mi east of Somerset Village, opposite the Willowbank Hotel, is the entrance to the **Heydon Trust Property**, which boasts both wide-open spaces and a tiny 1616 chapel. Around the bend on your left is **Fort Scaur**, a serene spot with sweeping views of the Great Sound. Linking Somerset Island with the rest of Bermuda is **Somerset Bridge**. Near it is the Somerset ferry landing, where you can catch a boat back to Hamilton. Across the bridge, Somerset Road becomes Middle Road, which leads into Southampton Parish.

TIMING   Allow a full day for exploring this area. Before setting out, you should check bus and ferry schedules carefully because, by water, the trip can take from 30 minutes to more than an hour depending on which ferry

The West End & Dockyard

Bermuda Maritime
Museum & Dolphin
Quest

Snorkel Park

Old Cooperage
Building

Ireland Island N.

Clocktower Mall &
Clocktower Parade

Pender Rd.

Royal Navy
Dockyard

Ireland Island S.

Cruise Ship
Dock

ATLANTIC OCEAN

Boaz
Island

Malabar Rd.

Long Bay
Park and
Nature
Reserve

Mangrove
Bay

Sea
Gardens

Somerset
Long Bay

Somerset
Village

Watford
Island

Great Sound

Daniel's
Head

Gilbert
Nature
Reserve

E. Shore Rd.

Watford
Bridge

Scott's Hill

Cavello
Bay

0   1/2 miles

0   1 km

SANDYS

Long Bay Ln.

Somerset Island

Heydon Trust
Property

KEY

Fort Scaur

Somerset Rd.

Ely's
Harbour

Ferry

Railway Trail

Tourist Information

Somerset
Bridge

TO
HAMILTON

you choose. There are, however, worse ways to spend your time than boating on Bermuda's Great Sound. Buses 7 and 8 depart from Hamilton about every 15 minutes, taking either South Road or Middle Road to the West End.

WHAT TO SEE

Bermuda Maritime Museum & Dolphin Quest. The Maritime Museum, ensconced in Bermuda's largest fort, displays its collections in a series of old munitions warehouses that surround the parade grounds and Keep Pond. Insulated from the rest of the Dockyard by a moat and massive stone ramparts, you'll enter by way of a drawbridge. At the Shifting House, right inside the entrance, you can wander through rooms filled with relics from some of the 350-odd ships wrecked on the island's reefs. Other buildings are devoted to seafaring pursuits such as whaling, shipbuilding, and yacht racing. More displays are in the 19th-century **Commissioner's House,** on the museum's upper grounds. Built as both home and headquarters for the Dockyard commissioner, the house later served as a barracks during World War I and was used for military intelligence during World War II. Today, after an award-winning restoration, it contains exhibits on Bermuda's social and military history.

Fodor'sChoice
★

After immersing yourself in maritime history, you can immerse yourself—literally—in the wonderful world of dolphins. **Dolphin Quest** (☎441/234–4464 ⊕*www.dolphin quest.org*) offers a range of in-water programs that allow adults and children ages five or older to pet, play with, and swim alongside Atlantic bottlenose dolphins in the historic Keep Pond. There are even specially designed sessions, conducted from a submersible bench, for younger kids. Since entry to the Dolphin Quest area is free with museum admission, anyone can watch the action. Participation in the actual programs, however, costs $150 to $285 and advance booking is recommended. ⊠*Maritime Museum, Dockyard* ☎*441/234–1418* ⊕*www.bmm.bm* ☎*$10* ☉*Daily 9:30–5, last admission 4.*

> **SOME ASSEMBLY REQUIRED**
>
> Though it may appear to be yet another stalwart stone building, the Commissioner's House is actually an engineering landmark. Designed by a naval architect, it was the world's first prefabricated residence. The component parts—made of cast iron rather than standard wood—were constructed in England between 1823 and 1827, then shipped to Bermuda where they were assembled and sheathed in local limestone.

Clocktower Mall & Clocktower Parade. A pair of 100-foot towers make it impossible to miss the Clocktower Mall. (Observant folks will note that one of them features a standard clock, the other a tide indicator!) Inside this 19th-century building, the Royal Navy's administrative offices have been replaced by distinctly Bermudian boutiques—including specialty shops and branches of Front Street favorites. These are particularly popular on Sunday because most stores outside the Dockyard area are closed. Just in front of the mall is the former military parade ground, which now hosts special events (like the Beat Retreat Ceremony) and is the site of a new **Visitor Information Centre** (☎*441/799-4842*). If you need pamphlets, bus and ferry tickets, or a phone card, the latter is open daily from 9 to 5. ⊠*Dockyard* ☎*441/234–1709* ☎*Free* ☉*Mid Apr.–Sept., Mon.–Sat. 9:30–6, Tues. 9:30–10, Sun. 10–5; Oct–mid-Apr., Mon.–Sat. 10–5, Sun. 11–5.*

Fort Scaur. The British chose the highest hill in Somerset for the site of this fort, built in the late 1860s and early 1870s to defend the flank of the Dockyard from possible American attacks. British troops were garrisoned here until World War I; and American forces were, ironically, stationed at the fort during World War II. Today its stone walls are surrounded by 22 acres of pretty gardens and the view of the Great Sound from the parapet is unsurpassed. Be sure to check out the early-Bermuda Weather Stone, which is billed as a "perfect weather indicator." A sign posted nearby solemnly explains all. ⊠*Somerset Rd., Ely's Harbour* ☎*441/234–0908* ☎*Free* ☉*Daily 8–4.*

Heydon Trust property. A reminder of what the island was like in its early days, this blissfully peaceful 43-acre preserve remains an unspoiled open space, except for a few citrus groves and flower gardens. Pathways with well-positioned park benches wind through it, affording some wonderful water views. If you persevere along the main path, you'll reach rustic **Heydon Chapel.** Built in the early 1600s, it's Bermuda's smallest church. Nondenominational services featuring stirring Gregorian chants are still held in the single-room sanctuary Monday through Saturday at 3. ⊠ *16 Heydon Dr., off Somerset Rd.* ☎ *441/234–1831* ⛶ *Free* ☉ *Daily dawn–dusk.*

Old Cooperage Building. Ready to do some shopping? Inside this former barrel-making factory, you can find the **Bermuda Craft Market** and the **Bermuda Arts Centre.** The former—arguably the island's largest and best-priced craft outlet—showcases the wares of more than 60 craftspeople, including quilters, candle makers, and wood carvers. The latter is a member-run art gallery that displays innovative high-end work. Exhibits change every six weeks and may include watercolors, oils, sculpture, and photography—much of which is for sale. Half-a-dozen artists also maintain studios on the premises, so leave some time to watch them at work. ⊠ *Dockyard* ☎ *441/234–3208 Craft Market, 441/234–2809 Arts Centre* ⊕ *www.artbermuda.bm* ⛶ *Free* ☉ *Craft Market: Apr.–Oct., daily 9:30–5; Nov.–Mar., daily 10–5. Arts Centre: daily 10–5.*

★ ⓒ **Snorkel Park.** Evidence of the Dockyard's naval legacy can also be viewed at this protected inlet, accessed through a stone tunnel adjacent to the Maritime Museum. Beneath the water's surface lie cast-iron cannons dating from 1550 to 1800, plus an antique anchor and gun-carriage wheel. The true attractions, however, are colorful fish (you might see more than 50 varieties) and other sea creatures including anemones, sea cucumbers, and assorted species of coral. Thanks to amenities like marked reef trails and floating rest stations, snorkeling could hardly be easier. But if you'd rather not swim you can always rent an underwater scooter—a battery-operated, fan-propelled gadget that would make James Bond proud. Kayaks, paddleboats, and paddle-bikes are also available for rent. ⊠ *Dockyard* ☎ *441/234–6989* ⛶ *Admission free, equipment rental extra, available Mon.–Sat. 10:30–6* ☉ *Apr.–Nov., daily 9–6.*

NEED A BREAK?
The super-size fireplace in which coopers used to forge their barrel bands is the focal point of the **Frog & Onion Pub** (⊠ *The Old Cooperage* ☎ *441/293– 1188* ⊕ *www.frogandonion.bm*). Architectural interest aside, this naval-theme pub makes a great place for a lunch break, an afternoon libation, or even a quick game of pool. The menu has traditional fare (think Cornish Pastie and fish-and-chips) as well as thirst-quenching ales made on-site by the Dockyard Brewing Company.

The West End is connected to the rest of Bermuda by **Somerset Bridge** and once you have crossed over it you're no longer, according to local lingo, "up the country." More than marking a boundary, Somerset Bridge is something of an attraction in its own right because it's reputed to be the world's smallest drawbridge. It opens a mere 18 inches, just wide enough to accommodate the mast of a passing sailboat. If your sojourn in the West End is limited to a quick ferry trip in and out of the Dockyard, you'll likely miss seeing the real thing; however, you can still catch a glimpse of this novel structure—assuming you haven't already spent all your cash on sightseeing and souvenirs. Just rifle through your wallet, dig out a Bermudian $20 bill, and flip it over. Somerset Bridge is pictured on the back.

Somerset Village. Its position on Mangrove Bay once made it a popular hideout for pirates. But judging by Somerset Village's bucolic appearance, you'd never guess that now. The shady past has been erased by shady trees, quiet streets, and charming cottages. As far as actual attractions go, this quaint one-road retreat has only a few eateries and shops—most of them offshoots of Hamilton stores. However, it provides easy access to the Gilbert Nature Reserve: a 5-acre woodland with paths that connect to some of the most scenic portions of Bermuda's Railway Trail.

> **TAKE A LOAD OFF**
>
> In a land where cars are limited to one per household, alternate means of transportation matter— which explains why Bermuda's efficient public transit system is so revered and why horse-drawn carriages still do a roaring business. Now **Segway Tours of Bermuda** (☎ 441/504–2581) adds a higher-tech option: 90-minute Dockyard tours conducted year-round on über-cool, two-wheeled Segway Human Transporters.

ELSEWHERE IN THE PARISHES

Bermuda's other points of interest—and there are many—are scattered throughout the nine parishes. This section, covering the length and breadth of the island, focuses on the major ones. Yet half the fun of exploring Bermuda is wandering down forgotten lanes or discovering little-known coves and beaches. A motor scooter, or bicycle if you don't mind hills, is ideal for this kind of travel. You can also take public transportation. Pick up ferry and bus maps and schedules at any visitor information center. A guided taxi tour (about $90 for three hours) is the quickest way to see the sights in all the parishes, and it's safer than biking. Many taxi-tour drivers are experienced, knowledgeable guides who will lead you along the roads less traveled for a look at real Bermudian life.

TIMING   With roads as narrow and winding as Bermuda's, it takes longer to traverse the island than you'd think. So it's smarter to stick with a couple of close-by sights rather than trying to cover them all in a single day. The parishes *are* less congested than the towns, but the area to the east of Hamilton—especially the traffic circle where Crow Lane intersects with the Lane and Trimingham Road—is very busy during morning (7:30–9) and afternoon (4–5:30) rush hours.

THREE GOOD TOURS

ST. GEORGE'S   Starting in the town of St. George's, walk north about 25 minutes on
PARISH   Duke of Kent Street, following the signs to **Fort St. Catherine**. (Those who would rather not hoof it can check at the visitor information cen-

tre to see if the minibus is operating from King's Square.) From here, fort aficionados may continue on to **Alexandra Battery** and **Gates Fort**. If you have a Wednesday morning free, you might also consider a guided tour of the **Bermuda Institute of Ocean Sciences (BIOS)**. To reach it, take a bus or taxi across the Ferry Reach to St. David's Road. Afterward, head east to explore quiet **St. David's Island.**

HAMILTON & SMITH'S PARISHES
Hamilton and Smith's Parishes encircle Harrington Sound. Starting on the northeastern end of the sound, take a bus, taxi, or scooter onto Wilkinson Avenue to access the millennium-old limestone formations in **Crystal Caves**. North Shore Road leads to Flatts Village, site of the **Bermuda Aquarium, Museum & Zoo**. Before leaving Flatts, stand on the bridge to watch the power of the water as it rushes through the narrows. Your next stop should be **Verdmont**, a historic home in Smith's Parish. If you have energy to spare at the end of the day, head down Collector's Hill to South Road, turn left, and in less than a mile you'll be at **Spittal Pond Nature Reserve.**

DEVONSHIRE, PAGET, WARWICK & SOUTHAMPTON PARISHES
If you're interested in botany, begin by nosing around the varied plant collections at the **Botanical Gardens**. Exiting through the north gate puts you on Berry Hill Road. From here you can take a bus, taxi, or scooter to **Waterville**, a harborside house that serves as headquarters for the Bermuda National Trust. Next, walk or ride along the lane, turning right at the traffic circle onto Harbour Road, then left onto Lover's Lane, which will take you to **Paget Marsh**, where you can see what Bermuda was like before settlement. Leaving the marsh, round the corner to Middle Road and catch the bus to **Gibb's Hill Lighthouse** in Southampton for breathtaking views.

WHAT TO SEE

🕲 **Bermuda Aquarium, Museum & Zoo.** The BAMZ, established in 1926, has
FodorsChoice always been a pleasant diversion. But following an ambitious decade-
★ long expansion program, it now rates as one of Bermuda's premier attractions. In the aquarium, the big draw is the Northrock Exhibit: a 140,000-gallon tank that gives you a diver's-eye view of the area's living coral reefs and the colorful marine life it sustains. The museum section has multimedia and interactive displays focusing on native habitats and the impact humans have had on them. The island-theme zoo, meanwhile, displays more than 300 birds, reptiles, and mammals. Don't miss the "Islands of Australasia" exhibit with its lemurs, wallabies, and tree kangaroos or "Islands of the Caribbean," a huge walk-through cage that gets you within arms-length of ibises and iguanas. Other popular areas include an outdoor seal pool and cool kid-friendly Discovery Room. ⊠ *40 N. Shore Rd., Flatts Village, Hamilton Parish* ☏ *441/293–2727* ⊕ *www.bamz.org* 🖃 *$10* ⊗ *Daily 9–5, last admission at 4; North Rock dive talk and seal feeding 1:10 daily Apr.–Sept.; Oct.–Mar., weekends only.*

Bermuda Institute of Ocean Sciences. In 1903—long before environmental issues earned top-of-mind awareness—scientists began studying marine life at this mid-Atlantic facility formerly known as the Bermuda Biological Station for Research. Now researchers from around the world come here to work on projects dealing with hot topics like global warming, marine ecology, and acid rain. You can learn all about them on a free 90-minute tour that starts Wednesday morning at 10 in the reception building. Tours cover the grounds and laboratory. You might also see the station's new 168-foot research vessel, *R/V Bank of Bermuda Atlantic Explorer,* if it happens to be docked that day. ✉*17 Biological Lane, Ferry Reach, St. George's Parish* ☎*441/297–1880* ⊕*www.bios.edu* ✉*Donations accepted.*

Botanical Gardens. Established in 1898, the Botanical Gardens are filled with exotic subtropical plants, flowers, and trees. The 36-acre property features a miniature forest, an aviary, a hibiscus garden

> ## GO FOR GOLD
>
> To sightsee like a VIP, sign up for the National Trust's guided Gold Tour, which runs every Wednesday morning from 9:30 to 12:30. The outing begins at Waterville with a "special-access" stroll through the historic house and surrounding gardens. After being served refreshments, groups continue on by taxi to Paget Marsh for an exclusive tour of the reserve. The $85 per-person price tag also includes admission to any two Trust museums. Contact the Bermuda National Trust at ☎441/236–6483 by 3 on the Tuesday prior.

with more than 150 species, and collections of orchids, cacti, fruits, and ferns. In addition to these must-see sights is an intriguing "must-smell" one: the Garden for the Sightless. Designed primarily for the blind, it has fragrant plants (like geranium, lemon, lavender, and spices), plus Braille signage. Weather permitting, free 60- to 90-minute guided tours of the Botanical Gardens begin at 10:30 Tuesday, Wednesday, and Friday. The gracious white house within the gardens is **Camden** (☎*441/236–5732*), the official residence of Bermuda's premier. Tours of the interior are given Tuesday and Friday noon to 2, except when official functions are scheduled. Behind Camden is the **Masterworks Arts Centre** (☎*441/236–2950* ⊕*www.bermudamasterworks.com* ✉*Free*), open weekdays from 10 to 4 and on Saturday by appointment. The theme of this not-for-profit foundation is "Bermuda through the Eyes of Artists," and it counts among its collection works by native-born painters as well as international figures such as Georgia O'Keeffe and Winslow Homer. These are slated to be moved into a new purpose-built museum (currently under construction nearby) late in 2007. ✉*169 South Rd., Paget Parish* ☎*441/236–4201* ✉*Free* ☉*Daily dawn–dusk.*

☾ **Crystal Caves.** Bermuda's limestone caves have been attracting attention
Fodor'sChoice since the island was first settled. As far back as 1623, Captain John
★ Smith (of Pocahontas fame) commented on these "vary strange, darke, and cumbersome" caverns. Nevertheless, it came as a surprise when two boys, attempting to retrieve a lost ball, discovered Crystal Cave in 1907. The hole through which the boys descended is still visible. But, thankfully, you can now view their find without having to make such a dramatic entrance. Inside, tour guides will lead you across a pontoon bridge that spans a 55-foot-deep subterranean lake. Look up to see

Elsewhere in the Parishes

ATLANTIC OCEAN

WEST END
Royal Naval Dockyard
Ireland Island N.
Cruise Ship Docks
Ireland Island S.
Boaz Island
Cobbler Island
Clarence Cove
Spanish
Watford Is.
Matabar Rd.
Spanish Point
North Shore R
Somerset Long Bay
Watford Bridge
PEMBROKE
Daniel's Head
Somerset Village
Hamilton
SANDYS
Great Sound
Wate
Somerset Island
Somerset Rd.
Hawkins Island
Hamilton Harbour
Front St.
Cruise Ship Dock
Somerset Bridge
Paget Marsh
Harbour Rd.
Middle Rd.
PAGET
Spring Benny's Bay
Middle Rd.
Little Sound
WARWICK
West Whale Bay
Middle Rd.
South Rd.
Warwick Long Bay
SOUTHAMPTON
Gibb's Hill Lighthouse
Horseshoe Bay Beach
Church Bay

Tobacco Bay Beach

Fort St. Catherine

ST. GEORGE'S

Fort St. Catherine Beach

Town of St. George

Alexandra Battery

St. George's Island

Mullet Bay Rd.

Gates Fort

Bermuda Institute of Ocean Sciences

St. George's Harbour

Cruise Ship Docks

Ferry Rd.

Kindley Field Rd.

St. David's Rd.

Bermuda Airport

St. David's Island

The Causeway

St. David's Island

Castle Harbour

Crystal Caves

Crawl Hill North

HAMILTON

Harrington Sound Rd.

Shelly Bay

Harrington Sound

Tucker's Town

rmuda Aquarium, Museum & Zoo

Flatts Village

Harrington Sound Rd.

John Smith's Bay

SMITH'S

Verdmont

Spittal Pond Nature Reserve

VONSHIRE

South Rd.

tanical rdens

ATLANTIC OCEAN

KEY	
⛴	*Cruise Ship Dock*
🚢	*Ferry*
┼─┼─	*Railway Trail*

0   2 miles

0   3 km

stalactites dripping from the ceiling or down through the perfectly clear water to see stalagmites rising from the cave floor. Amateur spelunkers can also journey through geologic time at Crystal's smaller sister cave, Fantasy. After being closed to the public for decades, it reopened in 2001. Set aside 30 minutes to see one cave; 75 minutes if you plan to take in both. ⊠ *8 Crystal Caves Rd., off Wilkinson Ave., Bailey's Bay, Hamilton Parish* ☎ *441/293–0640* ⊕ *www.bermudacaves.com* 🖾 *One cave $16; combination ticket $23* ⊙ *Daily 9:30–4:30, last combination tour at 4.*

| ATTEN-SHUN! |

The evolution of British military architecture between 1612 and 1956 can be traced through fortifications that dot the coast near St. George's. To get a sense of how diverse they are, follow your visit to Fort St. Catherine with a trip to **Alexandra Battery** (about a mile away along Barry Road) and nearby **Gates Fort**. The former, built in the mid-1800s, features Victorian "innovations" like cast-iron facings and concrete emplacements. The latter is a reconstruction of a small militia fort from the 1620s that was named for Sir Thomas Gates, the first survivor of the *Sea Venture* to reach dry land.

NEED A BREAK?

If the beauty of the caves doesn't leave you reeling, a rum swizzle certainly will. Bermuda's potent "national drink" was supposedly invented at the **Swizzle Inn** (⊠ *3 Blue Hole Hill* ☎ *441/293–1854*), about five minutes on foot from Crystal Caves. If you've got kids in tow—or are driving a scooter—you may want to skip the rum and stick to Bailey's—Bailey's Ice Cream (⊠ *2 Blue Hole Hill* ☎ *441/293–8605*), that is. The popular parlor, directly across from the inn, dishes up some two-dozen flavors of homemade all-natural ice creams, plus low-fat frozen yogurts and fat-free sorbets.

★ ☺ **Fort St. Catherine.** This restored hilltop fort is arguably the most impressive one on the island. Surrounded by a dry moat and accessed by a drawbridge, it has enough tunnels, towers, redoubts, and ramparts to satisfy even the most avid military historian—or adrenaline-fueled child. The original fort was built around 1614, but it was remodeled and enlarged at least five times. In fact, work continued on it until late in the 19th century. On site you can find detailed dioramas depicting island history, an audiovisual presentation about Bermuda's fortifications, and replicas of Britain's Crown Jewels. A collection of antique weapons is also on display. Standing out among the pistols and muskets is an 18-ton muzzle-loading cannon, which was capable of firing 400-pound shells a full half mile. ⊠ *15 Coot Pond Rd., St. George's Parish* ☎ *441/297–1920* 🖾 *$5* ⊙ *Daily 10–4.*

★ ☺ **Gibb's Hill Lighthouse.** The second cast-iron lighthouse ever built soars above Southampton Parish. Designed in London and opened in 1846, the tower stands 117 feet high and 362 feet above the sea. The light was originally produced by a concentrated burner of four large, circular wicks. Today the beam from the 1,000-watt bulb can be seen by ships 40 mi out to sea and by planes 120 mi away at 10,000 feet. The haul up the 185 spiral stairs is an arduous one—particularly if you dislike heights or tight spaces. But en route to the top you can stop to catch your breath on eight landings, where photographs and drawings of the lighthouse help divert attention from your aching appendages. Once on the balcony, you'll be rewarded by panoramic island views. ✉*68 St. Anne's Rd., Southampton Parish* ☎*441/238–8069* ⊕*www.bermuda lighthouse.com* 🖾*$2.50* ⊙*Daily 9–4:30* ⊙*Closed Jan.*

TIME FOR TEA

After Gibb's Hill was automated in 1969, the keeper's cottage at its base was converted into an eatery: the Lighthouse Tea Room. Owner Heidi Cowen (who descends from a line of lighthouse keepers dating back eight generations) serves breakfast and lunch each day, plus dinners on weekends May to October. If codfish croquettes and avocado omelets don't strike your fancy, you can always just order a drink. The "Pink Flip Flop" and "Bent Banana" are two house specialties. ✉*68 St. Anne's Rd.* ☎*441/238–8679* ⊕*www. lighthousetearoom.com* ⊙*Daily 9–4:45* ⊙*Closed Jan.*

Fodor'sChoice
★

Paget Marsh. Take a walk on the wild side at Paget Marsh: a 25-acre tract of land that's remained virtually untouched since presettlement times. Along with some of the last remaining stands of native Bermuda palmetto and cedar, this reserve—jointly owned and preserved by the Bermuda National Trust and the Bermuda Audubon Society—contains a mangrove forest and grassy savanna. These unspoiled habitats can be explored via a boardwalk that features interpretive signs describing the endemic flora and fauna. When listening to the cries of the native and migratory birds that frequent this natural wetland, you can quickly forget that bustling Hamilton is just minutes away. ✉*Lover's La., Paget Parish* ☎*441/236–6483* ⊕*www.bnt.bm* 🖾*Free* ⊙*Daily dawn–dusk.*

★ **Spittal Pond Nature Reserve.** This Bermuda National Trust park has 64 acres for roaming, though you're asked to keep to the well-marked walkways that loop through the woods and along the spectacular shoreline. More than 30 species of waterfowl—including herons, egrets, and white-eyed vireos—winter here between November and May, making the reserve a top spot for birders. Get your timing right and you may be able to spy migrating whales as well! History buffs may be more interested in climbing the high bluff to Spanish Rock. Early settlers found this rock crudely carved with the date 1543 along with other markings that are believed to be the initials "RP" (for *Rex Portugaline,* King of Portugal) and a cross representing the Portuguese Order of Christ. The theory goes that a Portuguese ship was wrecked on the island and that her sailors marked the occasion before departing on a newly built ship. The rock was removed to prevent further damage by erosion, and a bronze cast of the original stands in its place. A plaster-of-paris version is also on display at the Museum of the Bermuda Historical Society in Hamilton. Guided 90-minute tours are offered Tuesday afternoons, starting at 1:30 from Waterville. Tours cost $50 per person with transportation included. ✉*South Rd., Smith's Parish* ☎*441/236–6483* ⊕*www.bnt.bm* 🖾*Free* ⊙*Daily dawn–dusk.*

CLOSE UP

Slavery in Bermuda

Within a few years of the colony's founding, slavery had become a fact of life in Bermuda. As early as 1616, slaves—most of whom were "imported" as household servants and tradespeople rather than field workers—began arriving, first from Africa and then from the Caribbean. In the mid-1600s, they were joined by Native American captives (among them, the wife of a Pequod chief). The practice flourished to such an extent that by the time British legislation finally abolished it in 1834, slaves made up more than half of the island's population.

The date the abolition decree was issued, August 1, continues to be marked island-wide. Known as Emancipation Day, it's a time for cricket matches, concerts, and, of course, Gombey dancing: a colorful form of self-expression, rooted in African tradition, that slave owners had banned. If you can't time your trip to coincide with the festivities, you can still bone up on the backstory by following the African Diaspora Heritage Trail. Affiliated with UNESCO's international Slave Route Project, it highlights sites related to the Bermudian slave trade.

Some of the trail's 11 stops are already tourist staples. For instance, in St. George's, the slave graveyard at St. Peter's Church is a designated site; as is Tucker House, where Joseph Rainey (the first black man to be elected to the U.S. House of Representatives) sat out the Civil War. Also on the list is the Commissioner's House at the Royal Naval Dockyard, which has an exhibit that vividly evokes the age of slavery through artifacts like iron shackles and glass trade beads.

Other sites are obscure, but nonetheless illuminating. Take Cobb's Hill Methodist Church in Warwick Parish. Dedicated in 1827, seven years before Emancipation, it was the first sanctuary in Bermuda built by and for blacks. Because they struggled to complete it in their rare off-hours (often working by candlelight!), the church is both a religious monument and a symbol of human resilience. For further details on the African Diaspora Heritage Trail, click on ⊕ www.adht. net or pick up a brochure at any visitor information center.

–Susan MacCallum-Whitcomb

St. David's Island. In a place famous for manicured lawns and well-tended gardens, St. David's Island feels comparatively wild. The island was long populated by fishermen, so it seems appropriate that one of the top attractions here is the **Black Horse Tavern** (⊠101 St. David's Rd. ☎441/297–1991), which specializes in seafood concoctions like shark hash and curried conch stew. However, the real highlight is—quite literally—**St. David's Lighthouse.** Built in 1879 of Bermuda stone and occupying the tallest point on the East End, this red-and-white striped lighthouse rises 208 feet above the sea, providing jaw-dropping views of St. George's, Castle Harbour, and the reef-rimmed south shore. Since operating hours at the lighthouse are subject to change, it's advisable to check with the **Park Ranger's Office** (☎441/236–5902) before visiting. ⊠St. George's Parish ☎Free ☉Apr.–Oct., weekdays 8:30–5.

★ ☽ **Verdmont.** Even if you think you've had your fill of old houses, Verdmont deserves a look. The National Trust property, which opened as a museum in 1956, is notable for its Georgian architecture. Yet what really sets this place apart is its pristine condition. Though used as a residence until the mid-20th century, virtually no structural changes were made to Verdmont since it was erected around 1710. Former owners never even added electricity or plumbing (so the "powder room" was strictly used for powdering wigs!). The house is also known for its enviable collection of antiques. Some pieces—such as the early-19th-century piano—were imported from England. However, most are 18th-century cedar, crafted by Bermudian cabinetmakers. A china coffee service, said to have been a gift from Napoléon to U.S. President James Madison, is also on display. The president never received it, since the ship bearing it across the Atlantic was seized by a privateer and brought to Bermuda. ⊠ *6 Verdmont La., off Collector's Hill, Smith's Parish* ☎ *441/236–7369* ⊕ *www.bnt.bm* ✉ *$5; $10 combination ticket with Bermuda National Trust Museum in Globe Hotel and Tucker House* ☽ *Nov.–Mar., Wed.–Sat. 10–4; Apr.–Oct., Tues.–Sat. 10–4.*

Waterville. Bermuda's National Trust (the nonprofit organization that oversees the restoration and preservation of many of the island's gardens, open spaces, and historic buildings) has its offices in Waterville: a rambling estate overlooking Hamilton Harbour. Waterville was home to the Trimingham family for seven generations. In fact, their much loved (and dearly missed) department store started out here in 1842. The drawing and dining rooms, both laden with art and antiques donated by the family, are open to the public during business hours. Also worth seeing is a superb "showcase" garden planted by the Bermuda Rose Society. ⊠ *2 Pomander Rd., Paget Parish* ☎ *441/236–6483* ⊕ *www.bnt.bm* ✉ *Free* ☽ *Weekdays 9–5.*

Where to Eat

"We have had dinner at Fourways, Waterlot, and Aqua. I would choose Aqua. You can request a table outside, and have a beautiful view—practically right on the water. Even if you want to be inside, you will still have a beautiful view. The food is wonderful there as well!"

—1scs1

"The Speciality Inn on the Southshore has great breakfast and very cheap! Their banana pancakes are to die for! They also have good evening meals and make a great pizza!"

—Tanya

pdated by
irkka Huish

WHAT'S INCREDIBLE ABOUT THE BERMUDA RESTAURANT SCENE

isn't so much the number or high quality of restaurants, but the sheer variety of ingredients and cuisines represented on the menus, especially considering that Bermuda is such a tiny, secluded place. The island is host to a medley of global cuisines—British, French, Italian, Portuguese, American, Caribbean, Indian, Chinese, Japanese, and Thai—palatable reminders of Bermuda's history of colonization. Many superior, well-funded independent and resort restaurants attract a constant and steady stream of internationally acclaimed chefs, assuring that the latest techniques and trends are menu regulars. At the same time, virtually all restaurant menus list traditional Bermudian dishes and drinks, so you have the opportunity to taste local specialties at almost any meal.

> ### TOP 5 DINING
>
> ■ Eat-as-much-as-you-can Sunday brunch at the Fairmont Southampton Resort's Windows on the Sound restaurant.
>
> ■ A lazy afternoon at the Swizzle Inn with a huge plate of nachos— and a couple jugs of rum swizzle.
>
> ■ Grab some jerk chicken and rice n' peas from the Jamaican Grill and head to Horseshoe Bay for a picnic with friends.
>
> ■ A fish sandwich with plenty of mayo from Bouchée. Cheap and delicious!
>
> ■ Surf n' Turf at Waterlot Inn. Need we say more?

As you might expect, methods are not all that's imported. Roughly 80% of Bermuda's food is flown or shipped in, most of it from the United States. This explains why restaurant prices are often higher here than on the mainland. Nevertheless, there are a number of delicious local ingredients that you should look for. At the top of the list is extraordinary seafood, like lobster (September through March), crab, oysters, mussels, clams, red snapper, rockfish, tuna, and wahoo. Additionally, many chefs work with local growers to serve fresh, seasonal fruits and vegetables, such as potatoes, carrots, leeks, tomatoes, corn, broccoli, and Bermuda onions (one of the island's earliest exports); and in the dessert department, strawberries, cherries, bananas, and loquats (small yellow fruit used for preserves). Imports notwithstanding, Bermudian cuisine really begins and ends with local ingredients and traditional preparations, and therein lies the island's culinary identity.

WHAT IT COSTS IN U.S. DOLLARS					
	¢	$	$$	$$$	$$$$
estaurant	under $10	$10–$20	$21–$30	$31–$40	over $40

Prices are per person for a main course at dinner. The final tab usually includes a 15% service charge.

KNOW-HOW

RESERVATIONS

Reservations are always a good idea. We mention them only when they're essential or not accepted. Book as far ahead as you can and reconfirm when you arrive, especially in high season. Many restaurants close—or curtail hours, or days of service—in the off-season, so call ahead before setting out for lunch or dinner.

DRESS

Bermuda has had a reputation for strict sartorial standards, but most of the mid-price restaurants are much more casual these days. In many of the pubs and bars in town you would not be out of place in shorts and a T-shirt. It's a different story in more upscale restaurants, often attached to the hotels. Even when not required, a jacket for men is rarely out of place. In our res-taurant reviews, we mention dress only when men are required to wear either a jacket or a jacket and tie.

PRICES

Much harder to swallow than the delicious Bermuda fish chowder are the prices of dining out. Bermuda has never sought a reputation for affordability, and restaurants are no exception. A few greasy spoons serve standard North American fare (and a few local favorites) at a decent price, but by and large you should prepare for a bit of sticker shock. Don't be surprised if dinner for two with wine at one of the very top places—the Newport Room, for example—puts a $200–$300 dent in your pocket. A 15% service charge is almost always added to the bill "for your convenience."

HAMILTON & ENVIRONS

AFRICAN

$$–$$$ ✕**Café Cairo.** Experience the cuisine and ambience of North Africa at this relaxed restaurant. Boasting a menu of exotic flavors, this popular eatery shows Bermuda's culinary adventurous streak at its best, satisfying the well-traveled palates of both islanders and tourists. Specialties include Egyptian and Moroccan dishes; don't miss the hummus, kofta lamb and couscous, or the shish kebab. After your meal, settle in on the low-seated sofas and enjoy a pipe of sheesha (fruit tobacco) or Turkish coffee as belly dancers sashay around you. It's one of the few Front Street restaurants to serve food until the early hours of the morning, and the place becomes a lively nightspot after 10. ✉ *93 Front St., Hamilton* ☎ *441/295–5155* ▤ *AE, MC, V.*

AMERICAN

$$–$$$ ✕**Greg's Steakhouse.** A must for meat-lovers, Greg's is Bermuda's only steak house where you can tuck into certified Angus beef. Prepared to your liking, choose from filet mignon, T-bone, rib eye, or New York strip. The menu also offers plenty of international flair with fish, pasta, and vegetarian dishes. Watch the chefs prepare your food in the exhibition open-flame kitchen. The restaurant's bright and modern decor also features a bar and a more casual dining area on the first floor. Try the champagne Sunday brunch buffet for something different, and

for those sweet tooths out there, the dessert menu is to die for! ⊠*39 Church St., Hamilton* ☎*441/297–2333* ⊟*AE, MC, V.*

ASIAN

$$–$$$ ✕**L'Oriental.** Located above its sister restaurant, Little Venice, this Asian hot spot is a favorite among locals for its fresh sushi bar. Take the footbridge—over an indoor stream—to the raised seating at the lively teppanyaki table where trained chefs stylishly slice, stir, and season your steak and veggies onto your plate. Home to several "Best of Bermuda Gold Awards," the menu includes traditional Asian soups and entrées and a variety of Indonesian and Thai dishes (don't miss the curries!), as well as nightly specials. Choose from a selection of wines, sakes, and Japanese beers to wash it all down. The backdrop of colorful dragons and a handcrafted pagoda add to the Asian flavor. L'Oriental's Take Out Express location is on the corner of Church and Par-La-Ville Road. ⊠*32 Bermudiana Rd., Hamilton* ☎*441/296–4477* ⊟*AE, MC, V* ⊙*No lunch weekends.*

BERMUDIAN

★ **$$–$$$** ✕**Harley's.** Serene water views and gracious service combine with top-notch Continental and Bermudian cuisine to make Harley's one of the best restaurants in Hamilton. Dry-aged beef is always cooked to perfection. Try slow-cooked prime rib or grilled porterhouse, along with Harley's Mash—potatoes with caramelized onion, butternut squash, and black trumpet mushrooms. As for fish, Harley's chefs prepare a wonderful Bermudian specialty: almond-crusted and banana-glazed baked rockfish, which might be accompanied by a pumpkin risotto and sweet-pepper sauce. If you prefer something vegetarian, try hand-rolled cannelloni filled with ricotta cheese and grilled vegetables with a blackened-tomato coulis. The restaurant is bright and airy, and in summer, has the added bonus of a large outside canopy. ⊠*Fairmont Hamilton Princess Hotel, 76 Pitts Bay Rd., Hamilton* ☎*441/295–3000* ⊟*AE, DC, MC, V.*

> **GOOD TO GO**
>
> Miles Market, a gourmet grocery store, is a quick-hit spot for ready-to-go hot or cold eats, especially handy for a picnic on the beach or an in-room hotel feast. At the Waterfront (96 Pitts Bay Road in Hamilton), Miles supplies the local corporate sector with tasty but healthy lunch options like chicken dishes, pasta salads, wraps and sandwiches, fish, and steamed and grilled veggies. Be sure to use those spared calories on the selection of fresh pastries or at the smoothie or Godiva chocolate bar. Food is sold by the pound so watch how much you pile on your tray.

$$–$$$ ✕**Heritage Court.** Classic and conservative, with a refined afternoon tea service and piano music throughout the day, the Heritage Court is a calm, relaxing spot for any meal. Clinking china can be heard at breakfast and teatimes, while lunch and dinner bring businesspeople, hotel guests, couples, and families for reliable Bermudian—Continental fare and like—clockwork service. The Bermuda fish chowder, classic Caesar salad, and grilled tuna glazed with *mirin* (a sweet Japanese rice wine) are faultless. Some evenings a jazz band livens things up. Watch out for the hotel's Friday night happy hour, the revelers tend to take over the restaurant area. ⊠*Fairmont Hamilton Princess Hotel, 76 Pitts Bay Rd., Hamilton* ☎*441/295–3000* ⊟*AE, MC, V.*

$–$$ ✕**Bermuda Bistro at the Beach.** Despite what the name suggests, this restaurant is right in the heart of Hamilton. It's the ideal stop-off during a day of shopping, offering inexpensive food—and plenty of it. Whether you want a hearty three-course lunch or just an afternoon cappuccino and a cake, there's something on the extensive menu for everyone (and there's always a deal of the week). The restaurant's on-street patio is the perfect people-watching location. ⊠*103 Front St., Hamilton* ☎*441/292–0219* ⊟*AE, MC, V.*

$–$$ ✕**Bouchée.** Formerly known as Monty's, this once greasy spoon café has reinvented itself into a shiny new restaurant. It's worth the walk west out of Hamilton to see why this charming spot is a firm favorite with locals and tourists alike. The atmosphere is casual and the prices affordable. Recommended starters are crab cakes or fish chowder with sherry pepper sauce. For dinner, make the most of the local fish, cooked to your liking. What's more, you'll never go hungry as it's open all day, every day, serving breakfast, lunch, and dinner. The portions are a healthy size and the knowledgeable staff will keep you entertained. An easy-listening live duo also performs at dinner on Friday nights. ⊠*75 Pitts Bay Rd., near Woodburne Ave., Hamilton* ☎*441/295–5759* ⊟*AE, DC, MC, V.*

☻ **$–$$** ✕**The Pickled Onion.** This former whiskey warehouse is now a lively restaurant serving creative, contemporary Bermudian cuisine, as well as a handful of Latin- and Asian-flavored dishes. Try the flame-seared tuna, dressed with avocado, tomato, and cilantro salsa. If it's beef you're after, they grill it to perfection here. For those lazy weekends, they also do a great all-day Sunday brunch. For dessert, go straight for Melanie's Bermuda banana bread with brûléed bananas. Then sample a martini or two on the veranda overlooking Front Street and the harbor. A live band playing Tuesday to Saturday, from April to December, and a great cocktail list makes this a fabulous spot to hang out after dinner, too. The pub has recently undergone a complete renovation and now has a New York City wine bar feel. ⊠*53 Front St., Hamilton* ☎*441/295–2263* ⊟*AE, MC, V.*

$ ✕**Aggie's Garden & Waterside Café.**
Fodor'sChoice
★ The charm of this tiny restaurant is its location beside the water, just a few hundred yards from Hamilton.

SWEET TREATS

Double Dip Express. Mix and match every flavor of ice cream imaginable. We recommend the rum raisin or cookies and cream. ⊠*St. George's* ☎*441/293–5959.*

Lemon Tree Cafe. Stop off in the shaded garden and enjoy a French pastry or a fruit tart. ⊠*Hamilton* ☎*441/292–0235.*

Rock Island Coffee Café. Vanilla espresso and a scone is the perfect afternoon pick-me-up. ⊠*Hamilton* ☎*441/296–5241.*

Temptations Cafe & Bakery. The most perfect little finger sandwiches and cookies for teatime. ⊠*St. George's* ☎*441/297–1368.*

A brick stairway through fern-covered walls takes you to a harbor-side garden planted with herbs and flowers. The open kitchen—where cooking classes are taught at night—is on the harbor level of an old Bermuda home. The seating is mostly in the garden, with former church pews and umbrellas over the tables. The house and garden are quite an escape from the surrounding office blocks, and businesspeople often come here for lunch. Some patrons even moor their boats along the dock and skip the stairs altogether. The creative, seasonal menu lists soups, sandwiches, and salads made with locally grown produce, as well as grilled local fish, free-range chicken, and homemade pizza with organic toppings. Daily sweets, such as ginger or oatmeal-nut cookies, and fresh-fruit tarts are perfect with a cup of fair-trade tea or coffee. ⊠*Falconer House, 108 Pitts Bay Rd., Hamilton* ☎*441/296–7346* ▭*No credit cards* ☉*No dinner.*

BRITISH

$–$$ ✕**Hog Penny Pub.** Veterans of London pub crawls may feel nostalgic at this dark, wood-filled watering hole off Front Street. Those die-hard aficionados of old-style British comfort food will adore the Yorkshire pudding, shepherd's pie, steak-and-kidney pie, fish-and-chips, and bangers and mash. You can work up an appetite just decid-

> **OK, RACHAEL RAY!**
>
> If you've got an eye for bargains, the Hog Penny in Hamilton has been showcased on the Food Network's "$40 a Day." Rachael Ray said it was the place to go in Bermuda for a value-priced meal.

ing the impressive burger selection, and the British ale on tap will wash the food down nicely. This is Hamilton's oldest licensed establishment, opened in 1957. There's live, toe-tapping music most nights in summer and less frequently in winter. ⊠*5 Burnaby Hill, Hamilton* ☎*441/292–2534* ▭*AE, DC, MC, V* ☉*No lunch Sun.*

$ ✕**Docksider.** Locals come to mingle at this sprawling Front Street sports bar. It's generally more popular as a drinking venue, as it can get quite overcrowded and rowdy. But if you want to catch the game on the big screen with everyone else, standard pub fare is available, as well as local fish. Go for the English beef pie, fish-and-chips, or a fish sandwich and sip your dessert—a Dark 'n Stormy—out on the porch as you watch Bermuda stroll by. The pub has a good jukebox and there's often a DJ or a band on summer weekends. ⊠*121 Front St., Hamilton* ☎*441/296–3333* ▭*MC, V.*

CARIBBEAN

$–$$ ✕**Spring Garden Restaurant & Bar.** If you've never had Barbadian, or as Barbados natives like to call it, "Bajan" food, come sit under the indoor palm tree and try panfried flying fish—a delicacy in Barbados. Another good choice is the broiled mahimahi served in creole sauce, with peas and rice. During lobster season, an additional menu appears, featuring steamed, broiled, or curried lobster ($35 for the complete dinner). For dessert, try coconut cream pie or raspberry-mango cheesecake. ⊠*19 Washington Lane, off Reid St., Hamilton* ☎*441/295–7416* ▭*AE, MC, V* ☉*Closed Sun. Nov.–Apr. No lunch Sun. May–Oct.*

Where to Eat in Hamilton

2

CHINESE

☺ $-$$ ✕**Chopsticks.** The menu here is a mix of Szechuan, Hunan, Cantonese, and Thai favorites. Top Chinese choices include beef with vegetables in ginger sauce, sweet-and-spicy chicken, and sweet-and-sour fish. For Thai tastes, try beef with onion, scallions, and basil in hot chili sauce, or shrimp *panang* (in coconut-curry sauce). The food is good, but you won't get U.S. prices or portions. ⊠*88 Reid St., Hamilton* ☎*441/292–0791* ⊟*AE, MC, V.*

CONTINENTAL

$$$-$$$$ ✕**Ascots.** In an elegant former mansion just outside downtown Hamilton, Ascots gives you a wonderful excuse for leaving the city. When
Fodor'sChoice weather permits, meals are served on the covered terrace, with its stone
★ fountain, or on the front veranda, as well as indoors. You can assemble at the handsome cedar bar before and after meals. The high standards of owners Angelo Armano and Edmund Smith—the chef and manager, respectively—result in creative and seasonal menu offerings that incorporate fresh ingredients from local farmers and fishermen. You might find grilled grouper on panfried potatoes with spinach-and-crab rolls, or pan-seared lamb chops with vegetable risotto. An extensive wine list is available to complement your meal. ⊠*Royal Palms Hotel, 24 Rosemont Ave., Pembroke Parish* ☎*441/295–9644* ⊟*AE, MC, V* ☺*No lunch weekends.*

$$-$$$ ✕**The Red Carpet.** This tiny restaurant in the old Armoury is popular at lunch, especially among local politicians and businesspeople. But at dinner, the dining room is usually uncrowded, and the pace relaxes so that diners can take their time with the deliciously prepared meal. Among the culinary highlights are the grilled lamb chops with rosemary, grilled fresh Bermuda fish with fried banana and almonds, and the seafood kettle (mussels, shrimp, fish, scallops, and lobster tail in a creamy white-wine and curry sauce). ⊠*Armoury Bldg., 37 Reid St., Hamilton* ☎*441/292–6195* ⊟*AE, MC, V* ☺*Closed Sun.*

ECLECTIC

$ ✕**Coconut Rock and Yashi Sushi Bar.** Whether you're in the mood for shrimp tempura and sashimi served in a quiet room with black lacquer tables and paper lanterns, or you would rather have chicken chimichanga, fried tiger shrimp, or grilled sirloin steak surrounded by loud music videos on multiple screens at a popular nighttime venue—or if you want a little of both—these adjoining restaurants can satisfy. The underground restaurant is dark and dingy and remains well hidden beneath Hamilton's main shopping street. But it's an old favorite with locals, and the fusion of different flavors and good-size portions make it worth the wait for a table. ⊠*Williams House, downstairs, 20 Reid St., Hamilton* ☎*441/292–1043* ⊟*AE, MC, V.*

FRENCH

★ $$$-$$$$ ✕**Waterloo House.** This restaurant and small hotel in a former private house on Hamilton Harbour serves traditional Continental specialties, such as lamb and veal, plus a number of Bermudian dishes, including just-off-the-boat fish. The menu changes every day, and you can't go wrong with any choice. Fish can be grilled or panfried upon request.

QUICK BITES

Delicious, (☎441/295–5890) located inside the Washington Mall on Reid Street, offers a—you guessed it—delicious sandwich.

Cheap and cheerful **H20** (☎441/295–4903), inside the Hamilton Pharmacy on Parliament Street, is a good spot for a good burger. There are sandwiches, too, and the service is fast.

Kathy's Kaffee (☎441/295–5203), in the Emporium Building next to Bank of Butterfield on Front Street, serves robust breakfasts and satisfying lunches at reasonable prices.

Kentucky Fried Chicken (☎441/296–4532) on Queen Street between Front and Reid is always busy. Bring cash: they don't take plastic.

Watch your waistline with a tasty salad or sandwich from **Paradiso Café** (☎441/295–3263) on Reid Street. But be warned, this place is popular, and you'll probably have to wait for a table.

Anton Mosimann of Horizons is the restaurant's consultant chef. You can dine either on the waterside patio (in good weather) or in the more formal dining room, with its deep-raspberry walls, rich chintzes, and attractive lighting. Fodors.com users are full of praise for the menu, but have criticized the slow service. ⊠ *100 Pitts Bay Rd., Hamilton* ☎*441/295–4480 Jacket and tie after 6 pm* ▭*AE, MC, V.*

INDIAN

$ ✕**Bombay Palace/Jamaican Breeze.** This small eatery features two restaurants in one. Chef Nanak Chand of Bombay Palace whips up northern Indian cuisine and items cooked in the tandoor oven, whereas Jamaican Breeze offers traditional Jamaican food and natural juices. On a sunny day you may find Jamaican Chef Huntley Septimus—who is also a locally renowned musician—working up some tasty jerk chicken on the outdoor barbecue. He won't bite, so be sure to ask for a sample. Then grab a table in the relaxed dining room, or if the weather permits, sit on the outside patio. A delicious lunch buffet featuring favorites from both cuisines is offered every day for $12.95. Takeout is also available. ⊠ *60 North St., Hamilton* ☎*441/296–4094* ▭*AE, MC, V* ☯ *Closed Sun.*

$ ✕**House of India.** Slightly off the beaten track, this genuine Indian restaurant with Indian chefs is well worth the 10-minute walk or short cab ride from the town center. Start with vegetable *samosas* (small deep-fried turnovers), which are sure to whet your appetite. For your second course, you really can't go wrong with any entrée—meat, fish, or vegetarian. If you like spicy food, take on the chicken *chetanod.* It's hotter than a vindaloo, and it's the owners' proud boast that only two regular customers have the palate for it. All the *nan* (a flat, doughy bread) is freshly made in the tandoor, and the *lassi* (sweetened yogurt) drinks, particularly the mango, are delicious and refreshing. A filling weekday lunch buffet is worth every penny of the cost ($14.50). It's a small, busy restaurant, but if you can't get a table, you can opt for takeout. ⊠ *57 North St., Hamilton* ☎*441/295–6450* ▭*AE, MC, V* ☯ *No lunch weekends.*

ITALIAN

$$$–$$$$ ✕**Little Venice.** Little Venice is a little pricey, but it has fancy and flavorful Italian food. A stand-out starter is the antipasto plate with calamari, mozzarella, and salami, although the salads topped with Gorgonzola croutons are hard to resist. Good choices for a main course include thinly sliced grilled veal, duck with smoked bacon, and linguine with shellfish and calamari in tomato sauce. Bermuda's business elite fill the restaurant after work, making their way through the wine list that boasts 1,000 different wines from around the world. The less-than-filling average-size portions make the restaurant more suitable to clinch a business deal than enjoy a night out with the family. ⊠ *32 Bermudiana Rd., Hamilton* ☎ *441/295–8279* ⊙ *No lunch weekends* ⌂ *Reservations essential* ☰ *AE, MC, V.*

> **NOT-SO-FAST FOOD**
>
> If you think something may be missing from the horizon of Bermuda eateries, you are quite right. Apart from a lone Kentucky Fried Chicken (which snuck in sometime during the 1970s), you won't find any fast-food chains on the island. The majority of Bermuda's residents strongly believe that allowing American franchises onto the island would dilute Bermuda's distinctive foreign (and rather upscale) appeal, eventually leading to the island's resembling Anyplace, USA. Adjust your eyes (and belly) to the absence of big golden double arches!

$$–$$$ ✕**Ristorante Primavera and Omakase Sushi Bar.** High-backed, elegant banquettes and crisp, white tablecloths set the scene for delicious Italian meals delivered with superlative service. Those hankering for authentic Italian classics will love the beef carpaccio with Parmesan and pesto over arugula, and the *vongole al vino bianco* (baby clams sautéed with white wine, garlic, and parsley). Other excellent pastas here include the *penne al gorgonzola e noci* (penne sautéed with Gorgonzola and walnuts) and the *ravioli neri* (black ravioli) filled with lobster meat and served in a light, pink sauce. The sushi bar, Omakase, is upstairs, but you may order from downstairs as well. Delicacies include the Bermuda maki roll stuffed with crabmeat, avocado, and cucumber. Several vegetarian rolls, stuffed with asparagus or shiitake, are also on the menu. Worth every mouthful is the all-you-can-eat sushi bar special on Tuesday evenings. ⊠ *69 Pitts Bay Rd., Hamilton* ☎ *441/295–2167* ☰ *AE, MC, V* ⊙ *No lunch weekends.*

$–$$ ✕**La Trattoria.** Tucked away in a Hamilton alley, you can't go wrong with this no-nonsense trattoria, which is pleasant and unpretentious. Any of the pastas, such as lasagna, manicotti, and spaghetti with mixed seafood, can be served in smaller portions as appetizers. Fish fillets are generally panfried with olive oil, garlic, and herbs. La Trattoria's pizzas are cooked in Bermuda's only brick wood-burning pizza oven. About 20 inventive topping combinations (such as arugula and prosciutto) are on the menu, but the chef will mix and match whatever you like. ⊠ *22 Washington Lane, Hamilton* ☎ *441/295–1877* ☰ *AE, MC, V* ⊙ *No lunch Sun.*

$–$$ ✕**Portofino.** Bermuda's scaled down version of Ocean Avenue in South Beach, this is the place to see and be seen on a hot summer night.

The outside dining area is bustling most evenings, especially Friday, so arrive early. Inside, you'll be transported to Italy with little shuttered windows and traditional brick walls covered in pictures from the family album. Start with calamari or garlic bread, the two starters the restaurant is renown for. The pizzas are the best, and we especially favor the pepperoni and artichoke

GO ALL OUT

If you know you'll be overindulging with a huge meal, why not dance off the extra calories? If you dine at Portofino Italian restaurant on Bermudiana Road, you get free entrance to Splash nightclub next door.

variety. The Bistecca and the fettuccine Alfredo pasta are delicious. Prices and portions are good, too. A separate take-out section with its own entrance means you can get the good food while avoiding people-watchers. If it's busy, be prepared to wait. ⊠ *20 Bermudiana Rd., off Front St., Hamilton* ☎ *441/292–2375 or 441/295–6090* ⊟ *AE, MC, V* ⊗ *No lunch weekends.*

JAMAICAN

$–$$ ✕ **Jamaican Grill.** Journey outside the familiar city limits to Court Street and you'll find Jamaican food at its best. The owners are proud of their Jamaican heritage and want everyone to taste the Caribbean flavors with them. Classics like jerk and curry chicken, escovitched fish, hot wings, rice and beans, dumplings, and meat and veggie patties adorn the menu. Be sure to order Jamaica's own Ting grapefruit drink to wash down the tasty homemade cakes and cookies. It's no-frills food, but the prices are good and the take-out service makes for a great beach picnic. ⊠ *32 Court St., Hamilton* ☎ *441/296–6577* ⊟ *MC, V* ⊗ *Closed Sun.*

MEDITERRANEAN

★ $$–$$$ ✕ **Fresco's Wine Bar & Restaurant.** This cozy restaurant is tucked away, but well worth discovering for the way it mixes Mediterranean cuisine with a hint of Bermuda. Fresco's is known for its homemade pasta, seafood, and vegetarian specialties; consider the *tarte Provençal* (roasted vegetables and caramelized onions in a freshly baked pastry crust), panfried yellowtail snapper with zucchini-lime couscous and sweet red-pepper reduction, or lobster medallions roasted with vanilla. At lunch, ask for a table in the courtyard. With the fountain, palms, and flowers it's just like being in Europe. Before or after dinner, you can swirl a glass of *rosso* (red wine) beneath the vaulted ceiling of the wine bar, which boasts Bermuda's largest selection of wines by the glass. ⊠ *Chancery Lane, off Front St., Hamilton* ☎ *441/295–5058* ⊗ *Reservations essential* ⊟ *AE, MC, V* ⊗ *No lunch weekends.*

★ $$–$$$ ✕ **Harbourfront.** When you dine at a table beside the enormous open windows at Harbourfront, you might feel as though you were floating on the harbor yourself. Nearly every seat in the house has beautiful views of the quiet waters. Few Bermuda restaurants have menus as long and wide-ranging as this busy spot, where sushi is served alongside Continental and Mediterranean specialties. For lunch, you might have a good burger, a salad, or a couple of sushi rolls. For dinner, start

CLOSE UP

The Dish on Local Dishes

Shark hash made of minced shark meat sautéed with spices may not sound too appetizing but it's a popular Bermudian appetizer, usually served on toast.

Bermudians love codfish cakes—made of salted cod mashed with cooked potatoes and fresh thyme and parsley, then shaped into a patty and panfried. They taste great topped with a zesty fruit salsa and a side of mesclun salad.

The island's traditional weekend brunch is a huge plate of boiled or steamed salt cod with boiled potatoes, onions, and sliced bananas, all topped with a hard-boiled egg or tomato sauce, and, sometimes, avocado slices.

Cassava pie—a savory blend of cassava, eggs, sugar, and either pork or chicken—is a rich, flavorful dish (formerly reserved for Christmas dinner) often offered as a special side. More common is mussel pie, made of shelled mussels, potatoes, and onions, baked and seasoned with thyme, parsley, and curry.

As for Bermudian desserts, bananas baked in rum and brown sugar are to die for and loquat or banana crumble is sweet and rich.

---

with calamari or carpaccio, followed by lobster, buffalo steak, rack of lamb, or any of the excellent pastas. Sushi devotees can order miso soup, tempura, and sushi platters. Businesspeople and BUEI (Bermuda Underwater Exploration Institute) visitors alike partake of the delicious seafood. ⊠*Bermuda Underwater Exploration Institute (BUEI), East Broadway, Hamilton* ☎*441/292–6122* ▤*AE, MC, V* ⊘*Closed Sun.*

$$ ✗**Bolero Brasserie.** This newly opened restaurant has a real European feel to it with the waitstaff dressed in waistcoats, long white aprons, and red ties. Manager and chef Johnny Roberts takes great pride in preparing the finest food for his traditional bistro. The menu includes plenty of old-world-theme fare, but you must try the frogs' legs and snails with a twist. A tapas menu is also available between lunch and dinner. The impressive red decor includes a wall decorated with a multitude of various-size mirrors, and plenty of local artwork. There's also a balcony overlooking Front Street with great views of Hamilton Harbor. ⊠*Bermuda House Lane, 95 Front St., Hamilton* ☎*441/292–4507* ▤*AE, MC, V* ⊘*Closed Sun.*

SEAFOOD

$$$–$$$$ ✗**Barracuda Grill.** The tastefully decorated contemporary dining room—mahogany-framed chairs and banquettes, soft-gold lights over the tables—is reminiscent of sophisticated big-city restaurants, and the food that comes to the table is created by a culinary team dedicated to excellence. The island-style fish chowder and the steak-and-tomato salad with blue cheese and roasted garlic in balsamic vinaigrette are two good ways to start your meal. Moving on to entrées, you might try roasted salmon with caramelized onion, smoked bacon, and white-bean cassoulet; classically prepared rack of Australian lamb; or rigatoni Bolognese. If you save room for dessert, opt for the chocolate-banana bread pudding or perhaps the chocolate fondue for two.

There's also a great cocktail bar to sit at while you wait for your table. And if you're looking for a romantic dinner, reserve the "snug corner," which is a table for two, tucked away out of sight of other diners. ✉ *5 Burnaby Hill, Hamilton* ☎*441/292–1609* ▭*AE, MC, V* ⊘*No lunch weekends.*

> **IN THE KNOW**
>
> For the lowdown on where to eat in Bermuda, restaurant and menu guides are available at any Visitor Information Centres. The island's telephone directory also publishes a good selection of restaurant menus.

\$\$–\$\$\$
FodorśChoice
★

✕**Port O' Call.** Resembling the interior of a yacht, Port O' Call is a popular little restaurant. It's one of the few ground-level dining spots on Front Street, with an outdoor dining area reminiscent of a European sidewalk café. Fresh local fish—such as wahoo, tuna, grouper, and snapper—is cooked perfectly, and the preparations are creative. Consider the pan-roasted snapper, the seafood stir-fry, or the sesame-crusted tuna. ✉*87 Front St., Hamilton* ☎*441/295–5373* ▭*AE, DC, MC, V* ⊘*No lunch weekends.*

☾ \$\$ ✕**Lobster Pot.** Bermudians swear by this spot, where the maritime-theme dining room is filled with brass nautical gear, lobster traps, and sun-bleached rope. The fresh local lobster, available September through March, is most requested next to yellowtail or rockfish with bananas and almonds, all local favorites. The "Cup Match Special" is everything locals love about fried seafood dinners: crispy fish strips on a bun with a decent helping of coleslaw and fries. If you're looking for a good deal, there's also a limited-availability three-course set meal for about \$20. ✉*6 Bermudiana Rd., Hamilton* ☎*441/292–6898* ▭*AE, MC, V* ⊘*No lunch weekends.*

THAI

\$\$ ✕**Silk.** This culinary and aesthetic gem offers a unique Thai experience with a picturesque harbor view. One step inside the restaurant transports you into an authentically Asian environment. The colorful, trendy hangout is Bermuda's only Thai restaurant. The team of chefs from the Shangri-La restaurant in Bangkok concentrate more on taste than presentation. Menu options include plenty of Thai curries and noodle dishes. Don't miss the *Yam Ped Yang* (duck and mango salad) or *Ba-Miii Thalay* (fried noodles). Weather permitting you should dine on the covered patio for a superb view of Front Street and Hamilton Harbor. ✉*Masters Bldg., 55 Front St., Hamilton* ☎*441/295–0449* ▭*AE, MC, V* ⊘*Closed Sun. No lunch Sat.*

ST. GEORGE'S

BRITISH

\$\$–\$\$\$ ✕**Carriage House.** Hearty British fare is the daily bread at the Carriage House, an attractive slice of the restored Somers Wharf area. Try to secure a table outside on the patio or inside by a window so you can watch the action on the harbor. This is the place to tuck into roast prime rib, cut to order tableside, or roast leg of lamb with rosemary. But don't

2

overlook the fresh Bermuda fish, like panfried wahoo in lemon-butter sauce. Sunday the Carriage House lays out a generous brunch buffet that includes champagne, while a pianist plays background music. Afternoon tea with all the trimmings is served daily except Sunday. On Friday and Saturday nights, a jazz combo entertains. ⊠*Somers Wharf, Water St.* ☎*441/297–1270 or 441/297–1730* ⊟*AE, DC, MC, V.*

COOL YOUR CURRY!

If you find yourself sighing at the idea of eating indoors (and eating up valuable outdoor time) then grab your grub to go. **St. George's Curry House** (⊠ *14 York St.* ☎ *441/297–3170*) has hot spicy curry that tastes great washed down with a cool sea breeze on the nearby St. George's waterfront.

ITALIAN

☾ **$–$$** ✕**Cafe Gió.** This is waterside dining at its best with great views of St. George's Harbor. It's not unusual to see hungry boaters pull up and tie their vessels alongside the restaurant's sundeck. The popular spot offers tasty Italian cuisine, with the addition of a few Asian dishes, in a pleasant, romantic setting. The fettuccine is good and the Caesar salad is great. ⊠*36 Water St.* ☎*441/297–1307* ⊟*MC, V.*

ELSEWHERE IN THE PARISHES

THE CENTRAL PARISHES

AMERICAN

$$–$$$ ✕**Blu Bar & Grill.** This is a great spot for lunch or dinner with impressive views across the golf course and out to the sea. There's standard American cuisine, including steaks and ribs, but the eclectic chefs like to add bold flavors with lots of exotic herbs and spices. The wide variety of fresh seafood is your best bet. Follow up your fish chowder with lobster, yellowfin tuna, rockfish, snapper, or wahoo. ⊠*Belmont Hill Golf Course, 97 Middle Rd., Warwick Parish* ☎*441/232–2323* ⊟*AE, MC, V.*

BERMUDIAN

$$$$
Fodor'sChoice
★

✕**Horizons.** The dining room at Horizons cottage colony is one of Bermuda's most elegant, and reservations can be difficult to secure even weeks in advance. Chef Anton Mosimann's delicate, healthful, fusion cuisine brings the world's rich, famous, and trim to his table. Dinner is a five-course, prix-fixe (around $45) affair with a menu that changes nightly but may include vegetable terrine with basil oil and tomato coulis, and roasted snapper over sun-dried tomato polenta. The staff is, naturally, impeccably trained, swift, and discreet. You can linger over coffee on the terrace and listen to the sounds of the local tree frogs. ⊠*Horizons & Cottages, 33 S. Shore Rd., Paget Parish* ☎*441/236–0048* ⌂*Reservations essential Jacket and tie* ⊟*AE, MC, V.*

★ $$$–$$$$ ✕**Aqua.** Everything about Aqua is wonderfully romantic. Set on the island's southern coast, it has spectacular views overlooking a lovely beach and the endless Atlantic Ocean. Enjoy an unforgettable alfresco dining experience at one of the many tables on the large, covered deck, right next to the waves, or savor the view from the warmth of the dining room. The colors inside emulate the turquoise and deep-blue hues of the ocean. Blue glassware complements the white tablecloths, the white-wood beams, and slate flooring of the porch. The varied and ever-changing menu takes you on a journey through Europe, the Far East, and the Caribbean. For starters, the sugar-cured beef carpaccio

CELEBRITY HOTSPOT

It's not unusual to see Bermuda's most famous residents, Michael Douglas and Catherine Zeta-Jones, eating out. Their favorite hangout is Aqua, which is owned by the Douglas family. The Hollywood couple also likes to tuck into seafood at the Barracuda Grill.

on roasted peppers with cashews and parsnip chips is beyond compare. Seafood addicts should go for the panfried scallops on arugula. The choices of delectable entrées make a decision difficult: tandoori-spiced rack of lamb with citrus yogurt on cumin flat bread is a winner, as is panfried snapper on soba noodles with pickled-ginger sauce. Aqua is sometimes closed for lunch in winter. ☒ *Ariel Sands Hotel, 34 S. Shore Rd., Devonshire Parish* ☏ *441/236–2332* ▭ *AE, DC, MC, V.*

★ $$$ ✕**Seahorse Grill.** A chic, enduring restaurant with minimalist Bermuda stone walls and wood-beam interiors, Seahorse is a perennial favorite of local hipsters and professionals. The ever-changing menu showcases locally grown produce and fresh Bermuda fish prepared in a light, contemporary style with a nod to island tastes. On the menu, ingredients are described in detail, with even their geographic origins named. If it's listed, try the baked Caesar salad and anchovy tempura for an appetizer, and the seafood paella for a main course. The service can be island-time, so come prepared to linger between courses. Sunday brunch is divine. ☒ *Elbow Beach Hotel, 60 S. Shore Rd., Paget Parish* ☏ *441/239–6885 or 441/236–3535* ▭ *AE, MC, V.*

$$–$$$ ✕**Mickey's Bistro & Bar.** This is the place to go for alfresco dining— you can dine right on the sand. The no-fuss bistro serves inexpensive Continental and local dishes. It's the ultimate in relaxing dining with the waves almost at your toes. ☒ *Elbow Beach Hotel, 60 S. Shore Rd., Paget Parish* ☏ *441/236–9864 or 441/236–9107* ▭ *AE, MC, V* ⊗ *Closed Oct.–May.*

★ $$–$$$ ✕**Palms.** A low-key and romantic hideaway, this is the perfect place to escape the world. Dining can be outside by the pool overlooking the ocean or in the plant-filled garden dining room, with its wall of French doors that open to the outside. The menu is not extensive, but the dishes listed are all creative and flavorful. Popular appetizers include goat cheese, leek, and apple tart with saffron sauce, and fresh-vegetable-and-shrimp spring

LOVE IS IN THE AIR

For the ultimate romantic gesture, dine on your very own terrace overlooking the ocean. If you book in advance, Palms restaurant will set up its private clifftop terrace that's just big enough for two. There's nothing to interrupt your togetherness but the sound of the ocean waves. This is the perfect find for an anniversary, birthday, or even that all-important proposal.

roll with savory Asian-style sauce. When it's available, go for the signature rockfish entrée, cooked in a sumptuous blend of coconut curry and served with stir-fried vegetables. Another good entrée is the classic duck à l'orange. Desserts are worth every calorie—two of the best are the rum cake with rum-and-raisin ice cream and the crème brûlée of the day. ⊠*Surf Side Beach Club, 90 S. Shore Rd., Paget Parish* ☎*441/236–7100* ⊟*AE, MC, V* ۞*Closed Jan. and Feb.*

CONTINENTAL

★ $$$–$$$$ ✕**Fourways Inn.** Fourways has risen to preeminence as much for its lovely 17th-century surroundings as for its reliable cuisine. The elegant yet charming interior, with mahogany banisters, burgundy carpeting, impressionist prints, and silver-and-crystal table settings, evokes the image of a fine French manor. Traditional Continental dishes, such as veal scaloppine and roast duck, are beautifully presented and delicious. A pianist adds to the leisurely dining style. Be sure to visit the on-site "Peg Leg" bar for a step back in time. And definitely don't forget to stop in the on-site pastry shop, the chocolate dipped strawberries are a must. ⊠*1 Middle Rd., Paget Parish* ☎*441/236–6517 Jacket required* ⊟*AE, MC, V.*

ITALIAN

★ $$–$$$ ✕**Lido Restaurant.** On the beachfront terrace at the Elbow Beach Hotel, with waves breaking just below, Café Lido is often invoked as one of the island's most romantic settings. You could easily just stare out the window all evening. Food and service are top notch to give you a truly memorable dining experience. Items to try: the Angus rib-eye steak, Bermuda lobster, and the succulent roasted lamb. Dance off the desserts at the Elbow Beach complex disco, the Deep. It's best to reserve a table, but regardless, the place gets crowded and sometimes feels like you're on top of the other diners. ⊠*Elbow Beach Hotel, 60 S. Shore Rd., Paget Parish* ☎*441/236–9884* ⌑*Reservations essential* ⊟*AE, MC, V* ۞*No lunch.*

THE WESTERN PARISHES

AMERICAN

$$–$$$ ✕**Wickets Brasserie.** Simple but satisfying Italian and American fare and prompt service make this cricket-theme restaurant a great spot for families. You can find all the classics: salads, burgers, sandwiches, pastas, and pizza as well as good fish-and-chips, chicken cacciatore, and grilled steak. End your meal on a sweet note with delicious tiramisu and chocolate-crunch cheesecake. The casual restaurant offers all-day dining with great pool and ocean views. ⊠*Fairmont Southampton Resort, 101 S. Shore Rd., Southampton Parish* ☎*441/239–6969* ⊟*AE, DC, MC, V* ۞*Closed Jan.*

BERMUDIAN

$$$$ ✕**Coconuts.** Nuzzled between high cliff rocks and a pristine private beach on the southern coast, this outdoor restaurant is one of the best places to nab that table overlooking the ocean. The view is made even more dramatic at night by floodlights. The menu changes often, but

Where to Eat
in the Parishes

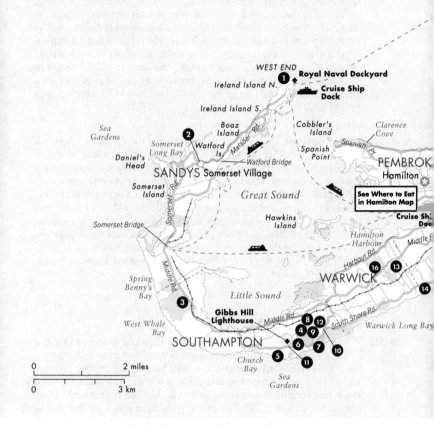

ATLANTIC OCEAN

WEST END
Royal Naval Dockyard
Cruise Ship Dock
Ireland Island N.
Ireland Island S.
Boaz Island
Watford Is
Malabar Rd.
Watford Bridge
Cobbler's Island
Clarence Cove
Spanish Point
Spanish Pt.
PEMBROK
Hamilton

Sea Gardens
Somerset Long Bay
Daniel's Head
Somerset Island
SANDYS Somerset Village

See Where to Eat
in Hamilton Map

Great Sound
Hawkins Island
Cruise Shi
Doc

Somerset Bridge
Somerset Rd.

Spring Benny's Bay
Middle Rd.
West Whale Bay
Little Sound

Gibbs Hill Lighthouse
Middle Rd.
SOUTHAMPTON
Church Bay
Sea Gardens

Hamilton Harbour
Middle R
Harbour Rd.
WARWICK
South Shore Rd.
Warwick Long Bay

0   2 miles
0   3 km

Fort St. Catherine

ST. GEORGE'S

27 28

St. George's
Island

Mullet Bay Rd.   Town of St. George

St. George's
Harbour   Cruise Ship
Dock

Ferry Rd.   St. David's Rd.

Kindley
Field Rd.

Sea
Gardens

Coney
Island   The
Causeway   **Bermuda
Airport**   St. David's
Island   26   **St. David's
Lighthouse**

Castle
Harbour

24

Crawl Hill North

25

**Crystal
Caves**   **Leamington Caves**

HAMILTON

Harrington
Sound Rd.

Shelly Bay

Harrington
Sound

Tucker's Town

**Bermuda
Aquarium,
Museum & Zoo**   Harrington
Sound Rd.

Flatts
Village   23   John Smith's Bay

evonshire
ock   North Shore Rd.   SMITH'S

DEVONSHIRE   22
21

Front St.   South Shore Rd.   20

PAGET

19
5

ATLANTIC OCEAN

KEY	
⛴	*Cruise Ship*
🛥	*Ferry*
├──	*Railway Trail*

Picnic Perfect

CLOSE UP

Ditch your proper place settings for a little sea breeze with that sandwich.

With verdant open spaces sprinkled with shady poinciana trees, the **Botanical Gardens,** on Middle Road in Paget, make a peaceful inland setting for a picnic. The gardens have a few picnic tables and plenty of benches, plus spacious lawns where you can spread a blanket. Bring your own supplies as there's no on-site café.

Clearwater Beach in St. David's is one of Bermuda's nicest picnic spots, with tables near to and on the beach. You can pick up picnic supplies at the grocery store about ¼-mi away or order lunch to go from one of St. David's casual eateries.

Just west of popular Warwick Long Bay, tiny, tranquil **Jobson Cove** beach

is backed by the dramatic cliffs and greenery of South Shore Park. There are no tables and no snack bars, and often no people—perfect for a private picnic on the sand.

If you want a tried-and-tested picnic spot, head to **John Smith's Bay** in Smith's Parish. The wooden picnic tables beneath the trees make it a popular spot for locals. Get there early if you want a good spot overlooking the beach.

Adjacent to a Bermuda Audubon Society nature reserve, **Somerset Long Bay Park** in Sandys has a semicircular beach, fluffy spruce trees, and shallow water. It's also a terrific place for birding: it borders on an Audubon Society sanctuary. You can find tables under the trees near the beach, and a grocery store less than ½-mi away.

you can always be sure of fresh, local produce, and fish prepared with a mix of contemporary Bermudian and international culinary styles. A fixed price of about $65 (including 15% gratuity) includes four courses at dinner. A simpler, less-expensive lunch menu includes daily specials, burgers, sandwiches, and salads. ⊠ *The Reefs, 56 S. Shore Rd., Southampton Parish* ☎ *441/238–0222* ⌂ *Reservations essential* ▤ *AE, MC, V* ⊘ *Closed Nov.–Apr.*

$$$$ ✕**Waterlot Inn.** This graceful, two-story manor house, which dates from
Fodor'sChoice 1670 and once functioned as a bed-and-breakfast, now holds one of
★ Bermuda's most elegant and elaborate restaurants. The service is impeccable, with waiters that have just enough island exuberance to take the edge off their European-style training. Nestled in Jew's Bay, the restaurant also offers breathtaking sunset views. The Bermudian–Continental menu changes every season, but always offers an excellent fish chowder. Seafood ravioli is another stellar appetizer choice. Grilled fish-of-the-day over a plate of local, colorful vegetables makes a perfect main course. Decadent desserts, like profiteroles in sweet vanilla cream, round off an extremely satisfying meal. The restaurant is also known for its fine wine list and its cigar selection. ⊠ *Fairmont Southampton Hotel, 101 S. Shore Rd., Southampton Parish* ☎ *441/239–6967 Jacket required* ▤ *AE, DC, MC, V* ⊘ *Closed Jan.–mid-Mar. No lunch.*

$–$$ ✕**Traditions.** Eat like a local. Fresh caught fish with crispy french fries, creamy homemade mac and cheese, or mushy peas and rice are just a few of the hearty homecooked local favorites waiting for you here on the West End of the island. You can also find the typical hamburgers, sandwiches, etc., but that would be depriving your taste buds of some good home cooking. ⊠ *2 Middle Rd., Sandys* ☎ *441/234–3770* ⊟ *AE, MC, V* ☾ *Closed Sun.*

BRITISH

☾ $$–$$$ ✕**Henry VIII.** As popular with locals as it is with vacationers from nearby Southampton resorts, the lively Henry VIII sports an Old English charm that stops just short of "wench" waitresses and Tudor styling. It's a bit pricey for what you get, but you can find a mix of English and Bermudian menu favorites, including steak-and-kidney pie, rack of lamb, and fish chowder. Save room for the sticky toffee pudding. Sometimes a strolling singer serenades diners. After dinner you can move along to the bar for a round of calypso. The outdoor tables have compelling views of the southern coast. There's live entertainment nightly from DJs and singers in season, and Sundays (when there's also a weekly brunch) are always popular with locals. ⊠ *69 S. Shore Rd., Southampton Parish* ☎ *441/238–1977* ⊟ *AE, MC, V.*

☾ $$ ✕**Somerset Country Squire.** Overlooking Mangrove Bay, this typically English tavern is all dark wood and good cheer, with a great deal of malt and hops in between. Much of the food isn't good enough to warrant a special trip across the island, but some of it is: Bermuda fish chowder, panfried mahimahi, and steak-and-kidney pie are all delicious. The in-house nightly specials—watch out for the Fish Friday deals, where you can get wahoo, tuna, dolphin, or rockfish for $15— are another draw. ⊠ *10 Mangrove Bay, Somerset* ☎ *441/234–0105* ⊟ *AE, MC, V.*

☾ $–$$ ✕**Frog & Onion Pub.** This is a pub lover's dream with everything on the menu named after old English pubs. The food is good, as is the ale and the atmosphere. With its vaulted limestone ceilings and thick walls, the former Royal Naval Dockyard warehouse is a fitting place for this nautically decorated pub and its large poolroom. The food caters to every palate, from hearty English pub fare and light European dishes to a selection of fresh local fish plates. Fodors.com users love the bangers and mash, the Argus Bank fish sandwich, panfried local rockfish or tuna, and the Frog & Onion burger. There's also a children's game room and a gift shop where you can purchase your hot toddy mix. ⊠ *The Cooperage, Dockyard* ☎ *441/234–2900* ⊟ *AE, MC, V.*

¢ ✕**Lighthouse Tea Room.** At the base of Gibbs Hill Lighthouse, in the old home of the former lighthouse keeper, this adorable little teahouse is the perfect place to rest after the climb up and down the tower's 185 spiraling steps. You can find expertly blended black teas and unusual herbal teas, such as dandelion and juniper berry, served iced as well as hot. A lunch menu lists homemade soups and sandwiches, smoked trout and pork pie with chutney, and a range of refreshing fruit smoothies. For dessert, try the fresh banana cake or gingerbread with lemon sauce. Dinner on Friday and Saturday, which is by reservation only, boasts a weekly changing menu, and breakfast is served daily. This is also a popular spot to enjoy romantic sunsets. ⊠ *68 St. Anne's Rd., Southampton Parish* ☎ *441/238–8679* ⊟ *AE, MC, V* ☾ *No dinner Dec.–Apr.*

FRENCH

$$$$
Fodor's Choice
★

✕**Newport Room.** Glistening teak and models of victorious America's Cup yachts give this fine restaurant a nautical theme. Each dish is beautifully presented, matching the clientele, which is made up of Bermuda's elite. The menu changes every season and the chef works with as much local produce as possible. Appetizers of Scottish smoked salmon, carved tableside, or Hudson Valley foie gras with a port sauce will send the taste buds

WORD OF MOUTH

"We went to Bermuda last year for my 40th and spent my actual birthday night at the Newport Room. It was outstanding, but very formal. It was very old world—very French and very special. If that is what you are looking for, I would definitely recommend it. "

–emcash

soaring. But it's the entrées that really shine. You might have panseared Arctic char and bay scallops in a lobster-vanilla sauce, or black Angus beef tenderloin with tomato tart, foie-gras mousse, and Madeira jus. For dessert, try the soufflé of the day or the ginger-and-lime crème brûlée with pineapple spears and red-currant frozen yogurt. ⊠ *Fairmont Southampton Resort, 101 S. Shore Rd., Southampton Parish* ☎ *441/239–6964 Jacket and tie* ▭ *AE, DC, MC, V* ✆ *Closed Jan. No lunch.*

ITALIAN

$$–$$$

✕**Bacci.** A winning combination of authentic Italian cuisine with fine dining is what you can find at Bacci. On the upper floor of the gold clubhouse, the restaurant is decorated in bright and bold colors with impressive golf course views. Bacci celebrates all that is great about Italy and the chefs are not afraid to experiment with the latest cooking trends. The menu combines traditional and modern Italian recipes with many dishes low in fat and carbohydrates. Make sure you leave room for dessert—there's a selection of more than 10 different gelatos and sorbets. It's a great place for families during the day, but at night the lights are dimmed and candles are lighted to create a more romantic atmosphere. ⊠ *Fairmont Southampton Resort, 101 S. Shore Rd., Southampton Parish* ☎ *441/238–2555* ⚅ *Reservations essential* ▭ *AE, MC, V* ✆ *No lunch.*

☾ $–$$

✕**Tio Pepe.** You don't have to spend much money for healthy portions of home-style cooking at this Italian restaurant with a Mexican name. The easygoing atmosphere makes it an ideal stop for bathers returning from a day at nearby Horseshoe Bay Beach—just grab a seat at one of the plastic tables on the porch and get ready to chow down. The pizzas are worth every bite (they're freshly made with superb sauces) and there's an extensive list of comforting, classic Italian dishes, including lasagna and spaghetti. ⊠ *117 S. Shore Rd., Southampton Parish* ☎ *441/238–1897 or 441/238–0572* ▭ *AE, MC, V.*

SEAFOOD

$$$–$$$$
Fodor's Choice
★

✕**Whaler Inn.** From your table overlooking the crashing surf, you can sometimes see fishing boats offshore, catching the seafood for this restaurant's next meals. The Whaler Inn is one of the top seafood res-

CLOSE UP

Where to Take Tea

When afternoon arrives, Bermuda, like Britain, pauses for tea. Usually, tea is served between 3 and 5, but teatime can mean anything from an urn or thermos and cookies sitting on a sideboard, to the more formal stiff-pinkie-presentation of brewed-to-order tea in a porcelain or silver teapot, served with cream and sugar on a tray, and accompanied by finger sandwiches and scones with clotted cream and jam.

Elbow Beach Hotel (⊠ *Paget Parish* ☎ *441/236–3535*) takes tea in the lobby. The $20 charge includes everything from cucumber and egg-and-tomato sandwiches to pound cake and French pastries.

Fairmont Hamilton Princess (⊠ *Hamilton* ☎ *441/295–3000* or *800/441–1414*) serves a posh afternoon tea in its Heritage Court, adjacent to the lobby and Japanese Koi pond. Fine Eastern teas are brought

to your Italian linen–covered table in shining silver teapots and poured into delicate Belgian china. The cost is $11 for tea, miniature sandwiches, and cakes.

Lighthouse Tea Room (⊠ *Southampton Parish* ☎ *441/238–8679*) has imported and special tea blends served with panoramic views at the hilltop. A pot of tea costs $8.

Waterloo House (⊠ *Hamilton* ☎ *441/295–4480*) serves a very proper English high tea. In summer, tea-takers sip from their cups in the coolness of the ocean breeze on the harborside terrace. A pot of tea costs $7 for nonhotel guests.

The **Willowbank** (⊠ *Sandys Parish* ☎ *441/234–1616*) tearoom features a slightly ersatz collection of Victorian memorabilia. High tea arrives on a triple-tiered china tray and at $13.50 for nonguests, it's one of the better tea-deals on the island.

taurants on the island, serving only the freshest of fish delivered daily by local fishermen. The grilled Bermuda seafood triangle of tuna and swordfish fillets, and shrimp on sugarcane brochette, each with a different sauce, gives the palate plenty to savor. If you prefer landside fare, go for the grilled pork chop with pumpkin-and-potato mash, or chicken breast stuffed with goat cheese and sun-dried tomatoes accompanied with corn risotto and spiced pineapple coulis. Desserts, such as the coconut-and-chocolate-brownie sundae, are unforgettable. The restaurant closes for one month in winter, usually January. ⊠ *Fairmont Southampton Resort, 101 S. Shore Rd., Southampton Parish* ☎ *441/239–6968* ▤ *AE, DC, MC, V* ☺ *No lunch Nov.–Mar.*

THE EASTERN PARISHES

BERMUDIAN

$$$$
Fodor'sChoice
★

✕ **Tom Moore's Tavern.** In a house that dates from 1652, Tom Moore's Tavern has a colorful past, thanks to the Irish poet for whom it's named. Tom Moore visited friends here frequently in 1804 and caused a scandal by writing odes to a local woman who was already married. Today, fireplaces, casement windows, and shipbuilders' cedar joinery capture a sense of history that in no way interferes with the fresh, light, and innovative cuisine. Broiled scampi, Bermuda lobster (in season), and sautéed-then-broiled Bermuda fish with pine nuts stand out. Soufflés are always excellent, as is the chef's pastry. Both change daily. Eat in one of five cozy rooms; by special arrangement, groups may dine alfresco on a terrace that overlooks Walsingham Bay. ⊠ *Walsingham La., Bailey's Bay, Hamilton Parish* ☎441/293–8020 *Jacket and tie* ☰*AE, MC, V* ☾*Closed Jan.–mid-Feb. No lunch.*

$$–$$$ ✕**North Rock Brewing Company.** The copper and mahogany tones of the handcrafted beers and ales are reflected in the warm interior of this bar and restaurant, Bermuda's only brewpub. Seating surrounds the glass-enclosed brewery where David Littlejohn, who runs North Rock with his wife, Heather, tinkers with the gleaming copper kettles. Sit in the dining room or outside on the breezy patio for fish-and-chips, codfish cakes, or prime rib. ⊠ *10 South Rd., Smith's Parish* ☎441/236–6633 ☰*AE, MC, V.*

$–$$ ✕**Black Horse Tavern.** Way off the main tourist trail in a remote corner
FodorsChoice of St. David's, the Black Horse is a dark horse, or at least a well-kept
★ local secret. Its beer garden overlooks a picturesque bay dotted with fishing boats and tiny islands. This is a great place for island originals: fish chowder and curried conch stew with rice are favorites, as are the straightforward renderings of amberjack, rockfish, shark, tuna, wahoo, and Bermuda lobster. Just about everything is deep-fried, so if that doesn't suit, then request it be cooked the way you like. ⊠ *101 St. David's Rd., St. George's Parish* ☎441/297–1991 ☰*AE, MC, V* ☾*Closed Mon.*

★ ☾ $–$$ ✕**Swizzle Inn.** No trip to Bermuda is complete without stopping off at the Swizzle. In fact, Swizzle Inn created one of Bermuda's most hallowed (and lethal) drinks—the rum swizzle (amber and black rum, triple sec, orange and pineapple juices, and bitters). This place is a Bermuda landmark with a warm and welcoming atmosphere, friendly staff, and plenty of affordable pub fare. Try a "Swizzleburger" (a bacon cheeseburger), or a huge plate of nachos and chili, which will challenge even the biggest of appetites. The Friday and Saturday barbecues with ribs, steaks, and seafood are a mouthwatering feast capable of satisfying any carnivore. With so many jugs of the island's national drink being consumed day and night, there's never a dull moment. It's also customary to leave your business card or scribble your name on the pub's colorful walls. A sister restaurant, Swizzle Inn South Shore, is now open in Warwick. ⊠ *Blue Hole Hill, Bailey's Bay, Hamilton Parish* ☎441/293–1854 ☰*AE, MC, V.*

ITALIAN

$$ ✕**Rustico Restaurant & Pizzeria.** At Rustico you can eat and drink in the quaint village of Flatts, across from the Bermuda Museum, Aquarium & Zoo. It's won a number of awards and is regularly fully booked during summer. Bermudian favorites are on the menu along with Italian specialties; the seafood pasta, or pasta *pescatore,* is well worth a try. The restaurant's casual and friendly atmosphere extends to its outside dining patio. ⊠ *8 N. Shore Rd., Flatts Village, Smith's Parish* ☎441/295–5212 ☰*AE, MC, V.*

CLOSE UP

Dining with Kids

Kids are people, too, and very hungry little people on a regular basis. Little-big eaters are usually banished to a far-flung corner away from all the action (which they'll then have to find, leaving a spaghetti trail behind), or forced to dine in fast-food restaurants for fear they'll actually express themselves. Well, Bermuda has no fast-food chains, except for a lone Kentucky Fried Chicken in Hamilton, but little diners and their big companions will have no trouble finding familiar foods in welcoming settings here.

Let the kids build up an appetite in the game room at the **Frog & Onion Pub** (☎ 441/234–2900). It's crammed full of games to keep children ages three and upward entertained—and their parents thankful for the peace and quiet. The pub also has a kids' menu containing all the tried and tested favorites.

Harbour Nights festival in Hamilton (Wednesday evenings April through October), lets kids eat on their feet. Choose fish sandwiches, patties, wraps, sweets, and more from booths and kiosks along Front Street.

Rather than just ordering a hamburger and fries, let your child watch it being cooked at the **Paraquet** (☎ 441/236–9742). This American-style diner's low counter with stools is ideal for little ones to watch what's going on in the kitchen. The large selection of kids' food and the well-priced menu make this a great spot for families.

Youngsters love being creative and eating with their hands, so let them have the best of both worlds by creating their own pizza. Head to **Pizza House** (☎ 441/293–0517) at South-side, St. David's to see who can come up with the tastiest combination of pizza toppings. Kids also enjoy watching the minibike racing at the nearby racetrack.

Children have the chance to splash about before dinner at **Sapori** (☎ 441/236–7201). The restaurant at Grape Bay, Paget Parish, is centered around its very own swimming pool, which is always a winner with youngsters in summer. Parents can relax on the terrace as their little ones play in the pool, before all coming together for some alfresco Italian cuisine. It's the ideal kid-friendly way to make a night of your meal.

Bermuda has the ideal picnic venue to keep the younger set entertained all day long. **Shelly Bay** in Hamilton Parish has a huge children's play area right next to its sandy beach, so little ones won't have time to be bored. Grab a bite to eat from the beach snack bar or bring a picnic, and prepare for a fun—and probably tiring—day by the ocean.

Let the kids knock 'em down with a family bowling challenge at **Warwick Lanes** (☎ 441/236–5290). The winner gets their pick off the menu at the on-site Last Pin restaurant. Kids' meals at the bowling alley in Middle Road, Warwick, include all the favorites: pizza, hamburger, chicken nuggets, and french fries.

2

☾ $ ✕ **Speciality Inn.** You may have to wait a few minutes for a table, but it's worth it. A favorite of locals and families, this south shore restaurant is cheerful and clean, with low prices, and always packed come dinnertime. The no-frills food is Bermudian with Italian and Portuguese accents. There's something for every diner with a sushi bar, tasty soups, and pizza. Carnivores should try the meaty Bermudian pizza. ✉ *Collectors Hill, 4 S. Shore Rd., Smith's Parish* ☎ *441/236–3133* ▭ *MC, V.*

Where to Stay

WORD OF MOUTH

"For a true Bermuda experience you may want to go for a cottage colony. My husband and I stay at the Pink Beach Club in quiet Tucker's Town. No TVs, but splurge for oceanfront, leave your French doors open, and fall asleep to the waves. Ahh . . ."

—thereadbaron

"The most central location is the Elbow Beach hotel or its neighbor, the Coco Reef. Elbow Beach, frankly, is the best beach on the island. Elbow Beach hotel has tennis courts, and golfing is nearby. Shopping in Hamilton is very close."

—fernlover

Updated by
Michael de
Zayas

FEW PLACES IN THE WORLD can boast the charm of Bermuda's curvaceous, colorful waterfront. It's a boon, then, that the lagoons, coves, coasts, as well as its inland sanctuaries are filled with equally colorful, alluring places to stay.

The quintessential accommodation on the island is a pink cottage—a cute, clean, unpretentious one-story house amid manicured gardens and coral stone pathways. Terraced whitewashed roofs (designed to capture rainwater) sit atop walls of pinks, peaches, and pastels, looking like cakes of ice cream in pink wafer sand. Add a waterfront setting, and voilà—the lure of Bermuda.

With nearly 60 lodging choices on the island, making a decision can seem daunting. Where, then, to stay? If you find yourself craving a beachfront resort, and you can afford it, several places in this chapter offer quality right-on-the-sand stays; another handful are a stone's throw away from the beach. If you find yourself craving a beachfront resort, and you *can't* afford it, don't despair. The island is blessed with clean, well-maintained public beaches. These are easily reached by bus, and aren't far from any point on the island. In this sense, selecting a hotel away from the beach will allow you to see more of the island, often leading to a more memorable trip.

> ### TOP 5 LODGING
>
> ■ Meet a living legend of eccentric hospitality: Salt Kettle House matriarch Hazel Lowe (and her cats and ducks!).
>
> ■ Breathe in the easygoing sophistication around the grounds of Waterloo House and Horizons and Cottages.
>
> ■ Dine right on the beach at the Reefs, decidedly marvelous.
>
> ■ Meander from beach to pool to tea to croquet at cottage colony Cambridge Beaches.
>
> ■ Live the fantasy of a Bermuda beachfront home at Grape Bay Cottage.

The majority of visitors to Bermuda these days are actually not beach lovers, but business travelers, brought in by the booming reinsurance business. These travelers almost always stay in Hamilton, though more and more are discovering the resort courtesy shuttles and excellent ferry system, which permits quick and scenic transport to Hamilton from any point on the island.

The capital city has many sophisticated choices, but vacationers who are looking for beachfront relaxation will be disappointed in beachless Hamilton. In fact, all noteworthy beaches are on the southern side of the island. With only a couple exceptions, beachfront lodging choices are along a 7-mi stretch of coast that runs along the central to western tail of the island, west from Paget to Warwick, Southampton, and Sandys. Lodging choices on the north coast of the island often are on glittering Hamilton Harbour or have deepwater access to the Atlantic, but not beaches.

Except for the older Fairmont Southampton, and the tall but unobtrusive larger main building at Elbow Beach, there are no highrises in Bermuda—and nowhere do neon signs sully the landscape.

Indeed, many of Bermuda's lodging properties are guesthouses, identifiable only by small, inconspicuous signs or plaques. Those who prefer bed-and-breakfasts will have no problem finding quaint retreats with local attention.

For the most part, lodging choices are conveniently placed on the island. However, Bermuda is so small that, no matter where you stay, you won't have to travel far to see and do everything you want.

WHAT IT COSTS IN U.S. DOLLARS					
	¢	$	$$	$$$	$$$$
FOR 2 PEOPLE	under $110	$110–$200	$200–$300	$300–$400	over $400

Prices are for two people in a standard double room in high season, excluding 7.25% tax and 10% service charge.

RESORTS & HOTELS

$$$$ □Coco Reef Hotel. Coco Reef is at one end of highly desirable Elbow Beach. Staying here, then, you get to enjoy the restaurants and explore the large grounds of the immediate neighbor, Elbow Beach resort. This would make it a bargain, except that Coco Reef, a much simpler hotel, still charges nearly as much as Elbow Beach. No matter, the views are dazzling: few rooms on the island are as closely set to the beach. A few steps beyond the multimirrored lobby is a pool terrace providing another dramatic vista. Two peach two-story buildings—one beachfront, the other slightly up hill—have tiled rooms with wicker furniture, colorful aqua-and-peach floral quilts, and plastic furniture on the outdoor patios and balconies. So what, the rooms aren't stylish, but the beach is, stretching almost a mile to Coral Beach Tennis Club. This is also the closest beach resort to Hamilton town. **PROS:** close to the beach, nice pool, steps from Elbow Beach's restaurants. **CONS:** limited restaurants on-site, expensive for what you get. ⊠*8 College Dr., Paget Parish PG04* ☎*441/236–5416* ⊕*www.cocoreefbermuda. com* ⟲*64 rooms* ⌂*In-room: safe, refrigerator. In-hotel: restaurant, bar, tennis courts, pool, beachfront, no elevator, laundry service* ▤*AE, MC, V* ℣❘*BP.*

★ ☾ **$$$$** □**Elbow Beach.** Some Mandarin Oriental properties are exercises in orchestrated perfection. This one trails far behind any such level of finesse, yet many highly appealing components still make Elbow Beach worth a stay. Foremost is its proximity to the beach, even if that means crossing a long series of lawns. In fact, these forced cross-campus walks give the property a breezier feel than the Fairmont Southampton, the island's other outsize upscale resort. Elbow's four restaurants have something for everyone, and there's poolfront service and a nightclub. Oddly enough the dining highlight may be breakfast at the Sea Horse Grill, where the service is impeccable. The spa is the most superlative in Bermuda because of its pervasive sense of tranquillity—it's here that the Mandarin touch is fully realized. Rooms off the main five-story building are all freshly furnished and have private sunning gardens—these are a breed apart. Some rooms in the main building are also renovated,

KNOW-HOW

Bermuda is a land of cottage colonies, cliff-top apartments, and beachfront resort hotels. Hidden along small parish roads, however, you can also find family-run, flower-filled guesthouses and simple, inexpensive efficiencies. The lodgings we list are the cream of the crop in each price category.

FACILITIES & SERVICES

Considering Bermuda hotel rates, it might come as a surprise that perks like 24-hour room service and same-day laundry service are rare. Fortunately, however, personalized attention, exceptionally comfortable rooms, and trim, scenic surroundings are not. The number and quality of facilities vary greatly according to the size and rates of the property. Resort hotels are the best equipped, with restaurants, pools, beach clubs, gyms, and (in the case of Fairmont Southampton) a golf course. Cottage colonies also typically have a clubhouse with a restaurant and bar, plus a pool or private beach, and perhaps a golf course. Each cottage has a kitchen, so you can cook your own meals, and housekeeping services are provided. Small hotels usually have a pool, and some have a restaurant or guest-only dining room, but few have fitness facilities or in-room extras like minibars. Efficiencies or housekeeping apartments almost always come with a kitchen or kitchenette. Some properties have pools, but you may have to take the bus or a scooter to get to the beach. Even the smallest property can arrange sailing, snorkeling, scuba, and deep-sea fishing excursions, as well as sightseeing.

All lodgings listed are equipped with private bathrooms and air-conditioning. In each review, we list the facilities that are available, but we don't specify whether they cost extra; when pricing accommodations, always ask what's included and what entails an additional charge. Most lodgings offer a choice of meal plans, several with "dine-around" privileges at other island restaurants. Under a Full American Plan (FAP), breakfast, lunch, and dinner are included in the hotel rate. A Modified American Plan (MAP) covers breakfast and dinner. A Breakfast Plan (BP) includes a full, cooked-to-order breakfast, and a Continental Plan (CP) means pastries, juice, and coffee. Unless otherwise noted, the rates quoted below are based on the European Plan (EP), which includes no meals at all.

PRICES

Rates at Bermuda's luxury resorts are comparable to those at posh hotels in New York, London, and Paris. A 7.25% government occupancy tax is tacked on to all hotel bills, and a service charge is levied. Some hotels calculate the service charge as 10% of the bill, whereas others charge a per-diem amount. Virtually every hotel on the island offers at least one vacation package—frequently some kind of honeymoon special—and many of these are extraordinarily good deals.

You can shave about 40% off your hotel bill by visiting Bermuda in low or shoulder seasons. Because temperatures rarely dip below 60°F in winter, the low season (November through March) is ideal for tennis, golf, and shopping.

with soothing blond- or dark-wood notes, luxurious marble floors and baths, and Caribbean hues. **PROS:** great beach, kids' activities, many restaurants to entertain. **CONS:** Somewhat generic, very expensive, huge property can mean a lot of walking. ⊠ *60 S. Shore Rd., Paget Parish PG 04* ☍ *Box HM 455, Hamilton HM BX* ☎ *441/236–3535, 800/223–7434 in U.S. and Canada* ⊕ *www.elbowbeach.com* ⇱ *169 rooms, 75 suites, 2 cottages* ☍ *In-room: safe, refrigerator, Ethernet, Wi-Fi. In-hotel: 4 restaurants, room service, bars, tennis courts, pool, gym, spa, beachfront, children's programs (ages 4–11), concierge* ⊟ *AE, DC, MC, V* ⑩ *BP, EP, MAP.*

> ## WE'RE NOT KIDDING
>
> Is Bermuda kid-friendly? Not so much. Don't believe it? Well, for starters, there isn't a single pool slide on the island. The only true exception is the Fairmont Southampton, which has a video game arcade and a real year-round kids' club with activities scheduled each day. Elbow Beach has less impressive kid activities, and Grotto Bay has a kids' club during summer months. Pompano Beach Club has an arcade room, and Pink Beach Club and Willowbank have playgrounds. Luckily the beach is fun for all ages—but don't forget the pails and shovels!

☺ $$$$ Fodor'sChoice ★ 🏨 **The Fairmont Southampton.** This is the island's most inclusive resort, with the best restaurants, the best kids' club, the biggest spa, the best hotel golf course, lobby, shops—and so on. If the lodgings, based in an older ¼-mi-long hotel, sat on a fine beach, and were a little less of a clunky high-rise, the Southampton would be the unchallenged island favorite. It does have a private beach—one of the very best in Bermuda—but it takes a quick shuttle or a five-minute walk to reach it from the vast grounds that stretch the entire width of the island. Still, there's much to recommend this hotel, as the island's most complete full-service resort, for those who like big hotels. The Willow Stream Spa has 15 treatment rooms, three lounges, two hot tubs overlooking the ocean, and an indoor heated pool with waterfalls. Ask to see a room before checking in—views vary—and avoid ones on the first three floors of the west and north wings, as they overlook a rooftop. **PROS:** all-year kids' camp with arcade, full-service resort with golf course, great restaurants, private beach. **CONS:** hotel building itself is unattractive and older, slightly long walk to beach. ⊠ *101 S. Shore Rd., Southampton Parish SN02* ☍ *Box HM 1379, Hamilton HM FX* ☎ *441/238–8000 or 800/441–1414* ⊕ *www.fairmont.com* ⇱ *594 rooms, 24 suites* ☍ *In-room: safe, kitchen (some), refrigerator, Ethernet. In-hotel: 7 restaurants, room service, bars, golf course, tennis courts, pools, gym, spa, beachfront, diving, water sports, children's programs (ages 4–16), laundry service, concierge, executive floor, public Internet, public Wi-Fi, some pets allowed* ⊟ *AE, DC, MC, V.*

☺ $$$$ 🏨 **Pompano Beach Club.** Pompano, which is passionately run by an American family, understands its customers—and those customers return year after year for the casual atmosphere and wonderful small beach. A new dining room with two-story glass windows seems to hover high over the ocean, making it one of the most dramatic dining

Where to Stay in the East & West Ends

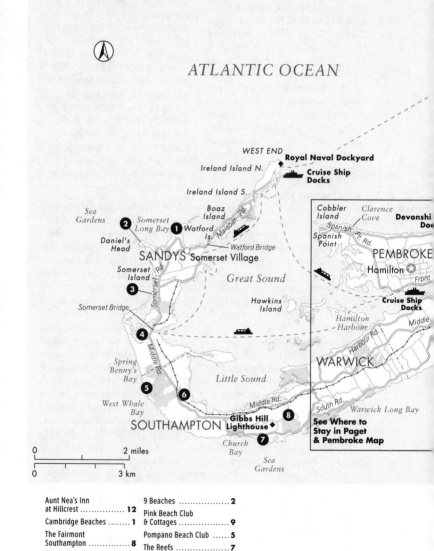

ATLANTIC OCEAN

WEST END
Royal Naval Dockyard
Ireland Island N.
Cruise Ship Docks
Ireland Island S.

Sea Gardens
Somerset Long Bay ❷
Daniel's Head
❶ Watford Is.
Boaz Island
Malabar Rd.
Cobbler Island Clarence Cove Devonshi
Spanish Pt. Rd.
Spanish Point
PEMBROKE
Hamilton
Front

SANDYS Watford Bridge
Somerset Village
Somerset Island
Somerset Rd.
❸
Great Sound
Hawkins Island
Cruise Ship Docks

Somerset Bridge
❹
Middle Rd.
Hamilton Harbour
Hamilton Harbour Rd.
Middle

Spring Benny's Bay
Little Sound
WARWICK

❺ West Whale Bay
❻
Middle Rd.
South Rd. Warwick Long Bay

SOUTHAMPTON Gibbs Hill Lighthouse ◆ ❽
❼
See Where to Stay in Paget & Pembroke Map

Church Bay
Sea Gardens

0 ___ 2 miles
0 ___ 3 km

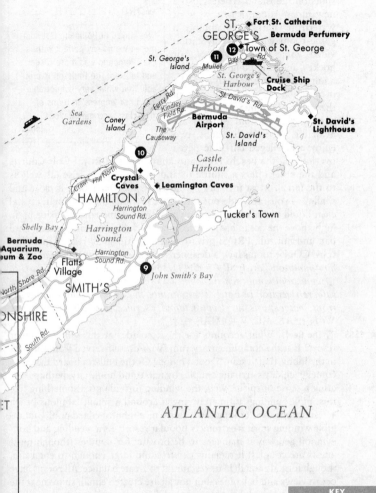

ST. GEORGE'S

♦ **Fort St. Catherine**

♦ **Bermuda Perfumery**

♦ **Town of St. George**

St. George's Island

11 *Mullet Bay*

St. Geo..s Rd.

St. George's Harbour

12

Cruise Ship Dock

St. David's Rd.

Ferry Rd.

Kindley Field Rd.

Bermuda Airport

St. David's Island

♦ **St. David's Lighthouse**

Sea Gardens

Coney Island

The Causeway

Castle Harbour

Crawl Hill North

10

♦ **Crystal Caves**

♦ **Leamington Caves**

HAMILTON

Harrington Sound Rd.

Harrington Sound

○ **Tucker's Town**

Shelly Bay

Bermuda Aquarium, ...eum & Zoo

Harrington Sound Rd.

Flatts Village

North Shore Rd.

9 *John Smith's Bay*

SMITH'S

...NSHIRE

South Rd.

...ET

ATLANTIC OCEAN

3

KEY	
	Cruise Ship
	Ferry
├—┼—┤	Railway Trail

spots on the island. There's also a new fitness room, a new wing of waterfront suites, and notably a game room with two PlayStation video game consoles, pool, air hockey, and ping-pong. (Games for adults or kids are hard to come by in Bermuda.) If you didn't come all the way to Bermuda to play video games, glass-bottom kayaks are available. Of three hot tubs, two enjoy a privileged cliff-side perch

WORD OF MOUTH

"We stayed at Pompano last summer—I would say perfect with kids. Pompano was more casual and relaxed. The trade-off is probably that while very comfortable, it did not 'impress' in terms of 'first class' accommodations."

–ilndlvr

overlooking the beach. Pompano abuts the Port Royal Golf Course, and the hotel offers a shuttle to and from the clubhouse (as well as to the ferry). Most memorable, however, the water here is clear and shallow—you can wade out through 250 yards of waist-high, crystal clear liquid to one of two floating platforms. A spacious cliff-side patio high above the ocean has a heated pool, a children's wading pool, pool bar, and hot tub. **PROS:** private and intimate small resort, three hot tubs. **CONS:** rooms lack a designer's style. ⊠*36 Pompano Beach Rd., Southampton Parish SB 03* ☎*441/234–0222, 800/343–4155 in U.S.* ⊕*www.pompanobeachclub.com* ⌂*58 rooms, 16 suites* ⌂*In-room: safe, refrigerator. In-hotel: 2 restaurants, bars, pools, gym, spa, beachfront, water sports, no elevator, laundry service, public Internet, public Wi-Fi* ⊟*AE, MC, V* ¦⊙¦*MAP.*

★ **$$$$** ⊡**The Reefs.** What accounts for the accolades at this wildly popular resort? Is it the complimentary rum swizzles, self-served from pitchers in the lobby, that sustain a jovial mood? Or the bulletin board that welcomes each day's arriving couples by name and home city, perhaps creating a sense of spirit? Well, the winning formula goes something like this: pink buildings intimately ringed around a small, fabulous beach + restaurants overlooking the water + nice infinity-edged pool + intangible winning spirit = extremely popular resort. As a wedding and honeymoon getaway it manages to be private; for families (though most guests are couples) it remains carefree and large enough to entertain, though formal enough in its restaurant to create balance. All rooms have ocean views and balconies, but not all are created equal: suites near the beach and overlooking the ocean each have a Jacuzzi tub, large walk-in shower for two, and complete entertainment system; for seclusion and tranquillity, the cliff-side rooms perched above wave-washed boulders at the far end of the resort are impeccable. **PROS:** intimate resort that caters to North American couples, cute beach. **CONS:** a small property like the Reefs can get repetitive. ⊠*56 South Rd., Southampton Parish SN 02* ☎*441/238–0222, 800/742–2008 in U.S. and Canada* ⊕*www.thereefs.com* ⌂*45 rooms, 4 suites, 8 junior suites, 8 cottage suites* ⌂*In-room: safe, DVD, VCR, dial-up. In-hotel: 3 restaurants, room service, bars, tennis courts, pool, gym, spa, beachfront, laundry service, public Internet, public Wi-Fi* ⊟*AE, MC, V* ¦⊙¦*MAP.*

$$$–$$$$
Fodor'sChoice
★

⊡**Waterloo House.** Its charms are as many as its years of service (Waterloo has been enchanting guests since 1929). Descriptives like warm, elegant, intimate, charming, tranquil, and indulgent will roll readily off

CLOSE UP

Spaaaah Resorts

Befitting their lovely island location, the best of Bermuda's hotel spas are spectacular in appearance, with white columns, marble floors, flowing linens, and burbling fountains. Bermuda has three full-service spas, located at the Fairmont Southampton, Elbow Beach, and Cambridge Beaches. Day spas are available at Ariel Sands, Pompano Beach, and the Fairmont Princess.

A favorite among Bermuda's society ladies, the day spa at the former **Ariel Sands** offers head-to-toe pampering in a lovely beachside-retreat setting. Although the cottage colony is currently closed, the spa is still open for blisstime.

Sunlight dapples the indoor swimming pools at the **Cambridge Beaches Ocean Spa,** inside a traditional, two-story Bermudian cottage with pink-stucco walls and a ridged roof. The glass dome that covers the pools is opened in warm weather, allowing salt-tinged ocean breezes to drift into the villa. The treatments offered here are hard to find outside Europe. Both

full-day and half-day packages include lunch on a bayside terrace.

The Fairmont Southampton's Willow Stream Spa is the island's largest facility. Besides a complete health club, including personal trainers, there's a garden-enclosed indoor pool, a sundeck overlooking the ocean, two Jacuzzis, three lounges, steam rooms, inhalation rooms, and 15 treatment rooms. Specially designed lengthy treatments combine baths, wraps, and massage conducted with the utmost skill.

The serene **Spa at Elbow Beach** offers personal and couples spa suites overlooking the Atlantic. The suites include personal showers, vanity area, and granite bath. Treatments are based on ayurvedic principles, and use ESPA products. This is the most lavish, personal, private, and relaxing spa on the island.

Serenity Spa at Pompano Beach Club offers a full range of individual and couple treatments from its four treatment rooms facing the ocean.

your tongue as you walk the rooms and grounds of this lovely property. Blessed with one of the island's best chefs, and an international, service-oriented staff, this place fares just fine on its own, but you get the additional value of the use of its sister properties on and near the south shore. This means you can play golf at Horizons and sign up for water sports at the otherwise private Coral Beach & Tennis Club. You can dine here as well with the $50 MAP supplement—a great deal. Rooms are individually fashioned: curtains, carpets, and fabrics are chosen by the owner, a woman who clearly is entranced by detail. Most rooms are in the main house, all have water views. ■TIP➔**Lunch on the sunny lawn at the marina's edge should not be missed. PROS:** stylish, intimate, right in the heart of Hamilton. **CONS:** not on a beach. ⊠*100 Pitts Bay Rd., Hamilton HM 11 ⌂Box HM 333, Hamilton HM BX* ☎*441/295–4480, 800/468–4100 in U.S. ⊕www.waterloohouse.com* ⌸*23 rooms, 6 suites ♿In-room: safe, refrigerator, Wi-Fi. In-hotel: restaurant, bars, pool, no elevator, laundry service, public Internet, public Wi-Fi ▭AE, MC, V ﹗BP, MAP.*

Where to Stay in Paget & Pembroke

$$$ The Fairmont Hamilton Princess.
The reigning royalty of Bermuda
lodging, the Princess boasts some
of the most comfortable rooms
on the island, especially at the
higher end. The hotel seems to
have no problem selling out all of
its rooms consistently, as it caters
to and pampers business guests
like no other hotel in the capital
can; indeed, it's the only full-ser-
vice resort in Hamilton. It's steps
away from the shops and liveliness
of Front Street, as well as the prin-
cipal insurance offices, on the edge
of Hamilton Harbour. Classy, con-
temporary rooms and suites have
elegant hardwood furnishings and
marble bathrooms. Fairmont Gold,
the chain's exclusive boutique hotel
within the larger property, is mem-
orable for its regal lounge, set in
the former ballroom. ■TIP➔ Take

WORD OF MOUTH

"Can anyone tell me their experi-
ences/opinion about the Fairmont
Hamilton Princess? My husband
and I are hoping to spend a long
weekend in Bermuda in May. We'd
like to stay at a nice hotel."
                            –jpetrocine

"My wife and I have been to Ber-
muda 3 times. We stayed at (Fair-
mont) Southampton the first time
then Hamilton the next. We really
like Hamilton because you could
walk to town to shop and/or dine.
You can have everything you need
right there except a beach and
you can take a shuttle to their SH
property to go to the beach."
                            –Ike

posh afternoon tea here complete with silver pots and fine china. Although
at the Princess, as in all Hamilton hotels, there's no beach, you can
walk off the dock onto a fun, twice-daily ferry (followed by a shuttle
ride) to Fairmont's south shore beach. Because it caters to business,
prices are lower on weekends. **PROS:** reliable first-rate rooms, only
full-service resort in the capital, attractive harborfront location. **CONS:**
mainly corporate guests, ferry or cab necessary to reach beaches. ⊠ *76
Pitts Bay Rd., Hamilton HM 08* ⌂ *Box HM 837, Hamilton HM CS*
☎ *441/295–3000 or 800/441–1414* ⊕ *www.fairmont.com* ⬐ *368
rooms, 42 suites* ⬳ *In-room: safe, Ethernet, Wi-Fi. In-hotel: 2 restau-
rants, room service, bars, pools, gym, spa, diving, laundry service, con-
cierge, executive floor, public Internet, public Wi-Fi, some pets allowed*
▭ *AE, DC, MC, V.*

$$$ Grotto Bay Beach Resort. Among
the most noteworthy aspects of this
resort's 21-acre setting, one—its
caves—was chosen to be featured
in its name. (Airport Bay does
sound remarkably less appealing.)
The beach here is satisfactory,
but is quite small for the number
of hotel units, and overlooks the
airport directly across Castle Harbour, a sad and continual reminder

WORD OF MOUTH

"I have stayed at Grotto Bay and
enjoyed it—very pretty grounds,
plain but comfortable rooms, liked
the food. Loved being close to the
Swizzle Inn (pub up the street)
and St. George's."
                            –sp

that you can't stay on this beautiful island forever. Perhaps for these
reasons the resort is inexpensive by Bermuda standards, and is popular
with packaged tour groups. The twin caves are indeed noteworthy: you

can swim in the lagoon of one. Or if you prefer, you can swim in a more traditional underground body of water: the resort pool. It's the center of the action here, next to an outdoor restaurant, hot tub, shuffleboard, and tennis courts. Kids marvel at the aquatic tussle of fish being fed from a small lagoon off the beach. For adults, sightseeing, scuba diving, and snorkeling cruises depart regularly from the on-site deepwater dock. **PROS:** kids' program in summer, on-site aquatic activities, caves. **CONS:** small beach, big complex, doesn't feel like much of Bermuda, rooms unexciting. ⊠ *11 Blue Hole Hill, Bailey's Bay, Hamilton Parish CR 04* ☎*441/293–8333 or 800/582–3190* ⊕*www.grottobay.com* ⮑*198 rooms, 3 suites* ⚐*In-room: safe, dial-up. In-hotel: 2 restaurants, room service, bars, tennis courts, pool, gym, beachfront, diving, water sports, laundry service, concierge, children's programs (ages 4–12), public Internet, public Wi-Fi* ☰*AE, MC, V.*

$$$ 🖵 **Willowbank.** Six acres of lovely waterfront property taper into a corner promontory, splitting two fine beaches, and leading to a wooden walk over the water. This scenic lookout has to be one of the more refreshing vistas on the island. Practicing Christians may appreciate knowing that this former estate was converted to a family-style hotel by a Christian trust. Morning devotions are held in a lounge and grace is said before supper (announced by an ancient ship's bell), which is served in the Loaves and Fishes dining room. But there's no proselytizing. Willowbank is simply a serene and restful alternative to glitzier resorts, with wonderful views and marvelous beaches. Guest rooms, many right on the ocean, have contemporary furnishings, but purposefully are devoid of phones and TVs. ■ TIP➡ **A free summer children's program includes crafts and trips around the island. PROS:** beautiful setting, two beaches, expansive grounds. **CONS:** religious environment might make some uncomfortable. ⊠*126 Somerset Rd., Sandys Parish MA 06* ⌂*Box MA 296, Sandys MA BX* ☎*441/234–1616 or 800/752–8493* ⊕*www.willowbank.bm* ⮑*64 rooms* ⚐*In-room: no phone, refrigerator, no TV, Ethernet, Wi-Fi (some). In-hotel: restaurant, tennis courts, pool, beachfront* ☰*MC, V* �託*MAP.*

$$–$$$ 🖵 **9 Beaches.** But who's counting? A campus of 84 small, freestanding solar-powered cabanas, each angled for dramatic sea views, will make some travelers feel, despondently, like they are at a deluxe summer camp on the beach, while others will rejoice at the simplicity and direct engagement with nature. Plainly furnished cabanas have verandas, wicker ceiling fans, and sides and ceilings made of a canvas material that rustles in the breeze like sailcloth. Guests swear by these—or at them (depending on how they sleep). The half-dozen cabanas perched over the water have glass floor panels that reveal the clear shallow waves underfoot. Though water sports (take a fishing tour and the chef will cook your catch for dinner) are the name of the game here, technology is nicely integrated with Wi-Fi hot spots, complimentary iPods, and cell phones to reach staff from any location. Kids under 16 stay free. This is Bermuda's only truly informal resort. **PROS:** scenic, great for water sports, nice beach. **CONS:** the name of the resort may oversell its small beaches. ⊠*4 Daniel's Head Lane, Sandys Parish MA 04* ☎*441/232–6655 or 866/841–9009* ⊕*www.9beaches.com* ⮑*84*

cabanas ☼ *In-room: safe, refrigerator, no TV, Wi-Fi. In-hotel: restaurant, bars, tennis court, pool, gym, beachfront, water sports, bicycles, concierge, children's programs (ages 1–12), laundry service, public Internet, no-smoking rooms* ⊟*AE, MC, V* ⧉*CP.*

$$–$$$ ▦ **Rosedon.** Expect a tranquil, refined environ and friendly service from longtime staff at this bright, blue-shuttered, white manor house directly across the street from the Princess in the center of Hamilton town. Inside the main house, built in 1906, three traditional rooms have 12-foot ceilings and antique and reproduction furniture, though no balconies. The two-story building behind the main house is newer and less distinguished, but set alongside a relaxing tropical garden. Rooms here have bamboo floors, and some have four-poster beds, love seats, and whirlpool baths. All rooms have either balconies or patios from which you can enjoy the garden setting and a central pool; it's easy to forget you're downtown. Rosedon has no restaurant, but a full breakfast is brought to your room or umbrella-shaded table. **PROS:** hotel pays cab fare to beach, nice gardens, complimentary tea service, central Hamilton location. **CONS:** no beach. ⊠ *57 Pitts Bay Rd., Hamilton HM 06* ✆*Box HM 290, Hamilton HM AX* ☎*441/295–1640, 800/742–5008 in U.S. and Canada* ⊕*www.rosedonbermuda.com* ⇱*44 rooms* ☼*In-room: safe, refrigerator, VCR (some), Wi-Fi. In-hotel: room service, bar, pool, laundry service, public Internet, public Wi-Fi* ⊟*AE, MC, V* ⧉*BP.*

$$–$$$ ▦ **Royal Palms Hotel.** You have to
Fodor's Choice love a hotel that takes its gardens
★ with a botanist's seriousness and yet has enough sense of humor to leave a rubber ducky on your bath mat. Royal Palms is a winner for having high standards, great service, and a welcoming touch, too—fresh-from-the-garden flowers celebrate

> **KNOW THIS**
>
> Stay at Royal Palms if you're doing business in town, or want to experience Hamilton (a five-minute walk) but don't want the city buzzing around you.

your arrival. The best perch might well be the front swing, from which you can survey the lush grounds, including two tall royal palms that give the hotel its name. Also wonderful is the sunny, all-glass breakfast room where you eat at 90-year-old Bermudian cedar tables. If you're looking for privacy, there are three buildings set around the gardens of the main 1903 building; many rooms here have private entrances. It's clear that brother-and-sister owners Richard Smith and Susan Weare put more detailed care into their property, and manage it better than just about anyone else in Bermuda. A final touch is Ascot's—one of the island's best restaurants. **PROS:** beautiful gardens, wonderful breakfast, terrific service, great restaurant. **CONS:** no pool, no beach, 10-minute walk to Hamilton. ⊠ *24 Rosemont Ave., Pembroke Parish HM 06* ✆*Box HM 499, Hamilton HM CX* ☎*441/292–1854, 800/678–0783 in U.S. and Canada* ⊕*www.royalpalms.bm* ⇱*27 rooms* ☼*In-room: safe, dial-up, Wi-Fi. In-hotel: restaurant, bar, pool, no elevator, laundry service* ⊟*AE, MC, V* ⧉*CP.*

$$ ▦ **Bay City Guest House.** Business guests will find this bright blue mansion—the island's newest hotel—a great value downtown. Bank executive Bernadette Footé purchased, renovated, and reopened the hotel in late 2005 to target business travelers looking for a good value in a small upscale hotel. Suites 9–12 have fine views of the harbor across the street, and are recommended; room 9 has a hot tub and nearly 180-degree views; room 12 (for $295, a relative bargain on the island) is a grand corporate suite with an ornamental fireplace surmounted by a 37-inch plasma screen, a king-size bed, and the dark wood and carpeting you can find throughout the hotel. Downstairs, the comfortable breakfast room, which also looks onto the harbor, is a pleasant place to start the day. For self-service types there's a shared kitchen. **PROS**: across from the harbor in Hamilton, spacious rooms. **CONS**: no pool, no beach, reception not always present. ⊠ *53 Pitts Bay Rd., Hamilton HM 06* ☎*441/295–1275* ⊕*www.baycity. bm* 🛏*10 rooms, 2 suites* ⊘*In-room: safe, Wi-Fi. In-hotel: bar, public Internet, public Wi-Fi* ⊟*AE, MC, V* ⦿*CP.*

WORD OF MOUTH

"Are taxis readily available at the Bermuda Airport?"
              –rholt

"I have been to Bermuda many times and never once have I had to wait for a taxi. However, when you are departing, make sure you order the taxi in advance. Don't expect taxis to be there in an instant, they are on Island time plus the traffic makes for slow driving—especially at peak times."
              –Tanya

$$ 🏨**The Wharf Executive Suites Hotel.** This harborfront hotel is all business. Designed strictly with the corporate client in mind, guests will find an ergonomic desk chair, fax/copier/printer, two-line speakerphone, iron, full kitchens, and a generally spotless new room. What more could you ask for? Wireless Internet and a bit of soul. The former is irresponsible in a business-minded hotel; the latter is a consequence of a formulaic approach to corporate room design. Luckily each of the 10 studios and five one-bedrooms come with a private balcony, and they look out over the marvelous harbor. You can watch your ferry make its way over to Darrell's Wharf, which is downstairs, and stroll down to catch it for the seven-minute ride to Hamilton. That's a saving grace. Corporate guests get a discount. **PROS**: great balconies over the harbor, next to ferry service. **CONS**: business hotel with no Ethernet or Wi-Fi, rooms are corporate with no warmth. ⊠ *1 Harbour Rd., Paget Parish PG 01* ☎*441/232–5700 or 866/782–9232* ⊕*www.wharfexecutivesuites.com* 🛏*15 suites* ⊘*In-room: safe, kitchen, refrigerator, dial-up. In-hotel: laundry facilities, laundry service* ⊟*AE, MC, V* ⦿*CP.*

COTTAGE COLONIES

$$$$ 🏨**Cambridge Beaches.** Cambridge Beaches has a coat of arms that reads PRIMA ET OPTIMA, or First and Best. The First? Yes—it's the island's oldest cottage colony. The Best? Well, if you want a pervasive sense of tranquillity and relaxed refinement, then that's a fact, too. No other Bermuda resort uses its privileged setting better—its 25 acres on a peninsula near the western end of the island creates a sense of meandering expansiveness. Many large properties on the island are centered

Fodor'sChoice
★

around one main beach, but Cambridge has five, including beautiful Long Bay Beach and Morning Beach (backed by a chic infinity pool unveiled in 2007). The complimentary daily tea service is a civilized affair, set in a beautiful lounge overlooking Mangrove Bay. The varying sizes, styles, and locations of the cottages and rooms make for a wide range of prices. Less-expensive rooms open onto lawns and gardens, but overlook the same wide ocean. Ocean Spa is among the very best in Bermuda. **PROS:** private, gamut of activities and beaches to choose from, beautiful grounds and beaches. **CONS:** far removed from rest of island, very expensive. ⊠ *30 King's Point Rd., Sandys Parish MA 02* ☎*441/234–0331, 800/468–7300 in U.S.* ⊕*www.cambridgebeaches. com* ⇄*66 rooms, 25 suites, 3 2-bedroom cottages* △*In-room: safe, refrigerator, DVD (some), Ethernet. In-hotel: 2 restaurants, room service, bars, tennis courts, pools, gym, spa, beachfront, diving, water sports, laundry service, public Internet, no kids under 5* ▤*AE, DC, MC, V* ⎮◎⎮*BP, MAP.*

★ **$$$$** ⊞**Horizons and Cottages.** Horizons is a dying breed of old Bermuda—in fact, at the time of this writing, the Four Seasons was rumored to be ready to purchase it and its sister property across the street, the Coral Beach and Tennis Club. Although some things at Horizons (like the nine-hole course) could use an upgrade to get back to its former Relais & Chateaux polish, it's worth a stay to experience the former plantation estate's core cottage colony experience. For decades vacationers before you have soaked up the convivial and social environment, highlighted by drinks in the curious downstairs pub with its vintage billiard games and dinner served in the main clubhouse. Rooms don't have TVs; a game of tennis and a swim across the street at Coral Beach will suffice instead. Although Horizons has many similarities to Cambridge Beaches, this property is more clubby. Oriental rugs, polished wood floors, cathedral ceilings, and open fireplaces are elegant reminders of the 18th century, when the main house in this resort was a private home. Most guest cottages have a large common room with a fireplace, a library, and board games, and all have terraces. **PROS:** beautiful grounds, two-in-one hotel stay courtesy of sister property, gorgeous beach. **CONS:** golf course in bad shape, upkeep is slacking while the hotel waits to sell. ⊠ *33 S. Shore Rd., Paget Parish PG 04* ⌖*Box PG 198, Paget PG BX* ☎*441/236–0048, 800/468–0022 in U.S.* ⊕*www. horizonscottages.com* ⇄*40 rooms, 5 suites* △*In-room: safe, kitchen (some), refrigerator (some), no TV, dial-up. In-hotel: restaurant, bar, golf course, tennis courts, pool, gym, laundry facilities, laundry service, public Internet* ▤*AE, MC, V* ⎮◎⎮*BP, MAP.*

★ **$$$$** ⊞**Pink Beach Club & Cottages.** Pink Beach Club is a Bermuda original. This secluded cottage colony, on the west side of the island, a few minutes from Mid Ocean and Tucker's Point golf courses, opened in 1947. The main house, where you'll find the reception restaurant, looks like a private club, with dark-wood paneling, a large fireplace, and beam ceilings. Paved paths wind through 16½ acres of gardens, leading to two pretty, private beaches and 25 pink cottages. Single-room suites are expansive, with king-size beds, pullout couches, and sitting areas. One- and two-bedroom suites have separate living rooms, and some have

CLOSE UP

Pretty in Pink

Long before Bermuda's tourism heyday, when only British aristocrats, Hollywood stars, and blue bloods from America's East Coast could afford to come to the island and disappear for a while, Bermuda's would-be hoteliers were sowing the seeds of one of the island's most important future economy bases. The beautiful people, with their well-lined pockets, were transforming Bermuda into a chic getaway destination, and this exclusive clientele would want seclusion, colonial sophistication, and traditional Bermudian hospitality. And so the cottage colony was born: a purpose-built resort that left no comfort unexplored, no luxury ignored—a plush home-away-from-home for those who could afford it.

The Bermuda Department of Tourism recognizes nine properties as cottage colonies: 9 Beaches, Ariel Sands (which is currently closed as it converts to a Hilton), Cambridge Beaches, Fourways Inn, Horizons & Cottages, Mid Ocean Golf Club, Pink Beach Club, the St. George's Club, and Willowbank. Despite the tourism department's demarcation, you might well be baffled by the island's numerous lodgings that have the word cottage in their names or descriptions, and that's before realizing that there are even more cottages (often private homes) that have been converted into lodgings, and which *might not* have the word cottage in their title.

Confused? The definitive line over what does and does not qualify to earn the title continues to blur, but generally speaking it describes a purpose-built beachfront collection of Bermudian cottages, separated from a main building that often houses the front desk, restaurants, bars,

and lounge areas. Often, twisting walkways connect the cottages to the main building and lead down to the beach, over to the tennis courts, and elsewhere on the property. Many of the cottages are pink (Bermuda's trademark color) or other pastel shades, and most have either stunning water views or lush, tropical garden settings. Traditionally, the cottages have Bermudian white stair-step roofs, terraces or balconies, cedar-beamed ceilings and furniture, and British country-style fabrics and ornaments. Newer complexes, however, may have much larger cottages of more modern design, divided into suites, or they may have attached apartments. Some may not even have kitchens—a staple of the traditional cottages.

Whatever a cottage colony is, it certainly isn't basic or budget. Bermuda's homegrown accommodations are some of the island's most exceptional—and expensive—and while many offer a unique holiday experience, they won't suit everyone. The emphasis is on peace and quiet, and they provide this admirably. Entertainment, children's programs, and other activities are not emphasized in many complexes, so they may not be ideal for those seeking a lively, fun-packed vacation.

Although the concept and reality of cottage colonies continues to evolve, the unabashed romance of these magical oases is alive and well. The pursuit of authentic Bermudian living, with a distinct British colonial tradition, still remains to transport guests into gracious lifestyle rather than simply a hotel room.

—Vivienne Sheath

two bathrooms. All have French doors that open onto a balcony or terrace and most have ocean views. **PROS:** near Mid Ocean and Tuckers Point golf courses and the airport, classic cottage colony, very formal and private, no TV. **CONS:** isolated from populated parts of island and other vacationers, more formal, no TV. ✉ *1016 S. Shore Rd., Tucker's Town, Smith's Parish HS 01* ✆ *Box HM 1017, Hamilton HM DX* ☎ *441/293–1666, 800/355–6161 in U.S. and Canada* ⊕ *www.pink-beach.com* ➦ *94 suites* ⚎ *In-room: safe, no TV, refrigerator, Ethernet (some), dial-up. In-hotel: restaurant, room service, bar, tennis courts, pool, gym, beachfront, water sports, bicycles, no elevator, laundry service, public Internet* ▤ *AE, MC, V* ⦿*MAP.*

$$$ ⛃ **The St. George's Club.** This time-share complex, which looks and feels like a 1990s condo community, is the closest thing to a modern hotel room in St. George's. (Aunt Nea's guesthouse is the only other lodging choice in this corner of the island.) The grounds are tidy, ample, and perched high above St. George's. A walk (or drive) down a gardened path takes you into town from the 18-acre campus. Clean one- and two-bedroom cottages come with a fully equipped kitchen and views of the ocean, one of three pools, or a public golf course designed by Robert Trent Jones. The sleek, three-story main building holds the lobby, business center, a convenience store where you can buy champagne and sunblock, and two restaurants: Griffin's, serving contemporary food, and Blackbeard's Hideout Beach Club, a summer-only pub by Tobacco Bay public beach and the golf course. **PROS:** only non-B&B in St. George's, nice views walking to town, private. **CONS:** no activities outside of the pool, feels more like a suburban development than a vacation spot, far from the rest of the island. ✉ *6 Rose Hill, St. George's Parish GE O5* ✆ *Box GE 92, St. George's GE BX* ☎ *441/297–1200* ⊕ *www.stgeorgesclub.bm* ➦ *72 cottages* ⚎ *In-room: safe, kitchen, refrigerator, DVD (some), Wi-Fi. In-hotel: 2 restaurants, bars, tennis courts, pools, gym, laundry facilities, laundry service, public Internet* ▤ *AE, MC, V.*

$$ ⛃ **Fourways Inn.** The main edifice at this mid-island cottage colony is a family home, which belonged to the owners of Harvey's Bristol Crème in the 1700s. It's with this gastronomic tradition in mind that this pretty but otherwise unextraordinary cottage colony comes to life. Like most on the island, the colony is set amid a profusion of greenery and flowers around a pool; its suites have marble floors and balconies or patios. In short, it's pleasant. The main draws are its top-notch Continental restaurant, which brings formal patrons to its large dining room and 6,000-bottle wine list; and its small pub, the Peg Leg Lounge, which, partly situated in the old home's kitchen, manages to feel like a classic old-world redoubt, with unpolished bronze chandeliers and an enormous fireplace, the home's former woodstove. **PROS:** inexpensive, can walk to beaches, great dining. **CONS:** middle of the island, no beach. ✉ *1 Middle Rd.,*

KNOW THIS

The beach is a five-minute bus ride away from Fourways, but once there, guests can use the facilities at Coco Reef.

Paget Parish PG 01 ☐*Box PG 294, Paget PG BX* ☎*441/236–6517, 800/962–7654 in U.S.* ⊕*www.fourwaysinn.com* ↩*6 rooms, 4 suites* ☖*In-room: kitchen, refrigerator. In-hotel: restaurant, bar, pool, laundry service, no-smoking rooms* ▭*AE, MC, V* ⍾*CP.*

HOUSEKEEPING COTTAGES & APARTMENTS

$$$

Fodor'sChoice

★

Grape Bay Cottage. Down a long and meandering private estate road lined with hibiscus-fronted mansions, you can find this perfectly simple, laughably cute cottage perched right at the edge of the soft sands of Grape Bay Beach. The two-bedroom cottage has an open fireplace, hardwood floors, a full-size kitchen, a king-size bed, a pull-out couch, and a lawn patio overlooking the beach. The area is quiet and secluded, ideal for beach-lovers who like to cook for themselves and do serious sand-and-surf time. The cottages are a bit costly for one couple (though cheaper than any resort in Bermuda), but for two or even three couples sharing expenses (extra cots are provided), this is an eminently affordable choice. Gwen, the friendly housekeeper, has welcomed guests here for years, and recounts with familial joy the latest news in the lives of regular visitors. Although you can't perhaps afford to purchase a beachfront home in Bermuda, this may be the next best thing. **PROS:** sharable with friends or family, beachfront, quiet. **CONS:** no pool. ⊠*Grape Bay Dr., Paget Parish* ☐*Box HM 1851, Hamilton HM HX* ☎*441/295–7017, 800/637–4116 in U.S.* 🖷*441/296–0563* ↩*1 cottage* ☖*In-room: kitchen, refrigerator, no TV. In-hotel: beachfront, laundry facilities* ▭*AE, MC, V.*

$$

Edgehill Manor. The first thing you notice is the color: pea green. It takes your eyes a minute to adjust to the grand colonial-style house, built around the turn of the 20th century, and its newer wing. But then you see the order that's kept here: spotless grounds, with notes of hung flower pots, an inviting pool surrounded by lush greenery, and handsome simple and clean rooms, all with private balconies. Central Hamilton is a short 10-minute walk downhill. French country–style furniture, small flat-screen TVs, and lots of bright florals fill the guest and common rooms. **PROS:** nice pool, well maintained, clean rooms. **CONS:** not a leisure destination, no beach. ⊠*36 Rosemont Ave., Hamilton HM EX* ☐*Box HM 1048, Hamilton HM EX* ☎*441/295–7124* ⊕*www.bermuda.com/edgehill* ↩*14 rooms* ☖*In-room: safe, kitchen (some), refrigerator (some), VCR (some), Wi-Fi. In-hotel: pool, no elevator, public Wi-Fi* ▭*AE, MC, V* ⍾*CP.*

$

Fodor'sChoice

★

Clairfont Apartments. Clairfont offers one of Bermuda's best values, and it's probably the island's best buy if you're on a budget and don't mind a five-minute walk to one of the island's best beaches. Furnishings, while not exactly fancy, are the best in this price category. Rooms offer a great value for spaciousness as well. But above all you'll want to kiss the finicky, cleaning-crazy manager Corrine Simons because the property is spotless. Kitchens and baths were upgraded in 2007. Choose between two studios or six one-bedrooms—all with fully equipped kitchens. The studios ($130 year-round) have king-size beds and separate kitchens. The four sunny upstairs units have balconies, and the downstairs apartments have patios, leading onto a communal lawn and a nice pool. The property welcomes a lot of families with children during the summer months and Warwickshire Long Bay Playground is a few minutes' walk away. Monthly rates in winter are an astonishingly low $1,250. Early booking is recommended. **PROS:** cheap, very clean and well maintained, large units. **CONS:** not beachfront. ⊠6 *Warwickshire Rd., Warwick Parish WK 02 ⌂Box WK 85, Warwick Parish WK 02* ☎441/238–3577 *⊕www.clairfontapartments.bm* ⌨8 *apartments ⟡In-room: kitchen, refrigerator, DVD, Ethernet. In-hotel: pool, laundry service* ⊟AE, MC, V.

$ **Erith Guest House.** You'll pay an extra 30 bucks to stay here than at the more B&B-like Pomander Guest House directly across the street, but what separates this bright, new, eight-room guesthouse from others in its class is the overall spic-and-span cleanliness, the pool deck, and the efficient service. Both are on quiet, one-way Pomander Road. Three rooms here have private balconies or patios that make for great sunning or lunching. Everyone has access to the spartan pool and hot tub, which overlooks the adjacent tennis club. **PROS:** clean and meticulous rooms. **CONS:** not waterfront, beaches far away. ⊠15 *Pomander Rd., Paget PG 05* ☎441/232–1827 *⊕www.erithguesthouse.com* ⌨7 *rooms, 1 suite ⟡In-room: refrigerator, Ethernet. In-hotel: pool, laundry service, public Internet* ⊟AE, MC, V ⧖MAP.

$ **Garden House.** Hospitable owner and manager, the eccentric Rosanne Galloway is a fervent gardener, and spends much time on this large property planting and pruning. The grounds aren't flawless; indeed there's a relaxed work-in-progress approach that is evident, but for the right traveler, the result is an underpriced stay with more space than you'll know what to do with. You'll have to walk a ways to a beach, but the long lawn extends to a path that reaches Ely's Harbour where you can swim, as long as you don't mind diving into deep water right off the shore. There are other exciting aspects of this oft-overlooked corner of the island: Wreck Road, a marvelous mansion-lined residential street that skirts Ely's Harbor, has a small beach at the far end; and Somerset Bridge is reached from a dirt path that leads to Middle Road. Rooms are furnished with Persian rugs and antique furniture. All units have patios that lead out to the gardens. Children under 12 stay free. **PROS:** inexpensive cottages and rooms, quiet, interesting corner of the island to explore, friendly hostess. **CONS:** few services, not beachfront. ⊠4 *Middle Rd., Sandys Parish SB 01* ☎441/234–1435 ⎙441/234–3006 ⌨3 *apartments, 2 cottages ⟡In-room: safe, kitchen, refrigerator, DVD (some), VCR. In-hotel: pool, laundry facilities* ⊟No credit cards ⊘Closed Dec.–Feb.

$ **Granaway Guest House.** One of the island's best values, Granaway is a 1734 manor house with villa-like lawn and gardens leading to a clear and well-maintained pool. Any of the outdoor chairs and lounges are great places to relax. The pink house is across the street from Hamilton Harbour and ferries to Hamilton. South shore beaches are a 30-minute walk, or a jaunt of a cab ride, so it's an affordable option if you don't have be on the beach. All rooms are distinct; the "yellow room" features original cedar beams, and the "pink room" has a private terrace

Fodor'sChoice
★

with harbor views. A private cottage, which maxes out at $280 a night in peak season, gives you your own small home with kitchen. **PROS:** great value, gardened terrace, relaxing lawn and pool area, historic property. **CONS:** not waterfront or easy walk to beaches, only Continental breakfast. ⊠*Harbour Rd., Warwick WK 533* ☎*441/236–3747 U.S.* ⊕*www.granaway.com* ⇖*5 rooms, 1 cottage* ◊*In-room: kitchen (some), refrigerator. In-hotel: pool* ⊟*AE, MC, V* ⊚|*CP.*

$ 🏠**Greenbank Cottages.** Greenbank has been family-run for 50 years, and this is what Bermuda vacations were like back then: by way of entertainment you had a due-west pier with two chairs to watch the sunset. A stay at Greenbank is a slow, relaxed experience. There's no beach here (and no TVs). Instead, you sit out on the harborfront lawn and take in the sun, or use the private dock for deepwater swimming. Or catch the ferry, just steps across the road, to explore the island. The waterside cottages, especially Salt Winds, have lovely harbor views. No two are alike—some were converted from old horse and buggy stations once used in transporting salt. All are clean and updated, with kitchens, private entrances, and shaded verandas. **PROS:** close to ferry, secluded neighborhood, relaxed place. **CONS:** no pool or beach. ⊠*17 Salt Kettle Rd., Paget Parish PG 01* ☐*Box PG 201, Paget PG BX* ☎*441/236–3615* ⊕*www.greenbankbermuda.com* ⇖*4 cottages, 5 studios, 2 rooms* ◊*In-room: kitchen (some), refrigerator, no TV, Wi-Fi. In-hotel: public Wi-Fi* ⊟*AE, MC, V.*

$ 🏠**Mazarine by the Sea.** This easy-to-miss guest cottage is right on the edge of a wild, windswept promontory over the sea. Though it's only a mile from the capital (a bus stops right in front on North Shore Road), it's on the less-traveled north side of the island, and feels remote. Swim in a pool perched on a cliff edge or stay in Unit 7—a separate cottage with a grassy patio lawn and a small pathway of steps down to a rocky ledge that lets

> **KNOW THIS**
>
> You can deepwater swim and snorkel at Mazarine. There's even a small dive center on the premises that offers scuba and snorkeling tours. For those inclined to more advanced ocean exploration, this do-it-yourself spot is unrivaled.

into the ocean. Five of seven units have ocean views. **PROS:** waterfront property, pool. **CONS:** no hotel-style services, residential area not near beaches and a bus ride from Hamilton. ⊠*91 N. Shore Rd., Pembroke Parish* ☐*Box HM 91, Hamilton HM AX* ☎*441/292–1659* ⊞*441/292–6891* ⇖*7 apartments* ◊*In-room: kitchen. In-hotel: pool, water sports* ⊟*AE, MC, V.*

$ 🏠**Paraquet Guest Apartments.** For those not picky about the room they stay in, Paraquet (pronounced "parakeet") provides a centrally located, motel-like, no-frills stay. Rooms are simple, clean, and unadorned. The biggest draw is, at its price, proximity to Elbow Beach, one of the prettiest beaches on the island—a mere five-minute walk away! The Paraquet Restaurant is reasonably priced and—surprise!—is an American-style diner, with milk shakes, straws in old jars, and low counter stools. You can also walk to the nearby supermarket and cook your

Bermudian Architecture

CLOSE UP

The typical Bermudian building is built of limestone block, usually painted white or a pastel shade, with a prominent chimney and a tiered, white-painted roof that Mark Twain likened to "icing on the cake." More than just picturesque, these features are proof that "Necessity" really is "the Mother of Invention." Limestone, for instance, was a widely available building material—and far better able to withstand hurricane-force winds than the old English-style "wattle and daub."

The distinctive roof, similarly, was not developed for aesthetic reasons. It's part of a system that allows Bermudians to collect rainwater and store it in large tanks beneath their houses. The special white roof paint even contains a purifying agent. If your visit includes some rainy days, you may hear the expression, "Good day for the tank!" This is rooted in the fact that Bermuda has no freshwater. It relies on rain for drinking, bathing, and cooking water, as well as golf-course and farmland irrigation. So residents are careful not to waste the precious liquid. The island has never run out of water, though the supply was stretched during World War II, when thousands of U.S. soldiers were stationed in Bermuda.

"Moongates" are another interesting Bermudian structural feature, usually found in gardens and walkways around the island. These Chinese-inspired freestanding stone arches, popular since the late 18th century, are still often incorporated into new construction. Thought to bring luck, the ring-shape gates are favored as backdrops for wedding photos.

Other architectural details you may notice are "welcoming arms" stairways, with banisters that seem to reach out to embrace you as you approach the first step, and "eyebrows" over window openings. Also look for "butteries": tiny, steep-roofed cupboards, separate from the house, and originally built to keep dairy products cool in summer. If you wonder why, in this warm climate, so many houses have fireplaces in addition to air-conditioners, come in January, when the dampness makes it warmer outside than in.

—revised by Susan MacCallum-Whitcomb

own meals in one of nine rooms with kitchenettes. **PROS:** convenient diner, affordable, close to the beach. **CONS:** no views, no pool, no amenities. ✉ *72 South Rd., Paget Parish PG 04* 🗁 *Box PG 173, Paget PG BX* 🖷 *441/236–5842* ⊕ *www.paraquetapartments.com* ↩ *18 rooms* ☖ *In-room: no phone (some), kitchen (some), refrigerator. In-hotel: restaurant, laundry facilities* ☰ *MC, V.*

$ ▦ **Robin's Nest.** This well-maintained valley property is a tad off the beaten path, in a quiet residential neighborhood about a mile north of Hamilton and within walking distance to a secluded beach cove. Behind the main house up a flight of stairs you'll likely be surprised to find the guest rooms in what looks like a two-story urban apartment complex. Studios here are new, with spacious and modern kitchenettes; upstairs studios have balconies, and the ground-floor studios open onto tranquil, intimate gardens and a pool. The small number of rooms means you're more than likely to enjoy the good-size pool and patio all to yourself. A short bus ride can take you to Hamilton, Admiralty Park, or north-shore snorkeling sites. To find Robin's Nest, take Ingham Vale from North Shore Road. **PROS:** well-kept rooms and grounds, pool. **CONS:** out of the way location. ⊠*10 Vale Close, Pembroke HM 04* ☎*441/292–4347* ⊕*www.robinsnestbda.com* ⤴*11 studio apartments* ⌂*In-room: kitchen, refrigerator. In-hotel: pool* ☰*No credit cards.*

$ 🏨 **Sandpiper Apartments.** The brochure for this simple, apartment-style property boasts "the finest in luxury." Well, ahem, Sandpiper is probably the *least* luxurious choice in all of Bermuda. That said, it's not bad if you're looking for an easygoing do-it-yourself kind of stay within walking distance to all south shore beaches. Spacious and basically decorated, the 14 whitewashed units include five one-bedroom apartments with full kitchens and nine studios with kitchenettes. Each has either a balcony or patio. Most can accommodate up to four people. Choose from rooms with names outside that read Estascy [sic], Lover's Lair, Twiddle-dom (Unit 5) or Twiddle-dee (Unit 5A). **PROS:** convenient to south shore beaches, inexpensive, pool. **CONS:** not beachfront, limited services. ⊠*S. Shore Rd., Warwick Parish* ✆*Box HM 685, Hamilton HM CX* ☎*441/236–7093* ⊕*www.sandpiperbda.com* ⤴*14 apartments* ⌂*In-room: safe, kitchen (some). In-hotel: pool, laundry facilities* ☰*AE, MC, V.*

$ 🏨 **Serendipity.** These two studio apartments in residential Paget don't appear on official Bermuda Department of Tourism accommodation catalogs; hence, perhaps, the name. For budget travelers who stumble upon one of these two rooms offered by Albert and Judy Corday, fortune is smiling. Judy's

> **A GOOD DEAL**
>
> From January 1 through March 30, the price at Serendipity is $110 a night, making it just about the cheapest stay on the island.

family has been on the island since 1612, and she welcomes return guests as part of that extended family. The real genius of this place, however, is value. Both ground-floor apartments are clean and spacious, if decorated on the older, homier side. They have fully equipped kitchenettes and private patios that overlook the pool and yard, which is canopied in summer by the red blooms of two magnificent poincianas. Grape Bay beach is a lovely 12-minute walk away. The home is next to the Railway Trail, and across the street from the Paget Nature Reserve. **PROS:** clean, private, friendly, spacious, cheap. **CONS:** have to walk to beach, no hotel-style services. ⊠*6 Rural Dr., Paget Parish PG 06* ☎*441/236–1192* ⤴*2 apartments* ⌂*In-room: safe, kitchen, refrigerator. In-hotel: pool* ☰*No credit cards.*

BED & BREAKFASTS

★ $$ 🏨 **Oxford House.** Oxford House is the only true bed-and-breakfast in the capital, and one imagines that even if it had competition, it would still be the best. Even executives staying in town should be impressed by the elegant pale-pink two-story town house, which is two blocks from the capital's shops, ferries, and buses. Rooms have Internet and

LODGING ALTERNATIVES

APARTMENT & VILLA RENTALS

If you want a home base that's roomy enough for a family, consider renting a private house or apartment. Furnished rentals can save you money, especially if you're traveling with a group. **BermudaGetaway** (⊕ www.bermudagetaway.com) lists a selection of high-standard properties but does not accept reservations. For that, you can contact the property owner directly. **Bermuda Accommodations** (☎877/730–1352 or 416/232–2243 ⊕www.bermudarentals.com) maintains an up-to-the-minute listing of available properties all over the island *and* makes reservations. The Web site has photos and good descriptions of what you can expect to find. **Coldwell Banker JW Bermuda Realty** (☎441/292–1793 ⊕www.bermuda-realty.com) requires you to register with the company before an agent will help you find a property that meets your requirements. You can also make reservations with **Villas International** (☎415/499–9490 or 800/221–2260 ⊕www.villasintl.com).

BED & BREAKFASTS

B&Bs in Bermuda range from grand, converted Victorians to a couple of rooms with shared bath in a small home. Breakfasts, too, run the gamut, though light Continental breakfasts with fresh fruit are more common than hearty bacon-and-eggs meals. Sometimes there is a pool on the property, but to get to the beach, you usually have to travel by bus or scooter. **Bermuda Accommodations** (☎877/730–1352 or 416/232–2243 ⊕www.bermudarentals.com) lists and takes reservations for rooms available in B&Bs.

HOME EXCHANGES

If you would like to exchange your home for someone else's, join a home-exchange organization, which will send you its updated listings of available exchanges for a year and will include your own listing in at least one of them. It's up to you to make specific arrangements. **HomeLink International** (☎954/566–2687 or 800/638–3841 ⊕www.homelink.org) charges $90 yearly for a listing. Searching properties is free.

desks. The 1938 inn is family-owned and -operated, and each room is individually decorated with pretty, matching fabrics and antique and reproduction furniture. Polished cedar floors, a fireplace, and handsome Chippendale chairs lend warmth to the breakfast room, where you can sample scones each morning. There are coffeemakers in the rooms as well. **PROS:** friendly and attentive service, clean and updated rooms, right in Hamilton. **CONS:** rooms more executive than cozy, no beach, no pool. ✉*20 Woodbourne Ave., Hamilton ⌂Box HM 374, Hamilton HM BX ☎441/295–0503, 800/548–7758 in U.S., 800/272–2306 in Canada ⊕www.oxfordhouse.bm ⟲12 rooms ⌂In-room: Ethernet, Wi-Fi (some). In-hotel: restaurant, no elevator, laundry service ⊟AE, MC, V ⫿CP.*

$ ▦ **Aunt Nea's Inn at Hillcrest.** Stroll down to Aunt Nea's and you'll be treated to the best of St. George's. A narrow winding alley leads to the gate of a long central walkway amid formal gardens and up to the entrance of this grand home. Your hosts, Delaey Robinson and

Andrea Dismont will enthusiastically guide you through their inviting 18th-century home. The excitement is justified: all the Jasmine rooms and suites (some with whirlpools) have gorgeous, old-fashioned bed frames, from wrought iron to solid-oak four-posters with canopies. Aunt Nea's is within putting distance of St. George's golf course and a five-minute scooter ride from Tobacco Bay Beach and the other secluded coves. **PROS:** quaint St. George's setting, quiet, spacious. **CONS:** no pool, far from other island destinations. ⊠*1 Nea's Alley, St. George's GE 05* 🖃*Box GE 96, St. George's GE BX* ☎*441/297–1630* ⊕*www.auntneas.com* ⇆*12 rooms, 6 suites* ♿*In-room: kitchen (some), refrigerator, DVD (some), Wi-Fi. In-hotel: laundry service, public Wi-Fi* ☰*AE, MC, V* ⦿*CP.*

$ ⛭ **Greene's Guest House.** On the Bermuda Railway Trail in the quiet western end of Southampton Parish, this large family-run guesthouse is a cheap stay in a tranquil area for those who don't mind an out-of-date bedroom. Whale Bay Beach is a 10-minute walk away, and the bus stops in front. The house is outsize and has a huge front and backyard where you'll be treated to beautiful views of the Great Sound. Breakfast is included; you can use the kitchen to prepare lunch or dinner. Rooms are clean and some have water views. A large swimming pool in the back overlooks the ocean. **PROS:** airy views, open spaces, quiet, bottom-dollar. **CONS:** feels like you're in a stranger's big weird house, away from island action. ⊠*Jennings Bay, Southampton Parish SN BX* 🖃*Box SN 395, Southampton SN BX* ☎*441/238–0834, 800/637–4116 in U.S.* 🖷*441/238–8980* ⇆*6 rooms* ♿*In-room: refrigerator, Wi-Fi. In-hotel: pool, laundry service, public Internet, public Wi-Fi* ☰*No credit cards* ⦿*BP.*

⛭ **Little Pomander Guest House.** You're welcomed to this circa-1600 house—one of the island's oldest—by a quaint driftwood sign above the door. "Little Pomander" has indeed modest ambitions, perhaps a natural extension of its mellow owner, Pat Harvey. It's on a quiet one-way residential street that edges along a narrow inlet of Hamilton harbor. The backside of the cottage has a lawn looking over the water to town; lawn chairs are set out and some guests make use of the barbecue. One much-requested room has a patio with steps leading down to the lawn. Another room with water views is divided by a large unlikely bulge—which turns out to be the house's old wood stove. Quirkiness ends at breakfast—with its humble selection of bagels and toast. **PROS:** inexpensive, residential area makes you feels like part of a community, nice waterfront views of Hamilton, 10-minute walk to Hamilton or beaches. **CONS:** no beach, rooms slightly aging, linens clean but not contemporary. ⊠*16 Pomander Rd., Paget Parish PG 02* 🖃*Box HM 384, Hamilton HM BX* ☎*441/236–7635* ⊕*www. littlepomander.com* ⇆*6 rooms*

KNOW THIS

Pomander—and Erith Guest House across the street—make sense for unfussy travelers who want to be near the capital. Both are on a quiet, one-way residential street skirting the harbor, a 12-minute walk—or a few minutes by bus—to the center of Hamilton. They're also a 15-minute walk to south shore beaches.

&In-room: refrigerator, Wi-Fi. In-hotel: public Wi-Fi ⊟AE, MC, V ⦿CP.

$ **Salt Kettle House.** Innkeeper Hazel Lowe has the warmth and personality that B&B aficionados dream about. This, coupled with the fact that her house and its cottages rest directly on a secluded bay adjoining Hamilton Harbour, make Salt Kettle House the most memorable stay on the island. Besides Ms. Lowe, dramatis personae include her friendly cats Willy and Milly; two ducks; books, which are everywhere; and returning patrons, who constitute 90% of guests. A cozy lounge inside the main entrance has a real fireplace where you can gather for cocktails and conversation. First-timers, "whether they like it or not," are given insightful tips by Ms. Lowe on the best of Bermuda. Four waterside cottages have shaded patios and lounge chairs, bedrooms, sitting rooms, and full kitchens. You can fish here and cook your catch, read on a lawn hammock, or have tea with Ms. Lowe, B&B rock star. **PROS:** steps form ferry, wonderful private setting, beautiful gardens, great hospitality. **CONS:** no beach, no pool. ⊠10 Salt Kettle Rd., Paget Parish PG 01 ☎441/236–0407 ⊕441/236–8639 ⌤3 rooms, 4 cottages &In-room: safe, kitchen, refrigerator, no TV (some). In-hotel: laundry facilities, public Wi-Fi ⊟No credit cards ⦿BP.

Fodor'sChoice ★

Nightlife & the Arts

WORD OF MOUTH

"I was told that Bermuda's nightlife is low-key but I went with a group of girlfriends and we had soooooooooo much fun. I guess you make your own fun. We danced 'till we dropped at Splash nightclub in Hamilton—great DJs! Another night we got to chat (and sing!) with the locals at the Pickled Onion. Bring the right attitude and you'll have fun wherever you go. We want to go back again for the Bermuda Music Festival in October."

—jemiejac

Updated by
Andrew Raine

BERMUDIANS LOVE TO DRINK. THAT'S the title of a popular local song, and it hits the nail right on the head. Yes, the island that gave the world the Dark 'n Stormy and the rum swizzle might not have the largest selection of hot spots in which to party the night away, but what Bermuda lacks in venues it makes up for in attitude. Tourists, expats, and locals all mix together to create a melting-pot social scene, especially on Friday nights—the unofficial party day for just about everyone living on the Rock. The vibe is civilized but still fun and friendly, and if you're not sure where you want to go, just ask around; people will be more than happy to give you their thoughts— they might even buy you a drink!

TOP 5 NIGHTLIFE

■ A jug of rum swizzle, some fine barbecued food, and decent live music at the Swizzle Inn.

■ Limbo dance with the local ladies at Hawkins Island.

■ Happy-hour drinks in the grand gardens of the Hamilton Princess, and admire the yachts in the harbor.

■ Chill out to the island's best jazz music at Hubie's.

■ Stomp the boards at Café Cairo after a few too many Dark 'n Stormy's.

4

If you prefer your nightlife have more culture than rum concoctions, there's still plenty to do. Hubie's Bar is host to the island's finest jazz artists, and City Hall provides a venue for visiting artists on an ad hoc basis. Dramatic productions take place across a variety of venues— anywhere from a hotel auditorium to the back of a Front Street pub.

For a rundown of what's hot and happening in Bermuda, pick up the Bermuda Calendar of Events brochure at any Visitor Information Centre. The free monthly *Preview Bermuda* magazine also lists upcoming island events and can be accessed online at ⊕*www.previewbermuda. com*. *The Bermudian* ($5), a monthly magazine, has a calendar of events, as does *RG* magazine, which is included free in the *Royal Gazette* newspaper on the first Thursday of the month. *This Week in Bermuda*, another free magazine, describes arts and nightlife venues. The *Bermuda Sun* newspaper has a Scene section on Friday, which includes an events calendar. It's also a good idea to check ⊕*www. boxoffice.bm* for upcoming show information.

Some hotels carry a TV station that broadcasts information about the island's cultural events and nightlife. Radio VSB, FM 1450, gives a lineup of events daily at 11:15 AM. You can also dial 974 for recorded information. Because the arts scene in Bermuda is so casual, many events and performers operate on a seasonal or part-time basis. Bulletin boards are also a good spot to check for upcoming events.

NIGHTLIFE

Hamilton is the island's central nightlife hub, with a smattering of decent bars and clubs, featuring live music and drink promotions. Outside of the city there's a thriving nightlife scene within the hotels. In summer, weekly cruises and beach bashes add to the party scene.

Don't overlook the work of local musicians: Bermuda has a long tradition of producing superb jazz artists and hosts an annual jazz festival in fall. One of the best places to catch a jam session is at Hubie's Bar on Friday night; it's a typical jazz bar that caters to the forty-plus crowd. Everyone knows where Hubie's is, so a cab can easily get you there—and it's the kind of place where your neighbor at the bar could be a mail carrier or a member of Parliament.

As a general rule, both men and women tend to dress smart-casual for clubs. This means you may not want to wear T-shirts, ratty jeans, or running shoes. Pubs and clubs begin to fill up around 9:30 or 10.

BARS & LOUNGES

Most bars serve light pub fare in addition to a mean rum swizzle or a Dark 'n Stormy, two local rum-based drinks. Too lazy to call a cab and too elegant to ride your moped? Some of the island's best nightlife takes place at hotel bars—so check yours. Nonhotel guests are always welcome, too.

HAMILTON

The Bistro (⊠ *103 Front St.* ☎ *441/292–0219*) is a cross between a café and a sports bar. It's clean and relatively cheap, with large television screens showing live sports during the day. At night it operates somewhere between a bar and a nightclub, attracting a mixed crowd of tourists and locals. It's open until 3 AM nightly and there's a covered seating area outside.

Owned and operated by a local comedian and radio personality, **Bootsie's Comedy Club** (⊠ *123 Front St.* ☎ *441/737–2668*) is worth a visit as much for the music as for the laughs. Talented jazz–reggae artists offer an authentic Bermuda experience and the crowd is mostly local, so it's good for a true taste of Bermudian nightlife.

Fodor'sChoice
★ Egyptian-theme **Cafe Cairo** (⊠ *93 Front St.* ☎ *441/292–4737*) is probably the most popular of Hamilton's nightspots. Decorated with North African furnishings, it's a great place for an early-evening meal. Eating later may lead to indigestion, as after 10 PM it transforms into a jumping nightclub that's often packed with both locals and tourists. Food and drink is served until 3 AM or later on weekends and there's a covered outside area where the adventurous can try smoking the water pipe.

With a trendy Bermudian restaurant in front and an even trendier sushi bar called Yashi in the back, **Coconut Rock** (⊠ *20 Reid St.* ☎ *441/292–1043*) has a relaxed and friendly buzz. Don't confuse this place with Coconuts, the upscale restaurant at the Reefs resort in Southampton.

Docksider (⊠121 Front St. ☎441/296–3333) attracts a mixed crowd of visitors and locals with 15 big-screen TVs. It's a no-frills bar with a good party atmosphere, a decent jukebox, and reasonably priced pub food. There's sometimes a cover charge for the back room's various theme parties, Brit-pop nights, and tie-ins with local sports events, organized at irregular intervals. Docksider is open until 1 AM Sunday through Thursday and 2 AM on Friday and Saturday.

★ **Fairmont Hamilton Princess** (⊠76 Pitts Bay Rd. ☎441/295–3000) is the life of the island on Friday nights from May through October, when management sets up an outdoor buffet, offers special drink prices, and occasionally schedules bands. The magnificent lawns of the famous hotel are packed with locals and tourists who equally enjoy a cold drink and an ogle at the elegant yachts in the harbor. The vibe is trendy, so save your most stylish duds for this night.

Flanagan's Irish Pub & Restaurant (⊠69 Front St. ☎441/295–8299), on the second floor of the Emporium Building, is a favorite for folks who like to dance and talk over drinks. Lots of exotic, fun beverages, like frozen mudslides, are served up and there's often live music or a DJ on weekends. Adjoining the Irish pub is its sister bar **Legend's Sports Bar,** at the same address. Giant screens flicker with live sports action and walls are plastered with photographs of sporting heroes. There's a pool table and a thriving poker league based at the bar. Both are open from 11 AM to 1 AM.

★ **Fresco's Wine Bar & Restaurant** (⊠2 Chancery Lane ☎441/295–5058) has the largest selection of wine-by-the-glass in Bermuda, plus desserts to die for. It's just undergone extensive renovations that have made it one of the trendiest places to start a Friday evening out. The crowd is sophisticated but buttoned down. If the weather's nice, try the outdoor bar where you can sip away and chat with your friends under the stars. Dinner is served at the bar until 10:30.

Small, cozy **Hog Penny**, aka the *Cheers* bar, ⊠5 Burnaby Hill ☎441/292–2534) was the inspiration for the Bull & Finch Pub in Boston. With dark-wood paneling and pub fare like steak-and-kidney pie and bangers and mash, the Hog Penny will likely remind you more of an English country pub than a Boston hangout. A singer plays most nights in summer (just Friday and Saturday in winter), when the floor is cleared for dancing. It's open nightly until 1, and it can be very busy.

Lemon Tree Café (⊠7 Queen St. ☎441/292–0235) is a popular happy-hour spot on Friday nights from around 9 PM to midnight. It's a good place to continue the party after Hamilton Princess's happy hour. Lemon Tree caters to a mixed crowd of expats, locals, and tourists who come either to dance to the DJ's disco-style tunes or to sit and chat in the outside area overlooking Victoria Park.

The Pickled Onion (⊠53 Front St. ☎441/295–2263) is a restaurant and bar that caters to a well-heeled crowd of locals and visitors. It's recently undergone a refurbishment that's glammed up the place and given it a cleaner, more sophisticated feel. Live music—usually jazz and pop—

plays nightly from about 10:30 to 1 in high season and irregularly off-season.

Casual, friendly **Robin Hood** (⊠ *25 Richmond Rd.* ☎ *441/295–3314*) is popular for inexpensive pub fare, pizza, and beer served on the patio under the stars. There's almost always something sports-related on the TV.

> **SMOKE-FREE**
>
> Following in the footsteps of New York and San Francisco, Bermuda passed a law in April 2006 making smoking in enclosed public places illegal.

OUTSIDE HAMILTON

After winter renovations, **Café Lido** and **Mickey's Beach Bar** (⊠ *Elbow Beach Hotel, 60 S. Shore Rd., Paget Parish* ☎ *441/236–9884*) are again open for business and look better than ever. With intimate dining areas and expansive bars, both establishments overlook the cool blue waters just beyond the south shore's Elbow Beach. This complex is perfect for a quiet evening for two.

Country Squire (⊠ *10 Mangrove Bay, Somerset* ☎ *441/234–0105*) is an unpretentious bar adorned with Nascar flags and other memorabilia, and great views of the water. It's a decent spot for a quiet pint in the West End and its sizable beer garden and pub menu makes it particularly popular in summer.

Frog & Onion Pub (⊠ *Cooperage Bldg., Sandys Parish* ☎ *441/234–2900*) serves a splendid variety of down-to-earth pub fare in a dark-wood, barnlike setting. If you're spending the day at Dockyard, it's a great place to recharge your batteries. It's also one of only two places on the island where you can buy Bermudian-brewed beer.

★ **Henry VIII** (⊠ *69 S. Shore Rd., Southampton Parish* ☎ *441/238–1977*) is a popular restaurant and bar with rich oak paneling, polished brass, and a good program of local or visiting entertainment almost every night. You can also find one of the island's most popular entertainers, piano player and singer Dave Bootel, here. The Sunday night Henry VIII–Southampton Princess Wine Cellar combination is a big crowd puller.

★ **Jasmine** (⊠ *Fairmont Southampton, 101 S. Shore Rd., Southampton Parish* ☎ *441/238–8000*) draws the smartly dressed to its lounge and dance floor. Definitely check out the Joe Wylie Trio in season. Sandwiches, salads, and other light fare are served until 1 AM.

The **Michael Douglas Bar** (⊠ *Ariel Sands Beach Resort, 34 S. Shore Rd., Devonshire Parish* ☎ *441/236–1010*), in the resort's clubhouse, is decorated with publicity photos of the actor and his family. That might sound a little bizarre, but it's not—the resort is owned by the famous actor's Bermudian ancestors, and given that Mr. Douglas spends large amounts of time at his Warwick home with wife Catherine Zeta-Jones, it's not impossible that you might see the real thing walking past the photos. Pull up a stool or relax on a couch beside the giant central fireplace while you wait.

As well as being a relaxed and traditional pub and restaurant, the **North Rock Brewing Company** (⊠ *10 S. Shore Rd., Smith's* ☎ *441/236–6633)* is one of only two places on the island to get a genuine Bermuda-brewed ale. Try a sampler for a taste of all six of North Rock's famous beers—ranging from the sharp St. David's Light Ale to the head-spinning Whale of Wheat. You might want to book a taxi back to your hotel.

The serious, dark-wood **Port O' Call** (⊠ *Cambridge Beaches, 30 King's Point Rd., Sandys Parish* ☎ *441/234–0331)* at the island's oldest cottage colony has live music nightly in summer and a lovely outdoor terrace. You'll mostly mingle with hotel guests at this secluded West End resort.

Salt Rock Grill (⊠ *27 Mangrove Bay Rd., Sandys Parish* ☎ *441/234–4502)* keeps locals and visitors alike coming back for more, with its fine cuisine (which includes sushi), water views, and reasonable prices. The cheap happy-hour drinks will lure you in, but the friendly staff and intimate dance floor will keep you there all night.

Fodor'sChoice
★ **Swizzle Inn** (⊠ *3 Blue Hole Hill, off North Rd., Bailey's Bay, Hamilton Parish* ☎ *441/293–1854)* has business cards from all over the world tacked on the walls, ceilings, and doors. "Swizzle Inn, swagger out" is the motto. As the name suggests, it's the best place on the island for a jug of rum swizzle. An acoustic guitarist plays a repertoire of classics most nights and even invites brave members of the audience to get up and sing with him. This place is famous and is an absolute must-do.

The **Veranda Bar** (⊠ *Elbow Beach Hotel, 60 S. Shore Rd., Paget Parish* ☎ *441/236–3535)* has a jazz-lounge feel and an outdoor patio, extensive rum menu, and separate cigar room. It's perfect for enjoying a relaxing drink while gazing over the south shore views, or into that special someone's eyes. Get your groove going to DJs on Wednesday and Friday nights and a live band on Saturday in summer.

The yachting crowd gathers at **Wharf Tavern** (⊠ *Somers Wharf, St. George's* ☎ *441/297–1515)* for rum swizzles, moderately priced pub fare, and nautical talk.

White Horse (⊠ *8 King Sq., St. George's* ☎ *441/297–1838)* is probably the most popular bar outside Hamilton. It's great for an afternoon pint on the wooden terrace overlooking the water, where swarms of fish fight for scraps thrown from the tables. There are large-screen TVs for sports fans and nightly entertainment for everyone else. It's packed every Tuesday night in summer, when the cruise ships are in port.

The Wine Cellar Bar (⊠ *Fairmont Southampton, 101 S. Shore Rd., Southampton Parish* ☎ *441/238–8000)* is a nightclub and sports bar within the Southampton Princess hotel. It's an authentic stone cellar with a decent-sized dance floor that vibrates to the sound of live music and DJs on a nightly basis throughout the summer. The place is particularly popular on Sunday and draws a mixed crowd of locals and hotel guests. Entertainment by either the popular live-music duo Prestige or DJs goes until 3 AM.

MUSIC & DANCE CLUBS

Bermuda's musicians have suffered in recent years with some of the mainstream bars now tending to rely on solo singers with backing tracks, but there's still quality, professional music to be found in some of the less obvious places. Hubie's Bar on Court Street in the "back of town" area is the surest place to find top-quality musicians, while Elbow Beach hotel also often hosts jazz nights. The island's clubs cater to a diversified local and visiting crowd, so you'll be sure to find something to suit your musical taste—be it reggae, calypso, hiphop, or techno. International artists occasionally perform in Bermuda, especially during the annual Bermuda Music Festival, which usually takes place during the first weekend in October.

> **SAY CHEESE!**
>
> During your wanderings through Hamilton's nightlife scene, don't be surprised to bump into the odd photographer asking if you want your picture taken. Bermuda has two party Web sites, **Bermynet** (⊕ www.bermynet.com) and **Black and Coke** (⊕ www.blackandcoke. com), which take hundreds of snaps of partying people in the island's bars every weekend. Be sure you're striking your best pose on the dance floor!

If you're looking for something a little more fast-paced than a pub or lounge, there's a thriving party scene with various organizers competing to host top nights out. Unite, Siren Productions, and Volcanic all cater to a trendy, friendly crowd with events ranging from beach parties to opulent color-theme extravaganzas at the Fairmont Southampton. There's no strict schedule or venue for these parties, so look for ads in the local press or check out ⊕ www.volcanic.bm and ⊕ www.unite.bm.

HAMILTON

The **Bermuda Folk Club** hosts monthly get-togethers, which usually take place at 8:30 PM on the first Saturday of the month and are often done on an open-mike basis. Note that musicians might perform any number of musical styles besides folk. Drinks are often served at happy-hour prices, and the cover is $6, but can rise to more than $20 for off-island acts. It's worth calling to inquire about nights other than first Saturdays, too, as unpublicized gigs and events sometimes pop up. Venues vary, call ☎ 441/799–2020 or check ⊕ www.folkclub.bm for details.

Fodor'sChoice   **Hubie's Bar** (✉ *10 Angle St., off Court St.* ☎ *441/293–9287*) books the
★   best jazz bands on the island for weekly sessions on Fridays from 7 to 10. Other kinds of live music or poetry readings might be on the schedule other nights—whatever it is, it's bound to be good. There's a $5 cover. The area is a bit dodgy, so it's best to take a cab to and from the bar.

Level Nightclub (✉ *Bermuda House La., off Front St.* ☎ *441/292–4507*) is a European-style dance club that fills up late on Friday and Saturday. An open-air courtyard with a video screen for larger than life music videos keeps the party going until 3 AM daily. When it rains, a canvas roof is pulled over the terrace.

Gombey Dancers

The Gombey dancer is one of the island's most enduring and uniquely Bermudian cultural icons. The Gombey (pronounced *gum*-bay) tradition here dates from at least the mid-18th century, when enslaved Africans and Native Americans covertly practiced a unique form of dance incorporating West Indian, British, and biblical influences. Nowadays, Gombeys mainly perform on major holidays. The Gombey name originates from a West African word, which means rustic drum. The masked, exclusively male dancers move to the accompaniment of Congolese-style drums and the shrill, whistle-blown commands of the troupe's captain. The dancers' colorful costumes include tall headdresses decorated with peacock feathers, and capes covered with intricate embroidery, ribbons, and tiny mirrors. It's traditional to toss money at the dancers' feet. Performance times and locations vary, but check out the No. 1 Shed on Front Street on Tuesday around 3 PM, or consult the visitors bureau.

Splash (⊠ *10 Bermudiana Rd.* ☎441/296–3849) is Bermuda's hottest nightclub. With a guest DJ spinning tunes each week in a variety of styles including techno, reggae, and dance, this Hamilton club is usually jam-packed and hopping by 11. The door policy is strict for nonmembers so you'll want to dress to impress. The cover charge is $20.

OUTSIDE HAMILTON

★ At **The Deep** (⊠*Elbow Beach Hotel, 60 S. Shore Rd., Paget Parish* ☎441/232–6969) you can dance the night away and sip drinks at tables overlooking the dance floor. The island's top DJs and bands often make appearances here, and the music and the comprehensive champagne, wine, and cocktail menu attract the fashionable people of Bermuda's social register. Dance the night away to techno or house music on Sunday night when large numbers of the island's hospitality staff gather to party. Entrance fees can vary depending on the day and your sex; females are usually not charged, males usually have to cough up $20.

The Don't-Stop-the-Carnival-Party at **Hawkins Island** (⊕*www.hawkinsisland.com*) in the Great Sound is a hugely popular party night. It runs throughout the summer and features a boat cruise to and from the island, an open bar, a sumptuous barbecue dinner, Reggae from Tropical Heat, and a show from the new Dark 'n Stormy Carnival limbo dancers. A boat leaves the main ferry terminal at Albouy's Point at 7 PM on Tuesday, Wednesday, Friday, and Saturday, returning at 10:30 PM. The all-inclusive price is $90 per person with tickets available at the **BIC** (⊠*Somers Bldg., 15 Front St., Hamilton* ☎441/292–8652).

THE ARTS

Bermuda's arts scene is concentrated in a number of art galleries—Masterworks in the Botanical Gardens, City Hall in Hamilton, and the Arts Centre in Dockyard are the best known—a handful of performance venues, and a few gathering spots, like Rock Island Coffee Café on Reid Street. For dramatic and musical performances, the City Hall Theatre and the Ruth Seaton James Auditorium host the country's best, including Bermuda Festival events. It's also home to the annual Bermuda Idol competition based on the popular American show.

DANCE

The **Bermuda Civic Ballet** (☎441/293–4147) performs classical ballet at various venues during the academic year. Internationally known artists sometimes appear as guests.

The **Bermuda School of Russian Ballet** (☎441/293–4147 or 441/295–8621) has been around for half a century and presents unique ballet and modern-dance performances. Showtimes and venues vary, so call for details.

The **National Dance Foundation of Bermuda** (☎441/236–3319 ⊕www.dancebermuda.org) funds workshops and develops local talent as well as attracting international dancers and putting on shows and fund-raisers. It draws support from all over the island and enjoys the patronage of Bermuda's most famous resident, Catherine Zeta Jones.

FILM

♥ Kids love Movie Day at the Youth Branch of the **Bermuda National Library** (⊠74 Church St., Hamilton ☎441/295–0487).

Liberty Theatre (⊠Union and Victoria sts., Hamilton ☎441/291–2035) is a 270-seat cinema with four daily showtimes, including a matinee. The area immediately outside the theater is safe during the day, but you should not linger in this neighborhood after dark.

The **Little Theatre** (⊠Queen St., Hamilton ☎441/292–2135) is a 173-seater across the street from Casey's Bar. There are usually three showtimes per evening.

Neptune Cinema (⊠The Cooperage, Dockyard ☎441/291–2035) is a 118-seat cinema that typically shows feature films twice nightly, with matinees Friday, Saturday, and Sunday.

Southside Cinema, the island's largest theater, is on the former U.S. military base near the airport. Showtime is usually 7:30. Advance tickets are available at **Unlimited Supplies** (⊠2 Woodlands Rd., Hamilton ☎441/295–9229).

MUSIC

The **Bermuda School of Music** (☎441/296–5100 ⊕www.musicschool.bm) was formed when the country's two leading music schools merged in 2001. Concerts are presented periodically at various venues. There's a guitar festival in May and various other events throughout the year.

CLOSE UP

Very Fine Arts Festivals

Bermuda Festival. In January and February, the Bermuda Festival brings internationally renowned artists to the island. The two-month program includes theater, as well as classical and jazz concerts. Most shows take place in City Hall, with additional lunchtime and cocktail-hour concerts at various venues. ☎ 441/292-8572 Dec.–Feb., 441/295-1291 Mar.–Nov.

Bermuda International Film Festival. This top-notch festival is a celebration of independent films from all over the world. There are screenings during a full week in mid-March at the cinemas in Hamilton. Tickets are sold for individual films as well as for workshops and seminars. Festival parties are also popular, as Hamilton mimics—for a few days at least—the glamour of Sundance, minus the fancy cars. ☎ 441/293-3456 ⊕ www.biff.bm.

Bermuda Music Festival. This festival kicks off each fall at Dockyard, usually during a long weekend in October. Local and internationally known jazz artists pump out the tunes, and tickets go fast. Shop around for hotel-and-festival combination packages. ☎ 441/295-4839, 441/292-0023 for information ⊕ www.bermudatourism.com/94.aspx.

Harbour Nights, a street festival featuring Bermudian artists, crafts, Gombey dancers, face painting, and the like, takes place every Wednesday night in summer on Front Street in the City of Hamilton. Other weekly summer fetes include the **St. George's Market Nights** and **Destination Dockyard** on Tuesday nights, and **Flatts Village Festival** on Monday nights.

4

READINGS & TALKS

The **Bermuda National Gallery** (⊠ City Hall, 17 Church St., Hamilton ☎ 441/295-9428) often hosts a series of lunchtime lectures on art and film. You can stop by or call the gallery for a schedule.

To showcase your talents, whether it be through music, spoken word, or dance, stop by **Champions Sports Bar** (⊠ 73 Reid St. Extension ☎ 441/295-1752 ⊕ www.chewstick.com) every other Sunday for **Chewstick**, Bermuda's most popular open mike, between 8 PM and midnight. Admission is free before 8 and $5 thereafter. Full bar service is available. With a usually full house, Chewstick is a great place to mingle with locals and witness raw Bermudian talent.

THEATER

The **Bermuda Musical & Dramatic Society** (⊠ 11 Washington St., Hamilton ☎ 441/292-0848 or 441/295-5584 ⊕ www.bmds.bm) has some good amateur actors on its roster. Formed in 1944, this active theater society stages performances year-round at their Daylesford headquarters, one block north of City Hall. The Christmas pantomime is always a sellout, as are most other performances. Visit or call the box office at Daylesford, on Dundonald Street, for reservations and information. Tickets are about $10.

Bermuda is the only place outside the United States where Harvard University's **Hasty Pudding Theatricals** (⊠*City Hall, 17 Church St.* ☎*441/295–1727*) performs. For almost 30 years this satirical troupe has entertained the island during Bermuda College Weeks (March through April). Produced by the Bermuda Musical & Dramatic Society, each of these Bermuda-based shows incorporates political and social issues of the past year. They're all staged at the **City Hall Theatre**. Tickets are about $20.

VENUES & SOCIETIES

The **Bermuda Society of Arts** (⊠*City Hall, 17 Church St.* ☎*441/292– 3824* 🖨*441/296–0699*) has outstanding gallery space in City Hall, and it's a good place to meet local painters and see some of their work.

City Hall Theatre (⊠*City Hall, 17 Church St.* ☎*441/295–1727*) is the major venue for top-quality cultural events each year.

★ **Rock Island Coffee Cafe** (⊠*48 Reid St.* ☎*441/296–5241*) is a good place to stop and ask what's going on. Not only is it the unofficial watering hole for Bermuda's eclectic group of artists—it also doubles as an informal art space.

Beaches, Sports & the Outdoors

WORD OF MOUTH

"There is a little cove on the right of the main Horse-shoe Bay beach where you can just stand in the water and see fish swim by. Cool but crowded. We walked left past the main beach and there are several smaller beaches (Chaplin and Stone-hall Bay beach). Very scenic and not crowded. There are lots of huge boulders scattered in the water and on the beach. The waves were a bit strong but we had a fabulous time. Great photo opportunity so make sure to take your camera."

—mnag

Updated by
Keisha Webb-
Gibbs

LONG BEFORE YOUR PLANE TOUCHES down in Bermuda, the island's greatest asset becomes breathtakingly obvious—the crystal clear, aquamarine water that frames the tiny, hook-shape atoll. So clear are Bermuda's waters that, in 1994, the government nixed a local scuba-diving group's plan to create a unique dive site by sinking an abandoned American warplane in 30 feet of water off the island's East End, fairly close to the end of the airport's runway. The government feared that the plane would be easily visible from above—to arriving passengers—and could cause undue distress. It's the incredible clarity of the water that makes Bermuda one of the world's greatest places for exploratory scuba diving and snorkeling, especially among the age-old shipwrecks off the island. The presence of these sunken ships is actually one of Bermuda's ironies—as translucent as the water is, it wasn't quite clear enough to make Bermuda's treacherous reefs visible to the hundreds of ship captains who have smashed their vessels on them through the centuries.

Thanks to Bermuda's position near the Gulf Stream, the water stays warm year-round. In summer the ocean is usually above 80°F, and it's even warmer in the shallows between the reefs and shore. In winter the water temperature only occasionally drops below 70°F, but it seems cooler because the air temperature is usually in the mid-60s. There's less call for water sports December through March, not because of a drop in water temperature, but because of windy conditions. The wind causes rough water, which in turn creates problems for fishing and diving boats, and underwater visibility is often clouded by sand and debris.

In high season, mid-April through mid-October, fishing, diving, and yacht charters fill up quickly. Three major water-sports outfitters on the island—Blue Hole Water Sports, Somerset Bridge Watersports, and Windjammer Watersports—provide most of the rentals. Many boats carry fewer than 20 passengers, so it's advisable to sign up as soon as you arrive on the island. The shoulder seasons are March through mid-April and mid-October through November. During the "golf and spa season," December through February, many operators close to make repairs and perform routine maintenance. Though a few operators stay open on a limited basis, most will only schedule an outing when there are enough people to fill a boat.

Bermudians take their onshore sports seriously, too. The daily newspaper's sports section is full of local coverage. Cricket and soccer, the two national sports, grab most of the headlines, but road running, golf, field hockey, rugby, and a host of other activities also get their share of space. Bermudian soccer stars, such as former Manchester City striker Shaun Goater, have delighted crowds in British and U.S. leagues through the years, and Bermudian sailors hold their own in world competition, as do runners, equestrians, and swimmers. Bermuda catapulted onto the squash world stage after holding the Bermuda Masters in 2005. Tennis is quite a big deal here, too, and with 70 courts packed into these 21.6 square mi, it's hard to believe there's room left for horseback riding, cycling, running, squash, and golf.

BEACHES

Bermuda's south-shore beaches are more scenic than those on the north side, with fine, pinkish sand, and limestone dunes topped with summer flowers and Bermuda crabgrass. The water on the south shore does get a little rougher when the winds are from the south and southwest, but mainly the pale-blue waves break at the barrier reefs offshore and roll gently upon the sandy shoreline. Because the barrier reefs break up the waves, surfing has not really taken off in Bermuda, though many locals—especially children—love to bodysurf at Horseshoe Bay. Kite-surfing is also becoming increasingly popular. Most Bermudian beaches are relatively small compared with ocean beaches in the United States, ranging from about 15 yards to half a mile or so in length. In winter, when the weather is more severe, beaches may erode—even disappear—only to be replenished as the wind subsides in spring.

TOP 5 OUTDOORS

■ Marvel at the sea life on the ocean floor aboard a glass-bottom boat.

■ Feel the wind whip through your hair on a rented Jet Ski.

■ Sit on the top deck of the public ferry and cruise from Hamilton to Dockyard.

■ Rent a Boston Whaler and tour the island.

■ Swim with the turtles at Turtle Beach.

The Public Transportation Board publishes *Bermuda's Guide to Beaches and Transportation,* available free in all visitor information centers and most hotels. A combination map and bus-and-ferry schedule, the guide shows beach locations and how to reach them. The Bermuda telephone directory, available in hotels, also has maps and public-transportation schedules, plus many other tips for how to get around and what to see.

Few Bermudian beaches offer shade, but some have palm trees and thatched shelters. The sun can be intense, so bring a hat and plenty of sunscreen. You can rent umbrellas at some beaches, but food and drink are rare, so pack snacks and lots of water.

NORTH-SHORE BEACHES

Clearwater Beach. On the eastern tip of the island in St. David's Clearwater is a long sandy strip of beach that's popular with serious swimmers and triathletes who use it as a training ground. But don't be intimidated, the young and old also flock here to wade in the shallow water, and there are buoy markers that identify where the beach becomes deeper. Clearwater is one of the few beaches in Bermuda that has an adjoining café, serving kid favorites such as burgers and fries. There's also an in-house bar when the five-o'clock-somewhere mood strikes. Beach bathrooms and lifeguards during the tourist season (April through September) make this a great choice for families. **PROS:** nearby paved road is great for evening strolls, small children's playground keeps kids busy, great beach to spot turtles, picnic area. **CONS:** lots of vehicle traffic, bathrooms can be stinky and often run out of toilet paper. ⊠ *Cooper's Island Rd., St. David's Island* Ⓜ *Bus 10 from Hamilton.*

★ **Fort St. Catherine Beach.** Fort St. Catherine is one of the larger north-shore beaches, and the water's deep enough for a serious swim. There's also beach rentals and a snack bar. If and when you get beach-bummed out, head over to the military fort next door, for which this beach is named. Nearby Blackbeard's Hideout is a great place for a refueling meal. **PROS:** beach snack shop and nearby restaurant are convenient, fort tours are great for a beach break. **CONS:** beach is far from nearest bus stop. ⊠ *Coot Pond Rd., St. George's Parish* Ⓜ *Bus 1, 3, 10, or 11 from Hamilton.*

☽ **Shelly Bay Beach.** Known for its sandy bottom and shallow water, Shelly Bay is a good place to take small children. It also has shade trees, a rarity at Bermudian beaches. A playground behind the beach attracts hordes of youngsters on weekends and during school holidays. A nearby soccer and cricket practice field and a public basketball court are handy when you want to blow off some steam. **PROS:** shallow beach and adjoining playground for kids, on-site Jamaican food eatery, fun water rentals. **CONS:** noisy street traffic, lots of kids during summer camps, good swimming spots are hard to find during low tide. ⊠ *North Shore Rd., Hamilton Parish* Ⓜ *Bus 10 or 11 from Hamilton.*

Somerset Long Bay. Popular with Somerset locals, this beach is on the quiet northwestern end of the island, far from the bustle of Hamilton and major tourist hubs. In keeping with the area's rural atmosphere, the beach is low-key. Undeveloped parkland shields the beach from the light traffic on Cambridge Road. The main beach is long by Bermudian standards—nearly ¼ mi from end to end. Although exposed to northerly storm winds, the bay water is normally calm and shallow—ideal for children. The bottom, however, is rocky and uneven, so it's a good idea to put on water shoes before wading. **PROS:** low-key. **CONS:** rocky bottom. ⊠ *Cambridge Rd., Sandys Parish* Ⓜ *Bus 7 or 8 to Dockyard or Somerset from Hamilton.*

Tobacco Bay Beach. The most popular beach near St. George's—about 15 minutes northwest of the town on foot—this small north-shore strand is huddled in a coral cove. Its beach house has a snack bar, equipment rentals, toilets, showers, changing rooms, and ample parking. It's a 10-minute hike from the bus stop in the town of St. George's, or you can flag down a St. George's Minibus Service van and ask for a lift ($2 per person). In high season the beach is busy, especially midweek, when the cruise ships are docked. **PROS:** beautiful rock formations in the water. **CONS:** so popular it becomes overcrowded. ⊠ *Coot Pond Rd., St. George's Parish* ☎ *441/297–2756* Ⓜ *Bus 1, 3, 10, or 11 from Hamilton.*

★ **Turtle Beach.** Down a stretch from Clearwater Beach, Turtle Beach offers the same tranquillity, but with a bit less traffic. The water's also a deeper turquoise color here. If you're lucky, you might even spot a turtle. There's also a lifeguard station with a guard on duty. When your tummy grumbles, it's a short walk to Gombey's Restaurant. **PROS:** quiet beach, popular for turtle sightings. **CONS:** little parking, moped traffic. ⊠ *Cooper's Island Rd., St. David's Island* Ⓜ *Bus 10 from Hamilton.*

SOUTH-SHORE BEACHES

Astwood Cove & Park. On the weekends, you can find lots of children and families at this popular beach. The Astwood Park area is shady and grassy, which makes it popular among locals for birthday parties and family picnics. **PROS:** shady park area. **CONS:** short walk from the park down to the beach area. ⊠ *Off South Shore Rd., Warwick Parish* Ⓜ *Bus 7 from Hamilton.*

Chaplin and Stonehole Bays. In a secluded area east along the dunes from Horseshoe Bay Beach, these tiny adjacent beaches almost disappear at high tide. An unusual high coral wall reaches across the beach to the water, perforated by a 10-foot-high, arrowhead-shape hole. Like Horseshoe Bay, the beach fronts South Shore Park. Wander farther along the dunes and you can find several other tiny, peaceful beaches before you eventually reach Warwick Long Bay. **PROS:** low-key atmosphere, adjoining beaches. **CONS:** beach shoes needed. ⊠ *Off South Rd., Southampton Parish* Ⓜ *Bus 7 from Hamilton.*

★ ☾ **Elbow Beach.** Swimming and bodysurfing are great at this beach, which is bordered by the prime strand of sand reserved for guests of the Elbow Beach Hotel on the left, and the ultra-exclusive Coral Beach Club beach area on the right. It's a pleasant setting for a late-evening stroll, with the lights from nearby hotels dancing on the water, but the romance dissipates in daylight, when the beach is noisy and crowded. Protective coral reefs make the waters the safest on the island, and a good choice for families. A lunch wagon sells fast food and cold drinks during the day, and Mickey's beach bar (part of the Elbow Beach Hotel) is open for lunch and dinner, though it may be difficult to get a table. **PROS:** beautiful stretch of beach, safest waters on the island. **CONS:** busy, parking fills up quickly. ⊠ *Off South Rd., Paget Parish* Ⓜ *Bus 2 or 7 from Hamilton.*

☾ **Horseshoe Bay Beach.** When locals say they're going to "the beach," they're generally referring to Horseshoe Bay Beach, the island's most popular. With clear water, a 1/3-mi crescent of pink sand, a vibrant social scene, and the uncluttered backdrop of South Shore Park, Horseshoe Bay has everything you could ask of a Bermudian beach. A snack bar, changing rooms, beach-rental facilities, and lifeguards add to its appeal. Outdoor concerts, events, crab racing, and the Good Friday Annual Kite Competition take place in the high and shoulder seasons. The undertow can be strong, especially on the main beach. A better place for children is **Horseshoe Baby Beach.** Before 2003's Hurricane Fabian, this beach was reached by climbing a trail over the dunes at the western end of Horseshoe Bay. Fabian's storm surge ploughed right through those dunes, creating a wide walkway for eager little beachgoers. Sheltered from the ocean by a ring of rocks, this cove is shallow and almost perfectly calm. In summer, toddlers can find lots of playmates. **PROS:** adjoining beach is perfect for small children, snack bar with outdoor and indoor seating. **CONS:** the bus stop is a long walk up a huge hill, gets very crowded, busiest beach on the island. ⊠ *Off South Rd., Southampton Parish* ☎ *441/238–2651* Ⓜ *Bus 7 from Hamilton.*

Fodor'sChoice
★

5

Beaches

ATLANTIC OCEAN

◺ **Constellation**

WEST END
Snorkel Park
Ireland Island N.

Ireland Island S.

Boaz Island

Somerset Long Bay

Watford Is.
Malabar Rd.

Watford Bridge

L'Herminie ◺

Somerset Village

Somerset Island
Somerset Rd.
SANDYS

Cobbler's Island *Clarence Cove*
Spanish Pt.
Spanish Point

PEMBROKE

Great Sound

Hamilton ✪
Fror

Somerset Bridge

Hawkins Island

Hamilton Harbour

Middl

Spring Benny's Bay

Middle Rd.

Little Sound

Harbour Rd.

WARWICK

West Whale Bay Park & Beach

Warwick Long Bay
South Shore Rd.

Astwood & Park

West Whale Bay

Middle Rd.

SOUTHAMPTON

Gibbs Hill Lighthouse ◆

Chaplin and Stonehole Bays

Church Bay

Horseshoe Bay Beach & Horseshoe Baby Beach

Sea Gardens

0		2 miles
0		3 km

Cristobal Colon

araquet

Tobacco Bay Beach

Fort St. Catherine

Fort St. Catherine Beach

ST. GEORGE'S

Gates Fort Park

St. George's Island

Mullet Bay Rd.

Town of St. George

St. George's Harbour

Ferry Rd.

Kindley Field Rd.

St. David's Rd.

Sea Gardens

Coney Island

Bermuda Airport

St. David's Island

St. David's Lighthouse

The Causeway

Castle Harbour

Clearwater Beach

Turtle Beach

Crawl Hill North

HAMILTON

Harrington Sound Rd.

Shelly Bay Beach

Harrington Sound

Tucker's Town

Bermuda Aquarium, seum & Zoo

Harrington Sound Rd.

Flatts Village

SMITH'S

John Smith's Bay

North Shore Rd.

ONSHIRE

Kate

South Shore Rd.

bow Beach

ermos

ATLANTIC OCEAN

KEY	
←•→	*Railway Trail*
◺	*Dive Sites/Wrecks*

5

☺ **John Smith's Bay.** This beach consists of a pretty strand of long, flat, open sand. The presence of a lifeguard in summer makes it an ideal place to bring children. The only public beach in Smith's Parish, John Smith's Bay is also popular with locals. Groups of young folk like to gather in the park area surrounding the beach for parties, especially on weekends and holidays, so if you're

> **DID YOU KNOW?**
>
> Many south-shore beaches suffered serious damage when Hurricane Fabian slammed the island in September 2003. But now it's back to normal, as the scars have swiftly faded into the spectacular landscape.

not in the mood for a festive bunch with loud radios, this may not be the place for you. There are toilet and changing facilities on-site, as well as moped parking. **PROS:** grassy picnic area, serene beach in the evening. **CONS:** rough waves at high tide. ⊠ *South Shore Rd., Smith's Parish* Ⓜ *Bus 1 from Hamilton.*

☺ **Snorkel Park.** This is a popular spot among local families who like to treat their children to a sandy white beach and pristine views of the water. Food and bar amenities are on-site with beach equipment rentals for the kids as well as parents. If your cruise ship docks in Dockyard, Snorkel Park is a short walk from the cruise terminal. A children's playground is just outside the park. Before you leave be sure to stop in the Clocktower Mall and the Craft Market. Also nearby is the Bone Fish Bar & Grill, the Frog & Onion Pub, and an ATM. **PROS:** park is perfect for children, nearby shopping area and restaurants. **CONS:** must rent beach equipment to use beach, can be busy with summer children's camps. ⊠ *31 Freeport Rd., Dockyard* ☎ *441/234–6989* Ⓜ *Bus 7 or 8 from Hamilton.*

Warwick Long Bay. Different from the covelike bay beaches, Warwick Long Bay has about a ½-mi stretch of sand—the longest of any beach here. Its backdrop is a combination of steep cliffs and low grass- and brush-covered hills. The beach is exposed to some strong southerly winds, but the waves are usually moderate because the inner reef is close to shore. A 20-foot coral outcrop less than 200 feet offshore looks like a sculpted boulder balancing on the water's surface. South Shore Park, which surrounds the bay, is often empty, a fact that only heightens the beach's appealing isolation and serenity. In summer, the Bermuda Department of Tourism hosts "Movies at The Beach." **PROS:** summer movies on the beach. **CONS:** strong southerly winds in winter months. ⊠ *Off South Rd., Southampton Parish* Ⓜ *Bus 7 from Hamilton.*

★ **West Whale Bay.** This beach can be a secluded oasis if you go at the right time: sunset. To get to the beach, you need to cross a huge field and walk down a natural rock formation path. **PROS:** romantic. **CONS:** a bit of a walk from the parking area. ⊠ *Off Whale Bay and Middle Rds., Southampton Parish* Ⓜ *Bus 7 or 8 from Hamilton.*

SPORTS & THE OUTDOORS

BICYCLING

The best and sometimes only way to explore Bermuda's nooks and crannies—its little hidden coves and 18th-century tribe roads—is by bicycle or motor scooter. Arriving at the small shore roads and hill trails, however, means first navigating Bermuda's rather treacherous main roads. They are narrow, with no shoulders, and often congested with traffic (especially near Hamilton during rush hours). Fortunately, there's another, safer option for biking in Bermuda: the Railway Trail, a dedicated cycle path blissfully free of cars.

Despite the traffic, bicycle racing is a popular sport in Bermuda, and club groups regularly whir around the island on evening and weekend training rides. Be prepared for some tough climbs—the roads running north and south across the island are particularly steep and winding—and the wind can sap even the strongest rider's strength, especially along South Shore Road in Warwick and Southampton parishes. Island roads are no place for novice riders. Helmets are strongly recommended on pedal bikes (it's illegal to ride without them on a motor scooter), and parents should think twice before allowing preteens to bike here.

BIKE PATHS

★ **The Railway Trail.** Running intermittently the length of the old Bermuda Railway (old "Rattle 'n' Shake"), this trail is scenic, paved, and restricted to pedestrian and bicycle traffic. You can ask the staff at any bike-rental shop for advice on where to access the trail. One especially lovely route starts at Somerset Bridge and ends 2½ mi later near the Somerset Country Squire pub. You can take your bike onto the ferry for a pleasant ride from Hamilton or St. George's to the Somerset Bridge stop. From there, bike to the bridge on the main road, turn right, and ride uphill for about 50 yards until you reach the sign announcing RAILWAY TRAIL. Turning onto the trail, you find yourself along a course with spectacular views of the Great Sound. Along the way you pass old Fort Scaur, several schools, and the large pink Somerset Cricket Club. Toward the end of the trail segment, you'll find yourself on Beacon Hill Road opposite the bus depot. Here you can turn around and head back to Somerset Bridge, or, for refreshment, turn left and ride to the main road (you can see Somerset Police Station), and make a sharp right turn to find Mangrove Bay Beach and the Somerset Country Squire pub and restaurant. Because the Railway Trail is somewhat isolated and not lighted, you should avoid it after dark.

South Shore Road. This main island road passes absolutely gorgeous

PEDAL POINTER

You can pick up the Bermuda Handy Reference Map for free at visitor information centres for Bermuda's bike routes, but it's not as detailed or clear as the Bermuda Islands map, available at the Bermuda Book Store in Hamilton. You won't be lost without a map, as bike-rental shops and hotel clerks can recommend bike routes, too, but serious cyclists may find them worth examining.

ocean views. South Shore Road—also known as South Road—is well-paved and, for the most part, wider than Middle Road, North Shore Road, and Harbour Road, with relatively few hills. However, it's one of Bermuda's windiest and most heavily traveled thoroughfares.

Tribe Road 3. Tribe roads are small, often unpaved side roads, some of which date to the earliest settlement of Bermuda. They make for good exploring, though many are quite short and lead to dead ends. Beginning at Oleander Cycles in Southampton, Tribe Road 3 steeply climbs the hillside just below Gibbs Hill Lighthouse, with views of the south shore below. It eventually leads to a point from where you can see both the north and south shores.

> **ROAD RASH**
>
> The Bermudian slang dictionary *Bermewjan Vurds* defines road rash (grazes received from sliding along Bermuda's roads in an accident) as "a skin disease common amongst tourists brave enough to rent mopeds."

BIKE RENTALS

In Bermuda, bicycles are called pedal or push bikes to distinguish them from the more common motorized two-wheelers, which are also called bikes. Some of the cycle liveries around the island rent both, so make sure to specify whether you want a pedal or motor bike. If you're sure you want to bicycle while you're in Bermuda, try to reserve rental bikes a few days in advance. Rates are around $25 a day, though the longer you rent, the more economical your daily rate. You may be charged an additional $15 for a repair waiver and for a refundable deposit.

Riding a motor scooter for the first time can be disconcerting, wherever you are. Here you have the added confusion that Bermudians drive on the left, and though the posted speed limit is 35 kph, the unofficial speed limit is actually closer to 50 kph (while many locals actually travel faster than that). At most rental shops, lessons on how to ride a motor scooter are perfunctory at best—practice as much as you can before going on to the main road. Though many tourists can and do rent motor scooters, the public transportation system (ferries and buses) is excellent and should not be ruled out.

Eve's Cycle Livery. In three convenient locations around the island, Eve's rents standard-size mountain bikes, as well as motor scooters, including your mandatory helmet. The staff readily supplies advice on where to ride, and there's no charge for a repair waiver. Eve's Cycles on Water Street is convenient if you arrive in Bermuda on a cruise docking in St. George's—the shop is literally a few yards away from the cruise terminal. ⊠ *110 Middle Rd., near South Shore Rd., Paget Parish* ☎ *441/236–6247* ⊠ *1 Water St., St. George's* ☎ *441/236–0839* ⊠ *Reid St., Hamilton* ☎ *441/236–4491.*

Oleander Cycles. Known primarily for its selection of motor bikes, Oleander Cycles also rents mountain bikes, though none for kids. A repair waiver is charged. Oleander Cycles' Southampton location is convenient to Pompano Beach resort guests; it's next door to the resort. ⊠ *8*

Middle Rd., west of fire station, Southampton Parish ☎441/234–0629 ⊕*www.bermuda.com/oleander* ⊠*Middle Rd. at Valley Rd., Paget Parish* ☎441/236–2453.

Smatt's Cycle Livery. Smatt's has two locations—one in Hamilton, next to the Fairmont Hamilton Princess, and the other on the west end of the island at the Fairmont Southampton Resort. The shop offers standard moped rentals with helmet. Before a moped is rented, you'll be asked to take a riding test for your safety. ⊠*74 Pitts Bay Rd., Hamilton* ☎441/295–1180 ⊠*Fairmont Southampton Resort* ☎441/238–7800.

Wheels Cycles. If you're staying in one of Bermuda's large resorts, chances are there's a Wheels Cycles right in the hotel. And even if you're not in a resort you may find a location nearby. The store has several branches all over the island, with mountain bikes for children and adults. ⊠*Front St., near docks, Hamilton* ☎441/292–2245 ⊕*www.bermuda.com/wheels*

BIKE TOURS

★ **Fantasea Cruises.** This comprehensive outfitter offers a 1½-hour bike tour along the Railway Trail. Your day will start with a short boat cruise to the trail, where you can pick up your bikes. After the ride, finish with a cool-off swim and a drink at 9 Beaches Resort in Somerset. Depending on the day, the tour will start from either Albuoy's Point, Dockyard, or the Waterlot Inn at the Fairmont Southampton. The total trip, including the cruise and biking, lasts three hours. The cost is $65 per person and includes equipment and drinks. ⊠*Albuoy's Point, Hamilton* ☎441/236–1300 ⊕*www.fantasea.bm.*

BIRD-WATCHING

Forty species of warblers have been spotted in Bermuda, especially in the casuarina trees along the south shore and West End. Other omnipresent species include kiskadee, swifts, cuckoos, flycatchers, swallows, thrushes, kingbirds, and orioles. Bird conservation is a big deal in Bermuda. You can see bluebird boxes on every island golf course, which act as safe nesting sites for this jeopardized species, threatened by development and the invasive sparrow.

The largest variety of birds can be spotted during fall migration, when thousands of birds pass overhead, stop for a rest on their way south, or spend the winter on the island. You might spot the rare American avocet or the curlew sandpiper. In spring look for brightly colored Central and South American birds migrating north. The white-tail tropicbird, a beautiful white bird with black markings and a 12- to 17-inch-long tail (locals call it a "longtail"), is one of the first to arrive. Summer is the quietest season for bird-watching in Bermuda. Late migrants, like the barn swallow and chimney swift pass by, and if you check the ponds you may see the occasional shorebird.

Bermuda Audubon Society. The society has an excellent book called *A Birdwatching Guide to Bermuda,* by president Andrew Dobson, published by the Arlequin Press. In it are maps, illustrations, and descriptions of birds and their habitats. Several birding events are organized throughout the year, including the Christmas Bird Count—Bermuda averages 74 species per count, although 200 species have been recorded. You can find a listing of the Audubon Society's events on their Web site as well as a bird-watching checklist. ☎*441/292–1920* ⊕*www.audubon.bm.*

Bermuda Institute of Ocean Sciences (BIOS). Birders may be interested in David Wingate's efforts to repopulate the native cahow bird (Bermuda petrel) population via artificial burrows and other means on Nonsuch Island. Tours of the island are arranged by the institute and cost $75 for three to four hours. These tours are on weekdays only, as BIOS is open weekdays 8:30 to 5. ✉*17 Biological La., Ferry Reach, St. George's Parish* ☎*441/297–1880* ⊕*www.bbsr.edu*

Seymour's Pond Nature Reserve. Seymour's Pond is smaller than Warwick and Spittal ponds, but it has the advantage of being a bit farther inland, and therefore better protected. Twenty-eight species of duck are recorded in Bermuda and you're quite likely to see many of them here. ✉*Middle Rd., near Barnes Corner, Southampton Parish*

Spittal Pond Nature Reserve. Stretching placidly within a 60-acre nature reserve, Spittal Pond is an excellent place to view wildlife, especially birds. As long as the water level is not too high, some 30 species of shorebird can be present on the margins of the pond. On a good day in September you might see more than 100 birds. Semipalmated sandpipers are perhaps the most abundant. In winter, herons and egrets roost serenely in the shallow water. You can tour the reserve unaccompanied, or take a scheduled tour with a park ranger, usually on Friday. ✉*South Rd., Smith's Parish* ☎*441/236–4201*

Warwick Pond. In a well-kept inland nature preserve, Bermuda's only natural freshwater pond is prime bird territory. Shorebirds and herons gather around its edges in fall and winter. ⚠ **In the heat of summer, the stagnant water lets off a rather putrid smell.** ✉*Middle Rd., near Ettrick Animal Hospital, Warwick Parish*

CHARTER BOATS & BOAT TOURS

Bermuda is gorgeous by land, but you should take to the water to fully appreciate its beauty. You can either rent your own boat *(see Aquatic Adventures)* or charter one with a skipper. There's literally scores of options to suit all tastes from champagne cruises at sunset to cruise and kayak ecotours.

CHARTER BOATS

More than 20 large power cruisers and sailing vessels, piloted by local skippers, are available for charter. Primarily 30 to 60 feet long, most charter sailboats can carry up to 30 passengers, sometimes overnight. Meals and drinks can be included on request, and a few skippers offer dinner cruises for the romantically inclined. Rates generally range from $300 to $450 for a three-hour cruise, or $650 to $1,500 for a full-day cruise, with additional per-person charges for large groups. Where you go and what you do—exploring, swimming, snorkeling, cruising—is usually up to you and your skipper. Generally, however, cruises travel

Good Cheap Fun!

Bermuda is notoriously expensive, so if you've blown most of your inheritance getting here you needn't splash the rest of it on having a good time.

Walking Along the South-Shore Beaches. There's a 2-mi stretch from Horseshoe Bay in Southampton right down to Warwick Long Bay, which with a bit of clambering and the odd paddle in the ocean you can comfortably negotiate. The quiet secluded spots along the rocks are great for bird-watching and there are a number of tiny coves where you can stop for a picnic.

Cup Match. If you want a real Bermuda experience come to the island during the annual Cup Match holiday—either the last weekend in July or the first weekend in August. It's essentially the all-star cricket game between the best of the west and the best of the east, but you don't have to like cricket to enjoy the atmosphere. Half the island trots through the ground at some stage during the four-day holiday to listen to the sound of the drums, sample the fried chicken, and wave a flag for Somerset or St. George's. It's also the one time of year when gambling is legal and thousands pack the Crown & Anchor tents to roll the dice for Bermuda's own unique

version of the casino favorite—craps. Entry is $10.

Snorkeling at Tobacco Bay. You don't have to rent a boat or even swim very far offshore to get a close-up look at some of Bermuda's wonderful marine life. Tobacco Bay in St. George's is a favorite spot, where colorful sergeant majors, parrot fish, and clown fish can be seen in the crystal clear water close to the rocks. John Smith's Bay in Smith's parish, where shoals of tiny fish cast large dark shadows across the bay, is another great spot.

Wildlife Photography. From a patient day's vigil with an ultralong lens, waiting for a shot of a humpback whale, to a frantic pursuit of a pair of longtails dancing in the summer sky, Bermuda is an amateur photographer's dream.

Rent a Bike. On an island where the speed limit is 20 mph there's no need to worry about renting a car. Bermuda's strict traffic control rules mean you're not allowed to anyway. A bicycle is the best way to discover for yourself the hidden nooks and crannies and secret beaches that the bus routes and the tourist cabs just won't take you to. It costs about $25 a day.

to and around the islands of the Great Sound. Several charter skippers advertise year-round operations, but the off-season schedule can be haphazard. Skippers devote periods of the off-season to maintenance and repairs or close altogether if bookings lag. Be sure to book well in advance; in the high season do so before you arrive on the island.

Adventure Enterprises. A 36-foot motorized timaran, the *Argo II*, can carry up to 36 people and rents for $250 per hour for sightseeing tours ⊠ *Ordnance Island, St. George's* ☎ *441/335–1382.*

★ **Bermuda Barefoot Cruises.** Skipper Doug Jones will accommodate your every need. He has two 32-foot boats, the *Minnow* and the *Veebyes*, available strictly by private charter, and he'll pick you up and take you anywhere you like. It's like hiring a limousine for a tour of a city, instead of taking a bus. Rates vary depending on the length of the sail. ☎441/236–3498 ⊕*www.bermudabarefootcruises.com*.

Restless Native Tours. Fresh batches of cookies baked on board at every sailing and washed down with lemonade or rum swizzles are the delicious trademark of this family-owned and -operated charter company. Restless Native is also unique in its educational approach to chartering—they offer a crash course on Bermuda's fish and a guided snorkeling trip. The 50- by 30-foot

WHALE-WATCHING
During March and April the majestic humpback whales pass Bermuda as they migrate north to summer feeding grounds. Watching these giant animals as they leap out of the ocean is an awe-inspiring spectacle. You can see them from Elbow Beach or West Whale Bay on a clear day, if you're prepared to wait. But if you want to get a close-up view you can book a tour with an operator like Fantasea or Charter Bermuda Ltd.

boat is excellent for dinner charters, evening cocktail cruises, birthday parties, and weddings. The owners can pick you up at any wharf on the island. ☎441/734–8149 *or 441/234–1434*.

★ **Rising Son Cruises.** The *Rising Son II* is a beautiful, 60-foot, 80-passenger catamaran with a full bar. Besides offering sailing, swimming, and snorkeling trips, Captain William "Beez" Evans and the accommodating crew can arrange for you to spend part of the day on Jet Skis, in kayaks, or with a parasailing outfitter. Rates start at $800 for the first hour and go up to $2,000 for four hours depending on the number of passengers (up to 80). You can also book one of the popular cruises, such as the Turtle Bay Catamaran Beach Trip. The boat cruises over a turtle sanctuary before anchoring off a quiet sandy bay for snorkeling and kayaking. The price is $65 a head. ⊠*Town Sq., St. George's* ☎441/232–5789 ⊕*www.charterbermuda.com*.

Tam-Marina. Founded in 1969, Tam-Marina has a reputation for lively dinner and cocktail cruises on a fleet of elegant white ships. *Lady Erica* and *Lady Tamara* often accommodate large private parties on the Great Sound, whereas *Lady Charlotte* is smaller and more luxurious. You can book online. ⊠*61 Harbour Rd., Paget Parish* ☎☎441/236–0127 ⊕*www.ladyboats.com*.

Wind Sail Charters. You can rent a 41-, 51-, or 60-foot Morgan yacht, including snorkeling equipment, from Wind Sail. Captain Mike or his daughter, Captain Melissa, will sail to your location and take you for a spin. The rates for six people are $350 to $500, depending on the boat, for three hours, making this one of the most affordable rides on the island. Lunch catering is available for an extra charge. ☎441/734–8547 ⊕*www.bermudawindsailcharters.com*.

CLOSE UP

For Love of Cricket

The Oval and Lords are names of English cricket grounds that evoke memories of Britain long ago, a time of cucumber sandwiches and tea poured from china pots—but the cricket scene in Bermuda is definitely Caribbean. The thwack of leather on willow is the same, but overcast skies and frequent breaks as the ground staff move quickly to put the rain covers in place are not for these players. The fans, gathered on grassy knolls and open terraces, are also far removed from those back in England, where the game originated. Polite clapping and hearty hurrahs are not to be heard here. Instead the air is filled with chanting and the grandstands reverberate to the sound of music. Allegiances are clearly defined, though few miles separate the opposing factions—mothers, fathers, sons, and daughters all cheering on their favorites. As the match comes to a conclusion, the setting sun falls low behind the clubhouse and players and fans mingle to await the dawn of another day of runs, catches, and cries of "Howzat."

CRICKET

Cricket is the number one pastime on this sports-mad island, a fact that was seen with the national celebrations that followed the island's qualification for the Cricket World Cup in 2007. Bermuda is the smallest country ever to make the finals of the competition and its cricketers are treated as heroes in their homeland.

Fodor'sChoice ★ On the local scene, **Cup Match** in late July or early August is *the* summer sporting event, played over two days. The event celebrates the emancipation of slaves in Bermuda, with the top players from around the island competing in two teams: the East End team and the West End team. Although the match is taken very seriously, the event itself is a real festival, complete with plenty of Bermudian food and music. Bermuda's only venue for legal gambling, the Crown & Anchor tent is pitched at the field each year. Thousands of picnickers and partyers show up during the two-day match. Although the players wear only white, fans wear colors to support their team—blue on blue represents the East End and navy on red represents the West End. A $10 entry fee is charged per day.

The regular cricket season runs from April through September. Contact the **Bermuda Cricket Board** (✉ *Gorham Rd., Hamilton* ☎ *441/292–8958* ⊕ *www.bermudacricketboard.com*) for information about the match and other events throughout the year. A welcome addition to the local cricket calendar is the **20/20 World Cricket Classic** (⊕ *www.worldcricketclassic.bm/index.html*) held on the island for the first time in April 2006. It's an annual event that attracts former stars for a weeklong festival of cricket. Tickets go from $35 and up.

FISHING

Bermuda's proximity to the deep ocean makes it one of the best places in the world for deep-sea fishing. Many of the International Fishing Association's world-record catches were hauled in a few miles off the Bermuda coastline. July and August is marlin season and anglers from all over the world come to the island in a bid to try and hook monster blue marlin in excess of 1,000 pounds. Deep-sea fishing is not just for the experts, though. Most charter companies are happy to teach amateurs how to hook and reel in a catch—whether it's tuna, wahoo, or even marlin. Some of the charter fishermen let you keep your catch but they're not obliged to do so. Many of the fishermen rely on sales to restaurants to bolster their businesses, so unless it's a good day they might not give much away. And don't be surprised to find fish you pulled out of the ocean that day on the menu in one of Bermuda's many restaurants that evening. As well as deep-sea fishing, shore fishing is also popular, while some fishermen trawl inside the reefs. If you've got the cash there's no substitute for the thrill of the open ocean. Scores of operators are on the island, about 20 of which are regularly out on the water. A full list is available at ⊕*www.bermudatourism.com/fishing_charter.html*. Prices vary depending on the size and quality of the boat.

REEF & OFFSHORE FISHING

Three major reef bands lie at various distances from the island. The first is anywhere from ½ to 5 mi offshore. The second, the Challenger Bank, is about 12 mi offshore. The third, the Argus Bank, is about 30 mi offshore. As a rule, the farther out you go, the larger the fish—and the more expensive the charter.

Most charter-fishing captains go to the reefs and deep water to the southwest and northwest of the island, where the fishing is best. Catches over the reefs include snapper, amberjack, grouper, and barracuda. Of the most sought-after deepwater fish—marlin, tuna, wahoo, and dolphinfish—wahoo is the most common, dolphinfish the least. Trawling is the usual method of deepwater fishing, and charter-boat operators offer various tackle setups, with test-line weights ranging from 20 pounds to 130 pounds. The boats, which range from 31 feet to 55 feet long, are fitted with gear and electronics to track fish, including depth sounders, global-positioning systems, loran systems, video fish finders, radar, and computer scanners.

Half-day and full-day charters are offered by most operators, but full-day trips offer the best chance for a big catch because the boat has time to reach waters that are less often fished. Rates are about $600 per boat for half a day (four hours), $1,000 per day (eight hours). For more information about chartering a fishing boat, you can request or pick up a copy of *What to Do: Information and Prices* at the Bermuda Department of Tourism.

★ **Atlantic Spray Charters.** Half-day and full-day year-round charters are available on Atlantic's 40-foot *Tenacious*. Rates are $650 for the four-hour half day, $850 for six hours, and $1,000 for the eight-hour full day, including all the equipment you need, soda and water, and, most importantly, the knowledge you need to catch the big fish. ⊠*St. George's* ☏*441/735–9444* ⊕*www.atlanticspraycharters.bm.*

Fish Bermuda. Allen DeSilva is one of Bermuda's most knowledgeable skippers. His Web site is a great source of information on fishing conditions in Bermuda and he guarantees a fun day out for beginners or serious anglers on his DeMako boat, based out of Mill Creek near Hamilton. It costs $1,600 to charter the boat for a nine-hour day. ■TIP➔ **Check out DeSilva's Web site for yummy recipes on how to cook up your local catch.** ⊠*Mill Creek, Pembroke* ☏*441/295–0835 or 441/505–8626* ⊕*www.fishbermuda.com.*

Messaround Charters. With half-day and all-day charters available from Messaround Charters, it's easy to get to some of the prime offshore fishing grounds. Skipper Willard Joe Kelly can show you the ropes. ☏*441/297–8093 or 441/234–8953* ⊕*www.fishandfun.bm.*

Overproof. Skipper Peter Rans is a regular in the big-game classic and a master at hooking monster marlin. He can take you to the best spots and help you reel in whatever game fish is in season. His rates vary from $850 for half a day to $1,350 for nine hours of serious marlin hunting. ⊠*136 Somerset Rd., Somerset* ☏*441/238–5663 or 441/335–9850* ⊕*www.overprooffishing.com.*

Playmate Fishing Charters. Father-and-son team Keith and Kevin Winter boast a combined total of 75 years fishing Bermuda's waters so you won't be stuck for experience on a Playmate charter. Rates go from $900 for half a day to $1,300 for the full day with extra costs for tournament fishing. ⊠*4 Mills Point Lane, Pembroke* ☏*441/292–7131 or 441/335–5172* ⊕*www.playmatefishing.com.*

SHORE FISHING

The principal catches for shore fishers are pompano, bonefish, and snapper. Excellent sport for saltwater fly-fishing is the wily and strong bonefish, which hovers in coves, harbors, and bays. Among the more popular spots for bonefish are West Whale Bay and Spring Benny's Bay, which have large expanses of clear, shallow water protected by reefs close to shore. Good fishing holes are plentiful along the south shore, too. Fishing in the Great Sound and St. George's Harbour can be rewarding, but enclosed Harrington Sound is less promising. Ask at local tackle shops about the latest hot spots and the best baits. You can also make rental arrangements through your hotel or contact Windjammer Watersports.

Windjammer Watersports. Rods and reels rent for $20 a day (credit card required to secure the rental). Squid bait and weights are sold here, and it's open seven days a week. ⊠*Dockyard Marina* ☏*441/234–3082* ⊠*Cambridge Beaches, Sandys Parish* ☏*441/234–0250.*

GOLF

For descriptions of and information about Bermuda's nine golf courses, see Chapter 6.

One Fish, Two Fish, Red Fish, World Cup Fish

Bermuda's angling competitions attract top fishermen from all over the world. The Bermuda Blast tournament over the July 4 weekend coincides with the World Cup—where anglers across the globe compete to land the largest fish on the planet between 8 AM and 4:30 PM. Each year more and more boats descend on Bermuda over the holiday weekend, with the winners having been pulled out of the island's waters three times since 2002. The biggest local tournament is the Bermuda Big Game Classic with many of the World Cup fishermen sticking around to take part in the three-day festival. The dates vary depending on when the weekend falls but it's usually around July 15. The lure of monster marlin in excess of 1,000 pounds keeps them coming for the third leg of the Bermuda Triple Crown, the Seahorse Anglers Club tournament, the following week. Marlin season is what a lot of Bermuda's sport fishermen live for. "It's the biggest, baddest fish in the ocean—there's no feeling like landing a marlin," explains Sloane Wakefield of Atlantic Spray Charters. The **Bermuda Sport Fishing Association** at ☎441/295–2370 is a good source of information about tournaments.

HELMET DIVING

A different, less technical type of diving popular in Bermuda is helmet diving, offered between April and mid-November. Although helmet-diving cruises last three hours or more, the actual time underwater is about 25 minutes, when underwater explorers walk along the sandy bottom in about 10 to 12 feet of water (depending on the tide), wearing helmets that receive air through hoses leading to the surface. Underwater portraits are available for an extra charge. A morning or afternoon tour costs about $50 for adults and includes wet suits when the water temperature is below 80°F. Note that not all outfitters permit children to helmet dive.

Bermuda Bell Diving. Trips are scheduled daily at 10 and 2, and cost $60 per person. It's recommended that you make reservations one month ahead of time, although they're willing to accommodate you on short notice if there's room on the boat. ✉ *Flatts Village, Smith's Parish* ☎ *441/292–4434* ⊕ *www.belldive.bm.*

Greg Hartley's Under Sea Adventure. The Hartleys schedule two diving trips per day, usually at 10 and 1:30, six days per week, in high season. Dives cost around $60 per person. Nondivers are not allowed to snorkel or swim in the same area as the divers, the theory being that fish that are used to helmet divers and approach them for food may endanger themselves by becoming used to snorkelers, swimmers, and eventually fisherfolk. ✉ *Watford Bridge, Sandys Parish* ☎ *441/234–2861* ⊕ *www.hartleybermuda.com.*

Peppercorn Diving. Affiliated with Triangle Diving, Peppercorn offers an introduction to the underwater world if you're not ready to take on scuba diving. ⊠*Grotto Bay Beach Hotel, 11 Blue Hole Hill, Hamilton Parish* ☎*441/293–7319.*

PARASAILING

Parasailing outfitters operate in the Great Sound and in Castle Harbour from May through October. The cost is about $45 per person for an eight-minute flight. Want to sail through the sky with your significant other under a single parachute? Two-person trips costs around $80.

Skyrider Bermuda. Skyrider tours over the Great Sound depart every hour on the hour and cost $50 ($15 if you just want to ride in the boat). ⊠*Dockyard Marina, Sandys Parish* ☎*441/234–3019.*

St. George's Parasail Water Sports Ltd. Open seven days a week, it's $50 for a short ride, $35 for children. ⊠*Somers Wharf, St. George's* ☎*441/297–1542.*

RUGBY

Bermuda's rugby season runs from September to April. The **World Rugby Classic** (☎*441/291–1517* ⊕*www.worldrugby.bm*), in November, brings erstwhile top players, now retired, to the island for a week of play and parties—it's a hugely popular event among Bermuda's expatriate community. A game pass for the week is $100, daily admission is $25. The Classic can provide information about other matches as well.

RUNNING & WALKING

Top runners flock to the island in January for the Bermuda International Race Weekend, which includes a marathon and 10-km races. Many of the difficulties that cyclists face in Bermuda—hills, traffic, and wind—also confront runners. Be careful of traffic when walking or running along Bermuda's narrow roads—most don't have shoulders.

Bermuda International Marathon, Half Marathon, and 10K Race. Part of International Race Weekend, held in mid-January, these races attract world-class distance runners from several countries, but they're open to everyone. ☎*441/236–6086.*

Bermuda Triathlons. These three-sport events are held about once a month from April to October. The events combine a swim, a cycling leg, and a run. ☎*441/293–2765* ⊕*www.bta.bm.*

Mid-Atlantic Athletic Club Fun Runs. These 2-mi sprints are held Tuesday evening April through October. Runs begin at 6 near the Berry Hill Road entrance to the Botanical Gardens. There's no fee. ☎*441/293–8103.*

The Railway Trail. Runners who like firm pavement are happiest and safest along this former train route, one of the most peaceful stretches of road in Bermuda.

South-Shore Beaches. If you like running on sand, head for the south shore. The trails through South Shore Park are relatively firm. A large

CLOSE UP

Wreck Diving

If you've heard the stories of the Bermuda Triangle then you won't be surprised to hear that there are more than 20 ships wrecked off the island. Actually it's got more to do with the craggy reefs that surround the island than that old myth, but each wreck has a story, and most dive operators here know it. Graham Maddocks, a 20-year veteran of Bermuda's waters and owner of Triangle Diving, gave us a history lesson on five of Bermuda's most interesting wrecks.

Constellation. "Jaws" author Peter Benchley based his follow-up novel *The Deep,* set in Bermuda, around the *Constellation* wreck. A cargo ship bound for Venezuela during World War II, she was carrying building materials, morphine, and 700 bottles of whiskey when her hull was broken apart on the reef. Some of the building materials remain, but the rest of her cargo is long gone.

The Cristobel Colon. This massive Spanish cruise liner is the biggest of Bermuda's shipwrecks, at 499 feet long. It crashed into the reefs off the North Shore in 1936 after its captain mistook an offshore communications tower for the Gibbs Hill Lighthouse. It was crewed by Spanish dissidents from the civil war in Puerto Rico. (They were eventually rounded up and hung for treason in Spain.) The *Cristobel* sat in Bermuda's waters for several years and many of its furnishings can be found in Bermudian homes today. The British eventually sank its empty shell by using it for target practice during World War II.

The Hermes. Probably the most popular wreck dive in Bermuda, the *Hermes* remains fully intact sitting in 80 feet of water off the south shore.

It's one of the few wrecks that you can actually get inside and explore. It arrived in Bermuda with engine trouble and was ultimately abandoned by its crew. The Bermuda Government took possession of the 165-foot steel-hulled ship and sank it as a dive site in the early 1980s.

The Pelinaion. This 385-foot Greek cargo steamer was another victim of World War II. The British had blacked out the lighthouse in a bid to stop the Germans from spying on Bermuda. The captain had a perfect record, had sailed past Bermuda many times, and was months away from retirement when he made this journey from West Africa to Baltimore in 1940, carrying a cargo of iron ore. Without the lighthouse to guide him he couldn't find the island until he struck the reef off St. David's. You can still see the ship's steam boiler and engine as well as some of the cargo of iron ore.

The Xing Da. A modern-day pirate ship, the *Xing Da* was carrying a "cargo" of Chinese immigrants to be smuggled into the United States in 1996. Crewed by members of the Chinese mafia, the Triads, it had arranged to meet a smaller boat 145 mi off Bermuda for the immigrants to be transferred and taken into the States. Instead they found themselves surrounded by the U.S. Marines. The boat was given to the government as a dive site in 1997.

number of serious runners can be seen on Horseshoe Bay Beach and Elbow Beach early in the morning and after 5 PM. Another beach for running is ½-mi Warwick Long Bay, the island's longest uninterrupted stretch of sand. The sand is softer here than at Horseshoe and Elbow, so it's difficult to get good footing, particularly at high tide. By using South Shore Park trails to skirt coral bluffs, you can create a route that connects several beaches. Note that the trails can be winding and uneven in some places.

> ### SEGWAY AWAY!
>
> Rent a Segway, a two-wheeled upright power scooter, and tour around historic Dockyard. Pick yours up at the old-fashioned double decker bus across from Dockyard Glassworks and Bermuda Rum Cake Company. Tours are 1½ hours long and cost $76, which includes Segway training. Times are 9:30, noon, and 2:30. ✉ *Corner of Camber Rd. and Dockyard Terrace* ☎ *441/504–2581.*

SAILING & YACHTING

Bermuda has a worldwide reputation as a yacht-racing center. The sight of the racing fleet, with brightly colored spinnakers flying, is striking even if it's difficult to follow the intricacies of the race. The racing season runs from March to November. Most races are held on weekends in the Great Sound, and several classes of boats usually compete. You can watch from Spanish Point and along the Somerset shoreline. Anyone who wants to get a real sense of the action should be on board a boat near the race course. The Gold Cup race is held in October, and International Race Week is held at the end of April. In June in alternating years, Bermuda serves as the finish point for oceangoing yachts in three major races starting in the United States.

RACES & EVENTS

Bermuda Ocean Race. This race, from Annapolis, Maryland, takes place every other year in June, with one in 2008. For information, contact **St. George's Dinghy & Sports Club** (☎ *441/297–1612*).

King Edward VII Gold Cup. This is the event of choice if you're more interested in racing than gawking at expensive yachts. Managed by the **Royal Bermuda Yacht Club** (☎ *441/295–2214*), the October tournament hosts many of the world's top sailors—some of whom are America's Cup skippers—and includes the elite among Bermudians in a lucrative chase for thousands in prize money.

Newport (RI)-to-Bermuda Ocean Yacht Race. Powerhouse yachtsmen flock to this event in June. The race takes place every two years, with one in 2008. Be sure to attend the after-race party—it's open to the public and is always extremely well attended. Contact the **Royal Bermuda Yacht Club** at (☎ *441/295–2214*).

Non-Mariners Race. Though not as prestigious as the rest, this annual race, which takes place in early August during Cup Match weekend (the annual cricket holiday), is one of the highlights of the year. Held out of the **Sandys Boat Club** (☎ *441/234–2248 or 441/234–4137*) at

Mangrove Bay, the goal of this race is simple: to see whose boat (constructed on the beach minutes before) can make it out of the harbor without sinking. Easy to watch as the boats never get very far from land, this race sets the stage for an afternoon of music, barbecue, local political satire, and merrymaking.

> ### GOOD TO KNOW
>
> If you rent a motorboat be sure to ask for directions to Castle Island Nature Reserve, one of the most secluded and beautiful spots on the island.

Legend has it that someone even tried to float an old bus one year. A good viewpoint from which to watch the race is the **Somerset Country Squire Pub** (☎️*441/234–0105*).

RENTALS

Outfitters like **SurfShack** and **Windjammer** *(see Aquatic Adventures)* have a range of crafts to rent and also offer lessons for beginners. It's also worth checking out **Paget Dinghy Club**, which is the main center for sailors in Hamilton and offers lessons for beginners. If you know what you're doing and fancy taking part in some amateur racing, this is the place to be on a Wednesday evening. Just turn up at the dock—skippers are always looking for willing crew members. ✉️*Mangroville, Paget* ☎️*441/236–3077* 🌐*www.rhadc.com.*

SCUBA DIVING

Bermuda has all the ingredients for classic scuba diving—reefs, wrecks, underwater caves, a variety of coral and marine life, and clear, warm water. Although you can dive year-round (you will have to bring your own gear in winter, when dive shops are closed), the best months are May through October, when the water is calmest and warmest. No prior certification is necessary. Novices can learn the basics and dive in water up to 25 feet deep on the same day. Three-hour resort courses ($95–$110) teach the basics in a pool, on the beach, or off a dive boat, and culminate in a reef or wreck dive.

The easiest day trips involve exploring the south-shore reefs that lie inshore. These reefs may be the most dramatic in Bermuda. The ocean-side drop-off exceeds 60 feet in some places, and the coral is so honey-combed with caves, ledges, and holes that opportunities for discovery are pretty much infinite. Despite concerns about dying coral and dwindling fish populations, most of Bermuda's reefs are still in good health. No one eager to swim with multicolor schools of fish or the occasional barracuda will be disappointed. ⚠️ **In the interest of preservation the removal of coral is illegal and subject to hefty fines.**

Dive shops around Bermuda prominently display a map of the outlying reef system and its wreck sites. Only 38 of the wrecks from the past three centuries are marked. They're the larger wrecks that are still in good condition. The nautical carnage includes some 300 wreck sites—an astonishing number—many of which are well preserved. As a general rule, the more recent the wreck or the more deeply submerged it is, the better its condition. Most of the well-preserved wrecks are to the north and east, and dive depths range between 25 feet and 80 feet. Several wrecks off the western end of the island are in relatively shallow water, 30 feet or less, making them accessible to novice divers and even snorkelers.

Blue Water Divers Ltd. The major operator for wrecks on the western side of the island, Blue Water Divers offers lessons, tours, and rentals. The lesson-and-dive package for first-time divers, including equipment, costs $99. From the Elbow Beach Hotel location, you can ride a diver-propulsion vehicle (DPV), which is like an underwater scooter, past a wreck and through caves and canyons. A one-tank dive for experienced divers costs $60, and a two-tank dive is $85. With two tanks you can explore two or more wrecks in one four-hour outing. For all necessary equipment—mask, fins, snorkel, scuba apparatus, and wet suit (if needed)—plan to spend about $40 more. Night dives are available, too. This operator is not to be confused with Dive Bermuda, despite the Web address. ⊠*Elbow Beach Hotel, Paget Parish* ☎*441/232–2909* ⊠*Robinson's Marina, Somerset Bridge, Sandys Parish* ☎*441/234– 1034* ⊕*www.divebermuda.com.*

Dive Bermuda was awarded National Geographic Dive Centre status in 2006 and is the only center on the island to offer courses sanctioned by the world-renowned environmental magazine. It also offers PADI (Professional Association of Diving Instructors) instructor-level courses for divers who want to take the next step in their training. Formerly known as Nautilus Diving, it has locations on the south shore and Hamilton Harbour out of the famous Fairmont hotels. A lesson-and-dive package typically costs $115 including equipment, the same as a single-tank dive. A double-tank dive costs $135. Group rates and multiple dives cost less. ⊠*Fairmont Hamilton Princess Hotel* ☎*441/295–9485* ⊠*Fairmont Southampton Hotel* ☎*441/238–2332* ⊕*www.bermudascuba.com.*

Fodor's Choice ★ **Triangle Diving.** For East End diving among wrecks and coral reefs, head for this outfitter in the Grotto Bay Beach Hotel. A range of dive tours is offered, as well as PADI certification courses. Friendly staff who really know their stuff and who never get tired of sharing their vast knowledge of Bermuda's wrecks make diving with this company all the more fun. The location also offers great access to one of Bermuda's most beautiful reefs at North Rock. At press time, the company was planning to bring cage-diving for sharks by January 2008. Give them a call and see if they're ready for you to get up close and personal with the most fearsome predators in the ocean. ⊠*Grotto Bay Beach Hotel, 11 Blue Hole Hill, Hamilton Parish* ☎*441/293–7319* ⊕*www.trianglediving.com.*

SCUBA NEWBIES

If you've never dived before but want to give it a try, Bermuda is a great place to start. All of the island's dive centers offer a Discover Scuba course, which allows first-time divers to take a brief lesson and follow an instructor on a shallow wreck or reef dive.

5

SNORKELING

The clarity of the water, the stunning array of coral reefs, and the shallow resting places of several wrecks make snorkeling in the waters around Bermuda—both inshore and offshore—particularly worthwhile. You can snorkel year-round, although a wet suit is advisable for anyone planning to spend a long time in the water in winter, when the water temperature can dip into the 60s. The water also tends to be rougher in winter, often restricting snorkeling to the protected areas of Harrington Sound and Castle Harbour. Underwater caves, grottoes, coral formations, and schools of small fish are the highlights of these areas.

Some of the best snorkeling sites are accessible only by boat. As the number of wrecks attests, navigating around Bermuda's reef-strewn waters is no simple task, especially for inexperienced boaters. If you rent a boat yourself, stick to the protected waters of the sounds, harbors, and bays, and be sure to ask for an ocean-navigation chart. These charts point out shallow waters, rocks, and hidden reefs.

For trips to the reefs, let someone else do the navigating—a charter-boat skipper or one of the snorkeling-cruise operators. Some of the best reefs for snorkeling, complete with shallow-water wrecks, are to the west, but where the tour guide or skipper goes often depends on the tide, weather, and water conditions. For snorkelers who demand privacy and freedom of movement, a boat charter (complete with captain) is the only answer, but the cost is considerable—$650 a day for a party of 18. By comparison, half a day of snorkeling on a regularly scheduled cruise generally costs $45 to $65, including equipment and instruction.

Fodor'sChoice   **Church Bay.** When Bermudians are asked to name a favorite snorkeling
★   spot, they invariably rank Church Bay in Southampton (at the western end of the south-shore beaches) at, or near, the top of the list. A small cove cut out of the coral cliffs, the bay is full of nooks and crannies, and the reefs are relatively close to shore. Snorkelers should exercise caution here (as you should everywhere along the south shore), as the water can be rough. A small stall often sells snorkeling equipment, underwater cameras, and fish food.

John Smith's Bay. This popular snorkeling spot off the south shore of Smith's Parish has several reefs close to the shore as well as the added safety of a lifeguard overseeing the beach. Beware, this site occasionally experiences rip currents.

Snorkel Park. Off a rocky beach surrounded by the walls of the fort in Dockyard, the snorkel park is a cool place for kids. With a sunken cannon and other underwater features it's worth a look if you're in the West End. There's a bar and you can rent umbrellas and snorkel gear for a small fee. The site is closed November through April.

Tobacco Bay. This beautiful bay is tucked in a cove near historic Fort St. Catherine's beach. Tobacco Bay offers wonderful snorkeling, public facilities, and equipment rentals, and there's a snack bar near the shore. This site is the most popular in St. George's.

Warwick Long Bay. On south shore in Warwick, this ½-mi of beach is usually secluded and quiet. After Hurricane Fabian in 2003, formerly popular snorkeling spot Church Bay was closed to the public and the snorkeling concession stand there (featuring a popular DJ) was moved to Warwick Long Bay until Church Bay could be reopened.

West Whale Bay. Tiny West Whale Bay, off the western shore near the Port Royal Golf Course in Southampton, is quiet and usually uncrowded. The beach disappears during high tide, though, so check tide times first.

KITEBOARDING

Also known as kitesurfing, this is one of the newest and fastest-growing extreme sports in the world. It involves using a large power kite to drag a small surf-board along the water. If you're interested in giving it a try head to SurfShack or check out ⊕ *www. bka.bm*. If extreme sports is not your thing, the sight of the giant kites dipping and rising in the breeze is still an awesome specta-cle if you're walking along Elbow Beach on a windy day.

SNORKELING CRUISES

Snorkeling cruises, offered from April to November, are a less expensive albeit less personal way to experience the underwater world. Some boats carry up to 40 passengers to snorkeling sites but focus mostly on their music and bars (complimentary beverages are usually served on the trip back from the reefs). Smaller boats, which limit capacity to 10 to 16 passengers, offer more personal attention and focus more on the beautiful snorkeling areas themselves. Guides on such tours often relate interesting historical and ecological information about the island. To make sure you choose a boat that's right for you, ask for details before booking. Most companies can easily arrange private charters for groups.

Hayward's Snorkeling & Glass Bottom Boat Cruises. Groups of about 35 people board Hayward's 54-foot glass-bottom *Explorer* for 3¾-hour snorkeling trips. Access into and out of the water from the boat is easy. Special excursions are arranged during the spring migration of the humpback whales. ⊠ *Adjacent to Hamilton Ferry Terminal* ☎ *441/236–9894* ☜ *$50* ⊙ *Daily 9:45 and 1:30.*

Jessie James Cruises. Half-day trips aboard the 40-passenger luxury Chris Craft *Rambler* cost $50, including gear and instruction. ⊠ *47 Front St., Hamilton* ☎ *441/236–4804* ⊕ *www.jessiejames.bm.*

★ **Restless Native Tours.** Captain Kirk Ward has regularly scheduled sailing and snorkeling trips to the outer reefs on a 50-by-30-foot catamaran. With a crash course in Bermuda's marine life, plus fresh cookies on board, it's hard to resist this popular outfitter. The tours depart from wharfs all over the island. ☎ *441/234–8149 or 441/234–1434.*

SNORKELING EQUIPMENT RENTALS

Snorkeling equipment and sometimes underwater cameras are available for rent at most major hotels and at several marinas, as well as from the snorkeling concession stand at Warwick Long Bay. The Grotto Bay Beach Hotel & Tennis Club and Fairmont Southampton have dive

CLOSE UP

Aquatic Adventures

Whether it's renting a glass-bottomed kayak for a gentle paddle over the reefs, taking a motorboat for a spin around hidden coves and inlets, or spending an adrenaline-filled afternoon wakeboarding, getting out on the water is an essential part of the Bermuda experience.

Bermuda Waterski Centre. Operated by international competitor Kent Richardson, this business, as the name suggests, is all about the waterskiing. Kent has represented Bermuda at nine World Championships and has also been in the PanAm games. He took a trick skiing bronze medal at the Latin American games, but don't be intimidated—he's also a patient teacher. He's got a ski-nautique-style boat with a full range of gear for wakeboarding, kneeboarding, and tubing. His business operates at the same location as Somerset Bridge Watersports on Robinson's marina from mid-April to October. It's $150 for the hour, $80 per half hour. That price is for the time, which is split among however many people are on the boat. He can take up to seven at a time, but three or four is usually a good number to allow a decent amount of time on the skis. ⊠ *Somerset Bridge, Sandys Parish* ☎ *441/234-3354.*

Blue Hole Water Sports. Blue Hole, based out of the beautiful Grotto Bay hotel, has you covered in the East End of the island. For the ultimate in relaxation you can cruise the blue-green waters and soak up some rays in a SunKat, a low-powered floating deck chair. You can rent a kayak or double-kayak for $20 per hour or join one of the center's nature tours ($35 per hour). Blue Hole also offers windsurfing and sunfish sailboat rentals for around $30 per hour. There's

a gorgeous sheltered beach with a small wreck sunk just off-shore for snorkelers. ⊠ *Grotto Bay Beach Hotel & Tennis Club, 11 Blue Hole Hill, Hamilton Parish* ☎ *441/293-2915 or 441/293-8333 Ext. 37* ⊕ *www.blueholewater.bm.*

Fantasea. As the name suggests this Bermudian company offers a comprehensive range of aquatic adventures. The whale-watching tours in March and April are immensely popular and with Captain Mike Moby Dick at the helm you get close to the majestic humpbacks as they migrate north. There are various Jet Ski packages, and you can take your pick of a cruise-and-kayak or boat-and-bike ecotour for a closer look at some of the prettiest spots on the island. As well as snorkeling tours and various other boat trips you could try Snuba—a kind of intermediate step between snorkeling and scuba diving. It involves a short training session and a shallow dive, usually at Daniel's Head Marine Park in Somerset. You don't need qualifications, experience, or too much cumbersome dive gear, so it's a popular option for people who have never dived before. ⊠ *Albuoy's Point, Hamilton* ☎ *441/236-1300* ⊕ *www.fantasea.bm.*

Kayak Bermuda. Paddle your way along lagoons and rock formations, guided by locals. You can receive instruction and practice paddling techniques, as well as an option at the end of the tour to continue kayaking on your own or to jump in the water and take a dip. Tour includes a complimentary bottled water and a safety vest. ⊠ *15 Mullet Bay Rd., St. George's* ☎ *441/737-7378* ⊕ *www.kayakbermuda.com.*

Pompano Beach Club. For a more relaxed aquatic experience check out Pompano Beach Club. Several low-powered vessels are available including Sun Kat cruiser ($35 per hour), E-Schooter boats ($30 per hour), sunfish sailboats ($20 per hour), and paddleboats ($15 per hour). Pompano also rents rafts and rubber tubes. ✉ 36 Pompano Beach Rd., Southampton Parish ☎ 441/234-0222.

Somerset Bridge Watersports. This West End outfitter rents 13- and 15-foot Boston Whalers and is right next to Somerset Bridge. Rates are $75 for two hours, $120 for four hours, $165 for six hours, or $200 for eight hours, plus the cost of gas. For the six- and eight-hour tours you'll need to schedule a morning departure. You can also take a speed tour of the western end of the island on a Jet Ski. The tour takes you through Ely's Harbour, Mangrove Bay, and above the Sea Gardens coral formations. Groups are kept small—no more than six Jet Skiers per guide. ✉ Somerset Bridge, Sandys Parish ☎ 441/234-0914 or 441/234-3145.

★ **SurfShack.** SurfShack, based out of 9 Beaches Resort in Somerset, is the newest water-sports center in Bermuda and is fast becoming the place to go for all things aquatic. The center offers instruction and rentals for wakeboarding, waterskiing ($175 for boat/pilot for an hour), kiteboarding, windsurfing (lessons from $50), and sailing. Surfshack is the only certified IKO kiteboarding center in Bermuda. Fully qualified instructors will show you the ropes in one of the world's newest and fastest growing water sports ($125 for a two-hour lesson). If you already know what you're doing and have your own gear, then this is still a good starting point to hook up with like-minded people. You can rent HobieCats ($40 to $60 per hour), kayaks ($15 for an hour), or go for a more leisurely ride in a Boston Whaler, with the nearby Vixen wreck—a major snorkeling attraction. Snorkel safaris, for groups of up to 12 people, take you to some of the most secluded and beautiful locations around the island on one- or two-hour Jet Ski tours. Another fun attraction is the fly-fish or manta ray inflatables that are towed behind Surfshack's jet boat. ✉ 9 Beaches Resort, Daniel's Head, Somerset ☎ 441/239-2995 ⊕ www.surfshack.bm.

Windjammer Watersports. Based in Dockyard, Windjammer offers just about everything there is to do on the water. Windsurfing, sailing, boat rentals, Jet Ski tours, kayaking, as well as instruction from experienced mariners. You're looking at around $60 per hour for a windsurfing lesson, or if you already know what you're doing and just need to rent a board, it's $35 for the first hour and $10 an hour after that. Dockyard is a good spot to rent a motorboat, and it's easy to get to with a fast ferry running from Hamilton every half hour during peak times. Windjammer rents 17-foot-long motorboats for $40 for the first hour, plus $20 for each additional hour. Mariners can take out a 17-foot sailboat at $65 for two hours, $90 for four, or $135 for eight. Fishing and snorkeling gear are also available. You can rent kayaks from Windjammer's Cambridge Beaches location. ✉ Dockyard Marina ☎ 441/234-3082 ✉ Cambridge Beaches, Sandys Parish ☎ 441/234-0250.

operators on-site. A deposit or credit-card number is usually required when renting equipment.

Pompano Beach Club Watersports Centre. Equipment at Pompano rents for $8 per day, or $4 per hour, for a mask, snorkel, and flippers. Each piece is also available separately. ⊠*36 Pompano Beach Rd., Southampton Parish* ☎*441/234–0222.*

Windjammer Watersports. You can rent mask, snorkel, and flippers here for $20 per 24-hour period. Two of three pieces cost just $10. ⊠*Dockyard Marina, Sandys Parish* ☎*441/234–0250.*

TENNIS

Bermuda has one tennis court for every 600 residents, a ratio that even the most tennis-crazed countries would find difficult to match. Many are private, but the public has access to more than 70 courts in 20 locations. Courts are inexpensive and seldom full. Hourly rates for nonguests are about $10 to $16. You might want to consider bringing along a few fresh cans of balls, because balls in Bermuda cost $6 to $7 per can—two to three times the rate in the United States. Among the surfaces used in Bermuda are Har-Tru, clay, cork, and hard composites, of which the relatively slow Plexipave composite is the most prevalent. Despite Bermuda's British roots, the island has no grass court.

Wind, heat (in summer), and humidity are the most distinct characteristics of Bermudian tennis. From October through March, when daytime temperatures rarely exceed 80°F, play is comfortable throughout the day. But in summer, the heat radiating from the court (especially hard courts) can make play uncomfortable between 11 AM and 3 PM, so some clubs take a midday break. Most tennis facilities offer lessons, ranging from $25 to $30 for 30 minutes of instruction, and racket rentals for $4 to $6 per hour or per play.

Coral Beach & Tennis Club. Introduction by a member is required to play at this exclusive club, which is the site of the annual XL Capital Bermuda Open tournament in April. Coral Beach has eight clay courts, three of which are floodlit. It's open daily from 8 to 8. Resident pro Derek Singleton is the man to talk to about scheduling lessons, which run $45 for a half hour. Tennis whites are required. ⊠*Off South Shore Rd., Paget Parish* ☎*441/236–2233.*

Elbow Beach Hotel. This facility is fortunate to have as its director of tennis David Lambert, who is also a former president of the Bermuda Lawn Tennis Association. There are five Plexipave courts on hand, three with lights, and hours of play are 8 AM to 9 PM daily. Courts cost $12 per hour. Lessons and match play can be arranged for hotel guests or other visitors at $30 per half hour. ⊠*Off South Shore Rd., Paget Parish* ☎*441/236–3535.*

The Fairmont Southampton. Despite their position at the water's edge, the Plexipave hard courts here are reasonably shielded from the wind, although the breeze can be swirling and difficult. Six courts are at hand, with fees ranging from $12 to $16 per hour on any of the three courts that have lighting. Hours of service are daily from 8 AM to 6 PM, extended until 8 in summer. Lessons from pro Mark Cordeiro are available at $40 per half hour or $75 per hour. ⊠ *South Shore Rd., Southampton Parish* ☎ *441/238–1005.*

Government Tennis Stadium. These are the busiest of Bermuda's tennis courts, their inland location ideal for combating strong winds. Of the eight all-weather courts available, five are Plexi-Cushion and three are Har-Tru. Three courts in the main stadium have floodlights. Hours are from 8 AM to 10 PM weekdays and from 8 to 6 on weekends. Rates are $8 per hour during the day and $16 per hour at night. Tennis attire is required, and lessons are available starting at $30 per half hour and $50 per full hour. ⊠ *2 Marsh Folly, Pembroke Parish* ☎ *441/292–0105.*

Grotto Bay Beach Hotel & Tennis Club. A little more than a stone's throw from the Bermuda International Airport, Grotto Bay has four Plexipave cork-based courts, two lighted, with an hourly rate of $12. It's open daily, 7 to 7, with a midday break. Lessons are $25 per half hour and $45 per full hour. Tennis attire is required. ⊠ *North Shore Rd., Hamilton Parish* ☎ *441/293–8333 Ext. 1914.*

Pomander Gate Tennis Club. There are five hard courts available (four with lighting) at this scenic club located off Hamilton Harbour. Temporary membership is available for $30 per couple per week. Hours of play are 7 AM to 11 PM on weekdays, until 10 PM on weekends. ⊠ *Pomander Rd., Paget Parish* ☎ *441/236–5400.*

Port Royal Golf Course. Port Royal has four hard courts, two of which are floodlit. A host of pros are on hand to offer instruction. Rates for court play are the cheapest on the island; $10 per hour in the day and $14 per hour at night—it's open until 10 PM. Arrangements can be made through the golf club from 10 AM. ⊠ *Off Middle Rd., Southampton Parish* ☎ *441/238–9430.*

TENNIS TOURNAMENTS

Bermuda Lawn Tennis Association. Established in 1964, the association hosts all the important tennis events on the island. Ask for an events calendar. ☎ *441/296–0834* ⊕ *www.blta.bm.*

XL Capital Bermuda Open. In April, the clay courts at the Coral Beach & Tennis Club host this ATP Tour, a USTA-sanctioned event with the world's top professionals. Big names, such as Patrick Rafter and Todd Eldridge, have played in this event, as well as several of Bermuda's own tennis stars, such as James Collieson. In November there's back-to-back tournament activity at the club, too. The action begins with the Bermuda Lawn Tennis Club Invitational followed by the Coral Beach Club Invitational.

Golf

WORD OF MOUTH

"Tucker's Point is outstanding. It's gorgeous to look at, and the new clubhouse is, too. Mid Ocean is very expensive, pretty, and super difficult."

—thereadbaron

"Port Royal is a nice course, and the 16th hole is the whole enchilada. I had to hit my tee shot toward the ocean because of the wind. I would also recommend St. George's. It's a short course but the views are awesome. One hole (mulligan hole, definitely) you can either hit your tee shot over an inlet (about 260 yards) or hit around it."

—iamawfull

Updated
by Dale
Leatherman

GOLF IS AN IMPORTANT FACET of Bermuda sporting life, where golf courses make up nearly 17% of the island's 21.6 square mi. The scenery on the courses is quite often spectacular, with trees and shrubs decked out in multicolor blossoms against a backdrop of brilliant blue sea and sky. The layouts may be shorter than what you're accustomed to, but they're remarkably challenging, thanks to capricious ocean breezes, daunting natural terrain, and the clever work of world-class golf architects.

Of the seven 18-hole courses and two 9-hole layouts on Bermuda, five are championship venues: Belmont Hills, the Mid Ocean Club, Port Royal, Riddell's Bay, and Tucker's Point. All are well maintained, but you should not expect the springy bent grass fairways and

> ### TOP 5 GOLF
>
> ■ **Mid Ocean.** Walk in famous footsteps with a caddy at your side.
>
> ■ **Port Royal.** A quintessential Robert Trent Jones Sr. design, it's a favorite for its spectacular cliffside holes.
>
> ■ **Riddell's Bay.** The island's oldest course has tight fairways to keep you on your toes.
>
> ■ **St. George's Bay.** Sometimes good golf comes in small packages.
>
> ■ **Tucker's Point.** A real class act, Tucker's Point is an entirely new layout on the old Castle Harbour track.

6

fast greens typical of U.S. golf courses. The rough is coarse Bermuda grass that will turn your club in your hands. Because the island's fresh water supply is limited, watering is usually devoted to the greens and tees, which means the fairways are likely to be firm and give you lots of roll. Expect plenty of sand hazards and wind—*especially* wind.

Most clubs have TifEagle or Tifdwarf greens—finer-bladed grasses that are drought-resistant and putt faster and truer than Bermuda grass. However, the greens at St. George's Golf Club are seashore paspalum grass, a fine-bladed, salt-resistant variety that is popular in the Caribbean. It's a user-friendly putting surface once you get used to the fact that the ball doesn't break as much as you expect. In any case, you'll want to spend time on the practice greens to get a better feel.

Most courses overseed with rye grass sometime between late September and early November to maintain color and texture through the cooler winter months. Some courses use temporary greens, whereas others keep their regular greens in play during the reseeding process. This makes for inaccurate putting situations, so if you're visiting in fall, call ahead to find out the condition of the greens. Though all courses now have carts, there's often a "cart path only" rule in force to protect the fairways, so expect to do some walking.

Many Bermudian tracks have holes on the ocean or atop seaside cliffs. They're wonderfully scenic, but the wind and that big natural water hazard can play havoc with your game.

All courses in Bermuda have dress codes: long pants or Bermuda (kneelength) shorts and collared shirts for both men and women. Denim is not allowed. All courses require soft spikes. ■TIP➜ **Bermudian men always wear color-coordinated knee-high socks with their shorts on other occasions, but it's okay to go bare-legged on the golf course.**

DID YOU KNOW?

Bermuda does not have rivers and streams, and has very few natural ponds, so any water hazards you encounter (other than the ocean) are likely man-made.

Courses in Bermuda are rated by the United States Golf Association (USGA), just as they are in the States, so you can tell at a glance how difficult a course is. For example, a par-72 course with a rating of 68 means that a scratch golfer (one who usually shoots par) should be four under par for the round. High handicappers should score better than usual, too.

Reserve tee times before you leave home or ask your hotel concierge to do so as soon as you arrive. This is especially necessary to access the private courses. "Sunset" tee times, available at lower greens fees, generally start at 3 PM, but call ahead to be sure.

Lessons, available at all courses, cost $35 to $60 for a half hour, and $60 to $100 for an hour. Club rentals cost $25 to $45 (except on the Horizons and Cottages "mashie" course, where $5 will get you the few irons and putter needed). Caddies are available only at the Mid Ocean Club, where you'll pay $30 per golf bag or $35 for a double carry, plus a tip of 10 to 15 percent.

GOLF COURSES & CLUBS

BELMONT HILLS GOLF CLUB

18 holes. 6,017 yards. Par 70. Rating: blue tees, 68.4; white tees, 66.8; red tees, 69.

Belmont Hills, opened in June 2003, was designed by California architect Algie Pulley Jr. and built on the site of the former Belmont Manor and Golf Club, a haven for celebrities in the early 1900s. "Hills" was added to the course name to reflect the dramatic design features that Pulley used to replace the previous, rather mundane layout. This is now a real shot-making test, heavily contoured and with more water than most other Bermuda courses. The sand in the bunkers is the same used at the famed Augusta National, site of the Masters. A waterfall connects two man-made lakes that can come into play on several holes. The final four holes are particularly challenging because of their tight landing areas bordered by out-of-bounds stakes. A bad hit or intervention by the ever-present wind can lead to lost balls and penalties. The pressure continues until the ball is in the hole, because the greens are heavily bunkered and multitiered. Putting surfaces are well-maintained TifEagle grass. Fairways are attractively defined by palm trees, and an automated irrigation system keeps everything lush. The course has the island's only double green, a 14,000-square-foot putting surface on holes 1 and 10.

CLOSE UP

Secrets from a Golf Pro

Golf courses elsewhere are often designed with the wind in mind—long downwind holes and short upwind holes. Not so in Bermuda, where the wind is anything but consistent or predictable. Quirky air currents make play on a Bermudian course different every day. The wind puts a premium on being able to hit the ball straight, and grossly exaggerates any slice or hook.

The hard ground of most Bermuda courses means you must abandon the strategy you use on heavily watered tracks. Your ball will run a lot in the fairway, so don't overestimate the distance to hazards. Around the greens, it's wise to run the ball to the hole rather than chipping. Not only will you find it difficult to get under the ball

on the firm fairways, but your shot will be subject to the vagaries of the wind. If you're in the clinging Bermuda grass rough, your club face is likely to turn if you try to swing through it.

So, how should you prepare for a Bermuda trip? Practice run-up shots from close-cropped lies using a 5- or 6-iron—or a putter from just off the green. Use mid-irons to practice punching shots from the rough, angling back into the fairway rather than trying to advance the ball straight ahead and risk landing in the rough again. Putting surfaces are often undulating and grainier than bent grass, so putts will break less than you expect. They'll also die much more quickly unless you use a firm stroke.

6

Highlight Hole: The 7th hole, a 178-yard par 3, is bordered by a waterfall.

Clubhouse: The main clubhouse stands on the site of the former Belmont Hotel, close to the 9th hole. The building has lovely views of the Great Sound and Hamilton Harbour, plus an airy lounge, bar, pro shop, and restaurant. **Blu'** (☎441/232–2323) is an extraordinary dining experience. Its eclectic menu includes fork-tender Angus steaks; innovative seafood dishes such as salmon, crab, shrimp, and avocado wrapped in a tortilla; and irresistible desserts. ✉97 Middle Rd., Warwick Parish ☎441/236–6400 ⊕www.belmonthills.com ✆Greens fees $103 daily, $60 sunset (walking only after 2 PM). Mandatory cart rentals $27 per person. Pull cart rentals (sunset only) $10. Shoe rentals $15. Club Rentals $45. Lessons $60 for 30 minutes, $100 per hour.

BERMUDA GOLF ACADEMY

☺ When you just want to practice or have some fun teaching the kids how to play golf in a relaxed environment, head for the Bermuda Golf Academy. The 320-yard driving range is floodlit at night until 10 (weekdays) or 10:30 (weekends) and there are 40 practice bays. ■TIP➔**If you get a rainy day, fine-tune your game in one of the 25 covered bays.** Elevated target greens are placed 75 to 230 yards from the tees. You can also work on sand shots in the practice bunker or sharpen your putting on a 3,000-square-foot practice green.

Especially attractive for families is the 18-hole miniature golf course, which features pagodas, a waterfall, waterways—even a drawbridge to hit over on the 16th hole. The minicourse is lighted at night and takes 45 to 80 minutes to complete. Adjacent is a new restaurant and small café, **East Meets West** (☎441/238–8580). As the name implies, the cuisine includes Japanese, Chinese, Balinese, English, Caribbean, Indian, and American. The café side has a wide range of hot sandwiches, wraps, salads, meins, noodles, and Indian dishes, plus full breakfasts. ✉ *10 Industrial Park Rd., off Middle Rd., Southampton Parish* ☎*441/238–8800* 🖳*Driving range $5, $6 after 5* PM. *Miniature golf $10 adults, $8 children. Lessons $40 a half hour, $70 per hour, or $100 per hour with a video analysis.*

FAIRMONT SOUTHAMPTON GOLF CLUB

18 holes. 2,684 yards. Par 54. Rating: 53.7.

> ## DON'T REPLACE YOUR DIVOTS
>
> Bermuda grass is so called because it came to the U.S. from Bermuda, but it actually originated in Africa, where it's called Devil's Grass or Wire Grass. The grass is considered holy in India, where it's used to feed sacred cows. In ancient times, Romans boiled it and used the juice to stop bleeding. Bermuda grass is a creeping plant, putting down roots where nodes touch the earth. Once dislodged by your stroke, the mat of grass will not reroot, so don't bother to replace your divots. Instead, fill them with the sand and seed mixture on your cart.

Spreading across the hillside below the high-rise Fairmont Southampton, this executive golf course is known for its steep terrain, giving players who opt to walk (for sunset tee times only) an excellent workout. The vertical drop on the first two holes alone is at least 200 feet, and the rise on the 4th hole makes 178 yards play like 220. The Ted Robinson design is a good warm-up for Bermuda's full-length courses, offering a legitimate test of wind and bunker play. The front nine has almost constant views of the ocean and is more difficult than the back nine, with tight holes calling for careful club selection.

Highlight Hole: The signature hole is the 214-yard 14th, but the most striking is the 174-yard 16th hole, which sits in a cup ringed by pink oleander bushes. The Gibbs Hill Lighthouse, less than a mile away, is the backdrop.

Clubhouse: Because the hotel and its restaurants are so close, there's no golf clubhouse per se, just a 10th-hole Golf Hut for snacks and drinks. The golf shop has a fine selection of quality golf wear and any essentials you might forget to bring. On the level above the golf shop is **Bacci** (☎*441/238–8000*), a fine Italian restaurant overlooking the course. If you have a yearning for steak, catch the hotel shuttle to the bottom of the hill, where the 320-year-old **Waterlot Inn** (☎*441/238–8000*) sits on the edge of the marina. It's unassuming from the outside, but inside it's all elegance, romance, and comfort, with beamed ceilings and windows overlooking the water and terrific sunsets. The Angus steaks here are among the best on the island and the seafood is

Golf Courses

ATLANTIC OCEAN

WEST END

St. George's Golf Club

Fort St. Catherine

Town of St. George

St. George's Island

St. David's Lighthouse

St. David's Island

Mullet Bay

Ferry Rd.

Kindley Field Rd.

Bermuda Airport

Castle Harbour

St. George's Harbour

St. George's Rd.

Harrington Sound Rd.

The Causeway

Crystal Caves

Leamington Caves

Tucker's Point Golf Club

Tucker's Town

Mid Ocean Club

Coney Island

Sea Gardens

Crow Hill North

Harrington Sound

Flatts Village

HAMILTON

SMITH'S

South Shore Rd.

Ocean View Golf Course

North Shore Rd.

DEVONSHIRE

PEMBROKE

Front St.

Hamilton

Hamilton Harbour

PAGET

Middle Rd.

Spanish Pt.

Clarence Cove

Spanish Point

Cobbler's Island

Hawkins Island

South Shore Rd.

Belmont Hills Golf Club

Horizons & Cottages Golf Course

WARWICK

Harbour Rd.

Riddell's Bay Golf & Country Club

Fairmont Southampton Golf Club

Little Sound

Middle Rd.

Great Sound

Ireland Island N.

Ireland Island Rd.

Ireland Island S.

Watford Bridge

Boaz Island

Mangrove Rd.

Watford Is.

SANDYS

Somerset Village

Somerset Rd.

Somerset Bridge

Spring Benny's Bay

Port Royal Golf Course

Bermuda Golf Academy

West Whale Bay

SOUTHAMPTON

Gibbs Hill Lighthouse

Church Bay

Sea Gardens

2 miles

3 km

KEY

┼──┼ Railway Trail

delectable, too. Try the seared scallop appetizer and the surf and turf. Both restaurants are open evenings only, from 6 to 10. ⊠*Fairmont Southampton, South Rd., Southampton Parish* ☎*441/239–6952* ⊕*www.fairmont.com/Southampton* ✉*Greens fees $79 with mandatory cart, $39 sunset walking. Pull-cart rental $7.50. Shoe rentals $10. Titleist-club rentals $25. Lessons $40 a half hour, $80 per hour.*

DID YOU KNOW?

Golf was introduced to Bermuda in the late 1800s, when British Army officers were stationed on the island. At the turn of the century there were two courses on the island, neither of which exists today.

HORIZONS & COTTAGES GOLF COURSE
☺ *9 holes. 756 yards. Par 27. Rating: none.*

On the grounds of the Horizons & Cottages colony, this "mashie" (irons only) course is a fun place to practice your short game or expose your kids to play on a nicely maintained quick course. Do keep up the pace of play, though, so as not to disturb those following you. Golf carts are not available—understandably, since the longest hole (4th) is just 122 yards and the shortest (7th) a mere 51. Hit a hole in one and your name will be added to the plaque in the Pub Bar, which, dating to 1710, is the oldest part of the main building.

Highlight Hole: The 8th green is the highest point on the property, with great views of the well-tended resort and the south shore. But don't be too distracted. The upcoming 9th hole is very tight.

Clubhouse: There's no clubhouse, but on the floor above the Pub Bar is a nameless delightful Relais & Chateau restaurant (☎*441/236–0048*). Enjoy a full English or Continental breakfast here 7:30 to 10 AM. Lunch is served on the Pool Terrace, Ocean Terrace, or main dining room from 12:30 to 3 PM, and dinner is from 7 to 9 on the Ocean Terrace, Barbeque Terrace, or in the Middleton Room. Fresh Bermudian fish is, of course, a highlight of the extensive menu, which also includes beef, duck, lamb, and lobster. ⊠*33 South Rd., Paget Parish* ☎*441/236–0048* ⊕*www.horizonscottages.com* ✉*Greens fees: $25 weekdays, $30 weekends. Club rentals $5. Lessons $35 a half hour, $60 per hour.*

MID OCEAN CLUB
★ *18 holes. 6,548 yards. Par 71. Rating: blue tees, 72.8; white tees, 70.7; red tees, 74.6.*

The elite Mid Ocean Club is a 1921 Charles Blair Macdonald design revamped in 1953 by Robert Trent Jones Sr. *Golf Digest* ranked it 45th in the top 50 courses outside the United States. Patrons include celebrities and politicians such as Michael Douglas and Catherine Zeta-Jones, New York City Mayor Michael Bloomberg, and Michael Jordan. Presidents Eisenhower, Bush Sr., and Clinton have also played here. The club has a genteel air, and a great sense of history. Even though it's expensive, you must play it at least once, walking it with a caddy to savor the traditional golf experience and the scenery.

There are many holes near ocean cliffs, but you'll want to linger on the back tee of the last hole, where the view up the coast is spectacular. You'll come away with memories of the course's many elevation changes and tight doglegs. One in particular is the 5th hole, Cape, where Babe Ruth is said to have splashed a dozen balls in Mangrove Lake as he tried to land too far down the fairway on the other side. Because Mid Ocean is the second-longest course on the island, the average woman player may have trouble reaching greens in regulation—and some men, too, especially when the wind is up.

If you haven't been here since 2006, you'll find the layout is now irrigated and the TifEagle greens are truer and faster than ever. Many trees were pruned or removed to increase airflow and encourage grass growth. This all happened in 2007 in preparation for the televised PGA Grand Slam, which the club hosted that October, and will host again in 2008. The tournament was held for years in Hawaii, so this was a coup for Mid Ocean and Bermuda.

Highlight Hole: The 433-yard 5th is a par-4 dogleg around Mangrove Lake. The elevated tees sit atop a hillside of flowering shrubbery, with the lake below. It's tempting to take a big shortcut over the water, but remember the Babe's experience. To the left of the green, a steep embankment funnels balls down into a bunker, setting up a delicate sand shot to the putting surface.

Clubhouse: Overlooking the 18th hole and the south shore, the Mid Ocean's peach-and-white clubhouse is classically Bermudian down to the interior cedar trim. You'll get a logo towel for your hefty greens fees, and there are other goodies available in the pro shop. Several of the club's rooms commemorate famous American and British 20th-century politicians who played the course—there's the Churchill Bar, the Eisenhower Dining Room, and the MacMillan Television Room. The latter two are for members only, but you can have a drink in the bar and choose from an international menu in the

Eden Room (☎ *441/293–0330*), which is open to nonmembers for breakfast and lunch on Monday, Wednesday, and Friday. The menu includes a wide selection of salads, soups, and sandwiches. ✉ *Mid Ocean Dr., off S. Shore Rd., Tucker's Town* ☎ *441/293–0330* ⊕ *www. themidoceanclubbermuda.com* ✉ *Greens fees $210 ($70 when playing with a member). Nonmembers must be sponsored by a club member (your hotelier can arrange this); nonmember starting times available Mon., Wed., and Fri. until noon, except holidays. After noon, every second tee time is available to nonmembers. Caddies $30 per bag, single, or $35 per bag, double (tip not included). Cart rental $25 per*

PINK BUNKERS

There is no lack of sand in Bermuda, and you'll find a fair share of it in the bunkers. The texture is fine and soft, with pulverized pieces of pink shell just as you'll find on the island's famous pink beaches.

person. Shoe rentals $6. Club rentals $40. Lessons $40 a half hour, $80 per hour.

OCEAN VIEW GOLF COURSE
9 holes. 2,940 yards. Par 35. Rating: 68 playing white then blue tees, 68.7 playing yellow then red tees.

If you want to play with locals or just mingle to talk golf, Ocean View is the place to be after the workday ends. Only 10 minutes from Hamilton, it's very popular. Switch tees on your second loop of the 9 holes for an 18-hole round

GOLF TOURNAMENTS

The Bermuda Golf Association stages a variety of tournaments beginning in March each year. Overseas entrants are actively encouraged, with the Goodwill Tournament in December being the main competition for overseas golfers. For more information contact the **Bermuda Golf Association** (☎ *441/295–9972* ⊕ *www. bermudagolf.org*).

playing 5,658 yards to a par of 70. The first hole is a tough par 5 with a long, tight fairway flanked by a coral wall on one side and a drop-off to the shore on the other. The course is aptly named; there are panoramas from many holes as well as from the clubhouse and the restaurant patio. The club has a 260-yard driving range where the wind is often at your back, giving you a pleasant feeling that your drives are longer than they really are.

Highlight Hole: The green on the 192-yard, par-3 9th hole is cut into a coral hillside that's landscaped with colorful plants. It's a demanding shot when the wind is gusting from the north or west.

Clubhouse: Inside Ocean View's modest clubhouse is the **Out of Bounds Restaurant and Bar** (☎ *441/295–9093*) overlooking the north shore. Open for breakfast and lunch, the small dining room has a menu with the usual burgers, sandwiches, and salads, as well as Bermudian favorites such as fish chowder and fish-cake sandwiches. ⊠*2 Barker's Hill, off N. Shore Rd., Devonshire Parish* ☎*441/295–9092* ⊕*www.ocean-view.bm* ▭*Greens fee (18 holes) $85 with cart, $60 walking before 3 PM, $60 sunset with cart or walking. Club rentals $25. Lessons $50 for half hour.*

PORT ROYAL GOLF COURSE
★ *18 holes. 6,561 yards. Par 71. Rating: blue tees, 72.6; white tees, 70.1; red tees, 73.7.*

You've probably heard about it and seen pictures of the 16th hole at Port Royal, arguably Bermuda's best-known golf hole. The green of the 176-yard par 3 occupies a treeless promontory with a backdrop of the blue waters and pink sands of Whale Bay. When the wind is blowing hard onshore, as it frequently does, this can be a tough green to reach. The holes leading up to the 16th are the icing on the cake, with ocean views on 7, 8, 9, and 15. One of three government-owned courses (Ocean View and St. George's are the others), Port Royal is a perennial favorite of locals and visitors. The 1970 Robert Trent Jones Sr. layout has many elevated tees and greens and some clever doglegs. There are plenty of hills, on the back nine in particular.

Highlight Hole: Like the much-photographed 16th hole, the 387-yard, par-4 15th skirts the windswept cliffs along Whale Bay. The well-preserved remains of the Whale Bay Battery, a 19th-century fortification, stand next to the fairway.

Clubhouse: With its coral walls and white roof and shutters, the Port Royal clubhouse has all the charm of a traditional Bermudian house. Open for breakfast and lunch (until 5 PM) is the **Eagle View Restaurant & Bar** (☎441/234–5078). Bermuda cedar beams run the length of the dining room, and there's a patio that overlooks the 9th and 18th greens and the sea beyond. Fresh Bermuda fish, burgers, peas and rice, and pasta are always on the menu. The bar, open from 11 AM to 8 PM Monday through Thursday, and later on weekends, usually tuned to sports events. ⊠ *Off Middle Rd., Southampton Parish* ☎*441/234–0974, 441/234–4653 for automated tee-time reservations* ⊕*www.portroyalgolf.bm* ✉*Greens fees: $140 including cart and practice balls. Sunset rates are $85 with cart, $70 walking in summer (Apr.–Oct.); and $65 with cart, $50 walking in winter (Nov.–Mar.). Pull cart rentals $10. Shoe rentals $15. Club rentals $37. Lessons $50 for half hour.*

RIDDELL'S BAY GOLF & COUNTRY CLUB
18 holes. 5,854 yards. Par 70 (72 for women). Rating: blue tees, 68.5; white tees, 66.9.

Opened in 1921, Riddell's Bay is Bermuda's oldest course and one of the island's "must plays" for its scenery and precise shot-placing demands. Designed by Devereaux Emmett, who went on to plot the Congressional Golf Club near Washington, D.C., it receives periodic fine-tuning and upgrading at the hands of Ed Beidel. Don't let the 5,800-yard length fool you; this tight layout is cleverly woven into a peninsula that is only 600 yards wide in some places. The first hole, a 424-yard par 4 (par 5 for women) doglegs to an elevated green, serving notice of difficulty to come. Positioned between Riddell's Bay and the Great Sound, and with Popplewell's Pond in the interior, the course has water views and a fair number of water encounters. For instance, the sea lies all along the right side of dogleg on hole 8, and the 9th demands a drive across an inlet. The 10th tee box perches above a beautiful inlet where boats are moored.

Highlight Hole: The 8th hole, a 360-yard par 4, doglegs along the water to a green near the brink. With a tailwind, big hitters often go for the green. The Gibbs Hill Lighthouse is a distant backdrop.

Clubhouse: The Riddell's Bay clubhouse, a 150-year-old farmhouse refurbished in 1998, has locker rooms, a well-stocked pro shop, a bar made of Bermuda cedar, a lounge overlooking the 18th green and 1st tee, and the **Riddell's Bay dining room** (☎441/238–1060 Ext. 112), open for breakfast and lunch. On the menu are salads (including a nice smoked salmon and goat cheese plate), sandwiches (the Riddell's Bay Fishcake is a signature dish), burgers and, of course, a fine fish chowder. The dining room is open 10 AM to 3 PM weekdays and 8 AM to 4 PM weekends. ⊠*Riddell's Bay Rd., Warwick Parish* ☎*441/238–1060*

6

From Tee Time to Bed Time

If you stay in a hotel with its own golf course or one that has agreements with some of the golf clubs, it cuts out much of the planning you'll have to make on your own. For instance, the Fairmont Southampton Princess has its own 18-hole executive course and access agreement with Riddell's Bay Golf & Country Club. Tee times are blocked for hotel guests and a shuttle is provided to and from the hotel.

At the Tuckers Point Club, which has a new hotel and spa opening at the end of 2008, you can contrast the old and the new in golf course designs without straying very far from the resort. On-site is Roger Rulewich's fabulous design, laid down atop the old Castle Harbour Golf Club, designed by his mentor, Robert Trent Jones Sr. Literally next door is the classic Mid Ocean Club, a Charles Blair Macdonald track redesigned by Jones in 1953. You will have seen Mid Ocean on television

during the 2007 PGA Grand Slam, and you'll be anxious to try your luck.

Then there's Cambridge Beaches, the island's oldest cottage colony, which occupies 25 acres on a promontory at the island's western end. Last year the hotel launched a Fairway to Heaven package that includes three rounds of golf at any of the island's courses, a golf massage, dinner on a private island and other extras. If you're staying at the Horizons & Cottages colony (see lodging listing page), a Relais & Chateaux property, you can sharpen your short game on the property's mashie course in preparation for playing one of the major tracks.

When you make your lodging arrangements, check to see what golf packages and perks are available. Many hoteliers are also members at the clubs and are happy to facilitate arrangements.

⊕*www.riddellsbay.com* ☒*Greens fees $145, including mandatory cart. Shoe rentals $15. Club rentals $40. Lessons $50 for half hour, $90 for hour.*

ST. GEORGE'S GOLF CLUB
18 holes. 4,043 yards. Par 62. Rating: blue tees, 62.8; white tees, 61.4; red tees, 62.8.

What a delight this short but daunting course is. The Robert Trent Jones Sr. creation dominates a secluded headland at the island's north-eastern end, with views of the Atlantic on every hole. It's the only course in Bermuda with greens turfed in seashore paspalum, a fine-bladed grass that thrives on saltwater. It putts faster and truer than Bermuda, but the breaks are not as pronounced. In early 2007, the bunkers were refurbished. Wind—especially from the north—sweeps and swirls over these short holes with their small, aggressively bunkered greens, confounding club selection. St. George's has light traffic midweek, so if you play then you'll be able to pause to enjoy the views.

Highlight Hole: The 9th hole is aptly named "Salt Spray." A par 3 playing 143 yards from the back tees and 106 yards from the forward tees, it's right on the ocean, so any ball to the left ends up in the Atlantic.

Clubhouse: Overlooking the 18th hole is the clubhouse, with locker rooms, pro shop, and **Mulligan's Restaurant** (☎441/297–1836). The cozy dining room-bar and patio, which are tended by a friendly and efficient staff, have a fine view of the north shore and the ramparts of Fort St. Catherine. Breakfast and lunch are served daily 8 AM to 4 PM, and dinner after 6 PM on Friday. The menu includes sandwiches and salads as well as many local favorites such as fish-and-chips, grilled fresh fish, steaks, the award-winning Alfred's Fish Chowder, and St. David's fish cake (a codfish-and-mashed-potato concoction flavored with parsley and thyme). ✉1 Park Rd., St. George's Parish ☎441/297–8353 pro shop, 441/234–4653 tee times ⊕www. stgeorgesgolf.bm ☜Greens fees $90 including cart, sunset $70 including cart. The same fees apply to walking, which is not allowed on weekends and holidays until after 3 PM. Shoe rental $15. Club rentals $35. Lessons $50 half hour.

> **BIRDIES**
>
> If you see yellow-crowned night herons on the fairways, tip your hat to the greenskeepers' best friends. The natural shellfish predators have a taste for the land crabs that once dug countless little craters in fairways and greens. Up until the mid-1970s, the crabs were controlled by pesticides that also had a dire effect on the bird population. Then Dr. David Wingate, president of the Bermuda Audubon Society, came to the rescue by importing several pairs of herons. They flourished, as have the bluebirds, who do their part by eating insects. All courses provide bluebird nesting boxes along the fairways.

6

Fodor$Choice ★
TUCKER'S POINT GOLF CLUB
18 holes. 6,361 yards. Par 70. Rating: blue tees, 71.5; white tees, 68.9; red tees, 68.5.

If you remember the old Castle Harbour Golf Club, you'll recognize some of the views, but not the holes. Roger Rulewich, a former senior designer for the late Robert Trent Jones Sr., mapped out a stunning site layout in 2002, making the most of elevation changes and ocean views. It's longer than nearby Mid Ocean, and holds more surprises. On many holes, you tee off toward the crest of a hill, not knowing what lies beyond. Topping the rise reveals the challenge, often involving a very elevated, sculpted green with a scenic vista. The course is fully irrigated and beautifully groomed. The final resort components—the Harbour Court Waterfront Villas and the 88-room Tucker's Point Hotel & Spa—are scheduled to open in fall 2008 and spring 2009, respectively.

Highlight Holes: There are many outstanding holes, but the par-4 17th is one of the most picturesque in Bermuda, with sweeping views of Tucker's Town and Castle Island. A rival is hole 13, where the perspective is the north coast and the Royal Navy Dockyard 20 mi away on the island's western tip.

Clubhouse: The 20,000-square-foot Tucker's Point Golf Clubhouse, a traditional Bermudian British–colonial design with covered verandas and tray ceilings, stands on a hilltop with a commanding view. Within are posh locker rooms, a large pro shop, and superb dining. You can relax with a cocktail or dine alfresco on the second-floor veranda while enjoying a panorama of Castle Harbour and Tucker's Town. **The Grill** (☎441/298–6983) an elegant yet comfortable dining area, has an extensive menu that

TAXI TO TEE

If you bring your own clubs, budget for taxis to get you to the various courses. It's dangerous to carry your golf bag on a scooter and clubs are not allowed on public buses. Taxis are expensive, but most rides are relatively short.

includes sublime fish chowder, lamb, salmon, and tuna tartare, as well as catch-of-the-day and omelet specials. Breakfast is served on weekends, lunch every day, and dinner Tuesday through Saturday in winter. In summer dinner is served at the Beach Club. ⊠*9 Paynters Rd., St. George's Parish* ☎*441/298–6970* ⊕*www.tuckerspoint.com* ⛳*Greens fees $224 with cart, $119 with cart for members' guests. Shoe rentals, $10. Club rentals $45. Lessons $55 for half hour, $90 for hour.*

Shopping

WORD OF MOUTH

"My favorite inexpensive souvenirs are cedar Christmas ornaments from the Bermuda Crafts Market in Dockyards, linen tea towels with Bermudian flowers, cottages, or birds from the Irish Linen Shop, and cute hand-painted pieces from the Island House. The Bermuda perfumery is great, too."

—cmcfong

"You won't find Versace, Tiffany, and Gucci here, but you will find some of the most exquisite inlaid coral, mother-of-pearl and tanzanite jewelry for modest prices, as well as great shopping for Burberry, Mason Pearson, and other fine British goods."

—katalina_g

By Suzy
Buckley

IF YOU'RE ACCUSTOMED TO SHOPPING in Neiman Marcus, Saks Fifth Avenue, and Bergdorf Goodman, the prices in Bermuda's elegant shops won't come as a surprise. Designer clothing and accessories, from MaxMara to Louis Vuitton, tend to be sold at prices comparable to those in the United States, but without the sales tax. Crystal, china, watches, and jewelry are often less expensive here and sometimes even on par with American outlet-store prices. Perfume and cosmetics are often sold at discount prices, and there are bargains to be had on woolens and cashmeres in early spring, when stores' winter stocks must go. The island's unforgiving humidity and lack of storage space means sales are frequent and really meant to sweep stock off the shelves.

> **TOP 5 SHOPPING**
>
> ■ Grab a fruit smoothie at Rock On for pre-shopping energy.
>
> ■ Ask the salesperson at Lusso to point out which Fendi handbags are on sale.
>
> ■ No need to buy a "Bermuda" sweatshirt that screams "tourist" when you can beat chills with a crocheted cardigan from Stefanel.
>
> ■ Gift-getting at Dockyard Glassworks and the Bermuda Rum Company: their traditional black rum cakes are to die for.
>
> ■ Buy a beautiful coffee-table book from Trustworthy Gift Shop and help the Bermuda National Trust.

Art galleries in Bermuda attract serious shoppers and collectors. The island's thriving population of artists and artisans—many of whom are internationally recognized—produces well-reputed work, from paintings, photographs, and sculpture to miniature furniture, hand-blown glass, and dolls. During your gallery visits, look for Bruce Stuart's abstract paintings, Graeme Outerbridge's vivid photographs of Bermudian architecture and scenery, and Chelsey Trott's slim wood and bronze sculptures.

Bermuda-made specialty comestibles include rum and rum-based liqueurs, and delicious local honey, which you can find in most grocery stores. Condiments from Outerbridge Peppers Ltd. add zip to soups, stews, drinks, and chowders. The original line has expanded to include Bloody Mary mix, pepper jellies, and barbecue sauce.

The duty-free shop at the airport sells liquor, perfume, cigarettes, rum cakes, and other items. You can also order duty-free spirits at some of the liquor stores in town, and the management will make arrangements to deliver your purchase to your hotel or cruise ship. If you choose to shop in town rather than at the airport, it's best to buy liquor at least 24 hours before your departure, or by 9:30 on the day of an afternoon departure, in order to allow enough time for delivery. With liquor, it pays to shop around, because prices vary. Grocery stores usually charge more than liquor stores. U.S. citizens age 21 and older who have been out of the country for 48 hours are allowed to bring home 1 liter of duty-free liquor.

SHOPPING DISTRICTS

Hamilton has the greatest concentration of shops in Bermuda, and Front Street is its pièce de résistance. Lined with small, pastel-color buildings, this most fashionable of Bermuda's streets houses sedate department stores and snazzy boutiques, with several small arcades and shopping alleys leading off it. A smart canopy shades the entrance to the 55 Front Street Group, which houses Crisson's. Modern Butterfield Place has galleries and boutiques selling, among other things, Louis Vuitton leather goods. The Emporium, a renovated building with an atrium, has a range of shops, from antiques to souvenirs.

St. George's Water Street, Duke of York Street, Hunters Wharf, Penno's Wharf, and Somers Wharf are the sites of numerous renovated buildings that house branches of Front Street stores, as well as artisans' studios. Historic King's Square offers little more than a couple of T-shirt and souvenir shops.

In the West End, Somerset Village has a few shops, but they hardly merit a special shopping trip. However, the Clocktower Mall, in a historic building at the Royal Naval Dockyard, has a few more shopping opportunities, including branches of Front Street shops and specialty boutiques. The Dockyard is also home to the Craft Market, the Bermuda Arts Centre, and Bermuda Clayworks.

DEPARTMENT STORES

Both A. S. Cooper & Sons and Gibbons Co. are coming into their own right with the closure of venerable department stores Trimingham's and H. A. & E. Smith's. Gibbons Co. also opened branches of MAC Cosmetics on Front Street and Nine West next to its main department store. A. S. Cooper & Sons has a great selection of Bermuda items in its brand new Front Street building, but many of the store's departments will stay in satellite locations on Front, Reid, and Church streets. Most of the sales staff at these department stores have worked here for two or three decades. They tend to be unobtrusive, but polite and helpful when you need them. Department stores advertise planned sales or discount days in the local newspaper.

A. S. Cooper & Sons. With branches in all major hotels, Cooper & Sons is best known for its extensive inventory of crystal and china, with pieces and sets by Waterford, Swarovski, Wedgwood, Royal Doulton, Lladro, and Villeroy & Boch, many sold at 15% to 20% less than U.S. prices. The store also carries tasteful Bermudian souvenirs in the Fine Jewelry & Gifts department on the lower level. In 2007, Cooper & Sons debuted a Cosmetics & Fragrances department in its new Front Street store. The main store also carries its private-label clothing collection for women and a ladies sportswear department, which carries Calvin Klein, Ralph Lauren, and other popular brands. The men's line can be found at the well-stocked A. S. Cooper Man store, just down the street. ⊠*59 Front St., Hamilton* ☎*441/295–3961* ⊕*www.coopersbermuda. com* ⊠*Clocktower Centre, Dockyard* ⊠*22 Water St., St. George's.*

KNOW-HOW

Clothing, china, and jewelry in Bermuda are sold at prices similar to those abroad, but since there's no sales tax, you can get good deals, especially on high-end goods. If you see something you like, go ahead and buy it—comparison shopping isn't fruitful on Bermuda, as prices are typically fixed island-wide. In all but a few stores, shoppers leaving the fitting rooms are expected to return unwanted items to the store floor. The island's bounty of craft markets and artists' studios offers a multitude of inexpensive souvenirs, from Bermuda honey to hand-painted pillows. Buyers and sellers don't really bargain, although a vendor may offer a discount if you buy something in bulk.

BUSINESS HOURS

Shops are generally open Monday to Saturday from 9 to 5 and closed on Sunday, although some supermarkets are open from 1 to 5 on Sunday. From April to October, some of the smaller Front Street shops stay open late and on Sunday. The shops in the Clocktower Mall at the Royal Naval Dockyard are usually open from Monday to Saturday 9:30 to 6 (11 to 5 in winter) and Sunday 11 to 5. Some extend their hours around Christmas. Almost all stores close for public holidays. Many of Bermuda's more exclusive shops have branches in the larger resort hotels.

KEY DESTINATIONS

Department stores such as A. S. Coopers & Sons and Gibbons Co. are excellent one-stop shopping destinations, but you may have more fun exploring the boutiques on Front Street, as well as Reid Street and streets branching off it. For crafts, head to the Royal Naval Dockyard, where you can find artisans' studios and a permanent craft market. The town of St. George's has a bit of everything, including lots of small, unique boutiques, where you can find the perfect island outfit or a Bermuda-cedar model of a famous ship.

SMART SOUVENIRS

Small cakes from the Bermuda Rum Cake Company in the Dockyard make popular gifts and cost $9 duty free. Men may want to pick up a pair of real Bermuda shorts, which come in an array of bright colors, such as hot pink or royal blue. They sell for about $30 in department stores. The Outerbridge line of sherry peppers and other sauces is available at grocery stores and souvenir shops. Locals use them to flavor fish chowder, among other dishes. A Bermudian cookbook makes a good accompaniment. An original photograph or painting is a meaningful, if expensive, souvenir. A coffee-table book of Bermudian art is another option.

WATCH OUT

It's illegal to take shipwreck artifacts out of the country without a special permit. Likewise, visitors who want to export a Bermuda cedar carving or item of furniture that's more than 50 years old must apply for a permit at **Bermuda Customs** (⊠ *40 Front St., Hamilton* ☎ *441/295–4816*). A few stores in Bermuda sell Cuban cigars, but you may not bring them back to the United States.

A. S. Cooper Children's. This kids' clothing shop has everything you'll need to dress your little one. From shorts and shirts in summer to long pants and jackets for Bermuda's rainy winter, it's all here. ⊠*27 Front St., Hamilton* ☎*441/295–3961.*

A. S. Cooper Express. Flirty, bright clothes for junior girls in the know, from DKNY jeans and T-shirts to a great selection by Guess? are stocked in this airy store. A full wall of accessories in a rainbow of colors is one of the many highlights here. ⊠*Washington Mall, Reid St., Hamilton* ☎*441/296–6525.*

A. S. Cooper Home. If a housewarming present is what you're looking for, this is the perfect place. Candles, decorative home gifts, and flowers fill this shop, alongside bedding and home accessories by Lladro and Villeroy & Boch. ⊠*26 Church St., Hamilton* ☎*441/295–2615.*

FodorśChoice
★ **A. S. Cooper Man.** This division of the classy department store is first-rate, with a staff that's reserved and courteous, but very helpful when needed. The store is the exclusive Bermuda supplier of Polo Ralph Lauren. ⊠*29 Front St., Hamilton* ☎*441/295–3961 Ext. 201.*

Harbourside. A. S. Cooper's ready-to-wear shop stocks women's clothing, including plus sizes, accessories, and its own line of fragrances. Bermuda shell pieces and other locally made gifts can also be found at this location. ⊠*Pier 6, Front St., Hamilton* ☎*441/296–1675.*

Gibbons Co. One of Bermuda's oldest retailers (still run by the Gibbons family) is a fairly casual department store that stocks a wide range of men's, women's, and children's clothing, with brands such as Calvin Klein and DKNY. There's a substantial lingerie section, as well as quality handbags, purses, scarves, and Monet fashion jewelry. Gibbons also has a sizable household department and is the exclusive supplier of Denby tableware, which sells at a much lower price than in Canada or the United States. The on-site Peniston Brown perfume shop stocks many French, Italian, and American lines. But most notable are the company's two intimate boutiques next door, housing Nine West and Twenty 5 Reid boutique. ⊠*21 Reid St., Hamilton* ☎*441/295–0022.*

Marks & Spencer. A franchise of the large British chain, Marks and Sparks (as it's called by everyone in Bermuda and England) is usually filled with locals attracted by its moderate prices for men's, women's, and children's clothing. Summer wear, including swimsuits, cotton jerseys, and polo shirts, is a good buy, as is underwear. The chain's signature line of food and treats, plus wine from all over the world, is at the back of the store. On the upper level you'll find a comprehensive selection of the Levi's and Dockers clothing lines. ⊠*18 Reid St., Hamilton* ☎*441/295–0031.*

7

SPECIALTY STORES

ANTIQUES

The Bermuda Railway Museum. An extensive collection of historical arti-facts from Bermuda's short-lived railway is housed here. The museum shop sells photos, maps, books, prints, antiques, jewelry, coins, stamps, and china. If you take the bus here, get off at the first stop after the Bermuda Aquarium. The shop is open Tuesday to Friday from 10 to 4 or by appointment with Rose Hollis. ⊠ *37 N. Shore Rd., Hamilton Parish* ☎ *441/293–1774.*

Thistle Gallery. Antique British furniture, porcelain, china, glassware, and silver are laid out for sale in this large cottage store. ⊠ *7 Park Rd., Hamilton* ☎ *441/292–3839.*

ART GALLERIES

Art House Gallery. Watercolors, oils, and color lithographs by Bermu-dian artist Joan Forbes are displayed in this gallery. It's open Monday, Wednesday, and Friday from 10 to 4 or by appointment. ⊠ *80 S. Shore Rd., Paget Parish* ☎ *441/236–6746.*

Fodor$Choice **Bermuda Arts Centre at Dockyard.** Sleek and modern, with well-designed
★ displays of local art, this gallery is housed in one of the stone build-ings of the former Royal Naval Dockyard. The walls are adorned with paintings and photographs, and glass display cases contain exquisitely crafted quilts as well as costume dolls, jewelry, and wood sculpture. Exhibits change frequently. Several artists' studios inside the gallery are open to the public. The center is open daily from 10 to 5. ⊠ *Museum Row, Dockyard* ☎ *441/234–2809.*

Bermuda Memories. Artist Jill Amos Raine displays her watercolors depicting Bermuda's houses, scenery, and wharfs in this small studio on the town square. ⊠ *7 King's Sq., St. George's* ☎ *441/297–8104.*

★ **Bermuda Society of the Arts.** Many highly creative society members sell their work at the perennial members' shows and during a revolving series of special group exhibits. You can find watercolor, oil, and acrylic paintings, and pastel and charcoal drawings, as well as occasional pho-tographs, collages, and sculptures. ⊠ *17 Church St., 3rd fl. West Wing, City Hall, Hamilton* ☎ *441/292–3824* ⊕ *www.bsoa.bm.*

Birdsey Studio. Renowned artist Alfred Birdsey died in 1996, but thanks to his daughter, Jo Birdsey Linberg, the studio remains open and the tradition continues. Watercolors cost from $80 and oils from $350 to $900. Birdsey's paintings are also available on note cards. The studio is usually open weekdays 10:30 to 1, but call before you visit to be sure. ⊠ *Rosecote, 5 Stowe Hill, Paget Parish* ☎ *441/236–6658.*

Carole Holding Print & Craft Shops. Commercial artist Carole Holding mass-produces watercolors of Bermuda's scenes and flowers; many of the same images are sold as signed prints and limited editions. Crafts by local artists are also available. Prices range from $15 for small prints to more than $3,000 for framed original watercolors. The art-ist's prints can also be found on clothing, including shirts and aprons.

✉ *King's Sq., St. George's* ☎*441/297–1373* ✉*Fairmont Southampton* ☎*441/238–7310* ✉*81 Front St., Hamilton* ☎*441/296–3431 or 800/880–8570.*

Kafu Hair Salon and Gallery. Proving that art can happen anywhere, artist and hairdresser Glen Wilks displays contemporary work, including paintings and sculpture, by local avant-garde artists at his salon. ✉*8 Parliament St., near Victoria, Hamilton* ☎*441/295–5238* ⊕*www. kafu.bm.*

Masterworks Foundation Gallery. The foundation, formed in 1987, exhibits art by well-known Canadian, British, French, and American artists, including Georgia O'Keeffe and Winslow Homer, who produced work inspired by Bermuda. The Bermudiana Collection contains more than 400 works in watercolor, oil, pencil, charcoal, and other media. The Bermuda National Gallery locations at City Hall, Camden House, Government House, and Waterloo House all display pieces from this collection. ✉*97 Front St., Hamilton* ✉*Botanical Gardens, 183 South Rd., Devonshire* ☎*441/236–2950* ⊕*www.bermudamasterworks.com.*

Omax Ceramics Studio. Christine Wellman shows her pastel ceramic tiles, mugs, vases, and crockery at her home studio in Southampton. An appointment is required. She may even agree to pick you up and take you on a tour to the vendors who sell her pieces. ✉*Southampton Parish* ☎*441/292–8478.*

Otto Trott Art Studio. Trott is known for his beautiful oil paintings of landscapes and local characters. His work can be found at other galleries, but often his best pictures are here. Small watercolors are priced at $50, oils from about $300 to $5,000. Mr. Trott also gives painting lessons. ✉*151 North Shore Rd., Crawl Hill, Hamilton Parish* ☎*441/293–1050.*

Picturesque. If you like photography, check out Roland Skinner's two shops. His shots of Bermuda beach scenes and wildlife sell at $95 to $800. ✉*129 Front St. E, Hamilton* ☎*441/292–1452* ✉*Clocktower Mall, Dockyard* ☎*441/234–3342.*

X-Clue-Sive Creations. Pick up Doris Wade's hand-painted pottery here or indulge your creative side and create your own Bermuda souvenirs. Choose from 100 bare shapes and paint to your heart's content. The studio will glaze and fire the piece in four to seven days. ✉*86 Reid St., Hamilton* ☎*441/296–1676.*

BEAUTY & PERFUME

Bermuda Perfumery. This popular destination has downsized but still remains an interesting, must-see spot. Free, regularly scheduled guided tours of the old St. George's building now housing the factory include an exhibit on the distillation of flowers into perfume and one about fragrance distribution and packaging. At the Lili Boutique gift shop you can purchase perfumes, including the factory's 11 fragrances, as well as imported soaps. ✉*Stewart Hall, 5 Queen St., St. George's* ☎*441/ 293–0627.*

The Body Shop. Pick up the fragrant skin, bath, and hair-care products you love so much at home at the Bermuda branch of this popular chain. ✉ *The Washington Mall, 7 Reid St., Hamilton* ☎ *441/292–5329.*

Peniston Brown Ltd.–The Perfume Shop. In addition to being the exclusive Bermuda agent for Guerlain products, Peniston Brown's boutique stocks an extensive selection of French, American, and Italian perfumes, as well as soaps, bath salts, and bubble bath. The main boutique on Front Street also stocks Guerlain's complete line of cosmetics and skin care. ✉ *23 W. Front St., Hamilton* ☎ *441/295–0570* ✉ *6 Water St., St. George's* ☎ *441/297–1525* ✉ *Gibbons Co. Perfume Department, 21 Reid St., Hamilton* ☎ *441/295–5535.*

Sunshine Co. Although this shop caters mostly to professionals, it's open to the public on weekdays. The fantastic selection of OPI nail polish sells at $5 a bottle. OPI lipstick, other nail-polish brands, manicure tools, blow-dryers, and curling irons are also available. ✉ *Dallas Bldg., 6 Park Rd., Hamilton* ☎ *441/295–6077.*

BOOKSTORES

Bermuda Book Store Ltd. Owner Hannah Willmott has expanded her bright little Hamilton bookstore to a location in the Clocktower Mall. The shops are stocked with best sellers, children's books, and special Bermuda titles (including some out-of-print books). ✉ *3 Queen St., Hamilton* ☎ *441/295–3698* ✉ *Clocktower Parade, Dockyard* ☎ *441/234–4065.*

The Book Cellar. In a small space underneath the Tucker House, this shop crams in a surprisingly large selection of books about Bermuda and an interesting assortment of novels in addition to contemporary best sellers. Coffee-table books and children's books are plentiful. Owner Jill White and her well-read staff will be happy to help you search for an obscure title. ✉ *5 Water St., St. George's* ☎ *441/297–0448.*

The Bookmart. The island's largest bookstore carries plenty of contemporary titles and classics, plus a complete selection of books on Bermuda. Paperbacks and children's books are in abundance, as well as every popular beauty, technology, and men's magazine you can think of. This is also the place to come for greeting cards, balloons, and little gift items. Don't forget to visit the Annex toy department on the lower level. ✉ *Brown & Company, 4 Reid St., Hamilton* ☎ *441/295–3838.*

Metaphysical Bookshop. This incense-scented store sells books on meditation, alternative medicine, numerology, and yoga. Owner Kelvin Richardson also offers a bountiful supply of wind chimes, cards, candles, and other gift items. ✉ *77 Reid St., Hamilton* ☎ *441/295–5683.*

CIGARS

House of Cigars: Chatham House. In business since 1895, this shop looks like an old-time country store. Thick, gray, lusty cigar smoke fills the air, and a life-size statue of a Native American princess greets you as you walk in. You can find top-quality cigars from the Dominican Republic, Jamaica, and Cuba (Romeo y Julieta, Bolivar, Partagas, Punch), Briar and Meerschaum pipes, Dunhill lighters, and Swiss Army knives.

Prices for handmade Cubans start at $5. ⊠*63 Front St., Hamilton* 🕾*441/292–8422.*

CLOTHING & ACCESSORIES

CHILDREN'S
CLOTHING

Family Clothing Shop. This tiny, inexpensive hideaway sells kids' clothes, sandals, and socks—perfect for stocking up on anything you left at home. ⊠*1 Water St., St. George's* 🕾*441/297–5517.*

IANA. Fine Italian clothing for girls and boys newborn to age 16 are sold here at prices matching the quality of goods. ⊠ *Walker Arcade, 12 Reid St., Hamilton* 🕾*441/292–0002.*

Pirate's Port Boys. Casual wear for boys is crowded into this small store and sold at very reasonable prices. **Pirate's Port Girls** has trendy, inexpensive clothes for toddlers to teens. ⊠*Washington Mall, Reid St., Hamilton* 🕾*441/292–1080.*

MEN'S
CLOTHING

David Winston. An upmarket spot owned by the island's English Sports Shop group, this handsome store carries European-designed men's clothing and accessories. Hugo Boss, Danish brand Matinique, and Profuomo are well represented, and it's a great spot to pick up mens' Italian shirts, ties, and belts. ⊠*2 Reid St., Hamilton* 🕾*441/295–4866.*

The Edge. You can find trendy, casual clothing for men at this nice shop, including brand names such as Quick Reflex and J. Lindeberg. ⊠*Washington Mall, Reid St., Hamilton* 🕾*441/295–4715.*

Flatts Mens Wear. Owner Mick Adderley runs the only shop on the island specializing in big-and-tall sizes for men. ⊠*13 N. Shore Rd., Flatts Village* 🕾*441/292–0360.*

The Sports Source. Popular with locals, the Sports Source offers men's and youth urban wear and hip-hop gear. The labels are trendy, but the prices are reasonable. ⊠*Washington Mall, Reid St., Hamilton* 🕾*441/292–9442.*

Taylor's. Although the main Archie Brown store in Hamilton is closed, Taylor's is still dedicated entirely to Scottish-made knits. You can also buy tartan by the yard, and mohair knits, skirts, and scarves. ⊠*30 Water St., St. George's* 🕾*441/297–1626* ⊠*49 Front St., Hamilton* 🕾*441/295–2672.*

MEN'S &
WOMEN'S
CLOTHING

Davison's of Bermuda. Davison's offers exactly what you would expect of an island clothing store—light, comfortable cotton shirts, pants, and shorts for adults and children. Sherry peppers, aprons, teddy bears, and a collection of stuffed trolls are among the gift items. There's a branch in the Fairmont Southampton, too. ⊠*93 Front St., Hamilton* 🕾*441/292–3826* ⊠*Water St., St. George's* 🕾*441/297–8363* ⊠*Clocktower Centre, Dockyard* 🕾*441/234–0959.*

English Sports Shop. This shop specializes in British knitwear. The store's own line of cotton sweaters is priced at $29.95, although cashmere sweaters start from $220. Upstairs is a good supply of men's business and formal wear, and children's clothes. Women's clothing and accessories are on the ground level. Another branch is in the Fairmont

CLOSE UP

Bermuda Shorts in the Office

You may have heard of Bermuda's peculiar business fashion, and you may even have seen pictures of businessmen in shorts and long socks, but nothing can quite prepare you for the first sighting. First-time visitors have been spotted sniggering in shop doorways after discovering the bottom half of a blazer-and-tie-clad executive on his cell phone. After all, where else in the world could he walk into a boardroom wearing bright-pink shorts without anyone batting an eyelid? Only in Bermuda. These unique, all-purpose garments, however flamboyantly dyed, are worn with complete seriousness and pride. Bermudians would go so far as to say it's the rest of the world that is peculiar, and they have a point—particularly in the steaming humidity of the summer months.

What is surprising is how the original khaki cutoffs evolved into formal attire. They were introduced to Bermuda in the early 1900s by the British military, who adopted the belted, baggy, cotton-twill version to survive the sweltering outposts of the Empire. By the 1920s Bermudian pragmatism and innovation were at play as locals started chopping off their trousers at the knees to stay cool. Tailors seized on the trend and started manufacturing a smarter pair of shorts, and men were soon discovering the benefits of a breeze around the knees.

But for an island that has a love affair with rules there was always going to be a right and a wrong way to wear this new uniform. Bermudas had to be worn with knee-high socks, and a jacket and tie were the only acceptable way of dressing them up for business. But it didn't stop there. Obsession with detail prevailed, fueled by gentlemen who were disturbed at the unseemly shortness of other men's shorts. A law was passed to ensure propriety, and the bizarre result was patrolling policemen, armed with tape measures and warning tickets, scouring the capital for men showing too much leg. Officially, shorts could be no more than 6 inches above the knee, while 2 to 4 was preferable.

Other rigid but unwritten rules made it unheard of to wear them in hotel dining rooms after 6 PM or in churches on Sunday morning, and even to this day they are out of bounds in the Supreme Court, although in 2000, legislation was changed to allow them to be worn, even by ministers, in the House of Assembly. Viewed as conservative and respectable menswear for almost any occasion, they can be seen paired with tuxedo jackets and are even acceptable (provided they are black) at funerals.

But if Bermuda shorts are practical, smart dress for men, where does that leave the island's women during the sticky summer months? Wearing brightly colored cotton dresses and skirts, it would seem. Shorts are not considered ideal business wear for women and are only really acceptable on the beach and while shopping (but again, not if they're skimpy). In a country where pink is a man's color and men's bare legs are all but mandatory for six months of the year, perhaps the men feel the need to stamp their masculine pride on their pants.

—Vivienne Sheath

Southampton. ⊠*49 Front St., Hamilton* ☎*441/295–2672* ⊠*Water St., St. George's* ☎*441/297–0142.*

French Connection. This chic, casual-wear shop carries trendy skirts, pants, tops, and accessories for day and night. ⊠*15 Reid St., Hamilton* ☎*441/295–2112 Ext. 113.*

Giorgio Beneti. This stylish boutique, opened in October of 2005, sells leather jackets, handbags, wallets, shoes, and belts imported from Argentina. ⊠*44 Reid St., Hamilton* ☎*441/296–8097.*

Makin Waves. Warm-weather sports clothing and swimsuits by Roxy and Quick Silver are sold at this beachy shop. There are also sunglasses, incense, shell jewelry, beach bags, flip-flops, and snorkeling and dive gear. ⊠*75 Front St., Hamilton* ☎*441/292–4609* ⊠*32 Water St., St. George's* ☎*441/297–0546* ⊠*Clocktower Mall, Dockyard* ☎*441/234–4319.*

Mambo. Need a slice of Italian chic? Stop by this tiny shop that stocks funky Italian labels such as Dolce & Gabbana, Miss Sixty, Diesel, Von Dutch, Page Premium Denim, and Just Cavalli. ⊠*Walker Arcade, 12 Reid St., Hamilton* ☎*441/296–9797.*

The Outlet. Reduced-price merchandise from the English Sports Shop, Aston & Gunn, Cecile, and Crown Colony, as well as some U.S. merchandise, are sold here for up to 75% off the usual prices. ⊠*30 Queen St., Hamilton* ☎*441/295–0084.*

Pier-Vu. Breezy beach clothes in natural fibers are the specialty at this small store. The flowing skirts, island shirts, and small, colorful tank tops are suitable for wearing on the beach or in town. Sunglasses are also for sale. ⊠*39 York St., St. George's* ☎*441/297–4299* ⊠*Clocktower Mall, Dockyard* ☎*441/234–6868.*

Sasch. Part of the six-store Stefanel group of boutiques, this store brings the very latest, hippest fashions in casual, business, and dress wear from Florence to Bermuda. The clothes are high quality, made of primarily natural fibers in neutral colors. Large men may have trouble finding a good fit—most sizes are for smaller frames, and some styles are body-hugging. There's also a small selection of trendy shoes and handbags. ⊠*12 Reid St., Hamilton* ☎*441/295–4391.*

27th Century Boutique. This is the perfect store to visit when in need of both casual and evening clothes for men and women. Khakis, polo shirts, and dress shirts predominate in the sizable men's section, and women can find sparkly tank tops and great-fitting black pants alongside office-appropriate blouses. Owner Sharon Bartram can help you assemble a perfect outfit—she has an excellent eye for style and detail. ⊠*92 Reid St., Hamilton* ☎*441/292–2628.*

WOMEN'S
CLOTHING **Benetton.** This branch of the international chain has a wide variety of casual, chic women's and children's clothing, in both brash, bright colors and more subdued tones. ⊠*24 Reid St., Hamilton* ☎*441/295–2112.*

Boutique C.C. This English Sports Shop–owned store sells quality formal and business wear for women of every age with a flair for fashion, but the selection of evening wear is the highlight of this beautifully renovated store. Look for reasonably priced cocktail dresses and classic suits along with stylish contemporary separates and trendy accessories. ⊠*1 Front St., Hamilton* ☎*441/295–3935.*

Fodor'sChoice **Calypso.** Bermuda's fashionable set comes to this boutique to spend
★ plenty of money on Italian leather shoes and sophisticated designer wear by Graham Kandiah. Calypso has the island's largest selection of swimwear, including Villegriquin. Pick up a straw hat and sunglasses to make the perfect beach ensemble. Eclectic novelty items from Europe make great gifts. Calypso's shop in Butterfield Place, **Voila!,** carries Longchamp handbags and Johnston & Murphy men's shoes. There are branches at the Coral Beach & Tennis Club, Fairmont Southampton, and Clocktower Mall at the Dockyard. ⊠*45 Front St., Hamilton* ☎*441/295–2112.*

★ **Cecile.** Specializing in upscale European designer fashions, Cecile carries such labels as Valentino Red, Tibi, Pucci, Louis Feraud of Paris, and the perennial resort-wear favorite, Lilly Pulitzer. There's a good selection of evening wear and swimwear, including swimsuits by Gottex. An accessories department carries shoes, scarves, jewelry, handbags, and belts. The boutique offers very favorable prices, often significantly lower than U.S. retail, on some of the world's foremost fashion names. ⊠*15 Front St., Hamilton* ☎*441/295–1311.*

Eve's Garden Lingerie. Silk and satin panties, boxers, brassieres, and nightgowns, in sizes small to full-figure, are tucked away in this discreet shop at the back of Butterfield Place. You can also find massage oils and an adult section. ⊠*Butterfield Pl., Hamilton* ☎*441/296–2671.*

Frangipani. Owned by A. S. Cooper, this little store sells colorful women's fashions with an island-resort look. Cotton, silk, and rayon leisure wear are the backbone of the stock. Frangipani also sells a collection of hand-strung, brightly colored, beaded necklaces, bracelets, and earrings. ⊠*16 Water St., St. George's* ☎*441/297–1357.*

Jazzy Boutique. Lots of spandex and jeans are sold at this trendy juniors' clothing store. Plastic purses, faux-gem jewelry, and other colorful accessories tempt preteens of every ilk. Fortunately, the prices are quite affordable. ⊠*Washington Mall, Reid St., Hamilton* ☎*441/295–9258.*

MaxMara. Prices for this Italian designer's clothing average about 20% less in Bermuda than in the United States, although the accessories sell at much the same as U.S. prices. Although the boutique is much smaller than its counterpart on Madison Avenue, it still has a good selection of conservative-casual wear and evening attire. ⊠*57 Front St., Hamilton* ☎*441/295–2112 Ext. 130.*

Revelation Boutique. Cool, contemporary linen clothing is the focus of Paulette Spence's small shop. ⊠*79 Reid St., Hamilton* ☎*441/296–4252.*

Secrets. Come to Secrets for sometimes understated, sometimes flashy, but always sexy lingerie. The shop also carries massage oils and adult games. ⊠*Lower level of Washington Mall, Reid St., Hamilton* 🕾*441/295–0651.*

★ **Stefanel.** This popular Italian chain is good for simple, stylish, modern women's clothes, mostly made from cotton and other natural fabrics. Its own line of jackets, crocheted sweaters, and camisoles is particularly worth a look. The colors are neutral, sometimes with delicate small prints. Prices are commensurate with quality, but seasonal sales are particularly rewarding. ⊠*12 Walker Arcade, Reid St., Hamilton* 🕾*441/295–5698.*

Vibe. Funky clothes, shoes, and accessories at reasonable prices make Vibe a choice shop for women who want to keep up with the latest styles. ⊠*5 Burnaby St., Hamilton* 🕾*441/296–4883.*

COINS

Bermuda Monetary Authority. This agency issues and redeems Bermuda currency, and also oversees financial institutions operating in and through Bermuda. At its offices in Hamilton, it sells collectors' coins, including replicas of the old Bermuda "hogge" money of the early 17th century. Tree-frog, spiny-lobster, and tall-ship coins are among the many other pieces for sale. ⊠*26 Burnaby St., Hamilton* 🕾*441/292–5278.*

CRAFTS

Bermuda Clayworks. Miniature lighthouses, customized house-number plaques, and tableware are among the brightly painted pottery pieces created in this little shop. You can even buy a plain bisque item to paint yourself. The owners fire and deliver it to your hotel or home. ⊠*Maritime Lane, Dockyard* 🕾*441/234–5116.*

Bermuda Craft Market. The island's largest permanent craft outlet is the Dockyard's old cooperage building, which dates to 1831. Dozens of artisans show their work here, and you can expect to find baubles and edibles, from Bermuda-cedar hair clips to Bermuda honey and jam. Quilts, decoupage, and hand-painted glassware are among the prettiest souvenirs and gifts in the marketplace. ⊠*The Cooperage, Dockyard* 🕾*441/234–3208.*

★ **The Bounty.** The spicy smell of cedar is the first thing to greet you in this tiny shop, where owner Kersley Nanette and his staff handcraft teak and cedar model ships. The focus is on tall ships of the 17th and 18th centuries. Prices range from $150 to $2,000. Models of the *Sea Venture* and *Deliverance* are especially popular. Call for an appointment. ⊠*2A Old Maid's Lane, St. George's* 🕾*441/297–2143.*

Fodor'sChoice **The Island Shop.** Brightly colored island-theme artwork for ceramics,
★ linens, and pillows are designed by owner Barbara Finsness. A number of her original watercolors are available for purchase. She also stocks the store with cedar-handle handbags embroidered with Bermuda buildings, shell napkin rings, plates, monogrammed guest towels, rugs, chunky jewelry, and elegant gifts, as well as candles and bath

7

products. A smaller selection of her gifts can be found in the Old Cellar on Front Street. ⊠*3 Queen St., Hamilton* ☎*441/292–6307.*

CRYSTAL & CHINA

Bluck's. A dignified establishment in business for more than 150 years, Bluck's is the island's only store devoted exclusively to the sale of crystal and china. Royal Doulton, Royal Copenhagen, and Herend china compete with Lalique, Waterford, Baccarat, and Kosta Boda crystal in glorious displays, and Limoges porcelain boxes sit primly in their display cases. The courteous staff provides price lists upon request. ⊠*4 W. Front St., Hamilton* ☎*441/295–5367* ⊠*Water St., St. George's* ☎*441/297–0476.*

Vera P. Card. Lladro and Swarovski silver crystal figurines are available at almost identical prices elsewhere, but this store has the largest selection, including open-edition and limited-edition gallery pieces. The shop's collection of more than 250 Hummel figurines is one of the world's largest. Limited-edition porcelain plates and vases depicting Bermuda scenes cost $59 to $300. There are also brightly painted chiming cuckoo clocks. ⊠*11 Front St., Hamilton* ☎*441/295–1729* ⊠*9 Water St., St. George's* ☎*441/297–1718.*

GIFTS & SOUVENIRS

All Wrapped Up. Greeting cards, wrapping paper, and little gift items like aromatherapy oils are sold here. ⊠*Washington Mall, Reid St., Hamilton* ☎*441/295–1969.*

Another World Gift Shop. You can find every permutation of gift in this shop—from "Bermuda" sweatshirts to plates to funky knickknacks. ⊠*7 King's Sq., St. George's* ☎*441/297–0670.*

Bee's Knees. This small shop has souvenir T-shirts displayed from floor to ceiling. You can also find sunglasses, postcards, key chains, and knickknacks of all kinds. ⊠*61 Front St., Hamilton* ☎*441/292–6454.*

Crackerbox. Shells, shells, and more shells are what you can find in this adorable souvenir shop. Big bins of them invite rummaging, and you can buy just one or a whole handful. Also for sale are charms and jewelry made from shells and sea glass (bits of colored glass worn smooth from tumbling in the ocean or machine-tumbled to look that way). The store has its own line of Tobacco Bay Chocolate Beach Stones (chocolate-candy color to look like beach stones), and Bermuda Summer Breeze candles. ⊠*15 York St., St. George's* ☎*441/297–1205.*

Fodor'sChoice ★ **Dockyard Glassworks and Bermuda Rum Cake Company.** This combination micro-bakery and glassblowing shop is a favorite among locals and visitors alike. Pull up an armchair and watch as artists turn molten glass into vases, plates, miniature tree frogs, and other collectibles. Afterward help yourself to the rum-cake samples. Flavors include traditional black rum, rum swizzle (with tropical fruit juices), rum and ginger, and rum and banana. You can buy the cakes duty-free for $11.95, $19.95, and $29.95. If you purchase glassware, the company will pack the purchase and deliver it to your hotel or cruise ship. A small outlet in St. George's sells a collection of glasswork in addition to the cakes.

✉1 *Maritime Lane, Dockyard* ☎441/234–4216 ✉3 *Bridge St., St. George's* ☎441/297–3908.

Flying Colours. This family-owned and -operated shop, established in 1937, has the island's largest selection of souvenir T-shirts, with creatively designed logos in hundreds of styles. The shop also carries everything for the beach—hats, towels, sarongs, toys for playing in the sand—plus other quality souvenirs, like shell jewelry. Educational toys are a specialty. ✉5 *Queen St., Hamilton* ☎441/295–0890.

Foreign Cargo. Candles, oils, and incense are among the offerings at this shop that also stocks larger wrought-iron home accessories. ✉15 *Burnaby St., Hamilton* ☎441/296–3054.

★ **Gosling's Black Seal Gift Shop.** The rum maker's signature shop sells bottles of plain and flavored rum and tins of rum cake, plus T-shirts, ties, hats, and more, all with the Gosling logo, a black seal. ✉97 *Front St., Hamilton* ☎441/295–1123.

Hodge Podge. This cluttered little shop, just around the corner from the Ferry Terminal and Visitors Service Bureau, offers pretty much what its name implies: postcards, sunblock, sunglasses, film, and T-shirts. It also sells imported shells and shell jewelry at low prices. ✉3 *Point Pleasant Rd., Hamilton* ☎441/295–0647.

Howe Lifestyle. A variety of modern gift items including candles, frames, cards, pillows, and photo albums may be found inside Howe's. The shop also carries some furniture and a good stock of Designer's Guild linens. ✉27 *Reid St., Hamilton* ☎441/292–1433.

Littlest Drawbridge Gift Shop. Bermuda-cedar bowls, pens, and sachets are the highlight of this closet-size shop. Hand-painted apparel and handcrafted pottery and wooden games are also on sale. ✉*Clocktower Mall, Dockyard* ☎441/234–6214.

The Living Centre. Although the Living Centre and its sister stores deal mainly in high-end furniture, visitors have been known to drop in for some comparison shopping and to pick up accessories, like china or mirrors. ✉41 *Victoria St., Hamilton* ☎441/296–5284 *Furniture Basics* ✉49 *Church St., Hamilton* ☎441/292–1844 *Four Seasons Furniture* ✉45 *Victoria St., Hamilton* ☎441/295–8267.

Onion Jack's Trading Post. Onion Jack's own line of sweet and spicy sauces is sold here, along with an assortment of flip-flops, beachwear, and sunglasses. ✉77 *Front St., Hamilton* ☎441/295–1263.

Otto Wurz. It's hard to miss this Front Street store. Joke signs proclaiming such witticisms as LAUGH AND THE WORLD LAUGHS WITH YOU, SNORE AND YOU SLEEP ALONE fill its windows. Inside is a collection of model ships, silver and pewter jewelry, children's wood toys, and English silverware. ✉3 *Front St., Hamilton* ☎441/295–1247.

★ **Pulp & Circumstance.** If it's an original, quality gift you're after, look no further. The Reid Street store sells exquisite, modern picture frames in all shapes and sizes and from all over the world, plus candles, bath products, gifts for babies, a great selection of Burt's Bees products, and greeting cards. The Pulp & Circumstance stationery store in Windsor Place, just behind the main one, sells photo albums, pens, and Bermuda-theme stationery. Delicate pastel notepaper engraved with pictures of Gombey dancers or dinghies sells for $35 per box. ✉ *Reid and Queen sts., Hamilton* ☎ *441/292–9586* ✉ *Windsor Pl. and Queen St., Hamilton* ☎ *441/292–8886.*

★ **Sail On and Shades of Bermuda.** Owned and operated by Hubert Watlington, a former Olympic windsurfer and top local sailor, this shop stocks a gigantic selection of sunglasses, outdoor clothing and swimwear from such brands as Patagonia and Helly Hanson, plus wacky toys and gifts. The store is tucked into a little alley, opposite No. 1 Shed and the cruise-ship dock. A larger selection of women's clothing, including floaty skirts and sundresses, can be found at the store's Washington Mall location on Reid Street. ✉ *Old Cellar Lane, off Front St., Hamilton* ☎ *441/295–0808.*

★ ♺ **Treats.** You can find bulk candy in just about every flavor here, but the greatest draw to this tiny store are the fun, seasonal gifts and cute baby toys. Look out for the ladybug rain boots and matching raincoat for kids. A selection of intricately designed Vera Bradly quilted bags is also available. ✉ *Lower level of Washington Mall, Reid St., Hamilton* ☎ *441/296–1123.*

★ **Trustworthy Gift Shop.** Proceeds from the sales of Bermuda-inspired coffee-table books, key chains, serving trays, spoons, pens, and bags at this gift shop benefit the Bermuda National Trust. ■ TIP➔ **This is where you can find some of the most upscale gifts to take back home.** ✉ *47 Old Cellar Lane, Hamilton* ☎ *441/296–4164.*

GROCERY STORES

Many of the accommodations on Bermuda allow you to do your own cooking. Considering how expensive the island is, this option has widespread appeal for travelers on a budget. Still, groceries are relatively pricey. A dozen imported large eggs cost about $2.50. Locally raised eggs are even more expensive, about $4 a dozen. A loaf of Bermuda-made bread is $2.50, whereas U.S. bread is $4. And a 13-ounce can of coffee is $8.50. Unless stated otherwise, grocery stores carry liquor. Many grocery stores offer 5% off cash purchases on Wednesday. It's customary to tip the person who bags your groceries $1 or $2 for their efforts. For a small purchase, spare change is fine.

A-One Paget. This grocery is near Barnsdale Guest Apartments and the Sky Top Cottages. Be warned, however, that the route between Sky Top and the store takes in a significant hill, which could make for a difficult hike if you buy a lot. ✉ *Middle Rd., Paget Parish* ☎ *441/236–0351.*

Down to Earth, Ltd. This natural-food and health shop sells everything from tea and supplements to organic body products and home cleaners. Don't leave without grabbing a fresh glass of a fruity blend from the juice bar in the corner. ✉ *56 Reid St., Hamilton* ☎ *441/292–5639.*

Esso Tiger Market. If you need sundries or munchies in the early hours of the morning, this 24-hour convenience store is the only place to go in Hamilton. Beyond cigarettes and frozen foods, it stocks film, aspirin, and coffee. ⊠*37 Richmond Rd., Hamilton* ☎*441/295–3776.*

Harrington Hundreds Grocery & Liquor Store. Harrington is a must for those observing special diets or seeking unusual ingredients. It has the island's best selection of wheat-free foods, including gluten-free pastas, breads, and cookies. It's close to Spittal Pond and Angel's Grotto, but not within walking distance. ⊠*99 S. Shore Rd., Smith's Parish* ☎*441/293–1635.*

Heron Bay Marketplace. Part of the island-wide Marketplace chain of stores, this one has a large selection of fresh vegetables. It's convenient to Longtail Cliffs and Marley Beach, but not on foot. ⊠*227 Middle Rd., Southampton Parish* ☎*441/238–1993.*

Lindo's Family Foods, Ltd. Lindo's is a medium-size store with a good selection of organic foods, fresh seafood, and fine imported French and Italian cheese and pâtés. It's within walking distance of the several Warwick accommodations. ⊠*128 Middle Rd., Warwick Parish* ☎*441/236–1344* ⊠*4 Watlington Rd. E, Devonshire* ☎*441/236–5623.*

The Marketplace. The island's largest grocery store, and the chain's headquarters, Marketplace offers homemade hot soups, stir-fries, salads, dinners, and desserts for about $7 a pound. This branch is also open Sunday 1–5. ⊠*Church St. near Parliament St., Hamilton* ☎*441/292–3163.*

★ **Miles Market.** Miles is Bermuda's Balducci's, with a large selection of upscale or hard-to-get specialty food items and high-quality imported and local meats and fish. Many items are on the expensive side, but the quality and selection here are unsurpassed in Bermuda. The market delivers anywhere on the island. ⊠*Pitts Bay Rd., near Fairmont Hamilton Princess, Hamilton* ☎*441/295–1234.*

Modern Mart. Part of the Marketplace chain, but smaller than its flagship Hamilton store, this location has all the essentials. It's easily accessible from Sky Top Cottages, Loughlands, and other south-shore hotels. ⊠ *104 S. Shore Rd., Paget Parish* ☎*441/236–6161.*

Robertson's Drug Store. Great cards, gifts, and drug-store items abound at this large, well-stocked, long-standing store. ⊠*24 York St., St. George's* ☎*441/297–1736.*

★ **Rock On–The Health Store.** Nutritional supplements, diet books, natural teas, natural remedies, and environmentally friendly toiletries are among the goods offered at one of Bermuda's few health stores. The knowledgeable staff will guide customers in their selections, but there are plenty of books available, too. ⊠*Butterfield Pl., 67 Front St., Hamilton* ☎*441/295–3468* ⊠*12 Church St., Hamilton* ☎*441/295–3468.*

Shelly Bay Marketplace. This branch of the Marketplace chain is the only large grocery on North Shore Road. ⊠ *110N. Shore Rd., Hamilton Parish* ☎*441/293–0966.*

Somerset Marketplace. The largest grocery store on the island's western end, it's convenient to Whale Bay Inn, but take a moped or taxi. ⊠ *48 Somerset Rd., Sandys Parish* ☎*441/234–0626.*

Somers Supermarket. Despite its small size, Somers has a large selection, with hot food, salads, and sandwiches made fresh daily. It offers free delivery service within St. George's, and it's open Monday to Saturday from 7 AM to 9 PM, and Sunday from 8 to 8. ⊠ *41 York St., St. George's* ☎*441/297–1177.*

The Supermart. English products, including the Waitrose brand, are the specialties of this store, which stocks all the usual groceries. You can pick up a picnic lunch at the well-stocked salad-and-hot-food bar. ⊠*Front St., near King St., Hamilton* ☎*441/292–2064.*

JEWELRY & WATCHES

★ **Astwood Dickinson.** Established in 1904, this store has built a reputation for its exquisite collection of unmounted stones; upmarket jewelry, including designs by Baccarat and Tiffany and Co., and a wide range of Swiss watches. Cartier, Oakley, Gucci, and Tag Heuer watches, among other famous names, are sold for up to 20% less than in the United States. The shop's Bermuda Collection, designed and created in the upstairs workshop, ranges from 18-karat gold charms to bejeweled pendants representing the island's flora and fauna. ⊠*83–85 Front St., Hamilton* ☎*441/292–5805* ⊠ *Walker Arcade, Hamilton* ☎*441/292–4247.*

Crisson's. The only store in Bermuda carrying Rolex, Curum, and Movado, Crisson's attracts well-heeled customers who come here to buy merchandise at prices 20% to 30% off those at home. Earrings are a specialty, and there's a large selection. The gift department carries gold bangles and beads. ⊠*55 and 71 Front St., Hamilton* ☎*441/295–2351* ⊠*16 Queen St.,* *Hamilton* ☎*441/295–2351* ⊠*20 Reid St., Hamilton* ☎*441/295–2351* ⊠*Elbow Beach Hotel, S. Shore Rd., Paget Parish* ☎*441/236–9928* ⊠*York and Kent sts., St. George's* ☎*441/297–0672* ⊠*Water St., St. George's* ☎*441/297–0107.*

> **WORD OF MOUTH**
>
> "My husband found a watch at Crisson's in Hamilton that he could not get his hands on in the U.S. He was smiling the rest of the trip."
>
> —mnag

E. R. Aubrey. Gold and tanzanite are the specialties of this Hamilton jeweler. The store also carries a large selection of certified diamonds and promises to match prices as long as they can be verified. ⊠*19 Front St., Hamilton* ☎*441/295–3826* ⊠*101 Front St., Hamilton* ☎*441/296–3171* ⊠*20 E. York St., St. George's* ☎*441/297–5059* ⊠*Clocktower Mall, Dockyard* ☎*441/297–5059.*

Everrich Jewelry. This bargain jewelry store stocks countless styles of basic gold and silver chains, earrings, bangles, and rings. ⊠*28 Queen St., Hamilton* ☎*441/295–2110.*

Gem Cellar. Jewelers here make Bermuda-theme charms selling for $40 to $200, and they can produce custom-designed gold and silver jewelry in one to two days. ⊠ *Old Cellar Lane, Hamilton* ☎*441/292–3042.*

Kirk's. Owner Kirk Stapff says he can design and produce any piece of jewelry you desire, "from A to Z." ⊠*67 Front St., Hamilton* ☎*441/ 296–9428.*

Sovereign. This fine-jewelry shop, which also carries a selection of Casio, Citizen, and Timex watches, used to be part of Trimingham's. ⊠*13 Reid St., Hamilton* ☎*441/292–7933.*

Solomon's. Manager Allan Porter and his skilled staff custom-design charming, one-of-a-kind pieces costing from $70 to upward of $100,000. ⊠*17 Front St., Hamilton* ☎*441/292–4742 or 441/295–1003.*

Swiss Timing. The staff offers jewelry repairs and custom designs, as well as pieces from Germany, England, and Italy. ⊠*95 Front St., Hamilton* ☎*441/295–1376.*

Vera P. Card. Known primarily for crystal and porcelain figurines, this shop also carries fine and costume jewelry, including an extensive tanzanite ring collection. ⊠*11 Front St., Hamilton* ☎*441/295–1729* ⊠*9 Water St., St. George's* ☎*441/297–1718.*

★ **Walker Christopher.** *The Bermudian* magazine has named this goldsmith the island's best for fine jewelry. You can work with a jeweler to design your own exclusive piece or choose from classic diamond bands, strands of South Sea pearls, and the more contemporary handhammered chokers. Walker Christopher is the only Bermuda retailer carrying the Galatea diamond and pearl collection. The workshop also produces a line of Bermuda-inspired gold jewelry and sterling silver Christmas ornaments. ⊠*9 Front St., Hamilton* ☎*441/295–1466* ⊠*A. S. Cooper, 59 Front St., Hamilton* ☎*441/295–3961.*

LINENS

House of Linens. A wide collection of hand-embroidered table, bed, and bath linens can be found at this shop, which also sells baby linens and infant wear. ⊠ *Washington Mall, Reid St., Hamilton* ☎*441/296–0189.*

Irish Linen Shop. In a cottage that looks as though it belongs in rural Ireland, this shop is the place for Irish linen tablecloths. Prices range from less than $10 to more than $3,000. Antique tablecloths can cost nearly $2,000. ■TIP➔ The best buys are the Irish linen tea towels for around $10. From Madeira come exquisite hand-embroidered handkerchiefs, plus linen sheets and pillowcases, and cotton organdy christening robes with slip and bonnet, hand-embroidered with garlands and tiers of Valenciennes lace (from $220 to more than $800). The store has an exclusive arrangement with Souleiado, maker of the vivid prints from Provence that are available in tablecloths, place mats, and bags, as well as by the yard—the last at a huge savings over U.S. prices. ⊠*31 Front St., Hamilton* ☎*441/295–4089.*

LIQUOR STORES

Bermuda liquor stores have a good selection of wine and spirits. Each has branches sprinkled around the island from St. George's to Somerset. Spirits are sold for the same prices in liquor stores and a bit more in grocery stores.

Bermuda Duty Free Shop. The airport store invites you to put together your own package of Bermuda liquors at in-bond (duty-free) prices. Gosling's Black Seal rum and rum cakes are among the native products. ⊠ *Bermuda International Airport, 3 Cahow Way, St. George's* ☎ *441/293–2870.*

Burrows Lightbourn. This chain has a comprehensive selection and stores all over the island. ⊠ *127 Front St., Hamilton* ☎ *441/295–0176* ⊠ *Harbour Rd., Paget* ☎ *441/236–0355* ⊠ *Water St., St. George's* ☎ *441/ 297–0552* ⊠ *Main Rd., Somerset* ☎ *441/234–0963.*

Front Street Wine & Spirits Here's your one-stop shop for candy, wines, beer, souvenirs, and assorted snacks. ⊠ *57 Front St., Hamilton* ☎ *441/ 292–6620.*

Gosling Bros. Ltd. The maker of Bermuda's Black Seal rum also stocks a full selection of wines and other liquors at its stores. The helpful and knowledgeable staff provides excellent advice. You can only buy one bottle of Black Seal rum to consume on the island and then another to export—you can even arrange to have it sent to the airport from the shop. The exported bottle will cost you less than the one you plan to drink in Bermuda. ⊠ *Front and Queen sts., Hamilton* ☎ *441/295– 1123* ⊠ *York and Queen sts., St. George's* ☎ *441/298–7339.*

LUGGAGE

Harbourmaster. Tumi luggage and briefcases, among other brands, are sold here. ⊠ *Washington Mall, Reid St., Hamilton* ☎ *441/295–5333.*

MUSIC

The Music Box. Stereos and other electronics are crammed into the window of this independent store. Inside is a small but diverse collection of new CDs (mostly R&B and hip-hop), cassettes, and DVDs. ⊠ *58 Reid St., Hamilton* ☎ *441/295–4839* ⊠ *York St., St. George's* ☎ *441/297–0484.*

Music World. Every genre from pop to gospel to local sounds may be found at this major store. ⊠ *Bermudiana Arcade, 27 Queen St., Hamilton* ☎ *441/292–8785.*

Sound Stage. Small but fairly comprehensive, Sound Stage stocks new-release, mainstream CDs and DVDs. ⊠ *Washington Mall, Reid St., Hamilton* ☎ *441/292–0811.*

PHOTO EQUIPMENT

P-Tech Digital 35MM cameras, point-and-shoot digital cameras, digital photo frames, camcorders, and other small electronics are all here. Brands to look for are Nikon, Canon, Olympus, Minolta, and Pentax. Check out the wide selection of sunglasses as well. ⊠ *5 Reid St., Hamilton* ☎ *441/295–5496.*

CLOSE UP

Yo, Ho, Ho & a Bottle of Rum

One of the distinct pleasures of a visit to Bermuda is getting to sample a bit of island rum and rum-based products. Gosling's Black Seal Rum is perhaps the best-loved by locals. It's darker and thicker than the usual stuff, with a hint of a caramel flavor—especially when mixed with carbonated ginger beer to make a Dark 'n Stormy, a famous Bermuda drink (treat it with respect and caution).

Gosling's is one of Bermuda's oldest companies, and its Hamilton liquor shop was established in 1806. Gosling's Black Seal Rum was sold in barrels until just after World War I and inherited its name from the black sealing wax that sealed the barrel corks. In its 151-proof variety, Black Seal will test the strongest drinker.

Many prefer to buy it in the standard 80 proof.

Bermuda's Rum Swizzle, another popular drink, also uses the ubiquitous Black Seal Rum, along with a splash of club soda, lime juice, and sugar. Gosling also produces three liqueurs that are big favorites—Bermuda Gold, Bermuda Banana Liqueur, and Bermuda Coconut Rum. These liqueurs can be ordered everywhere, from poolside bars to late-night jazz clubs. They're even found in cakes, as you soon discover in gift shops and on restaurant menus. Classic Bermuda rum cakes are a delicious, nontoxic way to taste the island's famous export. Fear not if rum's not your thing: Guinness and Heineken are among the widely available imported beers.

7

SHOES & HANDBAGS

Boyle, W. J. & Sons Ltd. Bermuda's leading shoe-store chain, Boyle's sells a wide range of men's, women's, and children's shoes. **Trends** on Reid Street has the most up-to-the-minute foot fashions, although the **Sports Locker** has a good stock of running shoes and flip-flops. The Church Street store specializes in children's shoes. ⊠ *Queen St., Hamilton* ☎ *441/295–1887* ⊠ *Mangrove Bay, Somerset* ☎ *441/234–0530* ⊠ *Water St., St. George's* ☎ *441/297–1922* ⊠ *Trends, the Walkway, Reid St., Hamilton* ☎ *441/295–6420* ⊠ *The Sports Locker, Windsor Place, 18 Queen St., Hamilton* ☎ *441/292–3300* ⊠ *Children's Shop, Church St., Hamilton* ☎ *441/292–6360.*

Calypso. Women looking for quirky, snazzy footwear should visit Calypso's main store first. The shoe and bag section is small but with choice, super-trendy, sometimes weird styles and colors. Items may cost a little more than you want to spend but you'll want them anyway. Serious bargains can be had during sales. Calypso has branches at Coral Beach & Tennis Club, Fairmont Southampton, and Clocktower Centre in the Dockyard. ⊠ *45 Front St., Hamilton* ☎ *441/295–2112.*

Locomotion Too. Italian, Spanish, and American shoes for women and children are sold in this small store. ⊠ *Washington Mall, Reid St., Hamilton* ☎ *441/296–4030.*

Louis Vuitton. Come here to find the famous monogram on ladies' handbags, men's and women's briefcases, carry-on luggage, wallets, credit-card cases, and other items. Prices here are the same as in the United States, except there's no tax. Small ladies' handbags start at about $750. Small, soft leather carry-ons cost up to $1,000, and natural cowhide briefcases start at $3,000. ⊠*Butterfield Pl., Front St., Hamilton* 🕾*441/296–1940.*

> ### QUIK FIX
>
> Local shoes-in-distress swear by the friendly expert same-day service at **Heel Quik.** The store also carries some luggage, shoe-care products, and umbrellas. ⊠*Upper level of Washington Mall, Hamilton* 🕾*441/292–3839.*

Fodor'sChoice   **Lusso.** This is the ultimate island
★   boutique for designer shoes and leather goods for men and women. Selections from Prada, Ferragamo, Moschino, and Fendi are stocked in this luxury store. ⊠*51 Front St., Hamilton* 🕾*441/295–6734.*

Kay Ri's Children's Shoes. This shop offers trendy, bargain-price shoes for children. The store has a great selection of formal sandals. ⊠*Washington Mall, Reid St., Hamilton* 🕾*441/292–9317.*

Quattro. For the latest shoe styles from Florence and Rome, check out this closet-size shoe shop. The men's and women's shoes are beautifully made, but prices can be high. ⊠*12 Reid St., Hamilton* 🕾*441/295–9815.*

Trends. Pick up recognizable American and European shoe and handbag brands at this friendly, service-oriented shop. Choose from comfortable brands such as Aerosoles and Enzo Angiolini to Dr. Scholl's and Joan & David. Colorful Dooney & Burke handbags look great on the preppy, pretty streets of Bermuda. ⊠*The Walkway, 22 Reid St., Hamilton* 🕾*441/295–9815.*

SPORTING GOODS

★ **The Dive Shop.** The best prices for dive gear are found, naturally, at Bermuda's most complete dive shop. The children's mask-and-snorkel set costs $30. You can find a large selection of wet suits, fishing gear, and camping supplies. ⊠*7 Park Rd., Hamilton* 🕾*441/292–3839.*

Fly, Bridge and Tackle. The only island store completely dedicated to fishing supplies, Fly, Bridge and Tackle offers everything a fisherman needs except the fish. Plus, the avid fishermen on staff offer excellent advice about fishing in Bermuda. ⊠*26 Church St., Hamilton* 🕾*441/295–1845.*

International Sports Shop. Frisbees, snorkel gear, exercise wear, and rackets are all available here. ⊠ *26 Bermudiana Rd., Hamilton* 🕾*441/295–4183.*

The Sports Locker. Here you can find athletic shoes, Teva sandals, and flip-flops. ⊠*Windsor Pl., 18 Queen St., Hamilton* 🕾*441/292–3300.*

Sports 'R' Us. This store has Bermuda's largest selection of running shoes, plus gear and equipment for most sports. ⊠*Shoppers Fair Bldg., Church St., near Queen St., Hamilton* 🕾*441/292–1891.*

SportSeller. Big-name exercise gear, knapsacks, and running shoes are available at this shop, which also sells Speedo swimwear and some sunglasses. ⊠ *Washington Mall, Reid St., Hamilton* ☎*441/295–2692.*

Upstairs Golf & Tennis Shop. Golf clubs, tennis rackets, and the accessories for those sports are the specialties of this store. You can find some of the best brands available, including Ping, Callaway, and Titleist for the golfer, and Yonex and Dunlop for the tennis player. Men's and women's sportswear is also sold. ⊠*26 Church St., Hamilton* ☎*441/295–5161.*

Wheels Cycles, Ltd. Here's where to rent a single- or double-seat electric scooter to explore Bermuda. The company will pick up and deliver cycles right to your door. ⊠*117 Front St., Hamilton* ☎*441/292–2245.*

Winners Edge. This store sells exercise wear, water bottles, and helmets, and it's the only store in Bermuda to sell Cannondale, Gary Fisher, and Trek equipment. ⊠*73 Front St., Hamilton* ☎*441/295–6012.*

STATIONERY & ART SUPPLIES

Artcetera. This is where you can buy pens, paint, charcoal, pastels, sketching pads, canvases, and almost anything else an aspiring artist might need to capture Bermuda in color or black and white. ⊠*34 Burnaby Hill, Hamilton* ☎*441/295–2787.*

Card Cove. This tiny cottage offers a good supply of cards, calendars, toys, and party supplies. ⊠*19 Queen St., Hamilton* ☎*441/295–0727.*

The Complete Office. This one-stop office shop is where you can find everything from toners and computer paper to pens and staples. ⊠*17 Reid St., Hamilton* ☎*441/292–4333.*

The Royal Gazette Stationery Store. Pens, envelopes, writing paper, and note pads are plentiful at this well-stocked stationery store. ⊠*32 Reid St., Hamilton* ☎*441/295–4008.*

TOYS

The Annex Toys. This large toy department has one of the best and most up-to-date selections of toys and games for all ages. There's also a good supply of kites and beach toys. ⊠*4 Reid St., Hamilton* ☎*441/295–3838.*

Jack 'N' Jill's Toy Shop. This cottage near Victoria Park is filled with traditional toys as well as newer, perhaps "cooler" toys. The store is also the island's exclusive retailer of Bruynzeel art supplies. ⊠*7 Park Rd., Hamilton* ☎*441/292–3769.*

Magic Moments. Party planners will find gift-bag loot, balloons, banners, feather boas, and almost anything else you might need for a theme party. ⊠*Washington Mall, Reid St., Hamilton* ☎*441/296–8848.*

Cruising to Bermuda

WORD OF MOUTH

"My husband and I are taking my 90-year-old parents on a cruise to Bermuda in October. We're looking for something to do with them when we dock at King's Wharf."

—ovingtonl

"Kings Wharf is mostly shops—if that's what they're into, great! My parents weren't, so we took the ferry to St. George's and then one to Hamilton. Both have carriage rides through town—very nice. The ferry was easy for my mom to negotiate. She loved St. George's because the town is small and everything is close by. We took a taxi to Queen Anne beach which has a snack bar and level terrace and beautiful view!"

—CDonahue

Updated by
Linda Coffman

WITH ONLY TWO WAYS TO get to Bermuda—by air or by sea—you might be tempted to ask, "Why take a ship when Bermuda is only a two-hour flight from most East Coast cities?" The logical answer is twofold. A cruise is more than simply transportation and there's nothing quite as traditional, or gracious, as a Bermuda arrival by sea. Three Bermuda harbors serve cruise ships: Hamilton (the capital), St. George's, and King's Wharf at the Royal Naval Dockyard.

Cruise lines have traditionally offered what is called a "classic" Bermuda cruise with ships calling in Bermuda during the week and sailing to and from the island on weekends. While in Bermuda, your ship acts as a floating hotel. Some ships may call at only one port city,

> ## TOP 5 CRUISING
>
> ■ Climb up Gibb's Lighthouse for expansive view of the inlets and harbors.
>
> ■ Absorb Bermuda's nautical and military history at the Bermuda Maritime Museum.
>
> ■ Ride on the ferries to rub shoulders with Bermudians.
>
> ■ Watch gossips and nagging wives get drenched in a dunking stool during the town crier's St. George's pierside show.
>
> ■ Marvel as cruise ships gingerly inch through the cuts at Hamilton and St. George's harbors with *very* little room to spare.

such as St. George's; others may split their time between the capital Hamilton and St. George's or, particularly in the case of the largest vessels, tie up only at the Dockyard in the West End.

In today's bigger-and-newer-is-better marketplace, major cruise lines are divesting their fleets of smaller and older ships. Unfortunately, those were the only cruise ships able to squeeze through the entrances into Hamilton and St. George's harbors. That narrows your selection to the rare mid-size ships, such as Norwegian Majesty and Norwegian Dream, which are still able to tie up in St. George's harbor and the larger vessels that dock only at King's Wharf. In any case, you'll have access to the entire island by taxi, moped, public bus, high-speed ferry, or shore excursion.

Departure points for Bermuda cruises run the length of the Eastern seaboard, including Baltimore, Boston, New York, Norfolk, and Philadelphia. Departures are sometimes scheduled from other mid-Atlantic ports, such as Charleston, as well as those in Florida, so check with the cruise line or your travel agent. The Bermuda cruise season runs from mid-April through mid-November. However, a few ships make occasional port calls during off-season months.

Increasingly popular are round-trip itineraries originating in northeastern embarkation ports that include a single day or overnight port call in Bermuda before continuing south to the Bahamas or Caribbean. In addition to these Bermuda/Bahamas and Bermuda/Caribbean itineraries, "special" voyages or one-way ship-repositioning cruises are often available at the beginning or end of the usual Bermuda season when cruise lines move their ships to the Caribbean for winter months.

CHOOSING A CRUISE

Your choice of cruise line to Bermuda is narrowed by the government's firm control over the annual number of cruise ships and visitors to the island. That figure has increased in recent years, allowing more passengers to experience all Bermuda has to offer while still receiving the best service and hospitality. Although most ships to Bermuda are big, floating-resort type vessels, each has its own personality, which is determined by its amenities, theme, and, of course, passengers.

Your cruise experience will be shaped by several factors. To decide whether a particular ship's style will suit you, you need to consider your lifestyle and vacation expectations and then do a bit of research: Is there a full program of organized activities each day? What happens in the evening? What kind of entertainment is offered after dark? How often will you need to dress up for dinner? Are there facilities for kids and teens?

Space and passenger-to-crew ratios are equally important. The latter indicates the number of passengers served by each crew member—the lower the ratio, the better the level of service. The space ratio (the gross tonnage of a ship divided by its passenger capacity) allows you to compare ships' roominess. The higher the ratio, the more spacious the vessel feels: at 40:1 or higher a ship will feel quite roomy. Less than 25:1 will cramp anyone's style.

ACCOMMODATIONS

CABIN SIZE

The term "stateroom," used on some ships, is usually interchangeable with "cabin." Price is directly proportional to size and location, and most cabins are more compact than you would expect. The higher you go in the ship, the more expensive the quarters tend to be; outside cabins (those with windows) are often bigger than inside ones (no windows).

Suites are the roomiest and best-equipped accommodations, but they may differ in size, facilities, and price even on the same ship. Steward service may be more attentive to passengers staying in suites; top suites on some ships are even assigned private butlers. Most suites have a sitting area with sofa and chairs, and some have two bathrooms, occasionally with a whirlpool bath.

LOCATION

Today's cruise ships have stabilizers that make seasickness mostly a problem of the past. However, if you're susceptible to motion sickness, try to book a cabin amidship (close to the middle of the ship) as the bow (front) and stern (back) pitch up and down far more when the waves are uncooperative. Ships also experience a side-to-side motion known as roll. The closer your deck is to the true center of the ship—which is halfway between the bottom of the hull and the highest deck and midway between the bow and the stern—the less you will feel the ship's movement. Some cruise lines charge more for cabins amidship; most charge more for higher decks.

Outside cabins have portholes or windows (which cannot be opened). Upper-deck views from outside cabins may be partially obstructed by lifeboats or overlook a public promenade. Because outside cabins are more desirable, most newer ships are configured with only or mostly outside cabins; outside cabins on upper decks are increasingly being built with private verandas. Cabins that overlook a public promenade have mirrored windows, so that passersby can't see in by day; after dark, you'll need to draw your curtains.

Inside cabins on older vessels are often smaller and some are oddly shaped. On newer ships, inside cabin floor plans are virtually identical to those of outside cabins. As long as you don't feel claustrophobic without a window—and most cruise lines hang curtains or place mirrors on the wall to create the illusion—inside cabins are generally an excellent value.

Cruise brochures in print and online show a ship's layout deck by deck, and include the approximate location and shape of every cabin and suite. Use the deck plan to make sure the cabin you choose is not directly above or below public rooms or near the ship's engine, both of which can be noisy; and make sure that you're close to stairs or an elevator if you want to avoid walking down a long corridor every time you return to your cabin. If you can access detailed layouts of typical cabins, you can determine what kind of beds each cabin has, whether it has a window or a porthole, and what furnishings are provided.

SHARING

Most cabins are designed to accommodate two people. When more than two share a cabin, the third and fourth passengers are usually offered a substantial discount, thereby lowering the per-person price for the entire group. An additional discount is sometimes offered when children share a cabin with their parents. There's usually a premium on cruising solo in accommodations designed for two; passengers traveling on their own must pay a single supplement, which usually ranges from 125% to 200% of the double-occupancy per-person rate. On request, some cruise lines will find same-sex roommates for singles; each then pays the per-person, double-occupancy rate.

COSTS

The average daily price of a Bermuda cruise varies dramatically depending on several circumstances. The cost of a cruise on a luxury line such as Regent Seven Seas Cruises or Crystal Cruises may be five or more times the cost of a cruise on a mainstream line such as Royal Caribbean, Celebrity, or Norwegian Cruise Line. Although Bermuda has a relatively short cruising season, rates are still higher during holiday periods. You can usually save money by cruising late in the season, but this is also the time when hurricanes are most likely.

Solo travelers should be aware that single cabins have virtually disappeared from cruise ships. Taking a double cabin can cost twice the advertised per-person rates (which are based on double occupancy). Some cruise lines will find same-sex roommates for singles; each then pays the per-person, double-occupancy rate.

> **FRUGAL FUN**
>
> Shop for picnic supplies and relax in the shady tranquillity of Par le Ville Park—only a short walk from the cruise-ship pier, yet light-years away from bustling downtown Hamilton.

EXTRAS

Aside from the cost of your cruise there are additional expenses to consider, such as airfare to the embarkation port city. These days, virtually all cruise lines offer air add-ons, which are sometimes less expensive than the lowest available airline fare. Shore excursions can also be a substantial expense; the best shore excursions are not cheap. But if you skimp too much on your excursion budget you can deprive yourself of an important part of the Bermuda cruising experience. Finally, there will be many extras added onto your shipboard account during the cruise, including drinks (both alcoholic and nonalcoholic), activity fees (you pay to play bingo), dining in specialty restaurants, spa services, and even cappuccino and espresso.

TIPPING

Tipping is another add-on. At the end of the cruise, it's customary to tip your room steward, dining-room waiter, and the person who buses your table. You should expect to pay an average of $10 to $12 per day in tips. Most major cruise lines do not use the traditional method of tipping the service staff in cash at the end of the cruise, opting instead to add the recommended amount per day to your onboard account, which you may adjust upward or downward according to the level of service you receive. Bar bills generally include an automatic 15%–18% gratuity, so the one person you don't need to tip is your bartender. Some high-end cruise lines have no-tipping-required policies, though most passengers tip anyway. Each cruise line offers guidelines.

THE BERMUDA CRUISE FLEET

To avoid overcrowding, the Bermudian government limits the number of regular cruise-ship visits to the island. Cruise lines with weekly sailings are Norwegian Cruise Line, Princess Cruises, and Royal Caribbean International. In addition, cruise lines such as Carnival Cruise Lines, Celebrity Cruises, Costa Cruise Lines, Crystal Cruises, Regent Seven Seas Cruises, and Holland America Line each have at least one Bermuda cruise or a Bermuda port call on their 2008 schedules.

MAINSTREAM CRUISE LINES

Generally speaking, the mainstream lines have two basic ship sizes—large cruise ship and megaship—in their fleets. These vessels have plentiful outdoor deck space, and many have a wraparound outdoor promenade deck that allows you to stroll or jog the ship's perimeter. In the newest cruise ships, traditional meets trendy. You can find atrium lobbies and expansive sun and sports decks, picture windows instead of portholes, and cabins that open onto private verandas. For all these resort-style innovations, the newest ships still feature onboard classics—afternoon tea, complimentary room service, and lavish pampering. The smallest cruise ships carry 1,000 passengers or less, whereas the largest accommodate more than 3,000 passengers and are filled with diversions.

If you're into big, bold, brassy, and nonstop activity, these huge ships offer it all. The centerpiece of most megaships is a 3-, 5-, or even 11-story central atrium. However, these giant vessels are most readily distinguished by their profile: the boxy hull and superstructure rise as many as 14 stories out of the water and are capped by a huge sun or sports deck with a jogging track and one or more swimming pools. From their casinos and discos to their fitness centers, everything is bigger and more extravagant than on other ships. You may want to rethink a cruise aboard one of these ships if you like a bit more intimacy, since you'll be joined by up to 3,000 fellow passengers. Keep in mind that megaships are limited to docking at the Royal Navy Dockyard—they are simply too big to slip into the harbors at Hamilton and St. George's.

NORWEGIAN CRUISE LINE

Fodor's Choice ★ Norwegian Cruise Line (NCL) was established in 1966, when one of Norway's oldest and most respected shipping companies, Oslo-based Klosters Rederi A/S, acquired the *Sunward* and repositioned the ship from Europe to the then-obscure Port of Miami. With the formation of a company called Norwegian Caribbean Lines, the cruise industry was changed forever. NCL launched an entirely new concept with its regularly scheduled cruises to the Caribbean on a single-class ship, with an informal kind of luxury. No longer simply a means of transportation, the ship became a destination unto itself, offering guests an affordable alternative to land-based resorts. The *Sunward*'s popularity prompted other cruise lines to build ships to accommodate the burgeoning market, eventually turning Miami into the world's number-one cruise ship embarkation port. NCL led the way with its fleet of sleek, new ships. In another bold move, NCL purchased the former *France* in 1979 and rebuilt the grand ocean liner for Caribbean cruising. Rechristened *Norway*, she assumed the honored position as flagship of the fleet until she was retired from service in 2003. The late 1980s brought new ships and a new corporate name when Norwegian Caribbean Lines became Norwegian Cruise Line in 1987. NCL continued its expansion by acquiring other cruise lines, stretching and refurbishing older ships, and building new megaships, including the line's newest, two 2,400-berth Freestyle Cruising ships, *Norwegian Pearl* and *Norwegian Gem*.

8

Freestyle Cruising created a sensation in the industry when Asian shipping giant Star Cruises acquired NCL early in 2000—the new owners were confounded that Americans meekly conformed to rigid dining schedules and dress codes. All that changed with NCL's introduction of a host of flexible dining options that allow passengers to choose open seating in the main dining rooms or dine in any of a number of à la carte and specialty restaurants at any time and with whomever they please. Although the Freestyle Cruising concept now applies to the entire NCL fleet, you'll still see fewer options on the smaller, older ships like the *Norwegian Majesty*; for 2008, *Norwegian Dawn* is the only NCL Bermuda ship built especially for Freestyle Cruising. The line has even loosened the dress code to resort casual at all times and relaxed the disembarkation process by inviting passengers to relax in their cabins until it's time to leave the ship (instead of gathering in a lounge to wait for their numbers to be called). NCL's passenger list usually includes a wide range of ages, including families and couples, mostly from the United States and Canada.

NCL applies a service charge to passengers' shipboard accounts: $10 per passenger per day for those 13 and older and $5 per day for children ages 3–12. A 15% gratuity is added to bar tabs and spa bills.

Norwegian Cruise Line ☎*305/436–4000 or 800/327–7030* ⊕*www.ncl. com.*

☪ **Norwegian Dawn.** One of the line's newest and largest ships, built specifically for Freestyle Cruising, *Norwegian Dawn* comes bedecked with one of the largest art collections afloat. Andy Warhol prints are hung in stairwells and priceless original oil paintings by impressionist masters can be found in the Le Bistro premium restaurant. Cabins are reasonably large, with stylish decor and nice-looking cherry-veneer cabinetry; minisuites with private verandas are especially nice. Most accommodations have compartmentalized bathrooms with toilet, sink, and shower separated by sliding-glass doors and many are family-friendly with interior connecting doors; all cabins have coffeemakers. Extensive children's facilities (including a children's pool), and separate teen disco are definite pluses, as is wireless Internet access throughout the ship. ⇥*1,112 cabins, 2,224 passengers, 11 passenger decks* ♨*4 specialty restaurants, 3 dining rooms, buffet, ice-cream parlor, pizzeria, Wi-Fi, in-cabin safes, in-cabin refrigerators, some in-cabin DVDs, 3 pools (1 indoor), children's pool, fitness classes, gym, hair salon, hot tubs, sauna, spa, steam room, 9 bars, casino, cinema, dance clubs, library, showroom, video game room, children's programs (ages 2–17), dry cleaning, laundry facilities, laundry service, computer room* ▤*AE, D, MC, V.*

Norwegian Dream. Launched in 1992, *Norwegian Dream* gained something of a split personality in 1998 after being "stretched" when a 130-foot midsection was added to increase her size. Although 251 staterooms and a new reception area were added, unfortunately most public rooms were not increased enough in size and can feel cramped when the ship is fully booked. Oddities are a way-too-small buffet restaurant and the passageways through the Four Seasons dining room and the show lounge to reach the forward staircase. Where *Norwegian Dream* shines is the abundance of outdoor forward-facing decks and a wraparound promenade deck.

GOOD TO KNOW

Guys, Bermuda shorts are not welcome in the ship's formal restaurant at dinnertime, even if worn with a coat, tie, and knee-high stockings.

↩874 *cabins, 1,748 passengers, 10 passenger decks* ☼2 *specialty restaurants, 2 dining rooms, buffet, ice-cream parlor, pizzeria, Wi-Fi, some in-cabin safes, some in-cabin refrigerators, some in-cabin DVDs, 2 pools, fitness classes, gym, hair salon, hot tubs, sauna, spa, 8 bars, casino, dance club, library, showroom, video game room, children's programs (ages 2–17), dry cleaning, laundry service, computer room* ▭*AE, D, MC, V.*

Norwegian Majesty. The *Majesty* was lengthened in 1999 with the insertion of a prefabricated midsection that added 112 feet to its length and 203 cabins; about 71% are outside. Other additions included a second pool, an additional dining room, a coffee bar, a casino, another outdoor bar, and NCL's hallmark Le Bistro premium restaurant, offering French classics and nouvelle cuisine. There's also significantly more deck space. During the conversion, all interiors were spruced up and refurbished. Some of the standard cabins are fairly small, and all have a shower only. Most ocean-view staterooms have refrigerators. Lower beds in most staterooms can be combined to form a queen-size bed. ↩731 *cabins, 1,462 passengers, 9 passenger decks* ☼2 *specialty restaurants, 2 dining rooms, buffet, ice-cream parlor, pizzeria, Wi-Fi, in-cabin safes, some in-cabin refrigerators, some in-cabin VCRs, 2 pools, children's pool, fitness classes, gym, hair salon, hot tubs, sauna, spa, 8 bars, casino, dance club, library, showroom, video game room, children's programs (ages 2–17), dry cleaning, laundry service, computer room* ▭*AE, D, MC, V.*

PRINCESS CRUISES

Rising from modest beginnings in 1965, when it offered cruises to Mexico with a single ship, Princess has become one of the world's most recognizable cruise lines. Its fleet sails to more destinations each year than any other major cruise line. Princess was catapulted to stardom in 1977 when its flagship became the setting for *The Love Boat* television series, which introduced millions of viewers to the still-new concept of a seagoing vacation. The name and famous "seawitch" logo have remained synonymous with cruising ever since. Nearly everything about Princess is big, but the line doesn't sacrifice quality for quantity when it comes to building beautiful vessels. Decor and materials are top-notch, and service, especially in the dining rooms, is of a high standard. In short, Princess is refined without being pretentious. Eight nine-night eastern Caribbean with Bermuda sailings are on Princess Cruises' 2008 season from New York.

All Princess ships feature the line's innovative "Personal Choice Cruising" program, an individualized, unstructured style of cruising that gives passengers choice and flexibility in customizing their cruise experience—multiple dining locations, flexible entertainment, and affordable private balconies are all highlights. For traditionalists, one dining room is reserved for two assigned dinner seatings. Enrichment programs featuring guest lecturers and opportunities to learn new skills or crafts are welcome additions to a roster of adult activities, which still include staples such as bingo and art auctions.

Princess passengers' average age is 45, but you see a mix of younger and older couples on board. The ships are some of the most accessible at sea, and passengers with disabilities can select from staterooms in a variety of categories that are tailored to their special needs.

Princess suggests tipping $10 per person, per day. Gratuities are automatically added to onboard accounts, which passengers can adjust at the purser's desk; 15% is added to bar bills.

Princess Cruises ☎661/753–0000 or 800/774–6237 ⊕www.princess. com.

♺ **Caribbean Princess.** With a dramatic atrium and Skywalker's Disco—the "spoiler" hovering 150 feet above the stern—*Caribbean Princess* is nearly identical to earlier Grand-class vessels, but with an additional deck featuring balcony staterooms. A giant poolside LED screen shows up to seven movies or events daily. After dark, lounge chairs are covered with special cushions and blankets, and free popcorn plus a variety of drink specials and movie nibbles are available. Inside spaces are quietly sophisticated with sweeping staircases and a marble-floored atrium. An entire accommodations deck features popular minisuites and more than 80% of outside staterooms have private balconies. Surprising intimacy is achieved on this large ship thanks to the high number of public rooms and restaurants that swallow up passengers. *⊅1,550 cabins, 3,100 passengers, 15 passenger decks ♺2 specialty restaurants, 3 dining rooms, buffet, ice cream parlor, pizzeria, Wi-Fi, in-cabin safes, in-cabin refrigerators, 4 pools (1 indoor), children's pool, fitness classes, gym, hair salon, hot tubs, sauna, spa, steam room, 9 bars, casino, outdoor cinema, 2 dance clubs, library, 2 showrooms, video game room, children's programs (ages 3–17), dry cleaning, laundry facilities, laundry service, computer room, no kids under 6 months* ▤AE, D, MC, V.

ROYAL CARIBBEAN INTERNATIONAL

Imagine if the Mall of America were sent to sea. That's a fair approximation of what the megaships of Royal Caribbean International (RCI) are all about. These large-to-giant vessels are indoor-outdoor wonders, with every conceivable activity in a resortlike atmosphere, including atrium lobbies, shopping arcades, large spas, expansive sun decks, and rock-climbing walls. Several ships have such elaborate facilities as 18-hole miniature-golf courses, ice-skating rinks, and in-line skating tracks. These mammoth ships are quickly overshadowing the smaller vessels in Royal Caribbean's fleet. Passengers now have five generations of megaships to choose from and, happily, RCI regularly rejuvenates its older vessels, adding new facilities to mirror the latest trends.

The centerpiece of Royal Caribbean megaships is the multideck atrium, a hallmark that has been duplicated by many other cruise lines. The brilliance of this design is that all the major public rooms radiate from this central point, so you can learn your way around these huge ships within minutes of boarding. Ships in the Vision series (which includes *Grandeur of the Seas*) are especially bright and airy, with sea views almost anywhere you happen to be. The main problem with Royal Caribbean's otherwise well-conceived vessels is that, when booked to over 100% capacity, there are too many people on board, making for an exasperating experience at embarkation and disembarkation. However, small annoyances aside, Royal Caribbean is one of the best-run and most popular cruise lines.

Although the line competes directly with Carnival and Norwegian Cruise Line for passengers—active couples and singles in their thirties to fifties, as well as a large family contingent—there are distinct differences of ambience and energy. Royal Caribbean is a bit more sophisticated and subdued, even while delivering a good time on a grand scale.

Royal Caribbean suggests the following tips per passenger: dining-room waiter, $3.50 a day; stateroom attendant, $3.50 a day; assistant waiter, $2 a day. Gratuities for headwaiters and other service personnel are at your discretion. A 15% gratuity is automatically added to alcoholic-beverage and bar bills. All gratuities may be charged to your onboard account.

Royal Caribbean International ☎ *305/539–6000 or 800/327–6700* ⊕ *www. royalcaribbean.com.*

Explorer of the Seas. Royal Caribbean's enormous Voyager-class vessels are among the world's largest cruise ships and represent the highest space-per-guest ratio in the RCI fleet. Innovative and eye-popping features include ice-skating rinks, basketball courts, shopping promenades, in-line skating tracks, 18-hole miniature-golf courses, and rock-climbing walls. Spectacular three-story dining rooms have two dinner seatings, but there are other options, both casual (an actual Johnny Rockets diner) and reservation-only (for an extra fee). As on all Royal Caribbean ships, accommodations are cheery; however, while cabins are larger than on earlier ships, the least expensive can be a tight squeeze for more than two occupants. Suites have the advantage of more floor space and larger closets; other cabins have twin beds convertible to a queen and bathrooms with hair dryers and sizable vanity areas; some inside staterooms have a view overlooking the gigantic atrium. RCI boasts that staterooms designed for families can sleep up to eight. ↩*1,557 cabins, 3,114 passengers (3,835 to 3,844 at full occupancy), 14 passenger decks* ♨*2 specialty restaurants, dining room, buffet, ice-cream parlor, pizzeria, Wi-Fi, in-cabin safes, in-cabin refrigerators, some in-cabin DVDs, some in-cabin VCRs, 3 pools, fitness classes, gym, hair salon, hot tubs, sauna, spa, steam room, 12 bars, casino, cinema, 2 dance clubs, library, showrooms, video game room,*

8

children's programs (ages 3–17), dry cleaning, laundry service, computer room ☐*AE, D, MC, V.*

GOOD TO KNOW

Duty-free prices at Bermuda liquor stores only apply when purchases are delivered directly to your ship. Carry-outs carry a premium price tag.

☾ **Grandeur of the Seas.** With a seven-story atrium anchored by an elegant Champagne Terrace, skylights, acres of glass windows, and a bi-level health club/spa, *Grandeur of the Seas* lives up to its Vision-class designation with vast ocean views from most public areas. The double-deck formal dining room serves dinner in two assigned evening seatings; Windjammer, the Lido buffet, is a casual option for all meals. A solarium with a retracting roof over one swimming pool was a first for Royal Caribbean on *Grandeur of the Seas* and her sister-ships that sail other itineraries. The Viking Crown Lounge, high atop the ship with sweeping 360-degree sea views by day, is a rocking late-night dance club where the ship's DJ spins popular tunes until well into the early hours of the morning. Accommodations are a bit larger than on earlier fleet-mates, and cabins on two entire decks have balconies. ⮑*975 cabins 1,950 passengers (2,446 at full occupancy), 11 passenger decks ☖Dining room, buffet, ice-cream parlor, in-cabin safes, Wi-Fi, 2 pools (1 indoor), fitness classes, gym, hair salon, hot tubs, sauna, spa, 6 bars, casino, dance club, library, showroom, video game room, children's programs (ages 3–17), dry cleaning, laundry service, computer room* ☐*AE, D, MC, V.*

BEFORE YOU GO

To expedite your preboarding paperwork, some cruise lines have convenient forms on their Web sites. As long as you have your reservation number, you can provide the required immigration information, reserve shore excursions, and even indicate special requests from the comfort of your home. Less "wired" cruise lines might mail preboarding paperwork to you or your travel agent for completion after you make your final payment and request that you return the forms by mail or fax. No matter how you submit them, be sure to make copies of any forms you fill out and to bring them with you to the pier to shorten the check-in process.

TRAVEL DOCUMENTS

After you make the final payment to your travel agent, the cruise line will issue your cruise tickets and vouchers for airport-to-ship transfers. Depending on the airline, and whether you have purchased an air-sea package, you may receive your plane tickets or e-ticket vouchers at the same time; you may also receive vouchers for shore excursions, although most cruise lines issue these aboard ship. Should your travel documents not arrive when promised, contact your travel agent or call the cruise line. If you book late, sailing documents may be delivered directly to the cruise terminal.

Children under the age of 18 who are not traveling with both parents almost always require a letter of permission from the absent parent(s). Airlines, cruise lines, and immigration agents can deny minor children initial boarding or entry to foreign countries without proper proof of identification and citizenship *and* a permission letter from absent or noncustodial parents. Your travel agent or cruise line can help with the wording of such a letter.

> **FRUGAL FUN**
>
> Riding the ferry is an outstanding—and inexpensive—way to see Bermuda from the water. Bus and ferry passes, while sold on board some cruise ships, are usually less expensive when purchased at the ferry landing.

A WORD ABOUT PASSPORTS

It is every passenger's responsibility to have proper identification. If you arrive at the embarkation port without it, you will not be allowed to board, and the cruise line will issue no fare refund. Most travel agents know the requirements and can guide you to the proper agency to obtain what you need if you don't have it.

In the past, cruise lines sailing to Bermuda rarely asked to see the passports of American passengers; proof of citizenship in the form of a certified birth certificate and government-issued picture ID were sufficient. However, passports may be required of all passengers, including U.S. citizens, as early as January 1, 2008. Apply for a passport as far in advance of your cruise as possible. The process usually takes at least six weeks and can take longer during busy periods. Keep in mind that if you should find it necessary to cut your cruise short and return to the United States by air from Bermuda, a passport is required.

8

WHAT TO PACK

Cruise wear falls into three categories: casual, informal, and formal. Cruise documents should include information indicating how many evenings fall into each category. You will know when to wear what by reading your ship's daily newsletter—each evening's dress code will be prominently announced.

For the day, you'll need casual wear, including swimwear, a cover-up, and sandals for pool and beach. Time spent ashore touring and shopping calls for shorts topped with T-shirts or polo shirts and comfy walking shoes. Conservative is a rule to live by in Bermuda, and mix-and-match will save room in your suitcase. Forget denim, which is too hot, and concentrate on lighter fabrics that will breathe in the heat. At night, casual means khaki-type slacks and polo or sport shirts for men and sundresses, skirts, or casual pants outfits for women. By sticking to a few colors and adding accessories, you can mix and match for a different look every night.

Crime on Board

CLOSE UP

Crime aboard cruise ships has occasionally become headline news, thanks in large part to a few well-publicized cases. Most people never have any type of problem, but you should exercise the same precautions aboard ship that you would at home. Keep your valuables out of sight—on big ships virtually every cabin has a small safe in the cabin. Don't carry too much cash ashore, use your credit card whenever possible, and keep your money in a secure place, such as a front pocket that's harder to pick. Single women traveling with friends should stick together, especially when returning to their cabins late at night. When assaults occur, it often comes to light that alcohol, particularly overindulgence in alcohol, is a factor. Be careful about whom you befriend, as you would anywhere, whether it's a fellow passenger or a member of the crew. Don't be paranoid, but do be prudent.

Your cruise is a wonderful opportunity to leave everyday responsibilities behind, but don't neglect to pack your common sense. After a few drinks it might seem like a good idea to sit on a railing or lean over to get a better view of the ship's wake. Passengers have been known to fall. "Man overboard" is more likely to be the result of carelessness than criminal intent.

Informal dress is a little trickier. It applies only to evening wear and can mean different things depending on the cruise line. Informal for women is a dressier dress or pants outfit; for men it almost always includes a sport coat, and a tie is optional. Check your documents carefully.

Formal night means dressing up, but these days even that is a relative notion. You will see women in everything from simple cocktail dresses to elaborate, glittering gowns. A tuxedo (either all black or with white dinner jacket) or dark suit is required for gentlemen. For children, Sunday-best is entirely appropriate.

Men can usually rent their formal attire from the cruise line, and if they do so, it will be waiting when they board. Be sure to make these arrangements in advance; your travel agent can get the details from the cruise line. But if you're renting a tux, buy your own studs: a surefire way to spot a rented tuxedo is by the inexpensive studs that come with it. Also, many men with a little girth consider a vest more comfortable than a cummerbund.

An absolute essential for women is a shawl or light sweater. Aggressive air-conditioning can make public rooms uncomfortable, particularly if you're sunburned from a day at the beach.

Put things you can't do without—such as prescription medication, spare eyeglasses, toiletries, a swimsuit, and change of clothes for the first day—in your carry-on. Most cruise ships provide soap, shampoo, and conditioner.

ACCESSIBILITY ISSUES

As recently as the early 1990s, "accessibility" on a cruise ship meant little more than a few inside staterooms set aside for passengers with mobility issues. Most public rest rooms and nearly all en suite bathrooms had a "step-over" threshold. Newer ships are more sensitive to the needs of passengers with disabilities, but many older ships still have physical barriers in both cabins and public rooms. And once you get off the ship your problems will be compounded.

All cruise lines offer a limited number of staterooms designed to be wheelchair- and scooter-accessible. Booking a newer vessel will generally assure more choices and better accessibility. Auxiliary aids, such as flashers for the hearing impaired and buzzers for visually impaired passengers, as well as lifts for swimming pools and hot tubs, are available upon request. However, more than the usual amount of preplanning is necessary for smooth sailing if you have special needs.

Some people with limited mobility may find it difficult to embark or disembark the ship when docked due to the steep angle of gangways during high or low tide at certain times of day. In some situations, crew members may offer assistance that involves carrying guests, but if the sea is choppy, that might not be an option.

Passengers who require continuous oxygen or have service animals have further hurdles to overcome. You can bring both aboard a cruise ship, but your service animal will not be allowed to go ashore with you in Bermuda without an import permit, which must be requested in advance.

8

ARRIVING & DEPARTING

Most cruise-ship passengers fly to the port of embarkation. If you book your cruise far enough in advance, you'll be given the opportunity to purchase an Air & Sea package, which sometimes saves you money on your flight. By making your own airline arrangements, though, you may find airfare low enough to cover a pre-cruise night in a hotel if you have the time to fly in a day early. With frequent flight delays and cancellations these days, it's always a good idea to arrive in your port city the day before sailing—you will be more refreshed at boarding time and you don't want to "miss the boat"!

If you buy an Air & Sea package from your cruise line, a uniformed cruise-line agent will meet you to smooth your way from airport to pier. You will need to claim your own bags and give them to the transfer driver so they can be loaded on the bus. Upon arrival at the pier, luggage is automatically transferred to the ship for delivery to your cabin. The cruise-line ground-transfer system can also be available to independent fliers. However, be sure to ask your travel agent how much it costs; you may find that a taxi or shuttle service is less expensive and more convenient.

Many people prefer to drive to embarkation ports if they are close enough to home; secure parking is always available, either within the port or nearby. Additionally, some nearby hotels might offer free parking while you sail if you spend one pre-cruise night there.

BOARDING

Once the planning, packing, and anticipation are behind them, veteran cruise passengers sometimes view embarkation day as anticlimactic. However, for first-time cruise travelers, embarking on their first ship can be more than exhilarating—it can be downright intimidating. What exactly can you expect?

CHECK-IN

Once inside the cruise terminal, you'll see a check-in line. Actual boarding time is often scheduled for noon, but some cruise lines will process early arrivals and then direct them to a "holding" area. During check-in, you will be asked to produce your documents and any forms you were asked to complete ahead of time, plus proof of citizenship and a credit card (to cover onboard charges). You're issued a boarding card that often also doubles as your stateroom key and shipboard charge card. At some point—either before you enter the check-in area or before proceeding to the ship—you and your hand luggage will pass through a security procedure similar to those at airports.

The lines for check-in can be long, particularly at peak times. If check-in starts at noon but continues to 4 PM, you can expect lines to trail off as the boarding deadline approaches. Everyone is anxious to get on board and begin their vacation, so if you arrive at one of the busy periods, keep in mind that this is not the time to get cranky if you have to wait.

BOARDING THE SHIP

Once boarding begins, you will inevitably have your first experience with the ship's photographer and be asked to pose for an embarkation picture. It only takes a second, so smile. You are under no obligation to purchase any photos taken of you during the cruise, but they are a nice souvenir.

Procedures vary somewhat once you're greeted by staff members lined up just inside the ship's hull; however, you'll have to produce your boarding card, and possibly a picture ID, for the security officer. At some point, either at the check-in desk or when boarding the ship for the first time, you may be photographed for security purposes—your image will display on a monitor when your boarding card is "swiped" into a computer as you leave and reboard the ship throughout the cruise. Depending on the cruise line, once aboard you will be directed to your cabin, or a steward will relieve you of your carry-on luggage and accompany you. Stewards on high-end cruise lines not only show you the way, but hand you a glass of champagne as a welcome-aboard gesture.

ON BOARD

Check out your cabin to make sure that everything is in order. Try the plumbing and set the air-conditioning to the temperature you prefer. Your cabin may feel warm while docked but will cool off when the ship is underway. You should find a copy of the ship's daily schedule in the cabin. Take a few moments to look it over—you will want to know what time the muster drill takes place (a placard on the back of your cabin door will indicate directions to your emergency station), as well as meal hours and the schedule for various activities and entertainments.

Rented tuxedoes are either hanging in the closet or will be delivered sometime during the afternoon; bon-voyage gifts sent by your friends or travel agent usually appear as well. Be patient if you're expecting deliveries, particularly on megaships. Cabin stewards participate in the ship's turnaround and are extremely busy, although yours will no doubt introduce himself at the first available opportunity. It will also be a while before your checked luggage arrives, so your initial order of business is usually the buffet. Bring along the daily schedule to examine in detail while you eat.

While making your way to the Lido buffet, no doubt you'll notice bar waiters offering trays of colorful and exotic drinks, often in souvenir glasses that you can keep. Beware—they are not complimentary! If you choose one, you will be asked to sign for it. Again, like the photos, you are under no obligation to purchase; however, the glasses are fun souvenirs.

Do your plans for the cruise include booking shore excursions and indulging in spa treatments? The most popular tours sometimes sell out, and spas can be very busy during sea days, so your next stops should be the shore-excursion desk to book tours and the spa to make appointments. You may even want to take care of those tasks on the way to the buffet.

Dining-room seating arrangements are another matter for consideration. Some people like to check the main dining room to determine where their table is located. If it's not to your liking, or if you requested a large table and find yourself assigned to a small one, you will want to see the headwaiter. He'll be stationed in a lounge with his charts handy to make changes. The daily schedule will indicate where and when to meet with him. If you plan to dine in the ship's specialty restaurant, make those reservations as soon as possible to avoid disappointment.

PAYING FOR THINGS ON BOARD

Let's step back a moment and take a look at what happened when you checked in at the pier. Because a cashless society prevails on cruise ships, an imprint was made of your credit card or you had to place a cash deposit for use against your onboard charges. Then you were issued a charge card that usually doubles as your stateroom key. Most onboard expenditures are charged to your shipboard account with your signature as verification, with the possible exception of casino gaming—even so, you can often get cash advances against your account from the casino cashier.

An itemized bill is provided at the end of the voyage listing your purchases. In order to avoid surprises, it's a good idea to set aside your charge slips and request an interim printout of your bill from the purser to insure accuracy. Should you change your mind about charging onboard purchases, you can always inform the purser and pay in cash or traveler's checks instead. If your cash deposit was more than you spent, you will receive a refund.

TIPPING

One of the most delicate—yet frequently debated—topics of conversation among cruise passengers involves the matter of tipping. Who do you tip? How much? What's "customary" and "recommended?" Should parents tip the full amount for children or is just half adequate? Why do you have to tip at all?

When transfers to and from your ship are a part of your Air & Sea program, gratuities are generally included for luggage handling. In that case, do not worry about the interim tipping. However, if you take a taxi to the pier and hand over your bags to a stevedore, be sure to tip him. Treat him with respect and pass along at least $5.

During your cruise, room-service waiters generally receive a cash tip of $1 to $3 per delivery. A 15% gratuity will automatically be added to each bar bill during the cruise. If you use salon and spa services, a similar percentage might be added to the bills there as well. If you dine in a specialty restaurant, it may be suggested that you extend a one-time gratuity for the service staff.

There will be a "disembarkation talk" on the last day of the cruise that explains tipping procedures. If you're expected to tip in cash, small white tip envelopes will appear in your stateroom that day. If you tip in cash, you usually give the tip envelope directly to each person on the last night of the cruise. Tips generally add up to about $10 to $12 per person (including children) per day.

Most lines now either automatically add gratuities to passengers' onboard charge accounts or offer the option. If that suits you, then do nothing further. However, you're certainly free to adjust the amounts up or down to more appropriate levels or ask that the charge be removed altogether if you prefer distributing cash gratuities.

DINING

All food, all the time? Not quite, but it's possible to literally eat away the day and most of the night on a cruise. A popular cruise directors' joke is, "You came on as passengers, and you will be leaving as cargo." Although it's meant in fun, it does contain an element of truth. Food—tasty and plentiful—is available 24 hours a day on most cruise ships, and the dining experience at sea has reached almost mythical proportions. Perhaps it has something to do with legendary midnight buffets, the absence of menu prices, or maybe it's the vast selection and availability.

RESTAURANTS

Every ship has at least one main restaurant and a Lido, or casual, buffet alternative. Increasingly

GOOD TO KNOW

It isn't stinginess on the part of the cruise line that forbids bringing snacks ashore. Fruits, vegetables, seeds, plants, and meat are not allowed to be removed from the ship by regulation of the Bermuda government.

important are specialty restaurants. Meals in the primary and buffet restaurants are included in the cruise fare, as are round-the-clock room service, midday tea and snacks, and late-night buffets. Most mainstream cruise lines levy a surcharge for dining in alternative restaurants that may, or may not, also include a gratuity, although there generally is no additional charge on luxury cruise lines.

You may also find a pizzeria or a specialty coffee bar on your ship—popular favorites cropping up on ships old and new. Pizza is complimentary, but expect an additional charge for specialty coffees at the coffee bar and, quite likely, in the dining room as well. You'll also be charged for alcoholic beverages and soft drinks during meals; iced tea, regular coffee, tap water, and fruit juice are the most common complimentary beverages.

There's often a direct relationship between the cost of a cruise and the quality of its cuisine. The food is sophisticated on some (mostly expensive) lines, among them Crystal Cruises and Regent Seven Seas Cruises. In the more moderate price range, Celebrity Cruises has gained renown for their culinary stylings. The trend toward featuring signature dishes and even entire menus designed by acclaimed chefs has spread throughout the cruise industry; however, on most mainstream cruise lines, the food is of the quality that you would find at any good hotel banquet—perfectly acceptable but certainly not gourmet.

SEATINGS

If your cruise ship has traditional seatings for dinner, the one decision that may set the tone for your entire cruise is your dinner seating. Which is best? Early dinner seating is generally scheduled between 6 and 6:30 PM, and late seating can begin from 8:15 to 8:45 PM. So the "best" seating depends on you, your lifestyle, and your personal preference.

Families with young children and older passengers often choose an early seating. Early seating diners are encouraged not to linger too long over dessert and coffee because the dining room has to be readied for late seating. Late seating is viewed by some passengers as more romantic and less rushed.

Cruise lines understand that strict schedules no longer satisfy the desires of all cruise passengers. Many cruise lines now include alternatives to the set schedules in the dining room, including casual dinner menus in their buffet facilities, where more flexibility is allowed in dress and meal times. À la carte restaurants are showing up on more ships and offer yet another choice, though usually for an additional charge.

Open seating is primarily associated with more upscale lines; it allows passengers the flexibility to dine any time during restaurant hours and be seated with whomever they please.

Led by Norwegian Cruise Line and Princess Cruises, more contemporary and premium cruise lines are exploring adaptations of open seating to offer variety and a more personalized experience. Carnival Cruise Line even has four seating times instead of the usual two, plus casual evening dining in the Lido buffet.

CHANGING TABLES Some cruise lines advise that, although dining preferences may be requested by your travel agent, no requests are guaranteed. Table assignments are generally not confirmed until embarkation; however, every effort is made to satisfy all guests. If there's a problem, see the headwaiter for assistance. Changes after the first evening are generally discouraged; however, there will be a designated place to meet with dining-room staff and iron out seating problems during embarkation day. Check the daily program for time and location.

SPECIAL DIETS

Cruise lines make every possible attempt to insure dining satisfaction. If you have special dietary considerations—such as low-salt, kosher, or food allergies—be sure to indicate them well ahead of time and check to be certain your needs are known by your waiter once you're on board. In addition to the usual menu items, spa, low-calorie, low-carbohydrate, or low-fat selections, as well as children's menus, are usually available. Requests for dishes not featured on the menu can often be granted if you ask in advance.

WINE

Wine typically costs about what you would expect to pay at a nice lounge or restaurant in a resort or in your local liquor store (depending on where you live). Wine by the bottle is a more economical choice at dinner than ordering it by the glass. Any wine you don't finish will be kept for you and served the next night. Gifts of wine or champagne ordered from the cruise line (either by you, a friend, or your travel agent) can be taken to the dining room. Wine from any other source will incur a corkage fee of approximately $10 to $15 per bottle.

THE CAPTAIN'S TABLE

Legend has it that a nouveau-riche passenger's response to an invitation to dine with the captain during a round-the-world cruise was, "I didn't shell out all those bucks to eat with the help!" Although there are some cruise passengers who decline invitations to dine at the captain's table, there are far more who covet such an experience. You will know you have been included in that exclusive coterie when an embossed invitation arrives in your stateroom on the day of a formal dinner. RSVP as soon as possible—if you are unable to attend, someone else will be invited in your place.

Who is invited? If you're a frequent cruiser, occupy an owner's suite, or if you hail from the captain's hometown and speak his native language, you may be considered. Honeymoon couples are sometimes selected at random, as are couples celebrating a golden wedding anniversary. Unattached female passengers often round out an uneven number of guests. Requests made by travel agents on behalf of their clients sometimes do the trick.

ENTERTAINMENT

It's hard to imagine, but in the early years of cruise travel, shipboard entertainment consisted of little more than poetry readings and recitals that exhibited the talents of fellow passengers. Those bygone days of sedate amusements in an intimate setting have been replaced by lavish showrooms where sequined and feathered showgirls strut their stuff on stage amid previously unimagined special effects.

Seven-night Bermuda cruises usually include two original production shows. One of these might be a Las Vegas–style extravaganza and the other a best-of-Broadway show featuring old and new favorites from the Great White Way. Other shows highlight the talents of individual singers, dancers, magicians, comedians, and even acrobats. Don't be surprised if you're plucked from the audience to take the brunt of a comedian's jokes or act as the magician's temporary assistant. Sit in the front row if appearing onstage appeals to you.

Whether it's relegated to a late-afternoon interlude between bingo and dinner, or a featured evening highlight, the passenger talent show is often a "don't miss" production. From pure camp to stylishly slick, what passes for talent is sometimes surprising but seldom boring. Stand-up comedy is generally discouraged; however, passengers who want their performance skills to be considered should answer the call for auditions and plan to rehearse the show at least once.

Enrichment programs have become a popular pastime at sea. It may come as a surprise that port lecturers on many large contemporary cruise ships offer more information on shore tours and shopping than insight into the ports of call. If more cerebral presentations are important to you, consider a cruise on a line that features stimulating enrichment programs and seminars. Speakers may include destination-oriented historians, popular authors, business leaders, radio or television personalities, and even movie stars.

LOUNGES & NIGHTCLUBS

If you find the show-lounge stage a bit intimidating and want to perform in a more intimate venue, look for karaoke. Singing along in a piano bar is another shipboard favorite for would-be crooners. Some passengers even take the place of the ship's pianist during breaks.

Drinking on Board

It's hard to avoid the ship's bars since they are social centers, but alcoholic drinks are not usually included in your cruise fare, and bar bills can add up quickly. Drinks at the captain's welcome-aboard cocktail party and at cocktail parties held specifically for repeat cruisers are usually free. But if you pick up that boldly colored welcome-aboard cocktail as your ship pulls away from the dock, you may well be asked to sign for it, and the cost will then be added to your shipboard account. You should expect to pay about the same for a drink on board a cruise ship as you would pay in a bar at home: $3 to $4 for a domestic beer, $4 to $9 for a cocktail, $5 to $9 for a glass of wine, $1.25 to $2 for a soft drink. On virtually all ships, an automatic 15% gratuity will be added to your tab. Also note that specialty coffees like cappuccino—even in the dining room after dinner—will add a $2 to $4 charge to your onboard account. To save money on your bar bill, you can follow a few simple strategies. In lounges, request the less-expensive bar brands or the reduced-price drink of the day. On some ships, discounted "beverage cards" for unlimited fountain soft drinks and/or a set number of mixed drinks are available.

In international waters there are, technically, no laws against teenage drinking, but almost all ships require passengers to be over 21 to purchase alcoholic beverages.

Other lounges might feature easy-listening music, jazz, or combos for pre- and postdinner social dancing. Later in the evening, lounges pick up the pace with music from the 1950s and '60s; clubs aimed at a younger crowd usually have more contemporary dance music during the late-night hours.

CASINOS

A sure sign that your ship is in international waters is the opening of the casino. On most ships, lavish casinos pulsate with activity. Exceptions at sea are the family-oriented ships of Disney Cruise Line, which shun gaming in favor of more wholesome pastimes. However, all ships currently offering Bermuda itineraries feature casinos.

The rationale for locating casinos where most passengers must pass either through or alongside them is obvious—the unspoken allure of winning. In addition to slot machines in a variety of denominations, cruise-ship casinos might feature roulette, craps, and a variety of poker games—Caribbean stud poker, Let It Ride, Texas Hold 'Em, and blackjack, to name a few. Cruise lines strive to provide fair and professional gambling entertainment and supply gaming guides that set out the rules of play and betting limits for each game.

Casino hours vary based on the itinerary or location of the ship; most are required to close while in port, whereas others may offer 24-hour slot machines. Every casino has a cashier for convenience, and you may be able to charge a cash advance to your onboard account.

OTHER ENTERTAINMENT

Most vessels have a room for screening movies. On older ships and some newer ones, this is often a genuine movie theater; on other ships it may be a multipurpose room. Over the course of a weeklong voyage a dozen films may be screened, each repeated several times. Theaters are also used for lectures, religious services, and private meetings.

With a few exceptions, cruise ships equip their cabins with closed-circuit TVs showing movies (continuously on some newer ships), shipboard lectures, and regular programs (thanks to satellite reception). Ships with in-cabin VCRs or DVDs usually provide a selection of movies at no charge (a deposit is sometimes required).

Most medium- and large-size ships have video arcades, and nearly all ships now have computer centers.

SPAS

With all the usual pampering and service in luxurious surroundings, simply being on a cruise can be a stress-reducing experience. Add to that the menu of spa and salon services at your fingertips and you have a recipe for total sensory pleasure. The spas have become among the most popular of shipboard services so book your blisstime as soon as possible. Some luxury cruise lines allow you to book services in advance.

Some of the more exotic spa offerings sound good enough to eat. A Milk and Honey Hydrotherapy Bath; Coconut Rub & Milk Ritual Wrap or Float; and a Javanese Steam Wrap incorporating cinnamon, ginger, coffee, sea salt, and honey are just a few of the tempting items found on spa menus. Not

> **GOOD TO KNOW**
>
> Your ship's spa treatments are often available at a significantly reduced price during port days. Pamper yourself—and your wallet.

8

quite as exotic-sounding, other treatments and services are nonetheless therapeutic for the body and soul. Steiner Leisure is the largest spa and salon operator at sea (the company even operates the Madara and the Greenhouse spas), with facilities on more than 100 cruise ships worldwide.

In addition to facials, manicures, pedicures, massages, and sensual body treatments, other hallmarks of Steiner Leisure are salon services and products for hair and skin. Founded in 1901 by Henry Steiner of London, a single salon prospered when Steiner's son joined the business in 1926 and was granted a royal warrant as hairdresser to Queen Mary in 1937. In 1956 Steiner won its first cruise-ship contract, to operate salons on Cunard Line ships. By the mid-1990s, Steiner Leisure began taking an active role in creating shipboard spas offering a wide variety of wellness therapies and beauty programs for both women and men.

SPORTS & FITNESS

Onboard sports facilities might include a court for basketball, volley-ball, tennis—or all three—a jogging track, or even an in-line skating track. Some Royal Caribbean ships offer such innovative and unexpected features as rock-climbing walls and ice-skating rinks. For the less adventurous, there's always table tennis and shuffleboard.

Naturally, you can find at least one swimming pool, and possibly several. Cruise-ship pools are generally on the small side—more appropriate for cooling off than doing laps—and the majority contain filtered saltwater. But some are elaborate affairs, with waterslides. Princess Grand–class ships have challenging, freshwater "swim against the current" pools for swimming enthusiasts who want to get their low-impact exercise while on board.

Golf is a perennial seagoing favorite of players who want to take their games to the next level and add Bermuda's most beautiful and challenging courses to their scorecards. Shipboard programs can include clinics, use of full-motion golf cages, and even individual instruction from resident pros using state-of-the-art computer analysis. Once ashore, escorted excursions include everything needed for a satisfying round of play, including equipment and tips from the pro, and prescheduled tee times at exclusive courses. Unless you find avid golfers with firsthand insight into Bermuda courses who are anxious to make up a group from the ship themselves, you may find it more expedient to book golf outings through the cruise line rather than take your chances at locating a course with a convenient tee time, arranging costly transportation, and being paired with strangers. You may not save time or money by letting the cruise line arrange a golf outing; however, when they do it, they handle the details and make sure you return to the ship on time.

FITNESS CENTERS

Cruise vacations can be hazardous to your waistline if you're not careful. Eating "out" for all meals and sampling different cuisines tends to pile on unaccustomed calories. But shipboard fitness centers have become ever more elaborate, offering state-of-the-art exercise machines, treadmills, and stair steppers, not to mention weights and weight machines. As a bonus, many fitness centers with floor-to-ceiling windows have the world's most inspiring sea views.

If you prefer a more social atmosphere as you burn off sinful chocolate desserts, there are specialized fitness classes for all levels of ability. High-impact, energetic aerobics are not for everyone, but any class that raises the heart rate can be toned down and tailored to individual capabilities. Stretching classes help you warm up for a light jog or brisk walk on deck, and sit-for-fitness classes are offered for mature passengers or those with delicate joints. Fees are sometimes charged for specialty classes, such as Pilates, spinning, and yoga. Most ships have personal trainers on board to get you off on the right foot, also for a fee.

SHIPBOARD SERVICES

COMMUNICATIONS

Just because you're out to sea does not mean you have to be out of touch. Ship-to-shore telephone calls can cost $5 to $15 a minute, so it makes economic sense to use e-mail to remain in contact with your home or office. Most ships have basic computer systems, whereas some newer vessels offer more high-tech connectivity—even in-cabin hook-ups or wireless connections for your own laptop computer or one you can rent on board. Expect charges in the 35¢ to $1 per minute range for usage. Ships usually offer some kind of package so that you get a reduced per-minute price if you pay a fee upfront; the more minutes in the package, the lower the per-minute cost.

The ability to use your own cell phone from the high seas is a relatively new alternative that is gaining popularity. It's also cheaper than using a cabin phone. It's a rather ingenious concept: the ship acts as a cell "tower" in international waters—you use your own cell phone and number when roaming at sea. Before leaving home, ask your cell phone service provider to activate international roaming on your account. When in port, depending on the agreements your mobile-service provider has established, you may be able to connect to local networks. Rates for using the maritime service, as well as any roaming charges from Bermuda, are established by your mobile-service carrier and are worth checking into before you leave home.

LAUNDRY & DRY CLEANING

Most cruise ships offer valet laundry and pressing (and some also have dry-cleaning) service. Expenses can add up fast, especially for laundry, as charges are per item and the rates are similar to those charged in hotels. If doing laundry is important to you and you do not want to send it out to be done, some cruise ships have a low-cost or free self-service laundry room (they usually feature an iron and ironing board in addition to washer and dryer). If you book one of the top-dollar suites, laundry service may be included for no additional cost. Upscale ships, such as those in the Regent Seven Seas Cruises and Crystal Cruises fleets, have complimentary self-service launderettes. On other lines, such as Princess Cruises and Carnival Cruise Lines, you can do your own laundry for about $3 or less per load. None of the vessels in the Norwegian Cruise Line or Royal Caribbean Bermuda fleets has self-service laundry facilities.

LIBRARY

Cruise-ship libraries run the gamut from a few shelves of relatively uninspiring titles to huge rooms crammed with volumes of travel guides, classics, and the latest best sellers. As a rule, the smaller the ship, the more likely you are to find a well-stocked library. The space allotted to the library falls in proportion to the emphasis on glitzy stage shows—on small ships

GOOD TO KNOW

Get walking tour maps and other Bermuda tourism information in the cruise terminal when you arrive.

the passengers are more likely to lean toward quiet diversions. On ships with sophisticated entertainment centers in staterooms, you may find videotape or DVD movies as well as books in the library.

PHOTO SHOP

A Bermuda cruise is a series of photo opportunities, and ships' photographers are on hand to capture boarding, sailaway, port arrivals, and other highlights, such as the captain's reception. Photographers seem to pop up everywhere and take far more pictures than you could ever want; however, they're a unique remembrance, and there's no obligation to purchase them. Prices for the prints, which are put on display, range from $10 to $25, depending on size.

Film, batteries, single-use cameras, and related merchandise may also be available in the ship's photo shop. Some ships' photography staffers are capable of processing your film or your digital prints right on board.

SHORE-EXCURSION DESK

Manned by a knowledgeable staff, the shore-excursion desk can offer not only the sale of ship-sponsored tours, but may also be the place to learn more about ports of call and garner information you'll need to tour independently. Although staff members and the focus of their positions vary widely, the least you can expect is basic information and port maps. Happily, some shore-excursion staff members possess a wealth of information and share it without reservation. On some ships the port lecturer may emphasize shopping and "recommended" merchants, with little to impart regarding sightseeing or the history and culture of ports.

SHORE EXCURSIONS

Shore excursions are optional tours organized by the cruise line and sold aboard the ship. Most tours last two to four hours and all are meant to optimize your time on the island—the cruise line does the research about what to see and do, and you just go along for the ride. You'll sometimes pay more for these ship-packaged tours than if

GOOD TO KNOW

You should find the port agent's address and telephone number in your ship's daily bulletin. Take that with you when going ashore—the port agent is your local contact in case of emergency.

you booked them independently, either before you leave home or after arriving in port. However, with only two or three days at your disposal, the convenience, and assurance that a spot on the tour you're looking forward to is available, may be worth the price. Popular tours often sell out and may not be obtainable at any price once you are ashore. Fees are generally $20–$25 per person for walking tours, $45–$75 per person for island tours, $50–$70 for snorkeling trips, and $75–$150 for diving trips. Prices for children are usually less. For exact durations and pricing, consult your cruise line. Also keep in mind that tour fees and time estimates can vary depending on where your ship is docked.

Naturally, you're always free to explore on your own. With its excellent taxi service, Bermuda is a good, although pricey, island for hiring a car and driver. A taxi tour of the island including admissions to the Bermuda Aquarium, Museum & Zoo, and the Crystal Caves costs about $60 per person. Public transportation, including buses and ferries, is convenient to all cruise terminals and the sale of all-day passes might even be offered by the shore-excursion desk on your ship.

GOING ASHORE

Ships calling in Bermuda dock alongside the pier, so you can walk right off the ship to the center of town and major attractions. In Hamilton, for instance, passengers walk off the ship right onto Front Street, with its shops and restaurants. Before anyone is allowed to proceed down the gangway, however, the ship must be cleared for landing. Immigration and customs officials board the vessel to examine passports and sort through red tape. It may be more than an hour before you're allowed ashore. Your ship ID acts as your boarding pass, which you'll need to get back on board.

WORD OF MOUTH

"My cruise ship will be docked one day each in Hamilton, St. George's, and King's Wharf. I want to go diving one day and would love to do a wreck and a reef. Does anyone have a recommendation for companies to go with? I don't want to book through the cruise ship."

–expatgal1

"I like Blue Water Divers. They have always been very professional (ie safety is the top priority) and knowledgeable. The best site can vary because of conditions. Bermuda has a lot of choices for great wrecks, not so much for reef. I would follow the suggestions of your dive master."

–cmcfong

One advantage of a Bermuda itinerary is that cruise ships remain docked at night, which affords the opportunity to dine ashore and sample the nightlife. There's a downside to onboard life, though. Although most shipboard services—dining, lounges, and the fitness center and spa—continue to hum along as usual, duty-free shops and casinos are required by Bermuda government regulations to remain closed when in port. In addition, professional entertainment in the show lounge is suspended, although a movie might be screened there instead. Some ships offer a "Bermuda Night" tropical-theme deck party; however, ships docked in Hamilton and St. George's will wrap up the outdoor festivities around midnight as a courtesy to local residents.

RETURNING TO THE SHIP

Cruise lines are strict about sailing times, which are posted at the gangway and elsewhere and announced in the daily schedule of activities. Be sure to be back on board at least a half hour before the announced sailing time or you may be stranded. If you're on a shore excursion that was sold by the cruise line, however, the captain will wait for your group before casting off. That's one reason many passengers prefer ship-packaged tours.

If you're not on one of the ship's tours and the ship sails without you, immediately contact the cruise line's port representative, whose phone number is often listed on the daily schedule of activities. You may be able to hitch a ride on a pilot boat, although that is unlikely. Passengers who miss the boat must pay their own way to the next port.

DISEMBARKATION

All cruises come to an end eventually, and it hardly seems fair that you have to leave when it feels like your vacation has just begun, but leave you must. The disembarkation process actually begins the day before you arrive at your ship's home port. During that day your cabin steward delivers special luggage tags to your stateroom, along with customs forms and instructions.

The night before you disembark, you'll need to set aside clothing to wear the next morning when you leave the ship. Many people dress in whatever casual outfits they wear for the final dinner on board, or change into travel clothes after dinner. Also, do not forget to put your passport or other proof of citizenship, airline tickets, and medications in your hand luggage.

After you finish packing, attach your new luggage tags (they are color- or number-coded according to postcruise transportation plans and flight schedules). Follow the instructions provided and place the locked luggage outside your stateroom door for pickup during the hours indicated.

A statement itemizing your onboard charges is delivered before you arise on disembarkation morning. Plan to get up early enough to check it over for accuracy, finish packing your belongings, and vacate your stateroom by the appointed hour. Any discrepancies in your onboard account should be taken care of before leaving the ship, usually at the purser's desk.

Room service is not available on most ships on the last morning; however, breakfast is served in the main restaurant and the buffet room. After breakfast, there's not much to do but wait comfortably in a lounge or on deck for your tag color or number to be called. Disembarkation procedures can sometimes be drawn out by passengers who are unprepared. This is no time to abandon your patience or sense of humor.

Remember that all passengers must meet with customs and immigration officials before disembarkation, either on the ship or in the terminal. Procedures vary and are outlined in your instructions. In some ports, passengers must meet with officials at a specified hour (usually very early) in an onboard lounge; in other ports, customs forms are collected in the terminal and passports or other identification papers are examined there as well.

Once in the terminal, locate your luggage and proceed to your motor coach or taxi, or retrieve your vehicle from the parking lot.

CUSTOMS & DUTIES

U.S. CUSTOMS

Before a ship lands, each individual or family must fill out a customs declaration, regardless of whether anything was purchased abroad. If you have less than $800 worth of goods, you will not need to itemize purchases. Be prepared to pay whatever duties are owed directly to the customs inspector, with cash or check.

U.S. Customs preclears many ships sailing in and out of certain ports. It's done on the ship before you disembark. In other ports you must collect your luggage from the dock and then stand in line to pass through the inspection point. This can take up to an hour.

U.S. CITIZENS Duties are the same for returning cruise passengers as for all other travelers, with a few exceptions. On certain Caribbean itineraries that include a visit to Bermuda, you're entitled to bring back $800 worth of goods duty-free. ⇨ *For general customs and duty information, see Customs & Duties in Bermuda Essentials.*

NON–U.S. CITIZENS If you hold a foreign passport and will be returning home within hours of docking, you may be exempt from all U.S. Customs duties. Everything you bring into the United States must leave with you when you return home. When you reach your own country, you will have to pay appropriate duties there.

SENDING PACKAGES HOME

You may also send packages home duty-free, with a limit of one parcel per addressee per day (except alcohol or tobacco products or perfume worth more than $5). You can mail up to $200 worth of goods for personal use, and $100 worth of goods as a gift. Mailed items do not affect your duty-free allowance on your return.

Bermuda
Essentials

PLANNING TOOLS, EXPERT INSIGHT, GREAT CONTACTS

There are planners and there are those who, excuse the pun, fly by the seat of their pants. We happily place ourselves among the planners. Our writers and editors try to anticipate all the issues you may face before and during any journey, and then they do their research. This section is the product of their efforts. Use it to get excited about your trip to Bermuda, to inform your travel planning, or to guide you on the road should the seat of your pants start to feel threadbare.

GETTING STARTED

We're really proud of our Web site: Fodors.com is a great place to begin any journey. Scan Travel Wire for suggested itineraries, travel deals, restaurant and hotel openings, and other up-to-the-minute info. Check out Booking to research prices and book plane tickets, hotel rooms, rental cars, and vacation packages. Head to Talk for on-the-ground pointers from travelers who frequent our message boards. You can also link to loads of other travel-related resources.

RESOURCES

ONLINE TRAVEL TOOLS

All About Bermuda One of the best Bermuda Web sites is ⊕www.bermuda-online.org. Supported by the Royal Gazette, it has information on every aspect of Bermuda, from history to transportation. The Department of Tourism's Web site ⊕www.bermudatourism.com is helpful during the initial stages of vacation planning. ⊕www.bermuda.com has a good search engine and links to a number of Bermuda-related Web pages. The Bermuda Hotel Association's ⊕www.experience-bermuda.com has a monthly events calendar and a search function that allows users to find events by date or type. There's also a good selection of maps. Gay visitors to Bermuda might find ⊕www.gaybermuda.com useful for finding gay-friendly hotels and nightlife venues. ⊕BlackandCoke.com and ⊕www.bermynet.com are online guides to entertainment events in Bermuda, with a complete listing of the island's bars, clubs, and pubs. To keep up with current affairs, check out the island's three newspapers: ⊕www.theroyalgazette.com for stories from the daily Royal Gazette and the weekly Mid Ocean News, and ⊕www.bermudasun.bm for the twice-weekly Bermuda Sun. Visit the Bermuda National Trust at ⊕www.bnt.bm for event, tour, and attraction information.

Safety Transportation Security Administration (TSA) (⊕www.tsa.gov)

Time Zones Timeanddate.com (⊕www.timeanddate.com/worldclock) can help you figure out the correct time anywhere.

Weather Accuweather.com (⊕www.accuweather.com) is an independent weather-forecasting service with good coverage of hurricanes. **Weather.com** (⊕www.weather.com) is the Web site for the Weather Channel.

Other Resources CIA World Factbook (⊕www.cia.gov/cia/publications/factbook/index.html) has profiles of every country in the world. It's a good source if you need some quick facts and figures.

WORD OF MOUTH

After your trip, be sure to rate the places you visited and share your experiences and travel tips with us and other Fodorites in Travel Ratings and Talk on www.fodors.com.

INSPIRATION

Bermuda Moods is a compilation of Bermuda snapshots taken by professional and amateur photographers. As the title suggests, the pictures were chosen to reflect the various characteristics of the island. The book is a huge success locally.

Shakespeare, an Island and a Storm by David F. Raine mixes historical research with poetic storytelling to link the story of the Sea Venture and Shakespeare's *The Tempest*, which is believed to have been inspired by accounts of the storms that greeted the island's first settlers.

The Story of Bermuda and Her People by William Sears Zuill gives one of the best historical accounts of the island and its inhabitants, starting from the wreck of the Sea Venture in 1609 and ending in the modern era.

The Deep, starring Robert Shaw and Jacqueline Bisset, shows the island through Hollywood's eyes. Older locals remember the 1970s filming with pride. Rest assured, the shady international criminals in the film are purely part of Peter Benchley's imagination!

The documentary *Rare Bird* has enjoyed an exceptional response from both the Bermudian public and the international film scene after premiering at the Bermuda International Film Festival in 2007. The film follows the history of the cahow (Bermuda's national bird) and its present day plight against extinction. It also explores the island's environmental and social issues, both past and present.

When Voices Rise tells the important but little-known story of how segregation was finally overcome in Bermuda in the late 1950s. The documentary has achieved widespread critical acclaim.

VISITOR INFORMATION

In Bermuda **Bermuda Department of Tourism** (☎441/292–0023 ⊕www.bermudatourism.com). **St. George's Foundation** (☎441/297–8043 ⊕www.stgeorgesfoundation.com).

In the U.S. **Bermuda Department of Tourism** (☎800/223–6106).

▌ THINGS TO CONSIDER

GEAR

As a rule of thumb, Bermudians dress more formally than most Americans. Leave your cutoffs, short shorts, and halter tops at home. In the evening, some of the more upscale restaurants and hotel dining rooms require men to wear a jacket and tie and women to dress comparably, so bring a few dressy outfits. However, increasingly, venues are more accepting of the trend toward "smart-casual." In this case, women should be fine with slacks or a skirt and a dressy blouse or sweater. Bermudian men often wear Bermuda shorts (and proper kneesocks) with a jacket and tie for formal events and business meetings.

During the cooler months, bring lightweight woolens or cottons that you can wear in layers to accommodate vaga-

ries of the weather. A lightweight jacket is always a good idea. Regardless of the season, pack a swimsuit, a beach-wear cover-up, sunscreen, and sunglasses, as well as a raincoat (umbrellas are typically provided by hotels). Comfortable walking shoes are a must. If you plan to play tennis, be aware that many courts require proper whites and that tennis balls in Bermuda are extremely expensive. Bring your own tennis balls if possible.

Bermuda-bound airlines commonly accept golf club bags in lieu of a piece of luggage, but there are fairly stringent guidelines governing the maximum amount of equipment that can be transported without an excess baggage fee. The general rule of thumb is one covered bag containing a maximum of 14 clubs, 12 balls, and one pair of shoes.

PASSPORTS & VISAS

As of January 2007, U.S. citizens arriving by air to Bermuda need a valid passport. U.S. citizens may need a passport as early as January 2008, when traveling by sea. U.S citizens do not need a Visa to enter Bermuda for a period less than 90 days.

PASSPORTS

A passport verifies both your identity and nationality—a great reason to have one. Another reason is that you need a passport now more than ever. At this writing, U.S. citizens must have a passport when traveling by air between the United States and several destinations for which other forms of identification (e.g., a driver's license and a birth certificate) were once sufficient. These destinations include Mexico, Canada, Bermuda, and all countries in Central America and the Caribbean (except the territories of Puerto Rico and the U.S. Virgin Islands). Soon enough you'll need a passport when traveling between the United States and such destinations by land and sea, too.

U.S. passports are valid for 10 years. You must apply in person if you're getting a passport for the first time; if your previ-

PACKING 101

Why do some people travel with a convoy of huge suitcases yet never have a thing to wear? How do others pack a duffel with a week's worth of outfits *and* supplies for every contingency? We realize that packing is a matter of style, but there's a lot to be said for traveling light. These tips help fight the battle of the bulging bag.

■ **Make a list.** In a recent Fodor's survey, 29% of respondents said they make lists (and often pack) a week before a trip. You can use your list to pack and to repack at the end of your trip. It can also serve as record of the contents of your suitcase—in case it disappears in transit.

■ **Think it through.** As you create your itinerary, note outfits next to each activity (don't forget accessories).

■ **Edit your wardrobe.** Plan to wear everything twice (better yet, thrice) and to do laundry along the way. Stick to one basic look—urban chic, sporty casual, etc. Build around one or two neutrals and an accent (e.g., black, white, and olive green). Women can freshen looks by changing scarves or jewelry. For a week's trip, you can look smashing with three bottoms, four or five tops, a sweater, and a jacket.

■ **Be practical.** Put comfortable shoes atop your list. (Did we need to say this?) Pack lightweight, wrinkle-resistent, compact, washable items. Stack and roll clothes, so they'll wrinkle less. Unless you're on a guided tour or a cruise, select luggage you can readily carry. Porters, like good butlers, are hard to find these days.

■ **Check weight and size limitations.** In the United States you may be charged extra for checked bags weighing more than 50 pounds. Abroad some airlines don't allow you to check bags over 60 to 70 pounds, or they charge outrageous fees for every excess pound—or bag. Carry-on size limitations can be stringent, too.

■ **Check carry-on restrictions.** Research restrictions with the TSA. Rules vary abroad, so check them with your airline if you're traveling overseas on a foreign carrier. Consider packing all but essentials (travel documents, prescription meds, wallet) in checked luggage. This leads to a "pack only what you can afford to lose" approach that might help you streamline.

■ **Rethink valuables.** On U.S. flights, airlines are liable for only about $2,800 per person for bags. On international flights, the liability limit is around $635 per bag. But items like computers, cameras, and jewelry aren't covered, and as gadgetry can go on and off the list of carry-on no-no's, you can't count on keeping things safe by keeping them close. Although comprehensive travel policies may cover luggage, the liability limit is often a pittance. Your home-owner's policy may cover you sufficiently when you travel—or not.

■ **Lock it up.** If you must pack valuables, use TSA-approved locks (about $10) that can be unlocked by all U.S. security personnel.

■ **Tag it.** Always tag your luggage; use your business address if you don't want people to know your home address. Put the same information (and a copy of your itinerary) inside your luggage, too.

■ **Report problems immediately.** If your bags—or things in them—are damaged or go astray, file a written claim with your airline *before leaving the airport*. If the airline is at fault, it may give you money for essentials until your luggage arrives. Most lost bags are found within 48 hours, so alert the airline to your whereabouts for two or three days. If your bag was opened for security reasons in the States and something is missing, file a claim with the TSA.

ous passport was lost, stolen, or damaged; or if your previous passport has expired and was issued more than 15 years ago or when you were under 16. All children under 18 must appear in person to apply for or renew a passport. Both parents must accompany any child under 14 (or send a notarized statement with their permission) and provide proof of their relationship to the child.

■**TIP→** Before your trip, make two copies of your passport's data page (one for someone at home and another for you to carry separately). Or scan the page and e-mail it to someone at home and/or yourself.

There are 13 regional passport offices, as well as 7,000 passport acceptance facilities in post offices, public libraries, and other governmental offices. If you're renewing a passport, you can do so by mail. Forms are available at passport acceptance facilities and online.

The cost to apply for a new passport is $97 for adults, $82 for children under 16; renewals are $67. Allow six weeks for processing, both for first-time passports and renewals. For an expediting fee of $60 you can reduce this time to about two weeks. If your trip is less than two weeks away, you can get a passport even more rapidly by going to a passport office with the necessary documentation. Private expediters can get things done in as little as 48 hours, but charge hefty fees for their services.

U.S. Passport Information U.S. Department of State (☎877/487–2778 ⊕travel.state. gov/passport).

U.S. Passport & Visa Expediters A. Briggs Passport & Visa Expediters (☎800/806–0581 or 202/464–3000 ⊕www.abriggs.com). American Passport Express (☎800/455–5166 or 603/559–9888 ⊕www.americanpassport. com). Passport Express (☎800/362–8196 or 401/272–4612 ⊕www.passportexpress.com). Travel Document Systems (☎800/874–5100 or 202/638–3800 ⊕www.traveldocs.com).

Travel the World Visas (☎866/886–8472 or 301/495–7700 ⊕www.world-visa.com).

TRIP INSURANCE

What kind of coverage do you honestly need? Do you need trip insurance at all? Take a deep breath and read on.

We believe that comprehensive trip insurance is especially valuable if you're booking a very expensive or complicated trip (particularly to an isolated region) or if you're booking far in advance. Who knows what could happen six months down the road? But whether you get insurance has more to do with how comfortable you are assuming all that risk yourself.

Comprehensive travel policies typically cover trip-cancellation and interruption, letting you cancel or cut your trip short because of a personal emergency, illness, or, in some cases, acts of terrorism in your destination. Such policies also cover evacuation and medical care. Some also cover you for trip delays because of bad weather or mechanical problems as well as for lost or delayed baggage. Another type of coverage to look for is financial default—that is, when your trip is disrupted because a tour operator, airline, or cruise line goes out of business. Generally you must buy this when you book your trip or shortly thereafter, and it's only available to you if your operator isn't on a list of excluded companies.

■**TIP→** OK. You know you can save a bundle on trips to warm-weather destinations by traveling in rainy season. But there's also a chance that a severe storm will disrupt your plans. The solution? Look for hotels and resorts that offer storm/hurricane guarantees. Although they rarely allow refunds, most guarantees do let you rebook later if a storm strikes.

If you're going abroad, consider buying medical-only coverage at the very least. Neither Medicare nor some private insurers cover medical expenses anywhere outside of the United States besides Mexico and Canada (including time aboard a cruise ship, even if it leaves from a U.S.

Trip Insurance Resources

INSURANCE COMPARISON SITES		
Insure My Trip.com	800/487–4722	www.insuremytrip.com
Square Mouth.com	800/240–0369	www.quotetravelinsurance.com
COMPREHENSIVE TRAVEL INSURERS		
Access America	866/807–3982	www.accessamerica.com
CSA Travel Protection	800/873–9855	www.csatravelprotection.com
HTH Worldwide	610/254–8700 or 888/243–2358	www.hthworldwide.com
Travelex Insurance	888/457–4602	www.travelex-insurance.com
Travel Guard International	715/345–0505 or 800/826–4919	www.travelguard.com
Travel Insured International	800/243–3174	www.travelinsured.com
MEDICAL-ONLY INSURERS		
International Medical Group	800/628–4664	www.imglobal.com
International SOS	215/942–8000 or 713/521–7611	www.internationalsos.com
Wallach & Company	800/237–6615 or 504/687–3166	www.wallach.com

ort). Medical-only policies typically reimburse you for medical care (excluding that related to preexisting conditions) and hospitalization abroad, and provide for evacuation. You still have to pay the bills and await reimbursement from the insurer, though.

Expect comprehensive travel insurance policies to cost about 4% to 7% of the total price of your trip (it's more like 12% if you're over age 70). A medical-only policy may or may not be cheaper than a comprehensive policy. Always read the fine print of your policy to make sure that you are covered for the risks that are of most concern to you. Compare several policies to make sure you're getting the best price and range of coverage available.

BOOKING YOUR TRIP

Unless your cousin is a travel agent, you're probably among the millions of people who make most of their travel arrangements online.

But have you ever wondered just what the differences are between an online travel agent (a Web site through which you make reservations instead of going directly to the airline, hotel, or car-rental company), a discounter (a firm that does a high volume of business with a hotel chain or airline and accordingly gets good prices), a wholesaler (one that makes cheap reservations in bulk and then resells them to people like you), and an aggregator (one that compares all the offerings so you don't have to)?

Is it truly better to book directly on an airline or hotel Web site? And when does a real live travel agent come in handy?

▌ONLINE

You really have to shop around. A travel wholesaler such as Hotels.com or Hotel-Club.net can be a source of good rates, as can discounters such as Hotwire or Priceline, particularly if you can bid for your hotel room or airfare. Indeed, such sites sometimes have deals that are unavailable elsewhere. They do, however, tend to work only with hotel chains (which makes them just plain useless for getting hotel reservations outside of major cities) or big airlines (so that often leaves out upstarts like jetBlue and some foreign carriers like Air India).

Also, with discounters and wholesalers you must generally prepay, and everything is nonrefundable. And before you fork over the dough, be sure to check the terms and conditions, so you know what a given company will do for you if there's a problem and what you'll have to deal with on your own.

▌TIP→ To be absolutely sure everything was processed correctly, confirm reservations made through online travel agents, discounters, and wholesalers directly with your hotel before leaving home.

Booking engines like Expedia, Travelocity, and Orbitz are actually travel agents, albeit high-volume, online ones. And airline travel packagers like American Airlines Vacations and Virgin Vacations—well, they're travel agents, too. But they may still not work with all the world's hotels.

An aggregator site will search many sites and pull the best prices for airfares, hotels, and rental cars from them. Most aggregators compare the major travel-booking sites such as Expedia, Travelocity, and Orbitz; some also look at airline Web sites, though rarely the sites of smaller budget airlines. Some aggregators also compare other travel products, including complex packages—a good thing, as you can sometimes get the best overall deal by booking an air-and-hotel package.

The Bermuda Hotel Association ⊕*www.experiencebermuda.com*, and Bermuda.com ⊕*www.bermuda.com* both have extensive lists of accommodations for varying budgets and tastes, from top resorts to friendly guesthouses, as does Bermuda 4u ⊕*www.bermuda4u.com*, which is particularly detailed, with notes on each property such as "Thomas Moore stayed here in 1804."

▌WITH A TRAVEL AGENT

If you use an agent—brick-and-mortar or virtual—you'll pay a fee for the service. And know that the service you get from some online agents isn't comprehensive. For example Expedia and Travelocity don't search for prices on budget airlines like jetBlue, Southwest, or small foreign carriers. That said, some agents (online or

Online Booking Resources

AGGREGATORS

Kayak	www.kayak.com	also looks at cruises and vacation packages.
Mobissimo	www.mobissimo.com	
Qixo	www.qixo.com	also compares cruises, vacation packages, and even travel insurance.
Sidestep	www.sidestep.com	also compares vacation packages and lists travel deals.
Travelgrove	www.travelgrove.com	also compares cruises and packages.

BOOKING ENGINES

Cheap Tickets	www.cheaptickets.com	a discounter.
Expedia	www.expedia.com	a large online agency that charges a booking fee for airline tickets.
Hotwire	www.hotwire.com	a discounter.
lastminute.com	www.lastminute.com	specializes in last-minute travel; the main site is for the U.K., but it has a link to a U.S. site.
Luxury Link	www.luxurylink.com	has auctions (surprisingly good deals) as well as offers on the high-end side of travel.
Onetravel.com	www.onetravel.com	a discounter for hotels, car rentals, airfares, and packages.
Orbitz	www.orbitz.com	charges a booking fee for airline tickets, but gives a clear breakdown of fees and taxes before you book.
Priceline.com	www.priceline.com	a discounter that also allows bidding.
Travel.com	www.travel.com	allows you to compare its rates with those of other booking engines.
Travelocity	www.travelocity.com	charges a booking fee for airline tickets, but promises good problem resolution.

ONLINE ACCOMMODATIONS

Hotelbook.com	www.hotelbook.com	focuses on independent hotels worldwide.
Hotel Club	www.hotelclub.net	good for major cities worldwide.
Hotels.com	www.hotels.com	a big Expedia-owned wholesaler that offers rooms in hotels all over the world.
Quikbook	www.quikbook.com	offers "pay when you stay" reservations that let you settle your bill at checkout, not when you book.

OTHER RESOURCES

Bidding For Travel	www.biddingfortravel.com	a good place to figure out what you can get and for how much before you start bidding on, say, Priceline.

9 WAYS TO SAVE

1. Join "frequent guest" programs. You may get preferential treatment in room choice and/or upgrades in your favorite chains.

2. Call direct. You can sometimes get a better price if you call a hotel's local toll-free number (if available) rather than a central reservations number.

3. Check online. Check hotel Web sites, as not all chains are represented on all travel sites.

4. Look for specials. Always inquire about packages and corporate rates.

5. Look for price guarantees. For overseas trips, look for guaranteed rates. With your rate locked in you won't pay more, even if the price goes up in the local currency.

6. Look for weekend deals at business hotels. High-end chains catering to business travelers are often busy only on weekdays; to fill rooms they often drop rates dramatically on weekends.

7. Ask about taxes. Verify whether local hotel taxes are included in quoted rates. In some places taxes can add 20% or more to your bill.

8. Read the fine print. Watch for add-ons, including resort fees, energy surcharges, and "convenience" fees for such things as unlimited local phone service you won't use or a free newspaper in a language you can't read.

9. Know when to go. If your destination's high season is December through April and you're trying to book, say, in late April, you might save money by changing your dates by a week or two. Ask when rates go down: if your dates straddle peak and nonpeak seasons, a property may still charge peak season rates for the entire stay.

not) *do* have access to fares that are difficult to find otherwise, and the savings can more than make up for any surcharge.

A knowledgeable brick-and-mortar travel agent can be a godsend if you're booking a cruise, a package trip that's not available to you directly, an air pass, or a complicated itinerary including several overseas flights. What's more, travel agents that specialize in a destination may have exclusive access to certain deals and insider information on things such as charter flights. Agents who specialize in types of travelers (senior citizens, gays and lesbians, naturists) or types of trips (cruises, luxury travel, safaris) can also be invaluable.

■TIP→ **Remember that Expedia, Travelocity, and Orbitz are travel agents, not just booking engines. To resolve any problems with a reservation made through these companies, contact them first.**

A top-notch agent planning your trip to Russia will make sure you get the correct visa application and complete it on time; the one booking your cruise may get you a cabin upgrade or arrange to have bottle of champagne chilling in your cabin when you embark. And complain about the surcharges all you like, but when things don't work out the way you'd hoped, it's nice to have an agent to put things right.

Low-cost airfares, particularly from the U.S. east coast, are becoming more prevalent, and with Bermuda's tourism department specifically citing this reduction in price as one of their priorities, prices will likely continue to tumble. That means for those who like to shop around, some great and relatively cheap deals can be found—especially if you're looking to stay in a guesthouse. However, if you're looking to stay in a higher-end resort, significant savings can be made through travel agents, who can also save large groups a fair amount of hassle in terms of travel to and from the airport.

Agent Resources **American Society of Travel Agents** (☎703/739–2782 ⊕www.travelsense.org).

ACCOMMODATIONS

Accommodation standards in Bermuda—whether you prefer a guesthouse or a five-star hotel—are generally high, and strongly regulated by the Bermuda Department of Tourism. However, prices tend to reflect this quality, and you should be warned that there are no true budget options. (Camping is not allowed and there are no hostels on the island.) Staying in a hotel can mean anything from a luxury resort setting to something more similar to a three-star hotel in the U.S. Another option is to stay in more home-like accommodations—either by renting a room in a guesthouse (a commercial establishment roughly similar to a room in a bed-and-breakfast, though some can be very upmarket) or a cottage.

Most hotels and other lodgings require you to give your credit-card details before they will confirm your reservation. If you don't feel comfortable e-mailing this information, ask if you can fax it (some places even prefer faxes). However you book, get confirmation in writing and have a copy of it handy when you check in.

■TIP→ Assume that hotels operate on the European Plan (EP, no meals) unless we specify that they use the Breakfast Plan (BP, with full breakfast), Continental Plan (CP, Continental breakfast), Full American Plan (FAP, all meals), Modified American Plan (MAP, breakfast and dinner) or are all-inclusive (AI, all meals and most activities).

Be sure you understand the hotel's cancellation policy. Some places allow you to cancel without any kind of penalty—even if you prepaid to secure a discounted rate—if you cancel at least 24 hours in advance. Others require you to cancel a week in advance or penalize you the cost of one night. Small inns and B&Bs are most likely to require you to cancel far in advance. Most hotels allow children under a certain age to stay in their parents' room at no extra charge, but others charge for them as extra adults; find out the cutoff age for discounts.

For price categories, consult the price chart found at the beginning of the "Where to Stay" chapter.

APARTMENT & HOUSE RENTALS

Rental houses, apartments, and villas are all over Bermuda and may be owned by individuals, consortiums, and developers, so booking might be anything from calling the owner in person to booking on a Web site. Bermuda.com ⊕*www.bermuda.com* has a fairly extensive list of the more well-known properties.

Contacts **Villas International** (☎415/499–9490 or 800/221–2260 ⊕www.villasintl.com).

BED & BREAKFASTS

If you're part of the "no-frills" crowd, guesthouses in Bermuda offer bed-and-breakfast style accommodation. Some have their own Internet sites; most are listed on Bermuda.com ⊕*www.bermuda.com*.

Reservation Services **Bed & Breakfast.com** (☎512/322–2710 or 800/462–2632 ⊕www.bedandbreakfast.com) sends out an online newsletter.

HOME EXCHANGES

With a direct home exchange you stay in someone else's home while they stay in yours. Some outfits also deal with vacation homes, so you're not actually staying in someone's full-time residence, just their vacant weekend place.

Exchange Clubs **Home Exchange.com** (☎800/877–8723 ⊕www.homeexchange.com); $59.95 for a 1-year online listing. **HomeLink International** (☎800/638–3841 ⊕www.homelink.org); $80 yearly for Web-only membership; $125 includes Web access and two catalogs.

10 WAYS TO SAVE

1. **Nonrefundable is best.** Just remember that you'll pay dearly (as much as $100) if you change your plans.

2. **Comparison shop.** Web sites and travel agents can have different arrangements with the airlines and offer different prices for exactly the same flights.

3. **Beware those prices.** Many airline Web sites—and most ads—show prices *without* taxes and surcharges. Don't buy until you know the full price.

4. **Stay loyal.** Stick with one or two frequent-flier programs. You'll rack up free trips faster and you'll accumulate more quickly the perks that make trips easier.

5. **Watch those ticketing fees.** Surcharges are usually added when you buy your ticket anywhere but on an airline Web site. (That includes by phone—even if you call the airline directly—and paper tickets regardless of how you book).

6. **Check early and often.** Start looking for cheap fares up to a year in advance. Keep looking until you find a price you like.

7. **Don't work alone.** Some Web sites have tracking features that will e-mail you immediately when good deals are posted.

8. **Jump on the good deals.** Waiting even a few minutes might mean paying more.

9. **Be flexible.** Look for departures on Tuesday, Wednesday, and Thursday, typically the cheapest days to travel. And check on prices for departures at different times and to and from alternative airports.

10. **Weigh your options.** What you get can be as important as what you save. A cheaper flight might have a long layover, or it might land at a secondary airport, where your ground transportation costs might be higher.

∎ AIRLINE TICKETS

Most domestic airline tickets are electronic; international tickets may be either electronic or paper. With an e-ticket the only thing you receive is an e-mailed receipt citing your itinerary and reservation and ticket numbers.

The greatest advantage of an e-ticket is that if you lose your receipt, you can simply print out another copy or ask the airline to do it for you at check-in. You usually pay a surcharge (up to $50) to get a paper ticket, if you can get one at all.

The sole advantage of a paper ticket is that it may be easier to endorse over to another airline if your flight is canceled and the airline with which you booked can't accommodate you on another flight.

∎ TIP➔ **Discount air passes that let you travel economically in a country or region must often be purchased before you leave home. In some cases you can only get them through a travel agent.**

∎ RENTAL CARS

You cannot rent a car in Bermuda. The island has strict laws governing overcrowded roads, so even Bermudians are only allowed one car per household. A popular, albeit possibly somewhat dangerous, alternative is to rent mopeds or scooters (⇨ *See By Moped & Scooter*), which are better for negotiating the island's narrow roads.

∎ VACATION PACKAGES

Packages *are not* guided excursions. Packages combine airfare, accommodations, and perhaps other extras (theater tickets, guided excursions, boat trips, reserved entry to popular museums, transit passes), but they let you do your own thing. During busy periods packages may be your only option, as flights and rooms may be sold out otherwise.

Packages will definitely save you time. They can also save you money, particularly in peak seasons, but—and this is a really big "but"—you should price each part of the package separately to be sure. And be aware that prices advertised on Web sites and in newspapers rarely include service charges or taxes, which can up your costs by hundreds of dollars.

■TIP➜ Some packages and cruises are sold only through travel agents. Don't always assume that you can get the best deal by booking everything yourself.

Each year consumers are stranded or lose their money when packagers—even large ones with excellent reputations—go out of business. How can you protect yourself?

First, always pay with a credit card; if you have a problem, your credit-card company may help you resolve it. Second, buy trip insurance that covers default. Third, choose a company that belongs to the United States Tour Operators Association, whose members must set aside funds to cover defaults. Finally, choose a company that also participates in the Tour Operator Program of the American Society of Travel Agents (ASTA), which will act as mediator in any disputes.

You can also check on the tour operator's reputation among travelers by posting an inquiry on one of the Fodors. com forums.

Organizations **American Society of Travel Agents** (ASTA) ☎703/739–2782 or 800/965–2782 ⊕www.astanet.com). **United States Tour Operators Association** (USTOA ☎212/599–6599 ⊕www.ustoa.com). ■TIP➜ Local tourism boards can provide information about lesser-known and small-niche operators that sell packages to only a few destinations.

WORD OF MOUTH

Did the resort look as good in real life as it did in the photos? Did you sleep like a baby, or were the walls paper thin? Did you get your money's worth? Rate hotels and write your own reviews in Travel Ratings or start a discussion about your favorite places in Travel Talk on www.fodors. com. Your comments might even appear in our books. Yes, you, too, can be a correspondent!

▌GUIDED TOURS

Guided tours are a good option when you don't want to do it all yourself. You travel along with a group (sometimes large, sometimes small), stay in prebooked hotels, eat with your fellow travelers (the cost of meals sometimes included in the price of your tour, sometimes not), and follow a schedule.

But not all guided tours are an if-it's-Tuesday-this-must-be-Belgium experience. A knowledgeable guide can take you places that you might never discover on your own, and you may be pushed to see more than you would have otherwise. Tours aren't for everyone, but they can be just the thing for trips to places where making travel arrangements is difficult or time-consuming (particularly when you don't speak the language).

Whenever you book a guided tour, find out what's included and what isn't. A "land-only" tour includes all your travel (by bus, in most cases) in the destination, but not necessarily your flights to and from or even within it. Also, in most cases prices in tour brochures don't include fees and taxes. And remember that you'll be expected to tip your guide (in cash) at the end of the tour.

▌CRUISES

For information about cruising to Bermuda, see Chapter 8.

TRANSPORTATION

∎ BY AIR

Flying time to Bermuda from most east coast cities is about 2 hours; from Atlanta, 2¾ hours; from Toronto, 3 hours; and 7 hours from London Gatwick.

Most flights arrive around noon, making for particularly long waits to get through immigration; however, British Airways flights and one American Airlines flight from New York arrive in the evening.

Flights to Bermuda are occasionally delayed or canceled due to high winds or crosswinds, particularly in late summer and fall. Before you leave home for the airport, you should always call to confirm whether or not there are Bermuda-bound delays.

Bermuda-bound travelers are rarely bumped, even during the island's busiest summer season. Instead, when overbooking occurs, some airlines switch to a larger aircraft.

Have your passport or government-issued photo ID handy. Bermuda is rather scrupulous about ID, and you'll be asked to show your passport when checking in and again when boarding.

At many airports outside Bermuda, travelers with only carry-on luggage can bypass the airline's front desk and check in at the gate. But in Bermuda, everyone checks in at the airline's front desk. U.S. customs has a desk here, too, so you won't have to clear customs at home when you land. Passengers returning to Britain or Canada will need to clear customs and immigration on arrival.

Airlines & Airports **Airline and Airport Links.com** (⊕www.airlineandairportlinks.com) has links to many of the world's airlines and airports.

Airline Security Issues **Transportation Security Administration** (⊕www.tsa.gov) has answers for almost every question that might come up.

AIRPORTS

Bermuda's gateway is L. F. Wade Airport (BDA), formerly Bermuda International Airport, on the East End of the island. It's approximately 9 mi from Hamilton (30-minute cab ride), 13 mi from Southampton (40-minute cab ride) and 17 mi from Somerset (50 minutes by cab). The town of St. George's is about a 15-minute cab ride from the airport.

Airport Information **L. F. Wade Airport (BDA)** (☎441/293–1640 ⊕www.bermudaairport.com).

∎TIP➔ **Ask the local tourist board about hotel and local transportation packages that include tickets to major museum exhibits or other special events.**

GROUND TRANSPORTATION

Taxis, readily available outside the arrivals gate, are the usual and most convenient way to leave the airport. The approximate fare (not including tip) to Hamilton is $25; to St. George's, $15; to south-shore hotels, $35; and to Sandys (Somerset), $50. A surcharge of $1 is added for each piece of luggage stored in the trunk or on the roof. Fares are 25% higher between midnight and 6 AM and all day on Sunday and public holidays. Fifteen percent is an acceptable tip.

Bermuda Hosts Ltd. provides transportation to hotels and guesthouses aboard air-conditioned six- to 25-seat vans and buses. Reservations are recommended. Prices are $25 per person to Hamilton or $30 per person to Southampton, so for most people a taxi is the wisest option.

Contacts **Bermuda Hosts Ltd.** (☎441/293–1334). **The Bermuda Industrial Union Taxi Co-op** (☎441/292–4476). **Bermuda Taxi Radio Cabs** (☎441/295–4141). **BTA Dispatching Ltd.** (☎441/296–2121 ⊕www.

FLYING 101

Flying may not be as carefree as it once was, but there are some things you can do to make your trip smoother.

■ **Minimize the time spent standing in line.** Buy an e-ticket, check in at an electronic kiosk, or—even better—check in on your airline's Web site before leaving home. Pack light and limit carry-on items to only the essentials.

■ **Arrive when you need to.** Research your airline's policy. It's usually at least an hour before domestic flights and two to three hours before international flights. But airlines at some busy airports have more stringent requirements. Check the TSA Web site for estimated security waiting times at major airports.

■ **Get to the gate.** If you aren't at the gate at least 10 minutes before your flight is scheduled to take off (sometimes earlier), you won't be allowed to board.

■ **Double-check your flight times.** Do this especially if you reserved far in advance. Schedules change and alerts may not reach you.

■ **Don't go hungry.** Ask whether your airline offers anything to eat; even when it does, be prepared to pay.

■ **Get the seat you want.** Often, you can pick a seat when you buy your ticket on an airline Web site. But it's not guaranteed; the airline could change the plane after you book, so double-check. You can also select a seat if you check in electronically. Avoid seats on the aisle directly across from the lavatories. Frequent fliers say those are even worse than back-row seats that don't recline.

■ **Got kids?** Get info. Ask the airline about its children's menus, activities, and fares. Sometimes infants and toddlers fly free if they sit on a parent's lap, and older children fly for half price in their own seats. Also inquire about policies involving car seats; having one may limit seating options. Also ask about seat-belt extenders for car seats. And note that you can't count on a flight attendant to produce an extender; you may have to ask for one when you board.

■ **Check your scheduling.** Don't buy a ticket if there's less than an hour between connecting flights. Although schedules are padded, if anything goes wrong you might miss your connection. If you're traveling to an important function, depart a day early.

■ **Bring paper.** Even when using an e-ticket, always carry a hard copy of your receipt; you may need it to get your boarding pass, which most airports require to get past security.

■ **Complain at the airport.** If your baggage goes astray or your flight goes awry, complain before leaving the airport. Most carriers require this.

■ **Beware of overbooked flights.** If a flight is oversold, the gate agent will usually ask for volunteers and offer some sort of compensation for taking a different flight. If you're bumped from a flight *involuntarily*, the airline must give you some kind of compensation if an alternate flight can't be found within one hour.

■ **Know your rights.** If your flight is delayed because of something within the airline's control (bad weather doesn't count), the airline must get you to your destination on the same day, even if they have to book you on another airline and in an upgraded class. Read the Contract of Carriage, which is usually buried on the airline's Web site.

■ **Be prepared.** The Boy Scout motto is especially important if you're traveling during a stormy season. To quickly adjust your plans, program a few numbers into your cell: your airline, an airport hotel or two, your destination hotel, your car service, and/or your travel agent.

taxibermuda.com). **First Step Taxi Service** (wheelchair accessible) (☎441/293-0301 or 441/735-7151).

FLIGHTS

Nonstop service to Bermuda is available year-round on major airlines from Atlanta, Boston, Newark (NJ), New York City, Washington, D.C., Baltimore, Philadelphia, Toronto, and London, and seasonally from Miami, Charlotte, Orlando, Detroit, and Halifax. Travelers from Australia and New Zealand must fly to Bermuda via London, New York, or Toronto.

Fares from New York City may be found for under $300 on some of the budget airlines but the average price is closer to $500 and can be as high as $800 in peak season, whereas fares from Toronto are typically about $600. Fares from Gatwick vary from $700 in low season to $1,200 in high season on British Airways, or can be as low as $500 on the twice-weekly low-cost airline Zoom. Flight regularity and price is subject to rapid change and airlines recommend that travelers check their Web sites for up-to-the-minute information.

Airline Contacts **Air Canada** (☎888/247-2262 ⊕www.aircanada.com). **American Airlines** (☎800/433-7300 ⊕www.aa.com). **Continental Airlines** (☎800/523-3273 for U.S. and Mexico reservations, 800/231-0856 for international reservations ⊕www.continental.com). **Delta Airlines** (☎800/221-1212 for U.S. reservations, 800/241-4141 for international reservations ⊕www.delta.com). **jetBlue** (☎800/538-2583 ⊕www.jetblue.com). **USAirways** (☎800/428-4322 for U.S. and Canada reservations, 800/622-1015 for international reservations ⊕www.usairways.com).

▌ BY BOAT

The Bermuda Ministry of Transport maintains excellent, frequent, and on-time ferry service from Hamilton to Paget and Warwick (the pink line), Somerset and the Dockyard in the West End (the blue line), Rockaway in Southampton (the green line), and, weekdays in summer only, the Dockyard and St. George's (the orange line).

A one-way adult fare to Paget or Warwick is $2.50; to Somerset, the Dockyard, or St. George's, $4. The last departures are at 9:45 PM from mid-April through mid-November, 9 PM from mid-November through mid-April. Sunday ferry service is limited and ends around 7 PM. You can bring a bicycle on board free of charge, but you'll pay $4 extra to take a motor scooter to Somerset or the Dockyard, and scooters are not allowed on the smaller Paget and Warwick ferries. Neither bikes nor scooters are allowed on ferries to St. George's. Discounted one-, two-, three-, four-, and seven-day passes are available for use on both ferries and buses. They cost $12, $20, $28, $35, and $45 respectively. Monthly passes are also offered at $55. The helpful ferry operators can answer questions about routes and schedules and can even help get your bike on board. Schedules are published in the phone book, posted at each landing, and are also available at the Ferry Terminal, Central Bus Terminal, Visitors Service Bureaus, and most hotels.

Information **Ministry of Transport, Department of Marine and Ports Services** (☎441/295-4506 Hamilton Ferry Terminal ⊕www.seaexpress.bm).

▌ BY BUS

Bermuda's pink and blue buses travel the island from east to west. To find a bus stop outside Hamilton, look for either a stone shelter or a pink or blue pole. For buses heading to Hamilton, the pole is pink; for those traveling away from Hamilton, the pole is blue. Remember to wait on the proper side of the road. Driving in Bermuda is on the left. Bus drivers will not make change, so purchase tickets or discounted tokens or carry plenty of coins.

In addition to public buses, private minibuses serve St. George's. The minibus fare depends upon the destination, but you won't pay more than $5. Minibuses, which you can flag down, drop you wherever you want to go in this parish. They operate daily from about 7:30 AM to 9 PM. Smoking is not permitted on buses.

Bermuda is divided into 14 bus zones, each about 2 mi long. Within the first three zones, the rate is $3 (coins only). For longer distances, the fare is $4.50. If you plan to travel by public transportation often, buy a booklet of tickets (15 14-zone tickets for $30, or 15 three-zone tickets for $20). You can also buy a few tokens, which, unlike tickets, are sold individually. In addition to tickets and tokens, there are one-, two-, three-, four-, and seven-day adult passes ($12, $20, $28, $35, and $45 respectively). Monthly passes are also available for $55 each. All bus passes are good for ferry service and are available at the central bus terminal. Tickets and passes are also sold at the Visitor Information Centres in Hamilton, post offices, and at many hotels and guesthouses. Passes are accepted on both buses and ferries.

Hamilton buses arrive and depart from the Central Bus Terminal. An office here is open weekdays from 7:15 to 5:30, Saturday from 8:15 to 5:30, and Sunday and holidays from 9:15 to 4:45; it's the only place to buy money-saving tokens.

Buses run about every 15 minutes, except on Sunday, when they usually come every half hour or hour, depending on the route. Bus schedules, which also contain ferry timetables, are available at the bus terminal in Hamilton and at many hotels. The timetable also offers an itinerary for a do-it-yourself, one-day sightseeing tour by bus and ferry. Upon request, the driver will be happy to tell you when you've reached your stop. Be sure to greet the bus driver when boarding—it's considered rude in Bermuda to ask a bus driver a question, such as the fare or details on your destination, without first greeting him or her.

Bus Information **Public Transport Bermuda** (☎441/292–3851 ⊕www.bermudabuses.com). **St. George's Minibus Service** (☎441/297–8199).

▌ BY MOPED & SCOOTER

Because car rentals are not allowed in Bermuda, you might decide to get around by moped or scooter. Bermudians routinely use the words "moped" and "scooter" interchangeably, even though they're different. You must pedal to start a moped, and it carries only one person. A scooter, on the other hand, which starts when you put the key in the ignition, is more powerful and holds one or two passengers.

Think twice before renting a moped, as accidents occur frequently and are occasionally fatal. The best ways to avoid mishaps are to drive defensively, obey the speed limit, remember to stay on the left-hand side of the road—especially at traffic circles—and avoid riding in the rain and at night.

Helmets are required by law. Mopeds and scooters can be rented from cycle liveries by the hour, the day, or the week. Liveries will show first-time riders how to operate the vehicles. Rates vary, so it's worth calling several liveries to see what they charge. Single-seat scooter rentals cost from $35 to $53 per day or from $136 to $181 per week. Some liveries tack a mandatory $20 insurance-and-repair charge on top of the bill, whereas others include the cost of insurance, breakdown service, pickup and delivery, and a tank of gas in the quoted price. A $20 deposit may also be charged for the lock, key, and helmet. You must be at least 16 and have a valid driver's license to rent. Major hotels have their own cycle liveries, and all hotels and most guesthouses will make rental arrangements.

GASOLINE

Gas for cycles runs from $3 to $4 per liter, but you can cover a great deal of ground on the full tank that comes with the wheels. Gas stations will accept major credit cards. It's customary to tip attendants—a couple of dollars is adequate.

PARKING

On-street parking bays for scooters are plentiful and easy to spot. What's even better is they're free!

ROAD CONDITIONS

Roads are narrow, winding, and full of blind curves. Whether driving cars or scooters, Bermudians tend to be quite cautious around less-experienced visiting riders, but crowded city streets make accidents all the more common. Local rush hours are weekdays, from 7:30 AM to 9 AM and from 4 PM to 5:30 PM. Roads are often bumpy, and they may be slippery under a morning mist or rainfall. Street lamps are few and far between outside of the cities, so be especially careful driving at night.

ROADSIDE EMERGENCIES

The number for Bermuda's emergency services is 911. Scooters are often stolen, so to be safe you should always carry the number of your hire company with you.

RULES OF THE ROAD

The speed limit is 35 kph (22 mph), except in the World Heritage Site of St. George's, where it is a mere 25 kph (about 15 mph). The limits, however, are not very well enforced, and the actual driving speed in Bermuda hovers around 50 kph (30 mph). Police seldom target tourists for parking offenses or other driving infractions. Drunk driving is a serious problem in Bermuda, despite stiff penalties. The blood-alcohol limit is 0.08. The courts will impose a $1,000 fine for a driving-while-intoxicated infraction, and also take the driver off the road for about one year. Despite much discussion, there's currently no law against using a mobile phone even while driving a scooter.

TAXI TRAVEL

When you take a taxi, ask for the driver's personal card so you can call them back later. Most drivers carry them, and it's a good way to avoid any lengthy waits, particularly late at night when there can be an excess of revelers waiting for what seems to be far less taxis.

Rental Companies Elbow Beach Cycles Ltd. (☎441/236–9237). **Oleander Cycles** (✉Paget ☎441/236–5235 ✉Hamilton ☎441/295–0919 ✉Southampton ☎441/234–0629 ✉Dockyard, Sandys ☎441/234–2764). **Smatt's Cycle Livery Ltd.** (☎441/295–1180). **Wheels Cycles** (☎441/292–2245). **World Distributors Ltd.** (☎441/295–2329).

▌ BY TAXI

Taxis are the fastest and easiest way to get around the island—and also the most costly. Four-seater taxis charge $5.35 for the first mile and $2 for each subsequent mile. Between midnight and 6 AM, and on Sunday and holidays, a 25% surcharge is added to the fare. There's a $1 charge for each piece of luggage stored in the trunk or on the roof. Taxi drivers accept only American or Bermudian cash, but not bills larger than $50, and they expect a 15% tip. You can phone for taxi pickup, but you may wait while the cab navigates Bermuda's heavy traffic. Don't hesitate to hail a taxi on the street.

For a personalized taxi tour of the island, the minimum duration is three hours, at $30 per hour for one to four people and $42 an hour for five or six, excluding tip. **The Bermuda Industrial Union Taxi Co-op** (☎441/292–4476).**Bermuda Taxi Radio Cabs** (☎441/295–4141).**BTA Dispatching Ltd.** (☎441/296–2121 ⊕*www.taxibermuda.com*).**First Step Taxi Service** (wheelchair accessible) (☎*441/293–0301 or 441/735–7151*).

ON THE GROUND

▮ COMMUNICATIONS

INTERNET
You should have no trouble bringing a laptop through customs into Bermuda, though you may have to open and turn it on for inspection by security officers. It's a good idea to bring proof of purchase with you so you will not run into any difficulty bringing the computer back to the States, especially if it's a new machine.

Most hotels charge connection fees each time a laptop is hooked up to the Internet ($3 to $10), with additional charges (10¢ to 30¢ per minute) during the connection. The Fairmont Southampton has a fully equipped business center where guests can use hotel computers for Internet access (connection charges still apply).

If you do not have an Internet connection at your hotel, there are a few places around the island where you can log on. But it will cost you—$12 an hour is an average rate.

Contacts **Cybercafes** (⊕www.cybercafes. com) lists more than 4,000 Internet cafés worldwide. **Coconut Rock** (☎441/292–1043). **Logic** (☎441/294–8888). **Silk Thai Cuisine** (☎441/295–0449). **Twice Told Tales** (☎441/296–1995).

PHONES
The good news is you can now make a direct-dial telephone call from virtually any point on earth. The bad news? You can't always do so cheaply. Calling from a hotel is almost always the most expensive option; hotels usually add huge surcharges to all calls, particularly international ones. In some countries you can phone from call centers or even the post office. And then there are mobile phones (⇨ *See Mobile Phones below*), which are sometimes more prevalent—particularly in the developing world—than landlines; as expensive as mobile phone calls can

be, they are still usually a much cheaper option than calling from your hotel.

Destination-specific international calling cards from North Rock Communications in Hamilton offer the cheapest way of calling. You can use them on any phones, including public pay phones and mobile phones. You can also get standard international cards from pharmacies, some supermarkets, and many gas stations, which will also get you a better rate than calling directly from the hotel.

The country code for Bermuda is 441. When dialing a Bermuda number from the United States or Canada, simply dial 1 + 441 + local number. You do not need to dial the international access code (011).

CALLING WITHIN BERMUDA
Telephone service in Bermuda is organized and efficient, though service may be interrupted during storms.

When in Bermuda, call 411 for local phone numbers. To reach directory assistance from outside the country, call 441/555–1212.

To make a local call, simply dial the seven-digit number.

You can find pay phones similar to those in the United States on the streets of Hamilton, St. George's, and Somerset as well as at ferry landings, some bus stops, and public beaches. Deposit 50¢ (U.S. or Bermudian) before you dial. Most hotels charge from 20¢ to $1 for local calls.

CALLING OUTSIDE BERMUDA
The country code for the United States is 1.

Most hotels impose a surcharge for long-distance calls, even those made collect or with a phone card or credit card. Many toll-free 800 or 888 numbers in the United States aren't honored in Bermuda. Consider buying a prepaid local phone card rather than using your own calling card. In many small guesthouses and apartments the phone in your room is a private line from which you can make only collect, credit-card, or local calls. Some small hotels have a telephone room or kiosk where you can make long-distance calls.

You can find specially marked AT&T USADirect phones at the airport, the cruise-ship dock in Hamilton, and King's Square and Ordnance Island in St. George's. You can also make international calls with a calling card from the main post office. You can make prepaid international calls from the Cable & Wireless Office, which also has international telex, cable, and fax services Monday through Saturday from 9 to 5.

To call the United States, Canada, and most Caribbean countries, simply dial 1 (or 0 if you need an operator's assistance), then the area code and the number. For all other countries, dial 011 (or 0 for an operator), the country code, the area code, and the number. Using an operator for an overseas call is more expensive than dialing direct. For calls to the United States, rates are highest from 8 AM to 6 PM and discounted from 6 PM to 8 AM and on weekends.

Access Codes AT&T USADirect (☎800/872–2881). MCI Call USA (☎800/888–8000 or 800/888–8888). Sprint Express (☎800/623–0877).

International Calls Main post office (☎441/295–5151). Cable & Wireless Office (☎441/297–7000)

CALLING CARDS
Buy a prepaid phone card for long-distance calls. They can be used with any touch-tone phone in Bermuda, although they can only be used for calls outside Bermuda. Rates are often significantly lower than dialing direct, but the down side is that some hotels will charge you for making the call to your card's 800 number. Phone cards are available at

pharmacies, shops, gas stations, and restaurants. The phone companies Cable & Wireless, TeleBermuda, and Logic Communications sell prepaid calling cards in denominations of $5 to $50. The cards can be used around the world as well as in Bermuda.

Phone-Card Companies Cable & Wireless (☎441/297–7022). Logic Communications (☎441/296–9600). North Rock Communications Ltd. (☎441/540–2700). TeleBermuda (☎441/296–9000).

MOBILE PHONES
If you have a multiband phone (some countries use different frequencies than what's used in the United States) and your service provider uses the world-standard GSM network (as do T-Mobile, Cingular, and Verizon), you can probably use your phone abroad. Roaming fees can be steep, however: 99¢ a minute is considered reasonable. And overseas you normally pay the toll charges for incoming calls. It's almost always cheaper to send a text message than to make a call, since text messages have a very low set fee (often less than 5¢).

If you just want to make local calls, consider buying a new SIM card (note that your provider may have to unlock your phone for you to use a different SIM card) and a prepaid service plan in the destination. You'll then have a local number and can make local calls at local rates. If your trip is extensive, you could also simply buy a new cell phone in your destination, as the initial cost will be offset over time.

■TIP➜ If you travel internationally frequently, save one of your old mobile phones or buy a cheap one on the Internet; ask your cell phone company to unlock it for you, and take it with you as a travel phone, buying a new SIM card with pay-as-you-go service in each destination.

Most travelers can use their own cell phones in Bermuda, though you should check with your provider to be sure. Cell

LOCAL DO'S AND TABOOS

CUSTOMS OF THE COUNTRY

Bermudians tend to be quite formal in attire as well as in personal interactions. Casual dress, including bathing suits, is acceptable at hotels and resorts, but locals seldom venture into Hamilton in anything less than long shorts and sports shirts for men, and slacks-and-blouse combinations or dresses for women. Some restaurants and clubs, particularly those connected to hotels, request that men wear jackets, and more formal establishments require ties during dinner, but there are plenty of places in Hamilton and beyond where you can dress casually and dine well. If you have dinner reservations you should arrive promptly on time, but be aware that in other situations a phenomenon known as "Bermuda time" exists. If you make plans to meet a local, don't be surprised if they're 20 minutes late.

In downtown Hamilton, the classic Bermuda shorts are often worn by banking and insurance executives, but the outfit always includes high black socks, dress shoes, and jacket and tie. When it comes to dress, err on the formal side. It's an offense in Bermuda to appear in public without a shirt, even for joggers. This rule may seem arcane, but most Bermudians appreciate this decorum. Decorum is also expected at the beach.

GREETINGS

Courtesy is the rule when locals interact among each other. In business and social gatherings use the more formal Mr. and Ms. instead of first names, at least until a friendship has been established, which sometimes takes just a few minutes. Always greet bus drivers with a friendly "Good morning" or "Good afternoon" when you board public buses. This is an island custom, and it's nice to see each passenger offer a smile and sincere greeting when boarding and exiting the bus. In fact, saying "Good morning" to people on the street is also a custom. Obviously if you're walking down a crowded street you needn't say it to everyone you pass, but in less crowded situations, especially when eye contact is made, some recognition should be given. You'll be surprised at the friendly response you receive.

In general, respect and appreciation are shown quite liberally to public servants in Bermuda. Although one underlying reason may be the fact that the residents of this small island seem to know everyone, and personal greetings on the streets are commonplace, it also seems that a genuinely upbeat and friendly attitude is part of the national character.

OUT ON THE TOWN

The key to interaction with any Bermudian is to be polite and formal, and that goes for your waiter or any other person serving you. Rudeness will get you nowhere. Public displays of affection are quite okay, but you might want to keep it in moderation; generally people are fairly reserved. Gay and lesbian travelers in particular may experience some negative reactions when showing affection in public, such as holding hands.

SIGHTSEEING

Bathing suits are best kept for the beach only and overly skimpy attire is traditionally frowned upon, though attitudes are more tolerant of tourists. While the problem is far less prevalent than in most places of the world, there are a few street beggars and it's best not to give them anything—for one, due to Hamilton's small size, you're likely to see the same beggar again and again and if you give them something once they'll repeatedly approach you. A firm, but polite, refusal is best. You shouldn't eat or drink on the buses, and you'll gain approval by giving up your seat for elderly or pregnant women.

phone rentals are available from stores in Hamilton, some of which will even deliver the phone to you. A typical charge is $2 a day for the rental while local calls will cost 60¢ a minute. Incoming international calls will also cost 60¢ a minute, but outgoing international calls will cost $1.10 a minute.

Contacts **Cellular Abroad** (☎800/287–5072 ⊕www.cellularabroad.com) rents and sells GMS phones and sells SIM cards that work in many countries. **Mobal** (☎888/888–9162 ⊕www.mobalrental.com) rents mobiles and sells GSM phones (starting at $49) that will operate in 140 countries. Per-call rates vary throughout the world. **Planet Fone** (☎888/988–4777 ⊕www.planetfone.com) rents cell phones, but the per-minute rates are expensive.

Rentals **BermudaCellRentals.com** (☎441/232–2355). **Internet Lane** (☎441/296–9972).

❙ CUSTOMS & DUTIES

You're always allowed to bring goods of a certain value back home without having to pay any duty or import tax. But there's a limit on the amount of tobacco and liquor you can bring back duty-free, and some countries have separate limits for perfumes; for exact figures, check with your customs department. The values of so-called "duty-free" goods are included in these amounts. When you shop abroad, save all your receipts, as customs inspectors may ask to see them as well as the items you purchased. If the total value of your goods is more than the duty-free limit, you'll have to pay a tax (most often a flat percentage) on the value of everything beyond that limit.

On entering Bermuda, you can bring in duty-free up to 50 cigars, 200 cigarettes, and 1 pound of tobacco; 1 liter of wine and 1 liter of spirits; and other goods with a total maximum value of $30. To import plants, fruits, vegetables, or pets, you must get an import permit in advance

from the Department of Environmental Protection. Merchandise and sales materials for use at conventions must be cleared with the hotel concerned before you arrive. Be prepared for a bit of a wait, as the Customs Office has a reputation for being very thorough. If there are a lot of passengers this process can add an hour or so if you're unlucky. It goes without saying, but you should definitely not bring in any drugs such as marijuana, as drug checks are very thorough and the penalties are harsh.

Information in Bermuda **Department of Environmental Protection** (☎441/236–4201 ⊕www.animals.gov.bm).

U.S. Information **U.S. Customs and Border Protection** (⊕www.cbp.gov).

❙ DAY TOURS & GUIDES

GARDEN & WILDLIFE TOURS

Free 75-minute guided tours of the Botanical Gardens depart from the visitor center Tuesday, Wednesday, and Friday at 10:30 AM. You can tour the premier's official residence in the gardens Tuesday and Friday at 2 PM.

In the 1960s, passionate environmentalist David Wingate began restoring the uninhabited Nonsuch Island to its 17th-century glory. Today the 15-acre nature reserve, which lies northeast of Bermuda, is a living museum of the original flora and fauna encountered in Bermuda by the first settlers. On the Nonsuch Island Field Trip, you can learn about the ecological relationships of Bermuda's various indigenous wildlife. Tours, lasting four hours and costing $75 per person, depart from the Bermuda Biological Station for Research (BBSR) every Thursday at 9 AM, returning at 1:30 PM. Ordnance Island in St. George's is the second pick-up point, with departures at 9:15 AM and returns at 1:15 PM. All proceeds help support environmental research and educational programs at BBSR.

In spring, the Garden Club of Bermuda arranges tours ($15) to three houses each Wednesday afternoon from 1 to 4.

The enjoyable walking tours organized by Native Adventures allow you to experience Bermuda's natural beauty and remote corners through the eyes of professional photographer Tamell Simons. He leads 2½- and 5-hour tours that include transportation, and cost $65 and $100, respectively.

Contacts **Botanical Gardens** (☎441/236–5291 or 441/236–4201). **Garden Club of Bermuda** (☎441/295–1480). **Native Adventures** (☎441/295–2957). **Nonsuch Island Field Trip** (☎441/297–1880).

HISTORICAL & SOCIAL TOURS

The Bermuda Department of Tourism publishes brochures with self-guided tours of Hamilton, St. George's, the West End, and the Railway Trail. Available free at all Visitor Information Centres and at hotels and guesthouses, the brochures also contain detailed directions for walkers and cyclists as well as historical notes and anecdotes. The BDT also coordinates walking tours of Hamilton, St. George's, Spittal Pond Nature Reserve, the Royal Naval Dockyard, and Somerset. The tours of Hamilton and St. George's, as well as most of the Royal Naval Dockyard tours, take in historic buildings, while the Spittal Pond and Somerset tours focus on the island's flora.

Out & About Bermuda leads walking tours through some of Bermuda's most scenic nature reserves, parks, residential neighborhoods, and historic areas. The tours are conducted for two to six people and cost $20 per person or $30 per couple.

Tim Rogers Tours are run by a witty British transplant who has lived in Bermuda for more than a decade. Rogers leads exceptional walks (and seated talks) about various Bermuda topics that other historians or guides sticking to their textbooks may be hesitant to discuss. His humorous and conversational tours cover intriguing historical material on piracy, local ghosts and lore, and the island's more interesting architectural motifs. A 90-minute walking tour costs $65 per couple and $10 extra for each additional person. Special group rates are also available.

The Walking Club of Bermuda is an exercise club that provides visitors with a social opportunity to meet Bermudians while seeing the island. Walks are of varied length and refreshments included in the fee are served afterward. A $20 yearly membership fee is required for regulars, but donations are welcome from nonmembers at the beginning of the walk.

Segways of Bermuda offer a historical tour of the Royal Naval Dockyard aboard a Segway—an electric two-wheel vehicle. The machines are the only vehicle that can tour the Maritime Museum. Sites include the Clocktower Mall, Casemates Prison, the Victualling Yard, the Glassblowing and Rum Cake Factory, and the Sail Loft. It's run by Robert Territo, a New Yorker of Italian descent who grew up in Bermuda. He is both knowledgeable and wildly humorous. The 90-minute tour includes a brief orientation of the vehicle and costs $75.

Contacts **Bermuda Department of Tourism** (BDT) (☎441/292–0023 ⊕www.bermudatourism.com). **Out & About Bermuda** (☎441/295–2595 ⊕www.bermudashorts.bm/outandabout). **Segways of Bermuda** (☎441/504–2581). **Tim Rogers Tours** (☎441/234–4082 ☐441/238–2773). **The Walking Club of Bermuda** (☎441/236–6034 or 441/737–0437 ⊕www.walk.free.bm).

HORSE-DRAWN CARRIAGE TOURS

You can hire carriages on Front Street in Hamilton—a Bermuda tradition among the just-married. Rates for a one- or two-horse carriage for up to four passengers are $30 for 30 minutes. Each adult is charged an additional $5 per half hour when more than five people ride in one carriage.

TAXI & MINIBUS TOURS

For an independent tour of Bermuda, a taxi is a good but more expensive alternative to a group tour. A blue flag on the hood of a cab indicates that the driver is a qualified tour guide. These cabs can be difficult to find, but most of their drivers are friendly and entertaining—they sometimes bend the truth for a good yarn—and well informed about the island and its history. Ask your hotel to arrange a tour with a knowledgeable driver.

Cabs seat four or six, and the legal rate for island tours (minimum three hours) is $30 per hour for one to four passengers and $42 per hour for five or six passengers. Two children under 12 equal an adult.

Taxi & Minibus Tour Operators **Bee-Line Transport Ltd.** (☎441/293-0303 🖷441/293-8015). **Bermuda Hosts Ltd.** (☎441/293-1334 🖷441/293-1335). **Destination Bermuda Ltd.** (☎441/292-2325 🖷441/292-2252). **Radio Taxis** (☎441/295-0041 🖷441/295-3988).

▌EATING OUT

Bermuda has a surprising amount of restaurants serving just about any type of foreign cuisine imaginable: Indian, Thai, Japanese, Chinese, British, French—you name it. Truly Bermudian cuisine is, however, harder to come by. Codfish and potatoes, the national dish, tends to appear on some pub food menus and also in a number of diner-style restaurants. Vegetarians are generally well catered to, and most places have no problem with young children, but check ahead at some of the higher-class establishments just to make sure.

For information on food-related health issues, see Health below.

WORD OF MOUTH

Was the service stellar or not up to snuff? Did the food give you shivers of delight or leave you cold? Did the prices and portions make you happy or sad? Rate restaurants and write your own reviews in Travel Ratings or start a discussion about your favorite places in Travel Talk on www.fodors.com. Your comments might even appear in our books. Yes, you, too, can be a correspondent!

MEALS & MEALTIMES

Unless otherwise noted, the restaurants listed in this guide are open daily for lunch and dinner.

A word of warning to those who are used to eating out late: it can be difficult to find a place that serves food after 10 PM. Your last option is a burger van called "Jorjays," which is usually open late into the night on Front Street.

PAYING

For guidelines on tipping see Tipping below.

It's customary to ask for your check when you're finished, instead of waiting for the server to bring it. All major credit cards are accepted island-wide.

For price categories, consult the price chart found at the beginning of the "Where to Eat" chapter.

RESERVATIONS & DRESS

Regardless of where you are, it's a good idea to make a reservation if you can. We only mention them specifically when reservations are essential (there's no other way you'll ever get a table) or when they are not accepted. For popular restaurants, book as far ahead as you can (often 30 days), and reconfirm as soon as you arrive. (Large parties should always call ahead to check the reservations policy.) We mention dress only when men are required to wear a jacket or a jacket and tie.

GETTING STARTED / BOOKING YOUR TRIP / TRANSPORTATION / ON THE GROUND

WINES, BEER & SPIRITS

Bermuda's two national drinks, the Dark 'n Stormy (dark rum and ginger beer) and the rum swizzle (a mixed fruit cocktail with dark and light rum), both rely on the locally produced Gosling's Rum. These drinks are everywhere—so watch out! The only locally produced beers are available at Northrock Pub in Smith's Parish or at the Frog and Onion Pub in Dockyard. Otherwise available beers are fairly standard North American and European brands, and wines are plentiful. Liquor can't be bought from a liquor store on a Sunday or after 9 PM any day of the week.

▌ELECTRICITY

The local electrical current is the same as in the United States and Canada: 110 volt, 60 cycle AC. All appliances that can be used in North America can be used in Bermuda without adapters. Winter storms bring occasional power outages.

▌EMERGENCIES

Police, ambulance, and fire services are all at 911. Pharmacies usually open around 8 AM, some stay open until 9 PM. People's Pharmacy in Hamilton is open from 10 AM to 2 PM on Sunday.

Doctors & Dentists **Government Health Clinic** (☎441/236-0224 🖷441/278-4900).

Foreign Consulates **American Consulate** (✉Crown Hill, 16 Middle Rd., Devonshire ☎441/295-1342 ⊕http://hamilton.usconsulate.gov).

General Emergency Contacts **Air/Sea Rescue** (☎441/297-1010 ⊕www.rccbermuda.bm). **Police, fire, ambulance** (☎911).

Hospitals & Clinics **King Edward VII Memorial Hospital** (✉7 Point Finger Rd., outside Hamilton near Botanical Gardens ☎441/236-2345 🖷441/236-3691).

▌HEALTH

The most common types of illnesses are caused by contaminated food and water. If you have problems, mild cases of traveler's diarrhea may respond to Imodium (known generically as loperamide) or Pepto-Bismol. Be sure to drink plenty of fluids; if you can't keep fluids down, seek medical help immediately.

Infectious diseases can be airborne or passed via mosquitoes and ticks and through direct or indirect physical contact with animals or people. Some, including Norwalk-like viruses that affect your digestive tract, can be passed along through contaminated food. Speak with your physician and/or check the CDC or World Health Organization Web sites for health alerts, particularly if you're pregnant, traveling with children, or have a chronic illness.

SPECIFIC ISSUES IN BERMUDA

Sunburn and sunstroke are legitimate concerns if you're traveling to Bermuda in summer. On hot, sunny days, wear a hat, a beach cover-up, and lots of sunblock. These are essential for a day on a boat or at the beach. Be sure to take the same kind of precautions on overcast summer days—some of the worst cases of sunburn happen on cloudy afternoons when sunblock seems unnecessary. Drink plenty of water and, above all, limit the amount of time you spend in the sun until you become acclimated.

The Portuguese man-of-war occasionally visits Bermuda's waters, so be alert when swimming, especially in summer or whenever the water is particularly warm. This creature is recognizable by a purple, balloonlike float sack of perhaps 8 inches in diameter, below which dangle 20- to 60-inch tentacles armed with powerful stinging cells. Contact with the stinging cells causes immediate and severe pain. Seek medical attention immediately: a serious sting can send a person into shock. In the meantime—or if getting to a doctor will take a while—treat the affected area liberally with vinegar. Ammonia is also an effective antidote to the sting. Although usually encountered in the water, Portuguese men-of-war may also wash up on shore. If you spot one on the sand, steer clear, as the sting is just as dangerous out of the water.

More recently, divers have encountered the highly poisonous lionfish, which is not a native of the waters. Swimmers will be extremely unlikely to come into contact with one, while divers should just exercise caution around the creatures, which are not aggressive unless provoked.

▌HOURS OF OPERATION

Most branches of the Bank of Bermuda are open weekdays from 9 to 4:30 and Saturday from 11 to 1. All branches of the Bank of Butterfield are open Monday through Thursday from 9 to 3:30 and Friday from 9 to 4:30. Bermuda Commercial Bank (at 43 Victoria Street in Hamilton) operates Monday through Thursday from 9:30 to 3 and Friday from 9:30 to 4:30. Capital G Bank (at 25 Reid Street in Hamilton) is open weekdays from 8:30 to 4:30 and Saturday from 8:30 to 3:30.

Many gas stations are open daily from 7 AM to 9 PM, and a few stay open until midnight. The island's only 24-hour gas station is Esso City Auto Market in Hamilton, near the Bank of Butterfield, off Par-La-Ville Road.

Hours vary greatly, but museums are generally open Monday through Saturday from 9 or 9:30 to 4:30 or 5. Some close on Saturday. Check with individual museums for exact hours.

Pharmacies are open Monday through Saturday from 8 AM to 6 or 8 PM, and sometimes Sunday from around 11 to 6 PM.

Most stores are open Monday through Saturday from around 9 until 5 or 6. Some Hamilton stores keep evening hours when cruise ships are in port. Dockyard shops are generally open Monday through Saturday from 10 to 5, Sunday from 11 to 5. The Bermuda government recently made it legal for all stores to open on Sunday, although most shops have yet to take advantage of the change. Those that are open—mainly grocery stores and pharmacies—have abbreviated hours.

HOLIDAYS

On Sunday and national public holidays, all shops, businesses, and many restaurants in Bermuda close. Buses and ferries run on limited schedules. Most entertainment venues, sights, and sports outfitters remain open. When holidays fall on a Saturday, government and commercial offices close the following Monday, but restaurants and shops remain open.

Bermuda celebrates a two-day public holiday for Emancipation Day/Somers Day and Cup Match in late July, when the whole island comes to a standstill for the annual cricket match between the East and West ends of Bermuda. National public holidays are New Year's Day, Good Friday, Bermuda Day (late May), Queen's Birthday (mid-June), Labour Day (early September), Remembrance Day (early November), Christmas, and Boxing Day (December 26).

▌MAIL

Mail services in Bermuda can be erratic, so the following should be taken with a pinch of salt. However, generally allow seven to 10 days for mail from Bermuda to reach the United States, Canada, or the United Kingdom, and about two weeks to arrive in Australia or New Zealand.

Airmail postcards and letters for the first 10 grams to the United States and Canada cost 70¢. Postcards to the United Kingdom cost 80¢, letters 85¢ for the first 10 grams. Postcards to Australia and New Zealand cost 90¢, letters 95¢ for the first 10 grams.

If you want to receive mail but have no address in Bermuda, you can have mail sent care of General Delivery, General Post Office, Hamilton HM GD, Bermuda.

Main Branches **International Data Express** (☎441/297–7802). **Parcel Post** (☎441/297–7875).

SHIPPING PACKAGES

Through Parcel Post at Bermuda's post office, you can send packages via either International Data Express (which takes two to four business days to the United States and Canada and three to seven days to the United Kingdom, Australia, and New Zealand) or Air Parcel Post (which takes seven to 10 business days to the United States, Canada, and the United Kingdom, or two weeks to Australia and New Zealand).

For the first 500 grams, International Data Express rates are $25 to the United States and Canada, $30 to the United Kingdom, and $38 to Australia or New Zealand. Air Parcel Post rates run $7.65 for the first 500 grams to the United States, $9.10 to Canada, $11.95 to the United Kingdom, and $14.95 to Australia or New Zealand.

Most of Bermuda's largest stores offer shipping of purchases. Some may ask you either to buy insurance or to sign a waiver absolving them of any responsibility for potential loss or damage.

Overnight courier service is available to or from the continental United States through several companies. Service between Bermuda and Canada takes one or two business days, depending on the part of Canada; between Bermuda and the United Kingdom, generally two business days; and between Bermuda and Australia or New Zealand, usually three.

In Bermuda, rates include pickup from anywhere on the island. Prices for a document up to the first pound range from $26 to $37 to the United States, from $30 to $38 to Canada, and from $35 to $50 to the United Kingdom, Australia, or New Zealand. For the fastest delivery, your pickup request must be made before about 10 AM. Note that pickups (and drop-off locations) are limited on Saturday, and there's no service on Sunday. Packages sent to Bermuda may take a day longer than documents.

Express Services **DHL Worldwide Express** (☎441/295–3300). **Federal Express** (☎441/295–3854). **International Bonded Couriers** (☎441/295–2467). **Mailboxes Unlimited Ltd.** (☎441/292–6563). **Sprint International Express** (☎441/296–7866). **United Parcel Service** (☎441/295–2467).

▌ MONEY

The Bermudian dollar is on par with the U.S. dollar, and the two currencies are used interchangeably. (Other non-Bermudian currency must be converted.) You can use American money anywhere, but change is often given in Bermudian currency. Try to avoid accumulating large amounts of local money, which is difficult to exchange for U.S. dollars in Bermuda and expensive to exchange in the United States. ATMs are plentiful as are the amount of venues that will accept credit cards, even for small items.

ITEM	AVERAGE COST
Cup of Coffee	$3
Glass of Wine	$11
Glass of Beer	$6
Sandwich	$7
One-Mile Taxi Ride in Capital City	$10
Museum Admission	Free–$20

Since Bermuda imports everything from cars to cardigans, prices are high. At an upscale restaurant, for example, you're bound to pay as much for a meal as you would in New York, London, or Paris:

on average, $60 to $80 per person, $120 with drinks and wine. There are other options, of course; the island is full of coffee shops, where you can eat hamburgers and french fries with locals for about $9. The same meal at a restaurant costs about $15.

Prices throughout this guide are given for adults. Substantially reduced fees are almost always available for children, students, and senior citizens.

■TIP→ Banks never have every foreign currency on hand, and it may take as long as a week to order. If you're planning to exchange funds before leaving home, don't wait until the last minute.

ATMS & BANKS

Your own bank will probably charge a fee for using ATMs abroad; the foreign bank you use may also charge a fee. Nevertheless, you'll usually get a better rate of exchange at an ATM than you will at a currency-exchange office or even when changing money in a bank. And extracting funds as you need them is a safer option than carrying around a large amount of cash.

■TIP→ PIN numbers with more than four digits are not recognized at ATMs in many countries. If yours has five or more, remember to change it before you leave.

ATMs are found all over Bermuda, in shops, arcades, supermarkets, the airport, and two of the island's banks. Both the Bank of Bermuda—a branch of HSBC—and the Bank of Butterfield are affiliated with the Cirrus and Plus networks. Note that both banks' ATMs only accept personal identification numbers (PIN) with four digits. Typical withdrawal amounts are multiples of 20 up to 100. Cash point robberies are a rarity in Bermuda, but if you're concerned, Reid Street and Front Street—which have the most banks—are Hamilton's busiest, and hence safest places to withdraw cash.

CREDIT CARDS

Throughout this guide, the following abbreviations are used: **AE**, American Express; **D**, Discover; **DC**, Diners Club; **MC**, MasterCard; and **V**, Visa.

It's a good idea to inform your credit-card company before you travel, especially if you're going abroad and don't travel internationally very often. Otherwise, the credit-card company might put a hold on your card owing to unusual activity—not a good thing halfway through your trip. Record all your credit-card numbers—as well as the phone numbers to call if your cards are lost or stolen—in a safe place, so you're prepared should something go wrong. Both MasterCard and Visa have general numbers you can call (collect if you're abroad) if your card is lost, but you're better off calling the number of your issuing bank, since MasterCard and Visa usually just transfer you to your bank; your bank's number is usually printed on your card.

If you plan to use your credit card for cash advances, you'll need to apply for a PIN at least two weeks before your trip. Although it's usually cheaper (and safer) to use a credit card abroad for large purchases (so you can cancel payments or be reimbursed if there's a problem), note that some credit-card companies *and* the banks that issue them add substantial percentages to all foreign transactions, whether they're in a foreign currency or not. Check on these fees before leaving home, so there won't be any surprises when you get the bill.

■TIP→ Before you charge something, ask the merchant whether he or she plans to do a dynamic currency conversion (DCC). In such a transaction the credit-card *processor* (shop, restaurant, or hotel, not Visa or MasterCard) converts the currency and charges you in dollars. In most cases you'll pay the merchant a 3% fee for this service in addition to any credit-card company and issuing-bank foreign-transaction surcharges.

Dynamic currency conversion programs are becoming increasingly widespread. Merchants who participate in them are supposed to ask whether you want to be charged in dollars or the local currency, but they don't always do so. And even if they do offer you a choice, they may well avoid mentioning the additional surcharges. The good news is that you *do* have a choice. And if this practice really gets your goat, you can avoid it entirely thanks to American Express; with its cards, DCC simply isn't an option.

Most Bermudian shops and restaurants accept credit and debit cards. Some hotels insist on cash or traveler's checks, so check in advance whether your hotel takes credit cards. The most widely accepted cards are MasterCard, Visa, and American Express.

Reporting Lost Cards **American Express** (☎800/992–3404 in U.S., 336/393–1111 collect from abroad ⊕www.americanexpress.com). **Diners Club** (☎800/234–6377 in U.S., 303/799–1504 collect from abroad ⊕www.dinersclub.com). **Discover** (☎800/347–2683 in U.S., 801/902–3100 collect from abroad ⊕www.discovercard.com). **MasterCard** (☎800/622–7747 in U.S., 636/722–7111 collect from abroad ⊕www.mastercard.com). **Visa** (☎800/847–2911 in U.S., 410/581–9994 collect from abroad ⊕www.visa.com).

CURRENCY & EXCHANGE

The local currency is the Bermudian dollar, which is on par with the American dollar. Both are accepted throughout the island. Bermudian dollar notes all feature the Queen's head and are smaller than their U.S. counterparts. It's worth being careful as both the $10 and the $20 notes are similar in color (light blue) and could be easily mistaken for one another.

If you need to exchange Canadian dollars, British pounds, or other currencies, for the most favorable rates change money through banks. Although ATM transaction fees may be higher abroad

WORST-CASE SCENARIO

All your money and credit cards have just been stolen. In these days of real-time transactions, this isn't a predicament that should destroy your vacation. First, report the theft of the credit cards. Then get any traveler's checks you were carrying replaced. This can usually be done almost immediately, provided that you kept a record of the serial numbers separate from the checks themselves. If you bank at a large international bank like Citibank or HSBC, go to the closest branch; if you know your account number, chances are you can get a new ATM card and withdraw money right away. **Western Union** (☎800/325–6000 ⊕www.westernunion.com) sends money almost anywhere. Have someone back home order a transfer online, over the phone, or at one of the company's offices, which is the cheapest option. The U.S. State Department's **Overseas Citizens Services** (☎202/647–5225) can wire money to any U.S. consulate or embassy abroad for a fee of $30. Just have someone back home wire money or send a money order or cashier's check to the state department, which will then disburse the funds as soon as the next working day after it receives them.

than at home, ATM rates are excellent because they're based on wholesale rates offered only by major banks. You won't do as well at exchange booths in airports or rail and bus stations, in hotels, in restaurants, or in stores. To avoid lines at airport exchange booths, get a bit of local currency before you leave home.

■**TIP→** Even if a currency-exchange booth has a sign promising no commission, rest assured that there's some kind of huge, hidden fee. (Oh . . . that's right. The sign didn't say no *fee*.) And as for rates, you're almost always better off getting foreign currency at an ATM or exchanging money at a bank.

TRAVELER'S CHECKS & CARDS

Some consider this the currency of the caveman, and it's true that fewer establishments accept traveler's checks these days. Nevertheless, they're a cheap and secure way to carry extra money, particularly on trips to urban areas. Both Citibank (under the Visa brand) and American Express issue traveler's checks in the United States, but Amex is better known and more widely accepted; you can also avoid hefty surcharges by cashing Amex checks at Amex offices. Whatever you do, keep track of all the serial numbers in case the checks are lost or stolen.

Traveler's checks are widely accepted throughout Bermuda. If lost or stolen, they can usually be replaced within 24 hours. To ensure a speedy refund, buy your own traveler's checks. Don't let someone else pay for them, as irregularities like this can cause delays. The person who bought the checks should make the call to request a refund.

Some hotels take personal checks by prior arrangement (a letter from your bank is sometimes requested).

American Express now offers a stored-value card called a Travelers Cheque Card, which you can use wherever American Express credit cards are accepted, including ATMs. The card can carry a minimum of $300 and a maximum of $2,700, and it's a very safe way to carry your funds. Although you can get replacement funds in 24 hours if your card is lost or stolen, it doesn't really strike us as a very good deal. In addition to a high initial cost ($14.95 to set up the card, plus $5 each time you "reload"), you still have to pay a 2% fee for each purchase in a foreign currency (similar to that of any credit card). Further, each time you use the card in an ATM you pay a transaction fee of $2.50 on top of the 2% transaction fee for the conversion—add it all up and it can be considerably more than you would pay when simply using your own ATM card. Regular traveler's checks are just as secure and cost less.

Contacts American Express (☎888/412–6945 in U.S., 801/945–9450 collect outside of U.S. to add value or speak to customer service ⊕www.americanexpress.com).

▌RESTROOMS

Toilet facilities in Bermuda venues are generally of a high standard and there are also free public facilities, which tend to be reasonable, though obviously not quite as spick-and-span as those in a private venue. Gas stations do not usually have restrooms. Attendants are rare, but when present, should be tipped a dollar or so.

Find a Loo The Bathroom Diaries (⊕www.thebathroomdiaries.com) is flush with unsanitized info on restrooms the world over—each one located, reviewed, and rated.

▌SAFETY

Crime, especially against tourists, is extremely low in Bermuda. Purse snatching is the most common crime tourists should watch out for. While rare, more serious incidents do happen occasionally, so you should guard against being overly complacent. Don't leave unattended valuables on the beach while going for a swim. Exercise commonsense precautions with wallets, purses, cameras, and other valuables. If you're driving a moped, always travel with your purse or bag concealed inside the seat. Always lock your moped or pedal bike, and store valuables in your room or hotel safe. Although an ocean breeze through a screen door is wonderful, close and lock your hotel room's glass patio door while you're sleeping or out of your room. The "back-of-town" area, in particular Court Street, has a bad reputation historically, though the government has made a number of efforts to clean the area up. However, if you do want to go to a venue there (such as the Fodor's Choice

Hubie's Bar) it's worth taking a taxi, just to be on the safe side.

TIP→ Distribute your cash, credit cards, IDs, and other valuables between a deep front pocket, an inside jacket or vest pocket, and a hidden money pouch. Don't reach for the money pouch once you're in public.

TAXES

Hotels add a 7.25% government tax to the bill, and most add a 10% service charge or a per-diem dollar equivalent in lieu of tips. Other extra charges sometimes include a 5% "energy surcharge" (at small guesthouses) and a 15% service charge (at most restaurants).

A $25 airport-departure tax and a $4.25 airport-security fee are built into the price of your ticket, as is a $4 passenger facility charge, whereas cruise lines collect $60 in advance for each passenger, again, normally included in the price of the ticket.

TIME

Bermuda is in the Atlantic time zone. Bermuda observes daylight saving time (from the second Sunday in March to the first Sunday in November), so it's always one hour ahead of U.S. eastern standard time. Thus, for instance, when it's 5 PM in Bermuda, it's 4 PM in New York, 3 PM in Chicago, and 1 PM in Los Angeles. London is four hours, and Sydney 14 hours, ahead of Bermuda.

TIPPING

Tipping in Bermuda is fairly similar to tipping in the United States. A service charge of 10% (or an equivalent per-diem amount), which covers everything from baggage handling to maid service, is added to your hotel bill, though people often still tip a few extra dollars. Most restaurants tack on a 15% service charge; if not, a 15% tip is customary (more for exceptional service).

TIPPING GUIDELINES FOR BERMUDA	
Bartender	$1 to $3 per round of drinks, depending on the number of drinks
Bellhop	$2 per bag, depending on the level of the hotel
Dive Instructor	5% to 10% of the total trip
Gas Station Attendants	$2
Grocery Baggers	$1 to $2 a bag
Hotel Maid	$10 at lower-end accommodations, $20 at higher-end accommodations
Porter at Airport or Train Station	$1 per bag
Taxi Driver	15%, but round up the fare to the next dollar amount
Waiter	15%; nothing additional if a service charge is added to the bill

INDEX

PHOTO CREDITS

7, *Howard Millard/viestiphoto.com.* 8, *Bermuda Department of Tourism.* 9 (left), *Homer Martin/age fotostock.* 9 (right), *Rolf Richardson/age fotostock.* 12, *Ken Ross/viestiphoto.com.* 13, *Bob Krist/eStock Photo.* 14 and 15 (left), *Bermuda Department of Tourism.* 15 (right), *Richard Cummins/viestiphoto.com.* 20 and 21, *Joe Viesti/viestiphoto.com.* 22 and 23 (left), *Bermuda Department of Tourism.* 23 (right), *Homer Martin/age fotostock.* 24, *Bermuda Department of Tourism.* 25 (left), *Ken Ross/viestiphoto.com.* 25 (right), *SuperStock/age fotostock.* 26, *Bermuda Department of Tourism.*

NOTES

NOTES

NOTES

NOTES

NOTES

ABOUT OUR WRITERS

Girl on the go, Suzy Buckley keeps busy: she hosts a travel/entertainment series called Living the Life; she's a frequent guest commentator on shows such as True Hollywood Story, Love Chain and The Fabulous Life Of; she's Lifestyle Editor at Ocean Drive Magazine, and Florida Regional Editor for Lucky magazine, and a regular contributor to New York Magazine, New York Post, Departures, Town & Country, Daily Candy, and Self. Suzy always makes time for shopping and she loves to escape hometown Miami heat with a quick jaunt to nearby Bermuda where it is "always sunny, crisp and feels like Palm Beach in December." Suzy updated us on the Bermuda shopping scene this year.

Cruise Diva Linda Coffman is a freelance travel writer who has been dishing out cruise-travel advice and information for over a decade. Her articles have appeared online and in national magazines and newspapers, including Porthole, Consumer's Digest, the Chicago Sun-Times, and USA Today. Who better than the Cruise Diva to update everything you need to know about cruising to Bermuda?

Michael de Zayas spent much of his childhood traveling in the Caribbean and grew up to write and edit over two dozen guides for Fodor's, including destinations like St. Martin, Anguilla, Cuba, Mexico, and the Bahamas. He's also written for newspapers like The New York Post and The Miami Herald. Bermuda is his favorite island in the world and he escapes here regularly as a break from his day job as the head of two internet companies he founded, Neighborhoodies and Amp Camp.

Bermuda has become home-away-from-home for England-born Sirkka Huish. Since 2006, she's worked as a Sub-Editor for the Bermuda Sun by day, and by night she trawls the streets for culinary master-pieces. Believing there's no point in knowing your way around the kitchen if your palate can navigate itself to the nearest restaurant, Sirkka needed no excuse to fill her stomach for our Where To Eat chapter. All in the name of research, she piled on a few pounds and now none of her clothes fit.

Dale Leatherman is a freelance travel writer specializing in golf, adventure, and the Caribbean. Her work appears in national publications such as Continental, The Robb Report, Links, and Caribbean Travel & Life. She plays golf in Bermuda often, enjoying the combination of tropical golf and British atmosphere. Dale applied her knowledge of the ups and downs, and ins and outs of Bermuda's courses to our Golf chapter.

When he's not busy editing the Arts & Entertainment section for the Bermuda Sun, Andrew Raine spends his time trawling the island and crawling its bars. That's if he's not scuba-diving its underwater wrecks, or lounging on his adopted stretch of Horseshoe Bay. London-born Andrew fell in love with island life while working in the Falklands as a teenager, but later decided to move to Bermuda for a suntan. He's since turned orange.

A born and raised Bermudian, Keisha Webb-Gibbs works as a Public Relations & Events Manager for a privately-owned island financial institution. Before making a career change to Public Relations/Marketing, Keisha worked her way up from a Proofreader to Editor at community newspapers in Georgia and North Carolina. Four years ago she gave up the daily commute in the southern U.S. for family and sun in Bermuda. She now lives on the island with her husband of 10 years and loves to write about people, places, and food. This year, Keisha updated our Beaches, Sports & the Outdoors chapter.

From her home base in Nova Scotia, Susan
MacCallum-Whitcomb has zipped around
the globe writing travel features for Canada's top-selling newspapers and magazines but she feels a special affection for
Bermuda. "Back in grade school," Susan
says, "the first plane I ever boarded took
me there. It also happens to be where I
later had my first taste of champagne—
and romance. So aside from appreciating
the sun, sand, and sights, I feel the pull of
the place on an emotional level." Susan
updated our Front Matter and Exploring
Bermuda chapters this year.